Russia's "Market" Economy

Russia's "Market" Economy:

A Bad Case of Predatory Capitalism

Stefan Hedlund

Uppsala University

First published 1999 in the UK and the USA by

UCL Press Limited
11 New Fetter Lane
London EC4P 4EE

The name of University College London (UCL) is a registered trade mark used by UCL Press with the consent of the owner.

UCL Press is an imprint of the Taylor & Francis Group

ISBNs: 1–84142–054–9 HB
       1–84142–053–0 PB

British Cataloguing-in-Publication Data
A catalogue record for this book is available from the British Library.

Library of Congress Cataloging-in-Publication
Data are available

Typeset in 10/12 Bembo by Graphicraft Ltd, Hong Kong
Printed and bound by T.J. International Ltd, Padstow, UK

For Lilian, with love

Contents

Preface

Those who steal from private individuals are placed in iron and chains, but those who steal from public coffers are dressed in gold and crimson.
                                                          Cato (the elder)

Sitting down to pencil a few introductory words to the reader, I cannot help but recall a passage from Lewis Carroll's *Through the Looking Glass*: "The time has come, the walrus said, to speak of many things". In the following we shall indeed be speaking of many things. We shall see great expectations and great failures. We shall delve deep into the grand themes of Russian history, and we shall apply the magnifying glass to some of the most recent events. We shall look at Western attempts to help out, and at Russian ambivalence towards such involvement. And we shall try to look into the future.

The book is structured into four sections, with four different objectives. The first is mainly introductory, seeking to present a *tour d'horizon* for the remaining chapters. Section two presents a framework for the subsequent analysis. It defines the focus of attention, by charting four different "zones of confrontation" where the executive power must engage other actors (in the legislature, the judiciary, the financial markets and the entrepreneurial sector). It looks at the prelude to events taking place under Gorbachev, and it presents the story of a growing involvement by the West in Russia's attempted reforms.

In section three the economic reform programme is presented. It looks at the first years of high inflation, which led to a massive redistribution of both wealth and incomes, moves on to the subsequent period of low inflation, when the government resorted instead to massive borrowing, and rounds off by looking at the political scandals that surrounded various privatization deals, at the financial pyramid games that collapsed in August 1998, and at the political leadership style of President Boris Yeltsin.

Section four contains the theoretical analysis. Using tools from institutional theory, it presents the outline of a powerful Russian path dependence. It is argued that Russia's current troubles have roots that may be traced back to old Muscovy, and it is shown that the parallel ambitions of economists to introduce market economy and of jurists to introduce the rule of law were seriously flawed.

The *leitmotif* of the book as a whole is also the main tenet of institutional theory, namely, that while formal rules may be changed overnight informal norms take longer to adjust. By totally ignoring such insights, the Russian reformers never really had any chance of success.

Although history will figure prominently throughout the text, there is no pretence of original historical research. We shall rely exclusively on the work of others, and in particular on what Richard Pipes has written about the "patrimonial society". And we shall select only those parts of history that are of relevance to the arguments pursued. Thus Russian history will appear at various points in the text.

In Chapter 1 there will be a very brief glimpse of some distinctive patterns of reform and reversal. Chapter 2 then goes into greater detail on the historical legacy that is relevant to each of the four zones of confrontation that were mentioned above, and in Chapter 4 a background is provided on Russian relations to the West. In Chapters 8 and 9 we return to history with a more analytical ambition, mainly using the tools of institutional theory.

As always in writing about Russia in foreign languages, transliteration poses a problem. Here we take the easy way out. Names of the great tsars will be given in their familiar English forms. All others will be transliterated. Thus it will be Alexander II but Aleksandr Rutskoi. Diacritical signs will be omitted throughout.

Bits and pieces of the text have appeared before, in articles, discussion papers and seminar presentations. Of the very many people who at various points have provided feedback that eventually went into this book, I would like to mention in particular Thráinn Eggertsson, Tim McDaniel, Douglass North, Mancur Olson and Leonid Polishchuk.

The final manuscript has been read, wholly or in parts, by Carl Linden, James Millar, Richard Pipes, John Richards, Steven Rosefielde, Peter Rutland, László Szamuely and Tsuneaki Tanaka. I owe them all, including two anonymous referees, a large debt for helpful comments and criticisms and will hold none accountable for remaining errors and omissions.

Stefan Hedlund
Sollentuna, 21 November 1998

I

Introduction

CHAPTER ONE

Russian riches mismanaged

Russia is a land of great riches. Across its eleven time zones stretches a variety and a wealth of natural resources that represent true abundance. If only these riches could have been tapped and managed in a reasonably efficient way, the peoples living on this land would have been living a good life indeed. Regrettably, however, Russia's long history is one of great mismanagement. The resources once given by God have not been put to their best use, to put it mildly, and the peoples of present-day Rus are not living the good life they could have been enjoying.

There are two important problems embedded in these observations. The first is theoretical and concerns the role of initial conditions in making forecasts for possible growth trajectories. In a case where there is both a wealth of natural resources and an educated workforce, two necessary conditions for positive growth have been fulfilled. But, and this is important, pointing at favourable initial conditions is far from sufficient. We must also be able to identify a production function that will make it possible to transform the initial endowments into a growing wealth of services and finished goods. And here the record of the Russian past is rather discouraging.

Over the centuries there have been many "windows of opportunity", where both foreign traders and domestic reformers have developed great plans to unlock and develop Russia's hidden wealth. For a variety of reasons, however, neither category has met with any great degree of success. The windows for trade have been narrow and the domestic spurts of reform activity have been brief.

To those who argue that present-day Russia is so richly endowed with resources that an economic boom simply has to follow, these observations do present a problem. If the argument is to be taken seriously, something will also have to be said about the "software" of the system, i.e. about the production function. This implies that the pre-conditions for reform must be placed in focus. It must be shown that Russia is finally ready to be integrated into the world economy and to go about its domestic business in a rational and efficient manner. In subsequent chapters we shall have a lot to say about this.

The second of our two problems mentioned above is empirical and relates to the nature of the Russian riches. Throughout much of her history, Russia has actually been a very poor country. This poverty had a great impact on the way the country developed and again we shall have more to say on that count below.

For the moment it will suffice to note that the overwhelming part of the present resource endowments is of a kind that was largely inaccessible before the twentieth century. It is modern technology that has placed oil, gas and minerals at the disposal of modern Russians. At the same time, however, Soviet technology has done much in order to diminish rather than augment the marketable value of those resources.

Although both Lenin and Stalin started out with favourable endowments, and although there followed several decades of emphasis on both general education and massive capital accumulation, the results were not encouraging. The reasons that may help explain why the Soviet economy eventually collapsed must thus be set aside from the initial conditions, as must the arguments that have supported predictions for a rapid post-Soviet economic recovery.

The fundamental question that will be posed in the following, with respect to post-Soviet growth prospects, must depart from these realizations. Pointing at Russia's current riches has little if any bearing on whether the economic system will be successfully transformed into a high-growth market economy. On the contrary, decades of predatory extraction may well have left Russia with poorer endowments today than at the time of introducing the Soviet system.

The latter is certainly true with respect to natural resources, most importantly so in ecology and in the agricultural sector. But perhaps it also holds true in the field of human capital, where the successes of basic and secondary education must be weighed against the informal learning of less useful "Soviet" work ethics and practices.

In subsequent chapters we shall thus disregard the riches and focus on the production function, that is, on the ability to establish an institutional structure that is conducive to an efficient transformation of available resources into marketable goods and services. In this endeavour, moreover, we shall not subscribe to the widely held belief that all of Russia's economic troubles in the post-war decades were uniquely related to the Soviet "command" economic system.

Given all the negative things that have been – rightly – said about this system, replacing it with a market-based system really *should* have led to rapid improvement. Instead of a Russian economic boom, however, we have witnessed a protracted period of hyperdepression,[1] followed by a financial meltdown. The logical conclusion, in all honesty, must be, therefore, that the reasons behind Russia's recent economic troubles have roots that go much deeper than merely to the Soviet system. The question is how deep.

In the following chapters, we shall repeatedly find reason to return to the past in order to look for Russian roots that may help explain the current problems. We shall not only subscribe to the loose notion that "history matters". We shall also attempt, however humbly, to uncover how, i.e. to find institutional lock-in effects or even "pathologies" in mental models that were created a long time ago and still have important consequences for current decision making.

Let us begin by making a first very brief review of some distinctively Russian patterns of self-imposed isolation and of failed domestic reforms.

At the fringe of Europe

In all discussions of economic growth, foreign trade must play a prominent role. By engaging in foreign trade, the opportunity set for domestic producers is broadened, technology is diffused and enhanced competition serves to stimulate greater efficiency. A long row of Third World experiments that were aimed at achieving self-sufficiency, with resultant effects of distorted exchange rates and costly import substitution, provides ample support for the case in defence of free trade and open economies. Isolation may bring rulers short-term political benefits, but it also carries a price tag in terms of economic backwardness.

Russian isolationism

In the Russian case the historical role of foreign trade has been weak, so weak in fact that Richard Pipes sees a direct link to the equally weak development of a domestic urban culture: "Russia is too remote from the great routes of international trade to have developed a significant urban civilization on the basis of foreign commerce. Three times in its history she was pulled into the mainstream of international trade; each time the result was the sprouting of cities; but each time, too, the urban flowering proved short-lived."[2]

The *first* of these three attempts by foreigners to draw the land of Rus into the orbit of international trade occurred between the ninth and the eleventh centuries. The trigger was the Muslim expansion in the eastern Mediterranean, which served to block the Christian trade routes. Although a substantial detour, the Russian waterways offered an alternative path to the Near East. This was the time when a great proportion of the major cities of old Russia were founded. It was brought to an effective end in the mid-thirteenth century, when the "Mongol Storm" severed all Russian trading links with Constantinople.

In the *second* phase it was the Hanseatic League that served as the engine of growth. Between the thirteenth and the fifteenth centuries, Novgorod was one of its most important members, so important in fact, that at a 1628 meeting of the League it was stated that "all of its great European commercial establishments were based on the trade with Novgorod".[3] This phase was in its turn brought to a forceful end with the capture and eventual destruction of Novgorod by the expanding Muscovy.

The decision by Grand Prince Ivan III, that the Hansa depot should be closed, reflected an underlying dilemma that was to face a long succession of Russian rulers. While foreign trade might bring economic advantage, it would also bring the contamination of dangerous foreign influences.[4] To Ivan the conclusion was obvious: in 1494 he ordered that all Hanseatic merchants on the territory of Novgorod should be arrested, their goods confiscated, and their yard and church be closed. Thus the window to the West was slammed shut.

In the *third* phase, the impetus came from the north. It began in 1553, when Richard Chancellor looking for a "Northeast Passage" discovered a sea route to Russia via the North Sea. Tsar Ivan IV gave him a warm welcome, and in 1556 he was granted extensive trading privileges for his "Russia Company". Again there was a lively growth of cities, this time along the roads and waterways leading from Moscow to the White Sea. Again, however, it was a short-lived experience. In the latter part of the seventeenth century, the trading privileges were withdrawn and commerce ground to a halt.

Towards the end of the nineteenth century, it finally looked as though Russia's relations to the West were about to enter a phase of normality. Domestic industry was booming, foreign investment was pouring in and the currency had been made convertible. From a counter-factual perspective it is fascinating to wonder if this really *could* have been the take-off for a period of true convergence between Russia and the rest of Europe. The implications for the twentieth century of a democratic and market-oriented Russia are certainly daunting.

As we know, however, that was not to be. With the imposition of Bolshevik rule, Russia's borders were sealed once again. For the coming seven decades, all trading links with the outside world would be operated via purposely-designed foreign trade organizations. Thus domestic producers were deprived of all opportunities of learning and developing through competition with other producers in the world market. When the system finally broke down, and its destructive consequences could be freely inspected, it was easy to establish a link between the self-imposed isolation and a serious technological lag behind the market economies of the West.

Viewed against this rather depressing historical background of centuries of isolation and xenophobia, the opening up of the Russian economy to outside influences that began under Mikhail Gorbachev and was brought to completion under Boris Yeltsin does represent an important break with the past. A question that remains to be answered is *how* important, i.e. what the increased openness has meant for the underlying ability to reform.

On the positive count, one may argue that this time the window to the West is likely to remain open – in the age of the Internet it would seem difficult to slam it shut again. But on a slightly less optimistic note we must question if this is enough of a basis for a positive forecast. Opening the borders to the outside world is certainly a necessary condition for economic recovery. But is it also sufficient?

In the following we shall focus much attention on the way in which domestic producers would adjust to the new opportunities that were now made available. This brings us over to the dimension of domestic reform, of domestic liberalization and of imposing market-oriented rules of the game. In this dimension, the heritage of the past is every bit as heavy as that of isolation from the outside world.

Reforms that never were

Looking back at the long list of domestic reformers who have sought to transform the inner workings of the Russian economy, we find a distinctive pattern of great expectations that have been repeatedly crowned with great failures and a return to the *status quo*. The various details in these developments will be discussed at length below, but it may be of some use already at this early stage to provide a brief overview of reforms and reversals.

There was Peter the Great, who sought to yank Russia into the modern world, who travelled abroad for inspiration, invited foreigners to come to his land and imitated foreign "models" for the running of his country. His was the first real attempt at "systemic change", and it was not a success. Five years after his death, the bureaucracy and the nobility had succeeded in reversing almost all of his reforms. The empire would remain, but so would all the problems of isolation and backwardness.

Then there was Peter III, who was the first to embark on a programme of what might be called "liberal" reforms, including an abolition of the secret police, an abolition of the obligation for the nobility to serve the tsar and a renewed decree inviting foreigners to settle in Russia. Faced with the threat of even more far-reaching reforms, however, the bureaucracy fought back. After merely half a year in power, the tsar was murdered.

And there was German-born Catherine the Great, who expressed great distaste at the Russian practice of serfdom and sought to bring Enlightenment to Russia. She drew inspiration from people like Voltaire and Montesquieu, introduced French at court, called a legislative commission and gave the nobility its Charter of Freedom – only to be frightened out of further reform by the bloody peasant uprising that was led by Yemiliyan Pugachev in 1773–5.

Perhaps most important of all, there was Alexander II, the great liberal reformer who set about emancipating the serfs, who introduced truly radical legal reforms and a system of local self-rule – all of this only to end his life in a terrorist bombing and to have his own son, Alexander III, reverse his reforms.

Then there was the "Bloody Sunday" of 1905, which compelled Nicholas II to introduce the October Manifesto, granting Russia the right to take a few cautious steps on the road towards a parliamentary democracy, and there was Pyotr Stolypin's great attempt at agricultural reform: "The government has placed its wager, not on the needy and the drunken, but on the sturdy and the strong – on the sturdy individual proprietor who is called upon to play a part in the reconstruction of our Tsardom on strong monarchical foundations."[5]

For a brief spell in 1917, after the abdication of the tsar in March, it looked as though the project might really succeed, but then there was Lenin and again the window to the West was slammed shut. Under the Bolsheviks, Russia was subjected to a new great attempt at yanking the country into the modern world (albeit somewhat differently defined than under Peter the Great). This renewed struggle for modernity, however, once again was based on isolation from the outside world and on a total repression of all that forms the basis of a market economy. The outcome was warped, to say the least.

In 1985 it finally looked as though Russia was once and for all about to cast off the heavy weight of its troubled history. Although, as we shall see below, the actual content of the reforms that were introduced by Mikhail Gorbachev left much to be desired, the associated "new thinking" did represent at least an attempt to achieve a profound mental reorientation. When Boris Yeltsin climbed on top of the famous tank outside the Moscow White House, to signal that the August 1991 *coup* had failed, he owed a debt to Gorbachev.

A process of preparing the mental grounds for embracing the institutions of democracy and the market economy had been set in motion. It would now be up to Yeltsin to make the best of it. Again, however, the outcome would be warped.

Boris Yeltsin – more of the same?

Looking back at Russia's troubled history of repeated attempts at modernization, many times undertaken at great cost to a suffering population, one is led to wonder whether the optimism that was to accompany this latest round of modernization policies had any solid foundation in fact. Have we merely been witnesses to repetition of old mistaken visions, or is something fundamentally new really about to happen?

The question is of some considerable importance, not only for the advancement of social science theories concerning the pre-conditions for successful institutional change and economic growth. Russia's future course also has obvious implications for the security of Europe as a whole. If it is merely repetition, we may look forward to a protracted period of reversals and destruction, but if it is a decisive break, then the Russians will finally be delivered out of a series of nightmares and Europe as a whole will benefit.

Which then will it be? By the end of 1997 the evidence was still mixed. There were signs saying that the economic decline had finally bottomed out, but by then the economy had been contracting for eight straight years and investment was down by three-quarters. Most importantly, the international markets had remained unconvinced of the wisdom of investing in Russia.

According to figures presented by the European Bank for Reconstruction and Development (EBRD), over the years 1989–96 the old Soviet Bloc as a whole had attracted merely $42.0 billion in foreign direct investment. Of this, $11.3 billion went to the former Soviet Union (excluding the Baltic republics) and $30.7 billion to Eastern Europe (including the Baltics). Placing these figures into context, we may note that measured per capita of the respective populations, Russia attracted $34, Estonia $459 and Hungary $1,288.[6]

Alternatively, we may note that in 1996 tiny Singapore attracted almost as much foreign direct investment as Central and Eastern Europe *as a whole* ($9,440 billion versus $12,261 billion), or that in the same year Peru attracted about twice as much foreign direct investment as Russia[7] ($3,556 billion versus $1,800 billion). Adding that the 1996 figure for Communist China was $42,300 billion provides further perspective on Russia's attractiveness.

During the first part of 1997, it gradually began to appear that the re-election and return to health of President Boris Yeltsin was restoring some faith in the Russian economy. The Moscow stock exchange was booming and foreign investment – both direct and portfolio – was rising. At the beginning of autumn, optimism about the future was approaching pure euphoria. Economic growth was seen to return and an investment boom was expected just around the corner.

Then came the financial crisis in Asia and the October "correction" on Wall Street. As *The Moscow Times* index entered a period of free fall, losing around 60 per cent over the coming three months, Russian euphoria ran into a brick wall. Foreign capital began to leave the country and the rouble was put under increasing pressure. In response, the Central Bank was forced to run down its currency reserves and to hike interest rates. Adding to the trouble, the economic reversals were compounded by political scandals involving the leading reformers, thus calling the whole reform project into question.

During spring 1998 the situation got gradually worse and despite a massive international bailout attempt in July, on 17 August the bubble burst. The rouble collapsed and foreign debt was frozen for 90 days. A new government was appointed to pick up the pieces.

The details of these latter developments will be dealt with at length in subsequent chapters. For the moment we will rest content with repeating our question from above. Did Boris Yeltsin's attempt to introduce "systemic change" represent something essentially new? Was Russia finally ready to undergo fundamental change, or will future historians put it down as just another in a long row of failures? Looking for an answer to these questions will be something of a *leitmotif* for this book.

Institutions and institutional change

Since systemic change really implies institutional change, the following chapters will have much to say about the work that has been done in institutional economics. Against this background it was somehow symptomatic that in March 1997, *Voprosy Ekonomiki*, the leading Russian economics journal, published an article by Douglass North, the pioneer of the institutional approach to economic analysis. In an introduction to the publication, Academician Leonid Abalkin made a number of interesting comments:

> Furthermore, the implementation of universal schemes for financial stabilization, which by their nature ignore the specific make-up of the concrete historical conditions of this or that country, is shown to be of little use. . . . No less important for growth are such parameters as historical traditions, the spiritual constitution of the population, norm systems, the level of legal consciousness, in a word, all that which appears as institutional factors in a socio-economic system.[8]

Given that the Russian project of systemic change provided perhaps the best ever laboratory in which to apply the theory of institutional change, it was certainly relevant to bring institutions into the picture. But the timing, unfortunately, was a bit off. It may be worth noting that North's main contribution to the theory of institutional change was already published in 1990, i.e. in the midst of the frenzy surrounding the Russian search for alternative reform paths.[9]

The frequently heard claims, that no appropriate theory was available to guide the "transition" from socialism, should be seen against this background. If claims of this kind were to be understood in the cookbook sense of providing detailed recipes for actual policy implementation, then there was indeed some truth involved.

Setting out, for example, to privatize in record time an entire economy in an environment where both capital, skills and legislation – not to mention the very notion of "property" – were seriously underdeveloped, certainly did represent an undertaking which had never been attempted before.

But arguing that this lack of previous experience was tantamount to a lack of suitable theory reflects a rather odd understanding of the role of economic theory. If the problem is turned around, and the project, for example, of Russian rapid privatization were to be looked at through the prism of existing theories, then much of the chaos and the plunder that resulted most certainly could – and perhaps even should – have been predicted.

This does not necessarily amount to a condemnation of the project of privatization as such. Given all the insider activities of asset stripping, stock watering and the like, all of which indicate a rather massive failure in the ambition of introducing effective corporate governance, it may still be argued that given the political restrictions at the time, what happened was the only possible way out, and that refraining from privatization would have led to an even worse outcome. We will return to this in a moment.

A crucial point at issue here concerns whether it is acceptable to argue that the plan as such was good, but that implementation failed because of unforeseen political opposition. Unless you are willing and ready to physically eliminate all those who raise objections to the proposed policy (this was Stalin's mode of shock therapy), then political opposition must surely be incorporated into the policy analysis and the appropriate conclusions drawn.

In the privatization debate, there was some explicit consideration of this type of problem, but it was of a very partial nature. Faced with fierce opposition to the project as a whole, the reformers concluded – early on – that the privatization programme would have to be designed in such a way that important groups of insiders were given tangible benefits.

This cynical conclusion, which foreclosed all potential ambitions of introducing legal impediments against plunder and abuse, was formulated rather bluntly by Andrei Shleifer and Maksim Boiko, two of the leading architects of the programme: "Unless these stakeholders are appeased, bribed or disenfranchised, privatization cannot proceed."[10]

If we look at the problem of privatization from a political economy point of view, it is obvious that proper analysis could have helped predict the outcome of the programme as it was designed. Since the debate on privatization has been fairly voluminous we shall provide just one small illustration of how political constraints might have been taken into a broader consideration than the one offered by Shleifer and Boiko.

The example is a paper by Gérard Roland, which begins by making a distinction between feasibility constraints and backlash constraints. The former are distribution-related restrictions which apply *ex ante* and are determined by the expectations of different actors as to winners and losers. This dimension was explicitly considered by Russian reformers, but not necessarily correctly so. Roland's argument is that a gradual approach of privatizing the best firms first would have been superior, both in dissolving the feasibility constraint and in building a constituency for further progress.

Since the process cannot be repeated we shall never know who is right on this count, but in the case of backlash constraints the situation is much clearer. Here we are dealing with restructuring-related restrictions that apply *ex post*, as special interest groups are formed to obstruct a crucially needed restructuring of privatized companies. And here the Russian reformers would run into formidable opposition.

The practical outcome of the programme for rapid mass privatization was that most of the lucrative assets were concentrated in a few hands. This not only served to create widespread dissatisfaction. It also blocked the needed hardening of budget constraints, the emergence of a sound private financial system and – above all – restructuring. According to Roland, it is the latter risks that are the really serious ones:

> In particular, we must warn about the danger of too rapid a privat-
> ization of companies where, for political reasons, the restructuring
> ought to be delayed. This can lead not only to partial redenation-
> alization, but can also destroy the emerging financial sector and
> lead to the prevention of the gradual elimination of the soft budget
> constraints.[11]

This brief example illustrates that relevant economic theory was indeed available, and could have helped provide important insights. We shall have a bit more to say about this in Chapter 4 below. Whether the decisions that actually were made on, say, privatization were the right ones or not is, however, a different matter altogether, which has less to do with theory. The apparent contradiction in this statement may be clarified by asking two different questions.

One the one hand we have the age-old Russian question "What should be done?" (*Chto delat?*), which had been asked by Nikolai Chernyshevskii in 1863 and again by Lenin in 1902. This is the policy question, which has its main roots in the political dimension.

On the other hand we have the more theoretical question "What will happen if?", which is the standard question in economic analysis – indeed the very rationale for the discipline. If all relevant variables are taken into account – including the political ones – proper analysis should be able to come up with a picture of likely consequences of certain policy choices.

11

The heated atmosphere that has marked most of the debates around the Russian economic reform process may be derived from precisely this distinction between which question is being asked – and answered. Though there have certainly been exceptions to the rule, participants may be roughly divided into two sides.

One side – the policy camp – advocated rapid transformation, be it "big bang", "cold turkey", "shock therapy" or whatever. Their main argument held that the initial situation was in two ways unique. While in a positive sense the collapse of the Soviet Union provided a political "window of opportunity" for fundamental reforms to be undertaken, in a negative sense the disintegration of the Soviet economy was accelerating at such a pace that the price of delay or inaction would be terrible. On both counts, very radical measures were seen to be necessary.

The other side – the theoreticians – set themselves the task of warning about the likely consequences of radical reforms. In order to show that the objections made by this camp did carry considerable weight we may listen to the voices of two winners of the Nobel Prize in economics during that period.[12]

In his 1991 Nobel Prize lecture, Ronald Coase spoke explicitly about the ongoing events in eastern Europe: "The value of including . . . institutional factors in the corpus of mainstream economics is made clear by recent events in Eastern Europe. The ex-communist countries are advised to move to a market economy, and their leaders wish to do so, but without the appropriate institutions no market economy of any significance is possible."[13]

The very same warning, about an inadequate institutional structure, was issued again in 1993 when the Nobel Prize was given to North (together with Robert Fogel). In his Nobel lecture, he spoke about the role of institutions and drew an important conclusion: "The implication is that transferring the formal political and economic rules of successful market economies to Third World and Eastern European economies is not a sufficient condition for good economic performance."[14]

In retrospect it is striking how little communication there was between these two camps.[15] One side kept on pleading what must be done, the other kept on warning about the consequences of the proposed actions. Although many early warnings about serious consequences were soon to be proven right, they had little or no impact on policy making. The reformers maintained that their road was the only road.

Thus, at a 1994 World Bank meeting Oliver Williamson again found good cause to bring up the same theme:

> "Getting the property rights right" seemed to be more responsive to the pressing needs for reform in Eastern Europe and the former Soviet Union . . . but the deeper problem is that getting the property rights right is too narrow a conception of what institutional

economics is all about. The more general need is to get the institutions right, of which property is only one part.[16]

(Logically, he then went on to cite both Coase and North.)
But what then was it that the institutional approach could have told the Russian policy-makers? The list of problems it could *not* have helped in any way to cure is long and merits at least a brief mention. No matter how successful the reformers might have been in transforming the software of the system that rests in the institutions, they would still have been left with a set of hardware that in large parts was practically useless and without much future.

No mental transformations conceivable would have solved the problems of what to do with derelict, value destroying industries; with resource extraction in places where nature precludes all sense of profitability; or with urban concentrations north of the Arctic circle, which under any remotely economically rational regime would never have been put there in the first place.

All this said, and recognizing that most of the latter problems could be made to go away only by means of massive investment, it remains a fact that the software would also have to play an important role in the transformation. At the very least, institutional change would be necessary in order to prevent good money from being thrown after bad, in misdirected ambitions of transforming the hardware. Thus, the remainder of this book will rest heavily on institutional theory.

In a highly condensed form, the central message of North's theory of institutional change is that the institutional matrix of a society consists of three different components. There are the formal rules, which may be changed overnight by political intervention. There are the informal norm systems, which change only gradually, and there are various mechanisms of enforcement, which make sure that the formal rules are upheld. It is the interplay between these three components that determines social change.

Even a casual application of these insights to the Russian reform project would have illuminated two great dangers. First, assuming that it is the norms that provide legitimacy for the rules, we may conclude that overly radical changes risk moving the rules too far away from the norms. Thus, the reform as such will be perceived as illegitimate and serious opposition will materialize. The Russian case provides ample illustration of this danger.

Secondly, in the absence of credible enforcement mechanisms, actors will consistently prefer to avoid a perhaps painful adjustment to new rules (be it, say, a new tax system), and if defection is allowed to become a dominant strategy, the reform will break down. Russian developments again bear witness to the reality of such risks.

In spite of all the high-profile political aspects, it thus follows that the technical dimension of how to devise changes in the formal rules really was a subsidiary problem. The issue that *should* have been dealt with first would have been to ask – very seriously – under what conditions individuals who have elaborated over time a certain set of informal norms will allow a radically changed environment to influence and transform their private mental models of the world around them.

It is by phrasing the question in this way that we may see a situation where pursuing *laissez-faire* in a post-Soviet Russian context was destined to generate radically different responses from those anticipated by policy makers trained in a Western mental universe. This, incidentally, is also a powerful argument against the use of foreign advisors – one, moreover, that was at the very heart of the successful Marshall plan for reconstruction of war-torn Western Europe after 1945.

The original version of that plan rested on careful preparation (almost a year was spent in negotiations). It featured training West European special-ists in the United States (more than 20,000 specialists were trained in bank-ing, industry and administration, and then sent back), and it emphasized linking economic support to highly restrictive conditions (most notably, the Europeans were discouraged from trading with the us). Simply put, the approach rested on self-help. When the first major deliveries of aid began to arrive, the success was already a fact.[17]

The proposals that were made in the early 1990s, for a Marshall plan of sorts for Russia, stand in sharp contrast to the original. Given the great haste, help to Russia would have had to be quickly concocted, it would have had to rely heavily on foreign advice, and it would have rested on a massive untied foreign economic support from day one. Whether it could have worked is a debatable point, but to conjure up the positive experi-ences of the late 1940s as support for the case in the 1990s was definitely misleading.

But *why* then did Russia opt for such a radical – indeed even brutal – break with the past? Let us take a closer look at the context in which the decision to go ahead with shock therapy was made.

Why shock therapy?

Boris Yeltsin, as we have noted above, was certainly not the first who set out ambitiously to change the inner workings of the Russian economic system. This is particularly true if we look at the decades that had passed since the death of Stalin. During this time, so many reform attempts were made, with such meagre results, that writing in 1979, Gertrude Schroeder found it warranted speaking of the Soviet economy as on a "Treadmill of Reforms".[18]

As we shall see in Chapter 2 below, the final year and a half of Gorbachev's rule would offer a real frenzy of further reform activity, no doubt prompted by the growing seriousness of the Soviet economic crisis.[19] But throughout the period leading up to 1991, none of these attempts at change within the system really did merit the label "reform".

Against this background, it was *politically* logical that Yeltsin would seek to implement the most radical break possible with the past. The risk of being viewed as just another tinkering partial reformer presented a serious threat to his own credibility as the leader of a new Russia, one that wanted to become a "normal society".

From the president's own political point of view it was thus understandable that Russia opted for a policy that was vaguely modelled on the previous Polish "big bang". Whether this was a good or a bad choice for the country has provoked harsh debates, both in Russia and in the West. Given the heavy Western political involvement in promoting and supporting the Russian reforms, it has also been a debate where high-level Western policy making has been taken to task. Much professional reputation and credibility has been at stake. While writing, it is still hard to see any consensus about to emerge.

But perhaps it does not matter much any more. When the dust has settled, historians will be better placed to make an objective assessment. In the following chapters we will thus seek to avoid, as far as possible, the debates on what *could* or *should* have been done, thus also largely avoiding both praise and recriminations. The reasons are fairly simple.

Let us begin by assuming that there actually *was* a better alternative. At a cursory glance, this would seem easy to accept. It is difficult indeed to imagine a policy (short of civil war) that would have led to an even greater destruction and suffering.[20]

Accepting this premiss would imply that shock therapy must be held responsible for most if not all of the failures of post-Soviet reforms. But how can that be led into evidence? If we admit that this is not a simple exercise in theoretical economics, but rather a complex implementation of political economy, it is obvious that there is no clear-cut answer. Since we cannot go back and try again, we will never know what actually *could* have been done, given the highly specific political and institutional restrictions at the time.

There is certainly merit in the theoretical debate on how a transformation from plan to market may be implemented, and it should be recognized that many valuable contributions have been made to this field, too many to list them here. The problem is that so much of the debate has been concerned not with theory, but with what was *politically* possible in late 1991.[21] In essence, we are speculating about the actual political motivations and ambitions of the Russian political elite in the autumn of 1991, and about their power and authority to implement whatever they might have wanted to do.

Given the turmoil at the time, it is obvious that this is a rather futile exercise. It might certainly be fun to speculate, and perhaps it might even improve our understanding of the political culture at the time, but it would not remove the distinction between what might have been a theoretically optimal design of the reform strategy and what was actually feasible at the time.

In consequence, however, this recognition also implies that we must question one of the most frequently heard arguments in defence of shock therapy, namely that what was done was the *only* thing that could be done – under the circumstances.

Take the case of a currency reform. In abstract economic terms it is obvious that a currency reform should have preceded price liberalization (more about this later). Taking into account the practical circumstances, however, it may be argued that there was no time, that the preparations would have leaked, etc. According to Yegor Gaidar, "Only one alternative remained, and that was to try to rapidly transform repressed inflation to open inflation."[22]

Or take the case of banks and enterprises. Under central planning there arose many cases of banks having large claims on enterprises that would stand no chance of being profitable under a market regime. Since financial relations of this kind had no real economic meaning in the absence of markets and property, the slate should have been wiped clean. As long as both banks and enterprises were still state owned, that would have been a simple technical exercise. It may be argued that not doing so was a big mistake, creating a situation of bad banks with bad claims on bad enterprises. But it may also be argued that there was no time, that there was no *apparat* capable of undertaking the task, etc.

Many similar illustrations may be advanced, all of which point in the direction outlined above. If all the political conditions at the time were to be taken into account, it is quite simply impossible to know what *could* have been done instead. Thus, our main ambition in the following will be to look at what *did* happen, and perhaps also to find out why. Before leaving these issues altogether, however, two reflections are due.

First, and rather humorously, it may be noted that those who argue that under the circumstances *laissez-faire*, or more properly *laissez-tomber*, was the only available option simultaneously reduce the achievements of the Russian reformers. If you agree that what *did* happen was the only thing that *could* happen, then the creation of a Russian market economy is no achievement at all. If you agree that what is happening in Russia today is indeed "market economy", then what else could it become, once the command structures had been effectively destroyed?

The second observation is perhaps a bit less humorous. While it is debatable to what extent foreign involvement in the Russian reform process has had an impact – positive or negative – on the evolution of the economy, the impact on the political process must be beyond doubt. Western "support" for the Russian reforms has been a long series of unprecedented meddling, to the point even of raising demands and setting conditions that no other country in the world would have found acceptable.

Assume, for example, that Russian authorities had made a practice of intervening in US presidential elections, and of repeatedly calling on the White House (the Washington one) to make policy changes or changes of senior staff members, in both cases with thinly veiled threats regarding the consequences of non-compliance.

All of this has been done in the other direction. It has not been equally well liked in all segments of the Russian population, and it may at some point in time have serious repercussions. To mention but one aspect of the problem, we may return to late 1997, to a time when the Russian government was under heavy pressure to improve tax collection.

In the midst of the political wrangling, *Nezavisimaya Gazeta* published a letter from IMF chairman Michel Camdessus. After some introductory courtesies about Prime Minister Viktor Chernomyrdin's excellent leadership, Camdessus goes on to hint that the IMF may approve releasing a promised credit – provided that Russia fulfils a set of 21 conditions (all listed by the newspaper).[23]

In a comment, the communist newspaper *Sovetskaya Rossiya* finds that "The question, however, is not only one of the IMF dictating its terms to Russia, because Russians are already used to this." The real point of anger concerns the question of who runs the Russian economy:

> As it turns out, from the Fund and the World Bank Russia can have no secrets. Messrs. Camdessus and Wolfensohn know everything that happens inside the Kremlin and the government. . . . the present government of Russia is merely an apparatus for monitoring the fulfillment of instructions from the IMF and other Western financial structures, and from them the government and the Kremlin have and can have no secrets.[24]

While it should be noted that conspiracy theories of various kinds tend to flourish in Russia, there do remain some important problems in relation to this type of interference, problems that are related to moral hazard. We shall have reason to pursue this line of argument further in Chapter 4 below.

Returning now to the main track of our argument in the present chapter, we again must ask whether Russia is finally about to break free from its historical heritage of gross mismanagement of truly amazing resource endowments. If the answer is yes, it implies that a majority of the Russian population are in a process of reorienting their mental models of the world that surrounds them. This would represent true institutional change.

The logical next question then is to ask what such a mental reorientation implies. How will those social and moral norm systems have to be transformed, which are to support the newly introduced formal rules of democracy, market economy and the rule of law?[25] And is such a trans- formation at all possible to achieve with public policy?

Perhaps most importantly of all, we must ask whether the prevailing norm systems that were now to be transformed were associated primarily with the Soviet order, or if they had deeper, Russian roots. Let us approach this issue by taking a closer look at what the planned economy was really about.

Kleptocracy Soviet style

The Soviet planned economy lasted for what was roughly equal to the average life expectancy of a Soviet male at the end of the 1980s. It was born in the autumn of 1928, with the introduction of the first five-year plan, and it went into its final coma in the autumn of 1991, when the Soviet state self-destructed and Russia declared its ambition to establish a market economy.

In its youth, it was – seemingly – both forceful and vital, an object of veneration and imitation from both near and afar. In its mature age, it was afflicted by repeated life crises, accompanied by failed attempts at medica- tion. In old age, it lapsed into protracted stagnation, frailty and senility. At the autopsy, it was shown that throughout its life-span it had been the carrier of an incurable virus. And it would have no offspring.

What then was it that was so wrong? And how could the disease have gone undetected for so long?

The command economy

With the onset of Mikhail Gorbachev's policy of glasnost, the old ideolo- gically determined images of the planned economy as a superior – indeed scientifically correct – system could suddenly be questioned and previously unthinkable critique could be presented. It was no longer certain that social- ism would be dancing on the grave of capitalism. Inspired by the new general secretary's example, Soviet social scientists went about their tasks of deconstruction with great energy.

The new trend was most noticeable in the use of a new language. In an echo of the terminology that had long been used by Western sovietologists to describe and analyze the Soviet "command economy",[26] Soviet sources began talking about "command-administrative methods".[27] Insights were spreading that the Soviet economy was a production system that might be capable, under certain circumstances, of producing large amounts of coal and steel, but which at the same time was inherently incapable of fine tuning and technological change.

While certainly important as such, these insights represented merely a beginning. There was still a long way to go to real analysis, and even longer to finding a working cure. This applied to both Soviet and foreign scholars.

During the post-war era, Western sovietology had sought in various ways to create a picture of the Soviet planned economy that was closer to reality than the official Soviet image of central planning as a scientific, stable and long-term undertaking.

One important approach had shown the economy to rest on a never-ending game of negotiations over resource allocation, where enterprise managers were pitted against planning bureaucrats. It was shown that the game was extremely short-sighted, and that both sides had clear incentives to play with hidden cards; the latter in particular had substantial implications for the capacity of the system to generate correct information regarding production possibilities.

It was also shown that during the plan period so many revisions were undertaken that there never really existed a "plan". This approach rested above all on the results from two major interview projects, where Soviet enterprise directors in emigration could convey important insights into the everyday life of a Soviet enterprise.[28]

Needless to say, there were many other approaches, focusing on various aspects of the reality that was to be found behind what was told in the official plan fulfilment documents, so many that seeking to hand out credits here would be rather pointless. There was, however, one common denominator. What most of these studies sought to explain were primarily consequences of deeper rooted problems.

Analyzing the consequences of certain manipulations – reforms – of the incentive systems that were embedded in the plans might, for example, help in understanding possible future directions of change. But it would say nothing about the hard core of underlying power preferences that determined the *shape* of the incentive systems, and thus formed the root cause of many of the at times rather odd manifestations of the economic and political systems.

An important step on the road towards a deeper understanding of these hard core preferences was taken by writers like Konstantin Simis, Arkadii Vaksberg and Mikhail Voslenskii.[29] It is in their accounts of the nature of Soviet corruption and criminality that we are beginning to approach real insights into the dominating rules and norms of the command system, insights that in turn may help us better to understand the subsequent problems of dismantling this system. Needless to say, such understanding may be further enhanced by turning to the literary world, to the works of Solzhenitsyn, Bulgakov, Orwell and many others.

The image of the Soviet economy that transpires here is that of a giant kleptocracy, i.e. a system whose dominating features are force, extortion and tribute, rather than voluntary exchange on a market. On the Western side, Gregory Grossman summarizes his own long-standing research into the "second economy" of the Soviet Union in precisely these terms:

> At the very least one can deduce that the purchase and sale of positions for large sums of money signifies the profound institutionalization in the Soviet Union of a whole structure of bribery and graft, from the bottom to the top of the pyramid of power; that considerable stability of the structure of power is expected by all concerned; and that very probably there is a close organic connection between political administrative authority, on the one hand, and a highly developed world of illegal economic activity on the other. In sum the concept of *kleptocracy*, developed by sociologists with reference to corrupt regimes and bureaucracies in underdeveloped countries, does not seem inapplicable.[30]

Previously, the term has been used primarily with reference to countries in the Third World, such as Haiti, where a ruling elite systematically plunders its own country and its own people. The Soviet case was in many respects different from the traditional model of a kleptocracy, or a predatory state, but as we shall see in a moment it also had traits which, in a long-term perspective, may turn out to have been even more destructive.

The economic structure of the Soviet kleptocracy resembled a pyramid. As Grossman notes, it began on the shop floor, where sales clerks offered part of the goods (often the better quality part) "on the side", known in Russian as *na levo*. The extra revenue that was thus generated was placed in a common pool from which distribution took place according to well established rules: one part for the employees, one part for the suppliers and one part upwards in the system, to officials higher up within the controlling bureaucracy.

Similar activities permeated all spheres of Soviet society. In all sectors there was an open economy, the results of which were laid out in plan fulfilment reports, and there was a hidden economy, where the real decisions were taken and where the real penalties and rewards were determined. At all levels officials controlled their part of the pyramid, making sure that no one took more than his or her fair share.

For a system of this kind to function, several conditions must be met. In both the traditional and the Soviet versions of kleptocracy, the ruling elite must have a secure grip on power and it must be able to prevent the victims of extraction from exiting. Thus violence or credible threats of violence in some form is needed.

A simple comparison on this count between the Soviet Union and, say, Haiti, presents the former as a vastly more refined system – one need only look at differences between the KGB and the *tonton macoutes*, the infamous terror police of Haitian dictator Duvalier.

But the degree of sophistication in brutality was certainly not the only dimension that set the Soviet kleptocracy apart from previous cases. In order to provide a better image, we may turn to János Kornai's classic account of the workings of the socialist economy.[31]

Body and soul

Kornai's main point is that the system evolves in an almost genetic sense, by creating a series of building blocks where one block being put in place conditions the creation of the next one in the chain. In the original formulation, there is a chain of five blocks; here we shall only be concerned with the first two.

The trigger, which serves to initiate the creation of the system as a whole, is the establishment of a monopoly on political power. It must, however, be something more than any old dictatorship. In order to function as a trigger for the remainder of the chain, the monopoly on power must also be linked to a totalitarian ideology. As Kornai puts it, together these two form the "body and soul" of the system.

Expanding on this point, we may look at the role of the totalitarian ideology in terms of Albert Hirschman's notions of exit, voice and loyalty.[32] Faced with deterioration in the performance of a state, an organization or a firm, voters, members or consumers have a choice between voting with their feet (exit) or seeking to influence those in charge (voice). Accepting that exit will abandon the organization to continued decline, system managers will seek to introduce a mechanism that serves to delay exit and thus to reinforce voice.

This, according to Hirschman, is the function of loyalty. To take a concrete example, the elaborate initiation rites that are practised by American university fraternities may be explained from precisely this perspective. Having paid a heavy price to become a member, the student will succumb to adaptive preference formation. Faced with decline in the performance of his fraternity, he will delay exit way beyond the point where an unprejudiced evaluation would have told him to get out. Thus the fraternity is given extra time in which to shape up.

The logic of this reasoning may be easily transferred to the Soviet case.[33] From the outset, the communist party was a vanguard organization. While membership was a pre-condition for successful advancement in both the military and the civilian spheres, it was not open to just anyone. You had to prove yourself worthy and earn the recommendations of two members. (In case of defection, they would be held responsible.) The initiation rite consisted in learning and practising marxism-leninism. (The fact that many Western intellectuals did this voluntarily has been difficult indeed for many Russians to understand.)

The resultant Soviet mechanism of loyalty became an effective instrument for weeding out potential heretics. Those who did not practise the gospel with sufficient enthusiasm could be taken to task and threatened with various sanctions, ranging from a halt in promotion to more tangible penalties. Being thus forced into line, members would be faced with characteristic cognitive dissonance. On the one hand was the normative reality that was held up by the party, on the other the actual observable reality.

In a free environment people may be expected to tell the truth, but having paid a heavy price for membership it was not only material considerations that would prompt communist party members into dissimulation. As Jon Elster points out, "one cannot indefinitely praise the common good '*du bout des lèvres*', for . . . one will end up having the preferences which initially one was faking".[34] Experience of self-contempt over past lies, or other unsavoury past behaviour, will trigger dissonance reducing mechanisms of adaptive preference formation: it is not so bad after all, it is worth it for the greater good, the problems are only local, etc.

The mental models of the world surrounding people who are submitted to such pressures will by necessity come to be marked by duality, by an experience of split realities. There is an official reality in which I exist when I am away from home, and there is a private reality that exists in my home and among my family.

Analytically, Soviet scholars have led this duality back to the duality between paganism and Christianity, known as *dvoeverie*, that marked the medieval Kiev Rus after its conversion to Christianity. While the official layer of social consciousness appeared to be Byzantine Christian, as far as ideology and value systems were concerned, the collective subconsciousness of Rus was pagan.[35]

The very same was reflected in the world of Soviet anecdotes. We may, for example, recall the man who enters a clinic and demands to see an "eye–ear" specialist, an *ukho-glaznik*. Informed that there is no such specialization, he can finally be persuaded to tell the nurse about his affliction: "Well, you see, I keep hearing one thing, but I see something totally different". Many similar jokes could be told, illustrating that the split reality was a well known phenomenon.

Returning now to Kornai, the second building block in his "genetic" programme represents a suppression of private property. This not only follows logically. It is also a pre-condition for the first building block to remain in place. If a sphere of private property were to be allowed, it would serve to erode not only the monopoly on power but even more so the totalitarian ideology.

With these two mutually supporting building blocks in place, the monopoly party elite can go about disposing of the country's assets without fearing either political or economic competition.

The absence of private property makes it impossible to eke out a living outside the party-controlled pyramid. Moreover, since it is the place within the monolith that determines the material well being of each individual, political submission becomes a must. The closer you get to the top, the greater will be the intensity of the dissonance reducing mechanisms that were outlined above. Whether in the end the system managers are transformed into true believers or totally callous cynics is beside the point.

The analytical content of the argument is that the totalitarian ideology becomes the glue that keeps the pyramid together. Each citizen must publicly declare his or her loyalty and submission – or face being branded as a heretic and driven off from both power and subsistence.

Returning again to Hirschman, there is an obvious limitation to the analogy in the sense that the Soviet system would allow neither exit nor voice, as these options are understood in a democratic, market-oriented context. Noting that the system managers had thus capped both options for giving vent to dissatisfaction would lead us to predict a dangerous build-up of pressures of discontent, which in the end would lead the system to explode.

In sharp contrast, however, in its final two to three decades the Soviet system exhibited a remarkable stability. In order to explain this seeming contradiction, we must recognize that there were indeed options for both exit and voice, albeit not of the open kind.[36]

On the former count, we may note the existence of the famed private plots in agriculture, and the *de facto* allowance of a number of semi-legal (*polulegalnye*) private activities. While activities of this kind offered the individual a mental exit from the system, a sense of working for the private good, they still remained within the official production system, compensating for, say, the failures of collectivized agriculture. It represented a "soft exit" in the sense that it was impossible to set up a truly autonomous and competing private venture.

On the latter count, there was a host of ways in which citizens could protest. One example is the "book of complaints" (*kniga zhalob i predlozhenii*) which was kept by all service establishments. Other examples are the writing of letters of complaints to be published in the media, or the lodging of complaints with various authorities. While these various options gave the individual some satisfaction of having given voice to protest, it was a "soft voice" in the sense that no aggregation or organization of protests was ever permitted.

It bears repeating that both of these "soft options" are defined *within* the system. The real hallmark of the Soviet case is that there was simply nowhere else to go. There was no real money to save or invest, no companies to own and run, no stocks or bonds, in short – no means for private wealth accumulation. Survival could be guaranteed only by advancement within the party-controlled hierarchy, or via illegal underground activity, which would also be under the control of the system managers, either directly or indirectly.[37]

A new theory of power

But what, then, does all of this imply for the project of radical economic reform that was launched after the implosion of the Soviet system? We mentioned at the outset of this chapter the paradox that lies in the fact that the introduction of market economy produced hyperdepression rather than an improved economic performance.

The very same paradox was addressed by Mancur Olson in a 1995 article. Comparing the pessimistic expectations that prevailed for post-war reconstruction in Germany and Japan to the optimistic expectations for reconstruction in post-communist Europe, he notes a stark contrast. While the former cases were so successful that they would become known as "economic miracles", the latter surprised in the opposite direction: "In fact, in most of the formerly communist societies economic performance so far has, paradoxically, been even worse than it was under communism. . . . there can be no doubt that economic performance in these countries after the collapse of communism has been dramatically below expectations."[38]

Adding to the complications, Olson also notes "another big surprise", in the form of an explosion of corruption and organized crime. Taken together, these observations prompt the need for a new theory of power, "a theory that focuses on coercive power (and the gains from wielding that power), on the incentives to acquire coercive power, and on the incentives facing those who have it".[39] Given that the analytical points raised by Olson will play a major role in our subsequent discussion of Russia's travails, we shall take some time here to recapitulate.

The main driving force behind the new theory of autocracy rests in the distinction between "narrow" and "encompassing" interests that was spelled out in Olson's earlier work on the *Rise and Decline of Nations*.[40] The logic, in a suggested criminal metaphor, is that an individual criminal operating in a populous society will carry only a minute part of the costs to society of his criminal activity – he thus has a *narrow* interest in not passing up any potentials for theft. On the contrary, a criminal who succeeds in monopolizing crime in his area will be forced to consider both costs and benefits. Since crime in various ways reduces the production possibilities, a criminal with an *encompassing* interest will have an incentive to suppress all other crime in his area, limiting himself to offering "protection".

The logical next step leads to the formation of a government, which succeeds in monopolizing theft on a long-term basis, thus having an incentive to optimize both taxation and the provision of public goods: "Most of the autocratic governments in history have in fact arisen from such seizures and conquests, and to a great extent their behavior is explained by modeling them as rational, optimizing, stationary bandits."[41]

The key here, which we shall have ample reason to return to in our subsequent argument, lies in the dimension of long-term security:

If an autocratic ruler has a short-term view, he has an incentive, no matter how gigantic his empire or how exalted his lineage, to seize any asset whose total value exceeds the discounted present value of its tax yield over his short-term horizon. In other words, just as the roving bandit leader who can securely hold a domain has an incentive to make himself king, so any autocrat with a short time horizon has an incentive to become, in effect, a roving bandit.[42]

Turning to apply this reasoning to the Soviet system, Olson brings forth a very special feature of Stalinism, an achievement that allowed the autocracy to extract without negative consequences for output. The key lies in simultaneously expropriating all productive assets and reserving the right to determine the rate of accumulation. The outcome was not only a high rate of investment, at the expense of consumption, but also an increase in extraction by adding all non-labour income: "In the long history of stationary banditry, no other autocrat had managed to do this."[43]

A more technical explanation derives from a distinction between marginal and inframarginal taxation. In a system of optimal extraction individuals would be faced with regressive tax rates, such that they are taxed heavily in the first bracket and not at all on their marginal income. This would provide strong incentives for extra effort, but it would also be impossible to introduce in a democratic setting, where all must face the same tax schedules. Those at the bottom would simply not have enough to survive.

To Stalin, that was not a problem. With basic wage rates set very low, and no alternatives being offered, the implied tax rate on low incomes was very high. To the strong, who were able to exert themselves, bonuses and perks of various kinds were offered. Perhaps the best illustration of Olson's model is that of Soviet agriculture. After putting in a day of labour for the collective, at little or no income, the peasants were allowed to continue working their private plots, and earn tax-free income. Thus exertion could be maximized.

There are two rather obvious problems with a model of this kind. One is that extracting hours is not necessarily the same as extracting effort; extra effort on the private plots may not compensate for sloppy work for the collective. The other is that all the distortions which resulted from suppressing markets would produce a lower total factor productivity – and a lower growth – than in a market economy at the same level of development. It is thus not surprising that economic stagnation was to become the true hallmark of the final decades of the Soviet system.

So far, however, we have merely been dealing with the superficial rules of the incentive system. The main thrust of Olson's theory of power lies in the introduction of a scope for collective action among the subordinates of the autocrat. The argument is built up in several steps.

Begin with the well known situation where subordinates within the bureaucracy have every incentive to shirk responsibilities and hide production possibilities. In order to explain how this system was able to survive, a countervailing force may be introduced in the form of competition among subordinates. There are two ways in which this may be exploited by the autocrat, or the central planner. One is to elicit better offers in the allocation of scarce resources, the other to encourage and reward denunciations of hoarding and shirking. Thus the absence of market-oriented incentives may be partly compensated for.

In a situation immediately after a shock or a shake-up, it would indeed seem reasonable to assume that there is a fair bit of competition among bureaucrats, who are all eager to shine by being in the vanguard of the new movement, say the cultural revolution in China. Gradually, however, as the situation stabilizes the incentives to collusion will gather strength: "Thus collusion or any kind of independent collective action among subordinates eliminates the competition that enables a Soviet-type economy to attain even modest degrees of productivity."[44]

The next step in the argument is to recognize that in contrast to a market-oriented setting, the Soviet environment is marked by an absence of money and property. Thus it will only be the autocrat, or the politburo, in which the property rights are vested, that will have an encompassing interest in making society work. Colluding groups will have quite narrow aims in pursuing their own special interests.

Step three is to introduce the notion of "market-contrary" economic policies, i.e. attempts by the autocrat, or the planner, to set prices, or introduce other regulations, that are far removed from the market solution. This implies that both parties to a transaction will have a common interest in hiding transgressions of the law, and in corrupting officials who are appointed to enforce it. Thus, "essentially all of the private sector incentives are on the side of undermining the rules".[45] This contributes to explaining the endemic corruption of the Soviet-type society, but it is far from the whole story.

It is the fourth step in the argument that really gets to the core of the system. By expropriating all productive assets, i.e. by eliminating private property, the stationary Soviet bandit also eliminates all self-interest among the subjects in guarding their property. In a market-oriented society, based on the rule of law, such self-interest is a powerful support for upholding the law. In a Soviet-type society it has no meaning.

With the autocrat, or the politburo, being the only actor in the system who has a clear interest in keeping resources from being stolen, it follows that an army of watchers must be created, which in turn must be watched by another army of watchers, and so on. Control logically becomes an obsession of the autocrat.

Returning to step one above, promoting competition among the guards would be a good way of making the system work. For the guards as a group, overthrowing the bandit and keeping the spoils for themselves would be the rational thing to do, but such an overthrow would represent a collective good, with all the associated problems of collective action. Thus it is more reasonable to expect the guards to collude in skimming off the take of the bandit, or the politburo. Gradually, such behaviour spreads to become endemic and thus to be viewed as both natural and right.

This brings us to the completion of Olson's theory of power, which is formulated as a "law of motion" of Soviet-type societies. Over time, collusive behaviour will not only generate increasing corruption and devour an increasing amount of resources in unproductive activities. It will also serve to produce informal norms supporting corrupt and criminal practices. Thus the system could not survive: "As communism devolved, it was bound to collapse".[46]

The real breaking point, which we shall have much more to say about in the following chapters, was that of money. By eliminating both property and money from the system, all exits could be effectively blocked. With all transactions (in money substitutes) going through one monolithic banking hierarchy, the autocrat, in this case the Gosbank, was in a good position to exercise control.

With the subsequent introduction of real money and real property, and with informal norm systems still being supportive of collusion and theft, the sluice gates were suddenly opened. With the autocrat, the politburo, being finally overthrown, nobody remained with an encompassing interest in making society work. Hyperdepression followed. As did massive wealth redistribution.

In the following chapters we shall set out to investigate how the introduction of market economy could bring about such a drastic breakdown for the real sector of the economy, and why it led to such massive redistribution of both wealth and incomes. In so doing, we shall place Olson's theory of power within the institutional context that has been briefly touched upon above.

One of the central tenets in the theory of institutional change concerns how the institutional matrix determines the pay offs in society, and thus also what people choose to do. If, for example, an economy is populated by pirates, this is because the institutional set-up rewards piracy: "The kinds of skills and knowledge that will pay off will be a function of the incentive structure inherent in the institutional matrix. If the highest rates of return in a society are piracy then organizations will invest in knowledge and skills that will make them better pirates."[47]

But why would a society have a pay off matrix that rewards piracy? Or, more properly, once created, how may such a situation be redressed? Both of these questions are intimately linked to the role of history. If a society does indeed exhibit an institutional matrix that rewards piracy, which we may interpret as roving banditry, the explanation must proceed in two steps. First, it must have begun with a situation of insecurity of property rights and a short time horizon. Secondly, we must be able to identify over time a path dependence whereby the society in question is locked into the inferior equilibrium.

The latter connection may be charted along two different tracks: one is the emergence of incentive systems that are marked by multiple equilibria, and are thus prone to "lock-in" effects, the other is the formation of norm systems, or "mental models", that may be associated with an inferior equilibrium.

This corresponds well with North's own formulation of the driving forces behind the process of institutional change. One relates to the pay off matrix: "The increasing returns characteristic of an initial set of institutions that provide disincentives to productive activity will create organizations and interest groups with a stake in the existing constraints." The other emphasizes the formation of norm systems: "The subjective mental constructs of the participants will evolve an ideology that not only rationalizes the society's structure but accounts for its poor performance. As a result the economy will evolve policies that reinforce the existing incentives and organizations."[48]

The main question, of course, both in theoretical terms and with respect to the concrete Russian case, is whether a society that has been locked into a situation of destructive roving banditry may actually find a way out. Briefly put, what type of shock may serve to generate a movement from the inferior to a superior equilibrium?

At this point we shall not attempt an answer, merely raise the crucial questions at hand. First, if we accept that mental models do influence the choice of player strategies, it follows that we must also spend some time thinking about how and when these models were created in the first place. Thus the need for a substantial historical background.

Turning then to the analytically challenging task of explaining how and when the population's mental models may be transformed, we must ask if such transformations take place only in reaction to observed transformations of surrounding reality, or if changes may be actively influenced by public policy?

Is it perhaps even the case that there exist "pathological" institutions, in the form of private mental models that are immune to public policy? The latter case, in which change will be difficult indeed to achieve, is highly provocative and will be dealt with at length below.

With this we shall conclude our discussion in this introductory chapter, and we shall do so in a fashion that has become distinctive of the discussion of Russia's economic reforms, namely by way of a metaphor.

Much as the yeast bacteria are diligently at work producing the alcohol that will spell their own destruction, the nature of the Soviet kleptocracy was such that it generated institutions – rules, norms and enforcement mechanisms – which served to erode the basis for its own long-term survival. As Olson also found, therefore, it was internally doomed to perish.

In an alternate biological analogy, the predatory state may be seen as an inferior form of parasite, one that draws so much blood that its host animal dies and its own survival is placed in danger.

Irrespective of analogies and metaphors, we may conclude that the Soviet economy perished not in competition with capitalism but from its own internal disease. The question that now remains to be asked is whether this was a Soviet or a Russian disease? Seeking to answer that question will be the purpose of the remaining chapters of this book.

Notes

1. Rosefielde, S. 1998a. *Efficiency and Russia's Economic Recovery Potential to the Year 2000 and Beyond.* Aldershot: Ashgate, p. xxvii.
2. Pipes, R. 1974. *Russia under the Old Regime.* New York: Charles Scribner, p. 9.
3. Ibid., p. 83.
4. Xenophobia was to be a prominent feature in subsequent Russian development. It is said, for example, that Tsar Michael (the first of the Romanovs) who reigned at the beginning of the seventeenth century had next to his throne a golden cup filled with water in which he could symbolically wash his hands after having received ambassadors from the contaminated West (Kochan, L. and Abraham, R. 1990. *The Making of Modern Russia.* Harmondsworth: Penguin, p. 94).
5. Robinson, G.T. 1932. *Rural Russia Under the Old Régime.* New York: Longmans, Green, p. 194.
6. EBRD 1997. *Transition Report Update.* London: EBRD, p. 12.
7. UN 1997. *World Investment Report 1997.* New York and Geneva: The United Nations, pp. 305, 307–8.
8. Abalkin, L. 1997. Insitutionalno-evolyutsionnaya teoriya i ee prikladnye aspekty, *Voprosy Ekonomiki* **3**, 4.
9. North, D.C. 1990. *Institutions, Institutional Change and Economic Performance.* Cambridge, Mass.: Cambridge University Press.
10. Shleifer, A. and Boycko, M. 1993. The politics of Russian privatization, in Blanchard, O. et al. (eds), *Post-Communist Reform.* Cambridge, Mass.: MIT Press, p. 39.
11. Roland, G. 1994. On the speed and sequencing of privatization and restructuring, *Economic Journal*, **104**, 1158.
12. See also Hedlund, S. and Sundström, N. 1996b. The Russian economy after systemic change, *Europe-Asia Studies*, **48**(6), 887–8.
13. Coase, R.H. 1992. The institutional structure of production, *The American Economic Review*, **82**(4), 714.
14. North, D. 1995. Economic performance through time, *The American Economic Review*, **84**(3), 366.
15. The increasing division of the economics profession into two camps was already highlighted in a 1994 article, where Richard Portes pointed at how

"Those who remained academics rather than advisors have adjusted expectations, looked for new models, may even have changed views", Portes, R. 1994. Transformation traps, *Economic Journal*, **104**, 1178.

16. Williamson, O.E. 1995. The institutions and governance of economic development. *Proceedings of the World Bank Annual Conference on Development Economics 1994*. Washington, DC: The World Bank, p. 173.

17. See further, Giersch, H., Paqué, K.-H. and Schmieding, H. 1992. *The Fading Miracle: Four Decades of Market Economy in Germany*. Cambridge: Cambridge University Press; and Goldman, M. 1996. *Lost Opportunity: What has Made Economic Reform in Russia so Difficult?*. New York: Norton, pp. 147–51.

18. Schroeder, G. 1979. The Soviet economy on a treadmill of "Reforms", in US Congress, Joint Economic Committee, *Soviet Economy in a Time of Change* (vol. I). Washington, DC: US Government Printing Office.

19. Goldman 1996, op. cit., p. 76, lists a total of 12 economic reform plans that were proposed and abandoned by Gorbachev.

20. Goldman, for example, finds that "given the distortions and abuses triggered by shock therapy, it is reasonable to ask if a more gradual approach to reform, as for example in China, would have produced distortions in Russia that were more disruptive than what actually took place. For example, would there have been more asset stripping? It is hard to see how that could have been". (Goldman, M. 1999. Can you get there from here: what must Russia do to become a normal market economy?, unpublished, p. 4.)

21. The case for the defence is laid out in great detail in Gaidar, Y. 1995. Russian reform, in Gidar, Y. and Pöhl, K.O. (eds), *Russian Reform/International Money*. Cambridge, Mass.: MIT Press.

22. Ibid., p. 26.

23. *Nezavisimaya Gazeta*, 18 December 1997.

24. *Sovetskaya Rossiya*, 20 December 1997.

25. On the various functions of norm systems, see also Elster, J. 1989. *The Cement of Society: A Study of Social Order*. Cambridge: Cambridge University Press, ch. 3 and *passim*.

26. The term was introduced in Grossman, G. 1963. Notes for a theory of the command economy, *Soviet Studies*, **15**(2).

27. One of the first Soviet analyses along these lines is Popov, G. 1987. S tochki zreniya ekonomista, *Nauka i zhizn*, **4**.

28. The first of these interview projects, the "Harvard Refugee Interview Project", was undertaken directly after World War II, and its results are presented above all in Berliner, J. 1957. *Factory and Manager in the USSR*. Cambridge, Mass.: Harvard University Press. The next big project, the "Soviet Interview Project", was undertaken in the 1980s and formed the basis for a number of important publications. Some of these have been collected in Millar, J. (ed.) 1987. *Politics, Work, and Daily Life in the USSR*. Cambridge: Cambridge University Press. Those living and working on the "inside", notably so in Poland and Hungary, were making parallel studies of the same problems but their results could not gain the same circulation.

29. Simis, K. 1982. *USSR: The Corrupt Society. The Secret World of Soviet Capitalism*. New York: Simon & Schuster; Vaksberg, A. 1991. *The Soviet Mafia*. New

York: St Martin's Press; Voslensky, M. 1984. *Nomenklatura: Anatomy of the Soviet Ruling Class*. London: Bodley Head.

30. Grossman, G. 1977. "The Second Economy" of the USSR, *Problems of Communism*, **26**(5), 32–3. In 1997, the chairman of the US House International Relations Committee, Benjamin Gilman, lifted this characteristic to the highest political level, by stating that Russia was "virtually a full fledged kleptocracy". (Quoted in CSIS 1997. *Russian Organized Crime: Global Organized Crime Project*. Washington, DC: Center for Strategic and International Studies, p. 2.)

31. Kornai, J. 1992. *The Socialist System: The Political Economy of Communism*. Oxford: Clarendon Press, ch. 15 and *passim*.

32. Hirschman, A. 1970. *Exit, Voice and Loyalty: Responses to Decline in Firms, Organizations and States*. Cambridge, Mass.: Harvard University Press.

33. See further Hedlund, S. 1989a. Exit, voice and loyalty – Soviet style, *Coexistence*, **26**(2).

34. Elster, J. 1985. *Sour Grapes: Studies in the Subversion of Rationality*. Cambridge: Cambridge University Press, p. 36.

35. See further, Gerner, K. and Hedlund, S. 1989. *Ideology and Rationality in the Soviet Model: A Legacy for Gorbachev*. London: Routledge, pp. 225–6.

36. See further, Hedlund, S. 1987. Soft options in central control, in Hedlund, S. (ed.), *Incentives and Economic Systems: Proceedings of the Eighth Arne Ryde Symposium*. London: Croom Helm.

37. Symptomatically, there are many accounts of how operators in the underground economy quite literally were forced to bury the proceeds from their activities in their back yards or hide them behind false walls (Voslensky, op. cit., ch. 5).

38. Olson, M. 1995. Why the transition from Communism is so difficult, *Eastern Economic Journal*, **21**(4), 437.

39. Ibid., p. 438.

40. Olson, M. 1982. *The Rise and Decline of Nations*. New Haven: Yale University Press.

41. Olson, 1995, op. cit., p. 440.

42. Ibid., p. 445.

43. Ibid., p. 446.

44. Ibid., p. 452.

45. Ibid., p. 454.

46. Ibid., p. 457.

47. North, D. 1993b. Towards a theory of institutional change, in Barnett, W.A., Hinich, M.J. and Scofield, N.J. (eds), *Political Economy*. Cambridge, Mass.: Cambridge University Press, p. 62.

48. North, 1990, op. cit., p. 99.

II

Framework

CHAPTER TWO

The heavy burden of history

There are certain points in time where decisive action, taken by a few individuals, may serve to change the course of history, be it for the better or for the worse. The months that followed in the wake of the failed August 1991 *coup* presented Russia's political elites with such a point of decision. Stating that the grand attempt at "systemic change", which was to follow, was an ambitious undertaking would certainly be no overstatement. But just how ambitious was it really? And why did it end in such a tragic failure?

The purpose of the present chapter is to map out in which dimensions the Russian reformers were to face their greatest challenges, thus placing ourselves in a better position to assess what it was that went wrong. Maintaining the institutional perspective that was outlined above, the reforms that were launched by Boris Yeltsin represented the imposition of a whole set of new formal rules of the game, namely those that are associated with democracy, market economy and the rule of law.

The question that will be asked below, and which really should have been asked by the Russian reformers themselves, concerns the following. In which respects would it be necessary for these new rules to be accompanied by a fundamental reorientation of the informal norms that had been associated with the old system, and with an equally fundamental transformation of the enforcement mechanisms that had been deployed by the old system managers?

The eventual outcome of the reform programme as a whole would be determined by the degree of successful interaction – or lack thereof – between these three processes of transformation. Thus the focus of our investigation has also been determined.

Once the role of informal norms has been brought into the picture, the role of history will also have to be approached. Thus we shall make substantial digressions into the Russian past, looking for Russian roots of the

Soviet system and for historical explanations to some of the difficulties facing the present-day reformers.

Before proceeding to this examination, there are, however, some terminological issues that first need to be clarified. Given the vital role of language as an instrument of thought and communication, it is important to note that many of the terms that were used to describe economic and political phenomena in the Soviet Union had Western connotations which frequently were very different from Soviet realities. This simple fact would add an extra dimension of complication, the importance of which has rarely been fully recognized.

An obvious example is the word "enterprise", which was used to translate the Russian terms *predpriyatie* or *obedinenie*. The problem here lies in the fact that a Soviet state owned enterprise had little in common with a Western market-oriented enterprise. It was not a legal person in its own right. It did not engage in either purchasing or marketing. It did not keep accounts, nor did it calculate costs and risks in order to persuade banks that it was creditworthy. It was quite simply nothing more than a workshop in the overall enterprise, which was sometimes referred to as "USSR Inc."

Similar comments can be made with regard to Soviet banks, which performed duties that had little indeed to do with banking in the market-oriented sense. They did not handle real money; there were no financial markets, no yield curves and no interest payments. Since there was no private property in either land or productive assets, it would, moreover, not even have been theoretically possible to offer serious collateral for a loan.

Moving into the domain of the Soviet political system, we may note that the very notion of a "one-party" state was a contradiction in terms; since "party" really means being but one part of the whole, if the whole is a monolith there can be no party. There were elections where the citizenry could vote (or not vote) for the officially approved list of candidates, but there was no choice. There were debates in thus "elected" bodies, but in any question of importance the outcome was predetermined. There were various interest organizations, such as labour unions, but they were all firmly integrated into the monolith.

In the legal sphere, finally, there was a superficial similarity with legal systems in the West. There were Soviet courts of law, with judges, prosecutors and defence counsel, which in trivial cases could work much as their Western counterparts. But in any case of economic or political importance, these courts were nothing more than obedient tools of relevant communist party supervisors. With a judiciary that was thus completely subordinated to the will of the party, it is debatable in which sense the word "justice" should be understood.

Bringing these observations together presents us with an image of a socioeconomic system that was fundamentally different from those institutional realities that have been at the focus of Western social science. Given that these differences were not reflected in the mirror of language, it is rather obvious that once systemic change was attempted a great deal of confusion was bound to arise – on both sides.

Above all, the underestimation of the true depth of the institutional differences between East and West would lead many to believe that the "transition" would not be all that difficult. The project as a whole could thus be conceived on the notion that *laissez-faire* would serve to liberate forces that were dormant under the surface.

If only all restraints could be freed, democracy, market economy and the rule of law would surge forth. One is tempted here to recall one of the battle cries of French students who spent a good part of 1968 tearing up the pavement in Paris streets: "*Sous les pavés il y a un plage!*" Bearing these observations in mind, let us now proceed to look at some very particular Russian complications.

Breaking up the monolith

If we are to fully appreciate the magnitude of the task that Boris Yeltsin set for himself – and for Russian society – when he launched his programme of building a democratic, power sharing, market-oriented state, based on the rule of law, we must begin by noting two fundamental Russian *differentiae specificae*. Both date back to the rise of Muscovy, in the fourteenth century, and both would have considerable impact on the way in which this latest in a very long row of Russian reform projects was to unfold.

The first lies in the fact that throughout the Russian tradition power has rested in the executive branch alone. A long succession of rulers, from tsars to general secretaries, have incorporated in themselves both the legislative and judiciary components of government. There are some short-lived exceptions to this rule, which will be discussed below, but in principle the statement stands.

The second and perhaps even more crucial Russian characteristic is that the dividing line between power and property has never been clearly and firmly drawn. The rulers have claimed not only absolute power but also exclusive property rights, thus making it exceedingly difficult to draw a line between politics and economics.

In his classic study of the "patrimonial society" in Russia, Richard Pipes places particular stress on the fundamental role that has been played by the institution of private property in Western society: "One may say that the existence of private property as a realm over which public authority normally exercises no jurisdiction is the thing which distinguishes Western political experience from the rest."[1]

In making this distinction, Pipes is also careful to underline that the patrimonial regime "is a regime in its own right, not a corruption of something

36

else". Where a despot, for example, violates the property rights of his subjects, the patrimonial ruler does not even acknowledge the existence of any such rights: "In a patrimonial state there exist no formal limitations on political authority, no rule of law, nor individual liberties."[2]

An immediate implication of these observations is that the current Russian process of systemic change must be distinguished from previous processes of twentieth century democratization. In his book about *Varieties of Transition*, Claus Offe makes this distinction very clearly. His background is that of previous comparative studies of countries which have undertaken a successful "transition to democracy".

The first such group is the "post-war democracies" (Italy, Austria, Japan and West Germany). In the 1970s three Mediterranean countries followed (Greece, Portugal and Spain), and in the 1980s a string of authoritarian regimes in Latin America collapsed (Argentina, Brazil, Chile, Paraguay and Uruguay).

Referring to the studies of these three groups of countries as an "important and highly successful research branch in the social sciences", Offe nevertheless cautions against extending the field into the post-socialist world: "The suggestive temptation to add a fourth group to these – that is, that of the Central and East European states – and to analyze them with the proven instrument supplied by this research tradition turns out, however, to be at least partly unsuitable and misleading."[3]

His reasons for this caution are that two serious complications have been added, namely territorial disputes and the need to reform the economy. Leaving the former aside, the latter does have some considerable relevance for the argument that is pursued here.

In all of the cases referred to above, the problem of transition was exclusively political and constitutional. Reformers were seeking to establish working democratic institutions, i.e. separating the executive part of government from the legislature and the judiciary. In the Russian case, we have the added complication of separating the political and legal sphere from the economy, i.e. the dual task of not only creating working democratic and legal institutions, but also the laying of the foundations for a working market economy. As we shall see below, that addition was to be no minor complication.

The roots of the Russian problem may be found in the rather curious blending of power and property that occurred early on in its history and would maintain its hold on Russian society for centuries to come. The essence of the patrimonial society was that the ruler combined in his person both the right to rule over all his subjects and the right to dispose of all property. He was thus not only a supreme ruler, a *samoderzhets*, but also the sole owner of the country's productive assets, thus rendering the very notion of "property" rather meaningless. Where there is no private property, it will also be impossible to draw a line between politics and the economy. All blends into one.

Seen from this perspective, the differences between old Russia and the modern Soviet state are not all that great. After removing some of the superficial decorations of the latter, we may find the same absence of private property, the same concentration of unaccountable power, the same subordination of justice, the same controls over freedom of speech and organization, and the same blending of politics and the economy. For all their outward manifestations of being worlds apart, the actual differences between these two systems may thus be reduced to matters of degree rather than of principle.

The implication of this miniature historical digression is that when Boris Yeltsin launched his "radical" reforms, he was dealing with a legacy that consisted not only of seven decades of destructive Soviet rule. In several important respects, which will be detailed below, he was also taking on a legacy of several centuries of failed Russian reforms. At the time, however, this latter complication was largely ignored. Under the circumstances of a rapidly collapsing Soviet system, it was all too easy to blame everything on communism, and to see *laissez-faire* as the one and only way ahead.

The implication of systemic change was that the Soviet monolith would have to be broken up and transformed into a pluralistic society, with clearly drawn dividing lines between the executive power and the four sectors that are illustrated in Figure 2.1 below, namely: a) the legislature, which was to make the new rules, b) the judiciary, which was to enforce them, c) the banks, which were to provide a financial system, and d) the enterprises, which were to tap the vast natural resources and set in motion a process of rapid high-tech economic recovery.

In all four of these directions, the executive would run into serious confrontations, thus indicating that the visions of a rapid "transition", with perhaps substantial but still brief suffering, had failed to take into account some very basic institutional realities. Some of these conflicts were of a technical nature, i.e. steps that were taken perhaps in great haste, that were

Figure 2.1   Four zones of confrontation

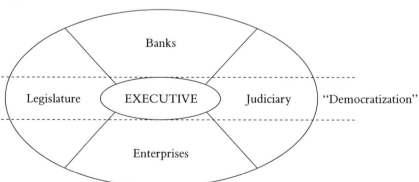

ill-advised. Others were linked to contradictory features in the political process, which were simply assumed out of existence. Yet others had their roots in the country's political culture, roots that go far back in history. All three will be mapped out in the following chapters.

In the present chapter, we shall trace the historical background to each of these four types of confrontation. Here it will be done in a mainly narrative form, with analysis and evaluation to follow in Chapters 8 and 9, once we have also taken a closer look at developments under Yeltsin's economic reforms.

We shall begin our investigation by looking at the background to the long row of confrontations that would be played out between the executive and the legislature, i.e. between President Boris Yeltsin and the Supreme Soviet and, later on, the State Duma. This was not only that part of the reform process which would have the highest political profile. By implication, it would also set an important example for actors moving in the other three zones of confrontation.

Above all, it was in this dimension that the president would feel most acutely the heavy burden that was placed on his own political leadership. It would now be up to him to uphold an arrangement of sharing his own political power with the members of the Supreme Soviet, i.e. those very men and women who – collectively – had subjected him to such humiliations in the past. This undertaking, as we now know, would be a tall order indeed.

The legislature

The conflict between the executive and legislative branches of power is basic, in the sense that it concerns the right to set the formal rules of the game. If this power is to be effectively shared, there has to be a fundamental ability and willingness on both sides to respect the rights of the other side, and to honour agreements made in situations of conflict.

This in turn requires that there is a certain amount of trust involved. If that trust is betrayed, such that the relation repeatedly degenerates into pure conflict, where agreements are made under duress only to be broken at the earliest convenience, then the very pre-conditions for power sharing are eroded, perhaps even fatally so. It is in this context that we must see the heritage from the past.

The patrimonial society

The roots of Russia's patrimonial society may be found in old Muscovy, at the time when the warring principalities around Moscow began to coalesce into a centralized state. It was a rather curious turn of history that eventually would transform a small remote town on the Moscow river into the capital city of a global superpower. There was little in the cards, neither resource wealth nor proximity to other great centres of trade or civilization, that would have led anyone to predict this transformation.

Pipes captures the essence of the paradox: "On the face of it, nature intended Russia to be a decentralized country formed of a multitude of self-contained and self-governing communities. Everything here militates against statehood: the poverty of the soil, remoteness from the main routes of international trade, the sparsity and mobility of the population."[4]

Moscow gets its first mention in the chronicles in 1147, at a time when the land of Rus, the *Kievskaya Rus*, was controlled from Kiev, the capital city of present-day Ukraine. At its height this was a great state, stretching from the Neva in the north to just east of Suzdal and Vladimir in the east and to just south of Kiev in the south. Most importantly, it was a state that from an institutional perspective was fundamentally different from its eventual northern successor.

The Kiev state was ruled by a prince, whose functions were primarily military and judicial. He exercised his power in a form of co-operation with a council of independent landowners, known as boyars, who in essence formed a nascent landed aristocracy. The prince was no absolute ruler, but more of a "first among equals", a *primus inter pares*. Urban government was conducted by a popular assembly, the *veche*, in which all free male adults had a voice.

In the countryside, the bulk of the population were known as *smerdi*, a form of free farmers owning their own homesteads, having their own land, animals and implements. All of this was property that could be bequeathed. In addition, the chronicles mention *zakupki*, legally free but landless peasants who were dependent on labour performed for others, and *kholopy*, who were either true slaves, taken in war, or peasants who by failing to fend for themselves had been reduced to near slavery.[5]

Before the rise of Muscovy we may thus talk of an embryonic system of power sharing and of a rather broad base of private property. For the princes who were to make Muscovy strong, there was challenge in both of these dimensions: to establish autocratic rule and to eradicate private property. If one name is to be associated with this task it has to be Ivan III, also known as Ivan the Great, the highly successful ruler of Muscovy in 1462–1505. But the rise of Muscovy would not have been possible without the prior decline of Kiev.

The beginning of the end for Kiev was signalled with the death of Yaroslav in 1054. Following the wish of their father, his five sons and a grandson undertook to rule the land collectively. The eldest son became the ruler of Kiev, with the title of Grand Prince, and the others received lesser towns and territories, known as appanages. This was the birth of "appanage Russia", an inherently unstable order that was bound to create disunity and weakness. By 1100 the once mighty Kiev state had broken down into 12 largely unconnected principalities.

This internal weakening made the land of Rus less capable of standing up to pressure from the outside. From the east barbarian raiders carried off thousands of Russians into slavery, to the south crusaders pushed Kiev out of the lucrative Mediterranean trade, to the southwest pressure was building from the Hungarians, and in the west Teutonic knights, Lithuanians and Swedes were advancing. For the peasantry of Rus, flight to the northeast was increasingly seen as the way out.

In 1169, Kiev was sacked by a coalition of 12 princes led by Andrei Bogolyubskii. The capital of Rus was moved to Vladimir, in Bogolyubskii's principality of Rostov–Suzdal. This increase in distance between Rus and Constantinople was the beginning of a trend of isolation, which reached a completion of sorts with the "Mongol Storm" of 1237–40. For the coming 240 years, the Russians would be ruled by the descendants of Ghenghis Khan. Under this "Mongol Yoke" all contacts with Western Europe were disconnected. In consequence, Russia would miss out on Renaissance, Reformation and Enlightenment.

It was in this context that the rise of Muscovy began. From their seat at Sarai, on the lower Volga, the Mongol khans ruled according to the classic principle of *divide et impera*. They took no great interest in colonization, but were all the more keen on collecting tribute and on demanding absolute obedience. Most importantly, the khans reserved for themselves the right to decide who would rule in the various Russian principalities.

For the Russian princes this implied a need to travel to Sarai, where they engaged in Byzantine intrigues and palace politics. The prize was an authorization from the khan, known as *yarlyk*, which confirmed the prince as ruler of his principality. Some 130 Russian princes are recorded to have made the pilgrimage, from which many never returned.

An important feature of this form of rule was that the Russian cities gradually lost their free urban institutions. Mongol troops, moreover, that were quartered in the principal Russian towns served not only to suppress frequent rebellions. They would also gladly intervene on one side or the other in local conflicts, being invited by one prince to help in defeating another (and in taking part in the loot). Thus the land of Rus was kept in a state of internal disunity.

The key to the rise of Muscovy to power over the other Russian principalities lies in its skilful manipulation of relations to the khans. The right to collect taxes from all of Rus was obtained already under Ivan Kalita (1325–41) and in 1353 Muscovy was acknowledged by the khan to have judicial authority over all the other principalities. In return, it was Prince Dmitry Donskoi of Muscovy who in 1380 fought and won the first decisive battle against the Mongols.

When Ivan the Great came to power there was, therefore, already considerable momentum to capitalize upon. By the end of his reign, the Mongols would no longer be a power to be reckoned with, and the might of Muscovy as a centralized state would be firmly entrenched. Turning now to see how this was done, we shall follow the distinction made above between power and property.

Ivan's main mission was that of regaining the "Patrimony of Yaroslav", i.e. of reconstituting – under Muscovy – a united Slav state. This implied not only a "gathering of the lands", i.e. uniting all the tiny Russian principalities, but also winning back land that had been taken by Lithuania after the Mongol invasion and breaking Mongol rule. Achieving these missions in turn implied a need to strengthen his own power.

The first step on the path towards the creation of a centralized Russian state was to break the appanage system, a task that Ivan completed by successfully attacking the power and privileges of his brothers and other appanage princes.[6] Thus the *primus inter pares* of old was transformed into a true autocrat. The confirmation of this process came in 1547, when Ivan IV, also known as Ivan the Terrible, was crowned Tsar of Russia.

Step two was to deal with the independent principalities, a task that Ivan the Great proceeded to undertake by both diplomacy and outright purchases. One by one they succumbed and recognized his rule. So far Muscovy had been growing peacefully. The real watershed came in the great stand-off with Novgorod.

Having obtained self-government from Kiev Rus already in 997, in 1136 "Lord Great Novgorod" gained complete independence. For more than three centuries to come, it would be a flourishing centre of trade and culture, one, moreover, which succeeded in preserving its old republican institutions.

The prince of Novgorod shared his power with the *veche*, which even had some legislative authority. The city was ruled by a mayor of sorts, known as *posadnik*. It was a major trading centre within the Hanseatic League and it had a relatively independent church. In short, it was a dangerous ideological rival to an increasingly autocratic Muscovy.

The fact that the Mongols had not conquered Novgorod did not mean that its independence was secure. On the contrary, it was conditioned upon balancing Lithuanians on the one side and Mongol-dominated Muscovy on the other. As long as the latter two were of reasonably equal strength Novgorod was doing fine. Faced with the growing strength of Muscovy, however, in 1471 pro-Lithuanian forces in Novgorod sought an understanding with Poland–Lithuania. In response, Ivan the Great launched a brief but successful military campaign, which put an effective end to the independence of Novgorod.

At the time of his death, Ivan had dealt successfully with both Novgorod and the Mongols, but the struggle with Lithuania was still to be settled. Under the subsequent reigns of Vasilii III and Ivan the Terrible, Muscovy would expand further, but only to the south and the east. For another century, Poland–Lithuania would remain in control of the lands from the Black Sea in the south to the Neva in the north. Subsequent rivalry between these two Slavic states would have far-reaching implications.

While the creation of a strong centralized Muscovy, with Ivan the Great in power as a true autocrat, did represent an important achievement in itself, it was the parallel ambition of suppressing the institution of private property that would lend to the state its most important *differentia specifica*.

As was noted above, Kiev Rus as well as early Muscovy rested on a system of hereditary private property. In the twelfth century Russian law code (*Russkaya Pravda*) it was stated that if a boyar died without sons, his daughters would inherit instead, "a provision which indicates that by this time the boyars were absolute owners of their properties".[7] The Russian name for this form of landholding was *votchina*, a name that is derived from the same root as the Russian word for "father" (*otets*). From a perspective of the rule of law, this implied that there was also a system of regulated individual rights.

It is a generally accepted fact that the boyars were independent freeholders rather than vassals in the Western feudalist sense. They were free to leave the service of one prince and enter into the service of another, without losing their property, and they could serve one prince while having landed property on the territory of another.

This custom of free service is documented in many sources: "Customary law guaranteed boyars the right to enrol in the service of the Russian prince of their choice; they could even serve a foreign ruler, such as the Grand Prince of Lithuania."[8] There was a standard phrase employed, stating that boyars should be free to choose "among us" whom to serve, and "Numerous surviving accords among princes . . . explicitly forbade the confiscation of the estates of departing boyars."[9]

In this sense, we may say that in medieval times Russia was actually ahead of Western Europe in the development towards market economy. But that was soon to change. Pipes captures the essence of this reversal of roles:

> One of the striking peculiarities of Russian history is that the development of property rights in that country ran exactly contrary to its course in Western Europe. In the West, conditional possession, embodied in the fief, gradually turned into outright ownership. In Russia, by contrast, absolute property evolved into conditional possession. This process occurred as a result of deliberate policy of Moscow princes to compel all secular land-holders without exception to render them service. As the grand princes of Moscow extended their authority throughout Russia, the principle of compulsory service became nationwide, providing a central pillar of the patrimonial state.[10]

The mechanisms by which this suppression of the institution of private property was achieved were of different kinds. The most important instrument was the introduction of a competing form of landholding, known as *pomestie*. The background was that the expansion of the state created a rapidly growing need for soldiers and bureaucrats, who somehow would have to be rewarded. These rewards would be offered in the form of land grants, with tenure for life conditional upon service to the tsar.

Ivan the Great laid the foundations for this policy by claiming personal property rights to all land, and he put it into systematic practice after the conquest of Novgorod.[11] Many of the local population were expropriated and deported, and their land handed over to loyal *pomeshchiki* from Moscow. Under Ivan the Terrible the practice of forceful deportations assumed proportions that would be paralleled only by Joseph Stalin.

The fundamental principle that was introduced by Ivan, as a rationale for this policy, was that land must not be separated from service (*zemlya ne dolzhna vykhodit iz sluzhby*). This principle would be of lasting importance for the coming three centuries. Its implication was that all landowners (except the church) were placed under an obligation to serve the prince (or the tsar, from Ivan the Terrible onwards). Ownership was thus fully conditioned upon service and surrounded by considerable arbitrariness.[12]

Often the rulers did not even bother to invent excuses for their expropriations. As Pipes notes, it was a political rather than a judicial process: "Landlords who for any reason did not satisfy the crown were evicted and their holdings confiscated. The decisive factor in confiscations was political, not juridical."[13] From a perspective of the rule of law, this was something very different from the regulated rights that had existed in Kiev Rus and in early Muscovy.

With the territorial expansion of Muscovy, the rulers found at their disposal more and more land that could be handed over to loyal supporters as *pomestie* land, on condition of continued service. Gradually, *pomestie* land thus came to dominate *votchina* land. It was, however, not a question of two separate classes of landowners. *Pomestia* were granted to holders of *votchiny* as well, and landholdings were widely scattered.

In the law code of 1550, the *tsarskii sudebnik*, Ivan the Terrible extended the service obligation to include *votchina* land. Thus the old Mongol principle of unquestioning and unqualified service to the ruler had been extended to cover all secular Russian landowners.

The church, though, remained an exception. Ivan did inquire of a church council whether church lands could be secularized but was turned down. In return, the church rendered excellent service as a propaganda machine for the tsar. It served to keep the state together, and no doubt was also helpful in extracting from the peasantry on behalf of the tsar.

With the extension of the service obligation, it was natural that many landowners would try to evade service by getting rid of their land, but this form of exit was soon to be blocked. The donation of *votchiny* to monasteries was prohibited, and if anyone tried to sell his *votchina* in order to avoid the service obligation he could be whipped "without pity" and be forced to hand over the property in question to the intended buyer without compensation.[14]

Perhaps the most important instrument in curtailing the institution of private property was that of a simple effect of lock-in. Although the technical right of boyars to depart without confiscation of their property would be honoured in name as late as 1530,[15] the territorial expansion of Muscovy eroded the actual contents of that right.

With the conversion of Lithuania to Catholicism, in 1386, this exit had been closed. Any boyar departing for Lithuania would automatically become an apostate and his property could be confiscated, together with those of his family and clan. And with Muscovy's triumph over Novgorod, Lithuania was the only place left to go. There was thus no place left to go.

Thus the *de facto* enserfment of the Russian nobility was completed, without any law restricting their movement ever having been passed. The term "service nobility" could be put to good use.

The practice of arbitrary expropriations and mass deportations became an essential feature of the system, so much so, in fact, that in 1729 the Russian government established "a bureau that must be unique in history, namely a Chancery of Confiscation (*Kantselaria konfiskatsii*)".[16]

It was under Peter the Great that the system of mandatory lifelong service to the tsar reached its completion. It was Peter who first laid claims to imperial stature, allowing himself in 1721 to be crowned "Imperator of all the Russias", and it was Peter who codified the total supremacy of the autocracy, albeit only in passing. In his military regulation from 1710, which was in force up until the early twentieth century, it was stipulated that "His majesty is an absolute monarch who is not obliged to answer for his actions to anyone in the world".[17]

But it was not simply a question of personal power for the autocrat. With the introduction in 1722 of the "Table of Ranks", the system of mandatory service was also brought to its highest point of refinement. The basic idea was to organize Russian society as a whole along the lines of service rather than blood. There were a total of 14 ranks, covering both the military and the civil service. Promotion from one rank to another was linked to performance, and hereditary nobility was awarded upon reaching the eighth rank (beginning at one). A Herald Master supervised the whole system. It would remain in place until the very end of tsardom.

A slow return to legal regulation

The post-Petrine period would be marked by a gradual erosion of patrimonialism. The growth of the empire had once and for all removed the constant threat of national extinction by foreign invasion. Why then should the nobility accept the hardships of lifelong service? Or, indeed, why should the autocracy rely on the services of often incompetent noblemen, when a professional apparat could be built to do the job?

The first major step on the road towards a regulated relation between the autocracy and the nobility came in 1736, in the reign of Anna, when compulsory service was reduced from life to merely 25 years. At the same time, it was also decided that if a father had two sons, one would be freed from service altogether.

But it was under Peter III that the nobility scored its first real victories. During his brief tenure of merely six months in 1762, a series of liberal decrees permitted the nobles to resign from state service, to travel abroad and to enter into the service of non-Russian powers (in peacetime). The necessary conditions for the establishment of private property and free enterprise had thus been fulfilled.

Under Catherine the Great, this process of liberation culminated with the introduction, in 1785, of her "Charter of the Nobility". In Article 11 of this important document it was stated that "A noble will not be deprived of his property without due process of law".[18] This was also the first time that the very notion of "private property" was introduced in the Russian language. Being of German extraction, Catherine made a direct translation from her own language. Thus *"Eigentum"* became *"sobstvennost"*.

Formally, Russia had thus been returned to the firm foundations of legal regulation and due process that had existed, if only embryonically, in old Kiev Rus. But it was late in the day. Catherine's charter was introduced nine years after the publication of Adam Smith's classic work *The Wealth of Nations*. In Western Europe, the market economy had been completed. In Russia there was still a long way to go.

The first part of the nineteenth century was heavily marked by the Napoleonic wars. At the beginning of his rule, in 1801, Tsar Alexander I was something of a liberal. He abolished the secret police (which had been reintroduced by Paul, the son of Catherine), removed the prohibition on foreign travel for the nobility and permitted the import of foreign publications. Gradually, however, the experience of the war convinced him that his mission as the saviour of Europe would not be compatible with any domestic reforms. He would end his rule in isolation, therefore, with dissent growing under the surface.

The death of Alexander I occurred in the midst of a conspiracy to take his life. The great war with Napoleon had brought many young Russian noblemen into contact with life outside Russia. Thus the seeds of a liberal opposition were sown. The first "sprouting" came with the abortive Decembrist revolt in 1825.

Although the *coup* as such was something of a non-event, followed by strikingly mild repression, it did serve to convince the new tsar, the 29 year old Nicholas I, of the dangers that surrounded the autocracy. His three decades in power would thus be characterized by a siege mentality, and his last words to his son were to "Hold on to everything!".

When Alexander II became tsar in 1855, he was not only the best-prepared heir thus far to ascend the throne. He was also the object of great expectations, from all those who had come to despair under Nicholas's conservative rule. His first acts also seemed to hold promise for great changes. In 1861, the system of serfdom was finally abolished. Shortly thereafter a system of local self-government, the *zemstvo*, was introduced, to be followed by profound legal reforms (more about the latter in a moment).

For all his reformist ambitions, however, Alexander II remained convinced about Russia's need for autocracy and his reforms were more a question of a delegation of power than of true reform. Given the rapid social changes that were taking place below the surface, most notably so in the form of an increasingly radical intelligentsia, the retreat of the autocracy was too little too late. Alexander II found himself increasingly isolated and finally ended his life in a terrorist bombing.

His son, Alexander III, was a powerful tsar with no reformist ambitions whatsoever. Under the influence of the reactionary lay head of the Orthodox Church, Konstantin Pobedonostsev, the new tsar set about reversing many of the reforms undertaken by his father, reforms that were branded by Pobedonostsev as "criminal errors".

The beginning of the twentieth century witnessed a gradual disintegration of the Russian autocracy. Shaken by the uprisings in 1905, Tsar Nicholas II was talked into granting a conditional form of democracy, spelled out in the famous "October Manifesto". Although he rapidly regretted his retreat, and proceeded to dilute some of the concessions, there was a succession of elections to a parliament of sorts that was known as the State Duma.

One of the restrictions imposed on the rights granted in the Manifesto was a provision for dissolution of the Duma, which was put to good use. The first Duma was dissolved after only 10 weeks, and the second after three months. After some rigging of the election rules, a third Duma was elected which was more malleable. This was one of the most important phases in Russian history, one that perhaps could have provided a true turning point.

Popular representation?

Looking back into history, the origins of the Russian Duma may be found in the Norman period, when it was customary for princes to hold consultations with the elder members of their *druzhiny*. Before the rise of Muscovy, the Duma was made up of servitors charged with administration and tax collection, but over time it became more aristocratic. Up until the reign of Ivan the Terrible it provided representation for the leading clans, but as their power waned it was increasingly merit rather than ancestry that decided who was to be asked.

Noting that Russian historians "have spilled much ink" over the question of whether the Duma had real legislative and administrative power, Pipes finds that evidence speaks against such an interpretation. Its composition was unstable, with membership varying over time from a high of 167 to a low of merely two. It had no calendar of sessions and no clear area of competence. It kept no record of debates, and left traces mainly in the form of a sentence often added to decrees: "the tsar ordered and the boyars affirmed". In 1711, Peter let it slip quietly into history, to be replaced by the Senate.

Recalling our perspective from above, of looking for an effective arrangement of power sharing between the executive and the legislature, this was obviously not even close: "For all these reasons, the Duma is best regarded not as a counterweight to royal authority but as its instrumentality; a proto-cabinet rather than a proto-parliament. Its main importance lay in the opportunity it afforded high officials to participate in the formulation of policies they were obliged to carry out."[19]

In addition to the Duma, there is another institution, known as the Assembly (*Sobor*), which also played a role that might be confused with popular representation. In contrast to the Duma, the Assembly was called primarily in times of national crisis. It consisted of the members of the Duma, plus the high clergy and regional representatives. Rather than holding elections, however, personal invitations were sent out.

The first known Assembly met in 1549, but it was not until the "Time of Troubles" (1598–1613) that it gained real prominence. In 1613 it elected the first of the Romanovs, Tsar Michael, and it then sat in almost continuous session until 1622. As the autocracy stabilized, however, the Assembly declined in importance. In 1648–9 it was convened to ratify the new law code, the *ulozhenie*, and in 1653 it met for the last time.

Pipes summarizes the limited importance of these experiences:

> In sum, the Duma and the Assemblies may best be viewed as expedients necessary to the state until such time as it could afford an adequate bureaucratic apparatus. The Duma provided a link between the crown and the central administration, the Assembly a link between the crown and the provinces. As the bureaucratic apparatus improved, both institutions were quietly dropped.[20]

The main characteristic of autocratic rule under Peter the Great was that of a more rational and professional bureaucracy, streamlined with the Table of Ranks. Its basic principle, however, was hardly that of participation. This was the time when the secret police was born, and when denunciation became an important instrument of exercising control over the subjects. And so it would remain until the end of tsardom.

It is against this background that the October Manifesto takes on such paramount importance. With the possible exception of the *zemstvo*, which was elected on a property franchise, this was the first time in Russian history that a popular assembly was elected on a general franchise. Needless to say, its first meeting with the tsar, in the Winter Palace, was a rather tense occasion, marked by fears of bombs being thrown.

Given the circumstances, it was perhaps not surprising that the political climate surrounding this experiment in democracy would be one of confrontation. Rather than choosing to work with the autocracy, seeking further reform, Duma members began asking for the impossible. Calls were issued for the government to resign, for political prisoners to be released, for the death penalty to be abolished, etc.

The general atmosphere of confrontation also served to sour relations between the autocracy and the government, or, more precisely, between the tsar and Prime Minister Sergei Witte, who had been instrumental in bringing about the October Manifesto: "Nicholas II loathed and hated Witte for divesting him of some of his inherited prerogatives particularly when he failed to restore order".[21]

Witte lasted only six months, but although his successor, the powerful Prime Minister Pyotr Stolypin, did succeed in restoring order, Nicholas does not seem to have shed many tears over his assassination: "Stolypin, the last considerable politician of Imperial Russia, died of a police agents' bullet in the autumn of 1911 – to the great relief of his master".[22]

The final days of the fourth Duma were rather characteristic. With the Great War having destroyed whatever confidence might have remained between the government and the people, attempts were made to force the Duma to take power. For this purpose, on 14 February, Aleksandr Kerenskii took the tribune and called for the tsar to be murdered.

Although this rather unorthodox parliamentary move did serve to produce major strikes and demonstrations, the Duma would not allow itself to be pushed into – illegally – assuming power. Instead, on 27 February it was dissolved by the tsar, who himself would be forced to step down on 2 March.

The period leading from the abdication of Nicholas II to the Bolshevik *coup d'état*, i.e. from February to October 1917 (old style) was to form a sort of "democratic parenthesis" in Russian history. For the first time in centuries there was a popularly elected assembly with no superior power in control. Conceivably, this could have provided the real breakthrough for Russian democracy. But that was not to be.

One of the reasons for the eventual failure of this attempt at democracy was the political weakness of the "Provisional Government" that was formed under Aleksandr Kerenskii. Caught in the crossfire between the Duma and the Petrograd Soviet, Kerenskii could never free himself from a feeling that the real threat came not from the left but from Monarchist forces planning a counter-*coup*. Thus his leniency towards the Bolsheviks, which paved the way for Lenin.

The decisive moment came not with the Bolsheviks' October *coup*, but in January 1918, when the newly elected Constituent Assembly gathered for its first meeting. Here the Bolsheviks found themselves in the minority, having won only 175 seats against the 350 seats of the Socialist-Revolutionaries. Having lost the very first vote, Lenin decided to put an end to the show. The delegates were sent home and that was it. The Red Guards took over. Russia's first attempt at introducing a system of power sharing, based on the rule of law, had ended in failure.

The Soviet order

When the Bolsheviks subsequently launched their project of creating a "Soviet" society, the real essence of their programme was to restore both the autocracy and the patrimonial society. Although it was nominally done in the name of "the people", the professional party elite displayed a clear ambition of establishing a system that rested on unaccountable power and an effective elimination of all private property in the means of production. With the 1921 prohibition on factions within the party, these ambitions reached their formal completion. Unbridled red terror would deal with all forms of opposition to the new order.

Throughout the Soviet period, the system was based on a formal division of power, but that was mere decoration. There was a legislature, the Supreme Soviet, and there was a government, the Council of Ministers, but in practice all important issues (and most certainly a host of unimportant ones too) were decided by the party apparatus.

Soviet administration rested on the somewhat fuzzy principle that the party "leads but does not govern" (*rukovodit no ne upravlyayet*). The idea behind this formulation was that the party should be charged with overall strategy, leaving day-to-day management to the state apparatus. But what that meant more precisely in a concrete situation was never made clear. The absence of clear-cut rules in fact was one of the hallmarks of Soviet politics.

While the Supreme Soviet, for example, formally was an elected body, the politburo, which was the real centre of power, practised an unregulated form of co-optation. The formation of a separate Western scholarly discipline, known as Kremlinology, which sought to penetrate behind the shrouds, illustrates that this system was not all that different from the games of "*neglasnost*" that had been played by the tsars and boyars of old Muscovy.[23]

When Mikhail Gorbachev introduced his policy of "*glasnost*", the shrouds were torn down and many (though not all) of the secrets of the party's sordid past were brought out into the open. But, as we shall see in the following chapter, openness was not to be sufficient. For all his talk about "democratization", Gorbachev would never demonstrate any serious inclinations towards a political system that was based on a true division of power.

Most importantly, he would never take the risk of facing his people in an open election. When he was appointed president of the Soviet Union it was done by decree, and when he held elections to a newly created Congress of People's Deputies, blocks of seats were reserved for various categories, such as high party officials.

With the possible exception of the "democratic parenthesis" of 1917, it would thus be correct to say that up until the open Russian presidential election in 1991, which was won by Boris Yeltsin, Russia had never experienced anything but indivisible and unaccountable power. At times that power had been partly delegated, but it had never been contested in an open election. The experiences of 1917, moreover, provided some important insight into the difficulties of establishing a functioning separation of power, based on trust and honouring agreements.

After the failed *coup* of August 1991, the challenge to Russian president Boris Yeltsin, himself a former senior member of the communist party politburo, was to create a system of checks and balances between the legislature and his own executive power. Simply put, he would have to introduce constraints on his own ability to dominate and control the very body that incarnated all he had struggled against.

The American way of doing this would have been to produce a written constitutional arrangement, to which both parties could have pledged their allegiance. But there are many European alternatives to this emphasis on formal rules, indicating that functioning "checks and balances" may be created only if the political culture is amenable to that form of contract. And then we are back to Thomas Hobbes, who will figure prominently in our later chapters.

By now we have entered into the second of our four zones of confrontation, that of separating the judiciary from the executive, and of somehow making sure that the latter would respect the new arrangement. Compared to the task of separating the executive and legislative branches of government, this would prove to be even more challenging.

The judiciary

The institution of an independent judiciary was a Roman invention, dating back to the second century BC. By the late Middle Ages it had spread to most of the countries of Western Europe, but until the judicial reforms of Alexander II, in the 1860s, Russia had known nothing of independent justice. Russia, according to Pipes, "in this respect resembled rather the ancient oriental monarchies where royal officials typically dispensed justice as part of their administrative obligations".[24] The reforms of Alexander II would, moreover, in some respects be short-lived indeed.

In order to fully appreciate the heavy weight of his historical heritage, we may add that "Until the 1860s Russian jurisprudence did not even recognize the distinction between laws, decrees, and administrative ordinances, all of which, once approved by the sovereign, were treated with equal solemnity". Laws concerning fundamental issues were treated on a par with insignificant instructions: "Indeed, most of the fundamental laws affecting Russia's system of government and the status of its citizens were never at all promulgated in any formal way".[25]

It is a fact, for example, that no laws were ever passed to introduce serfdom, to mandate compulsory service to the tsar, to regulate the landlord's authority over the peasants, to stipulate that civil servants be promoted on the basis of seniority, or to confine Jewish inhabitants to a restricted area (the "Pale of Settlement"). Ivan the Terrible introduced his "*Oprichnina*" without legal basis, as did Peter the Great with his secret police, the "*Preobrazhenskii Prikaz*", and the unaccountability of the autocracy is mentioned only in passing, in the sentence from Peter's military regulation that was quoted above.

All are slaves

Under the old patrimonial regime it was natural that the ruler both made and enforced his own rules, most often in a rather wilful fashion. After all, both the country and its population were the property of the ruler. The whole culture of old Muscovy was permeated by this mentality. It was customary, for example, for even senior boyars to address their sovereign not only in the third form diminutive, but also to add "your slave". It might thus be: "I, Ivashka, your *kholop*." It would not be until the reign of Peter the Great that this practice was abolished.[26]

In the early sixteenth century, Grand Prince Vasilii III, the successor to Ivan the Great, could state that "all are slaves", and it would not be until 1785 that the nobility were exempt from corporal punishment. Peter the Great, for example, is said to have been quite inclined to personally beating even senior members of his entourage. In such an environment the notion of "rights" for individuals makes little sense. And where there are no individual rights, there is not much need for an independent judiciary.

This important point may be highlighted by returning to the contrast that was made above between the rise of Russian patrimonialism and the development of feudalism in Western Europe. There are two crucial areas of difference, namely stratification and reciprocity.

On the first count, while the Russian development was marked by an ambition of the autocrat to treat all his subjects as serfs, poignantly expressed in the above quote from Vasilii III, Western feudalism was layered. At the bottom were the peasants, then came the vassals and at the top there was the lord. One consequence of this difference was that cities in Western Europe could rise to prominence, with rights and charters for merchant guilds. In the Russian case, as we have seen above, the Mongols were instrumental in ensuring that the cities of Muscovy lost all autonomous urban institutions. As a result, Russia would never develop a solid bourgeoisie.

The second difference, that of reciprocity, is of perhaps even greater importance. While the Russian rulers followed the Mongol example of insisting on absolute obedience from below, with no accompanying sense of reciprocal responsibilities, Western feudalism was marked by a strong sense of both rights and obligations, i.e. of contractual relations.

Pipes places particular emphasis on the latter: "This mutual obligation, formalized in the ceremony of commendation, was taken very seriously by the parties concerned and by society at large. Violation of its terms by either party nullified the contract. . . . What do we find in Russia? Of vassalage, in its proper sense, nothing."[27]

While Western feudalism went through a process of gradual strengthening of the rights of vassals and subjects, which eventually led to the end of feudalism, Russia went through a process of retrogression, where the power of the tsar was gradually strengthened, to the point where feudalism degenerated into complete submission of the whole population.

The overriding ambition by a series of Russian rulers to eradicate all sense of rights or contractual obligations was manifested above all in the process of removing private property in land, which was roughly completed in the sixteenth century. The next step was that of fixing the peasantry to the soil, a process that was accomplished in a series of laws on the capture of runaway serfs.

Although serfdom as such was never regulated by law, in 1597 a law was issued that allowed the capture by force of serfs who had left their landlords within the past five years. In the *ulozhenie* of 1649, the time limitation was removed, thus establishing full rights of the landlords to their serfs. In 1658 a decree provided for special officials that would help in tracking down fugitive serfs, and in 1661 both flogging and heavy fines were introduced as penalties for landlords who were caught protecting fugitives.

This gradual tightening of the screw on the peasantry led to hostilities, which in 1661 erupted in the violent rebellion of Stenka Razin, a Don Cossack who kept the tsar's troops busy for a whole decade. This was neither the first nor the last massive peasant revolt. Rebellion was to be an integral part of a pattern of complicated relations between the autocracy and the peasantry.

These observations point at some fundamental features of the role of law in Russian tradition. While in the Western – Roman – case, law has rested on contractual foundations, i.e. rules are made by the elected representatives of the people in order to regulate both relations among themselves and relations to their government, in the Russian case law has always been an instrument of power in the hands of the ruler. The Russian jurist Aleksandr Yakovlev explains this distinction by using the mirror of language.

The English word "truth", for example, may be given two different Russian translations. One is *pravda*, which represents a moral, subjective or spiritual truth. The other is *istina*, which represents a factual, scientific or objective truth. Putting it briefly, the latter represents something that *does* exist, the former something that *must* exist. Thus the name of the main daily paper of the communist party was "Pravda". Using this background, Yakovlev makes a crucial point:

> The basic cultural fact of Russian history is that in the people's consciousness, the law never was associated with the moral truth. Of course it existed "out there", in reality, but reality for the majority of the people was harsh and oppressive, unjust and cruel. The law was presented to the peasantry – the predominant part of the population – as the law of serfdom. It was reality, it was *istina* (factual truth), but obviously it was not *pravda* (moral truth).[28]

As legislation was used as an instrument of power, with no sense of mutual obligation, it was understandable that many Russians came to view both the state and the law "as sinful because these institutions justified the enslavement of the mind and the people." Such impressions were fortified by the experience of a consequently chronic Russian problem – the lack of any kind of legal order. This was not rule *of* law; it was rule *by* law. The importance of this distinction can hardly be exaggerated.

In the words of Owen, "the various codes of laws issued from 1497 onward, indicated the vigour with which tsarist bureaucrats sought to regiment society by means of statutory compulsion and restriction. The law functioned as an administrative device, not as a set of rules to be obeyed by state officials."[29]

In order to drive his point home, Yakovlev returns to the mirror of language, to show how the English word "justice" may also be rendered in Russian in two very different ways. One is *yustitsiya*, which is derived from the Latin and represents the official, legal system of justice. The other, *spravedlivost*, represents the everyday understanding of fairness. Thus the Justice Department is *Ministerstvo Yustitsii*, not *Ministerstvo Spravedlivosti*.

The implication, according to Yakovlev, is that in Russian public consciousness there is a very specific cultural duality. On the one hand, there is "an idea of justice as an objectively existing web of social relations in real life situations." On the other, there is a parallel "notion of justice as the set of political, state-bound institutions." His conclusion is rather to the point: "Historically, law was considered as being not an ingredient of normal life, but rather as something imposed from above and, more often than not, as a burden if not a yoke."[30]

Writing about the state of the peasantry up until 1917, Pipes lends support to this interpretation:

> Among the abstractions the peasant could not comprehend was law, which he tended to confound with custom or common sense. He did not understand due process. Russian customary law, enforced by village communities, recognized the accused person's confession as the most satisfactory proof of guilt. . . . Similarly, the peasant had great difficulty comprehending "property", confusing it with usage or possession.[31]

If we link Yakovlev's emphasis on the role of law as a basis for society to what has been said above about the weak – or non-existent – role of private property, we may clearly see some of the most salient features of the Russian mental universe. We see a reflection of the vertical society, where might is always right, where the law is an instrument in the hands of power and where individuals may be given mercy and privilege but never rights.

In Byzantium there was also a notion of the obligation to obey, but it was conditioned on the righteous behaviour of the emperor. If he started to behave like a tyrant it was right to rebel. There is an obvious correspondence here to the sense of contract and mutuality in Western feudalism. In Russia, however, there was never any notion of the righteous ruler, only of the legitimate, who for dynastic reasons had a right to the throne.

Therefore, "while the system could operate under weak or incompetent Grand Princes – and even under mad ones – it could not tolerate 'tsarlessness' (bestsarstvie), nor could it tolerate the factional struggles that would attend the decision to replace an ailing or incompetent Grand Prince".[32] And so it would remain to the present day.

Law was used in Russia exclusively in the punitive sense. It provided rights for the agents of the autocracy to punish "without any mercy" all forms of challenge to the "sovereign honour" of the Muscovite state. As illustration, James Billington uses the law code of 1649, which was to be in force until 1833:

> Unable to understand, let alone deal with the changes taking place about them, Russians resorted to violence and clung desperately to forms and distinctions that had already lost their meaning. Russia's first printed law code, the *Ulozhenie* of 1649, was elaborately and rigidly hierarchical and gave legal sanction to violence by explicitly denying the peasantry any escape from their serfdom and by prescribing corporal – even capital – punishment for a wide variety of minor offenses. The knout alone is mentioned 141 times.[33]

In this context, it is also important to note that Russia was the first country to develop institutions that would later come to be known as the "police state", i.e. a separate police force to protect the rulers against the people: "This political policing was a Russian invention; Russia was the first country to have two police systems, one to protect the state from its citizens, and the other to protect the citizens from each other. Subsequently, this dual structure became a fundamental feature of totalitarian states."[34]

As noted above, the first step on this road was taken under Peter the Great, with the introduction of the *"Preobrazhenskii Prikaz"*. But this was not a definitive step. The secret police was dismantled under Peter III, and neither Catherine II nor Alexander I showed any great interest in restoring it. In 1811 a special ministry of police was introduced, but it was disbanded eight years later. It would not be until the reign of Nicholas I that this institution became a permanent feature of the Russian government. In the meantime, a cautious process of moving towards greater legality had been initiated.

Autocracy under the law?

It is not surprising that the first hesitant steps towards introducing legal regulation of a Western kind were taken in the reign of German-born Catherine the Great. As we have noted above, it was she who brought the first flickering rays of Enlightenment to Russia. She introduced French as the language of the court and corresponded regularly with people like Voltaire and Diderot.

Influences of this kind served to produce the Charter of the Nobility. And when the tsarina decided, in 1767, to call a legislative commission to provide advice on the collection of a new code of laws, she drew much inspiration from Montesquieu's *L'Esprit des Lois*. But the context was still that of Russia. The work that was undertaken by the commission would be important mainly in the sense of preparing the ground for subsequent work.

The process of thinking about constitutional reform was continued under Alexander I, who charged Mikhail Speranskii with working out plans for an improved system of government. In the resulting proposal, which was presented in 1809, the autocracy was to be somehow reconciled with a system of separating the executive, legislative and judiciary dimensions of power.

The counterbalance to the tsar would be a new State Duma. Although it was to be elected on a property franchise, thus excluding the vast majority of the population (notably so the peasantry) it would still have represented a truly radical change. In the end, however, it all came down to nothing more than an advisory State Council, which was appointed by the tsar. Disappointment over this turn of events helped fuel the dissent that led to the Decembrist revolt.

The reign of Nicholas I would be characterized by a siege mentality, the discipline of the camp. Often regarded as the last true autocrat of Russia, Nicholas ruled his country via a "Personal Chancellery of His Imperial Majesty". It had a First Section, which was charged with supervising promotions to all important offices and positions, a Second Section, which continued the effort of collating Russian laws, and a Fifth Section, which pursued some careful probes into the problem of serfdom.

But by far the most important was the infamous Third Section, which was charged with maintaining internal security. Under the stern leadership of Count and General Benckendorff, who had succeeded, in the wake of the Decembrist revolt, in convincing the tsar of the need for such an apparat to complement the existing police, the Third Section kept a close watch on all signs of subversive activity. It consisted of a uniformed gendarmerie, organized along military lines, and a corps of secret informers infiltrating all public and private gatherings where dissent might be brewing.

Although the authority of the Third Section was vaguely defined, it did include some judicial capacity, such as rights to punish and exile. Like Peter's *Preobrazhenskii Prikaz*, it was also exempt from control by other arms of the government. Its general attitude is reflected in a statement once made by Benckendorff himself: "Laws are written for subordinates, not for the authorities".[35]

The real watershed, as we have noted above, came with Alexander II. Having finally brought about a formal end to the system of serfdom, he proceeded in 1864 to introduce his Judiciary Reform, the most sweeping legal reform ever in Russian history.

Before 1775, there had been neither courts nor specialized officials dispensing justice. Such functions had been carried out by administrators who also had other duties to perform. With the reforms of Catherine the Great, a court system of sorts was introduced, but it too suffered from severe limitations.

To begin with, each of the three estates – gentry, merchants and state peasants – had their own hierarchies of courts, leaving serfs to be dealt with by the gentry. Furthermore, far from being independent the new courts were placed under the supervision of governors, which meant that justice remained within the sphere of the executive. According to Peter Solomon, "The typical judge was uneducated in law, depended on his clerks to explain cases, and accepted bribes".[36] Proceedings, finally, were based on inquisitorial practice, relying on written documentation. As there were no trials, there was little need for either prosecutors or lawyers. Since proof was needed to convict or acquit, in the absence of confession, cases would typically end inconclusively with the accused "remaining under suspicion".

With the reforms of Alexander II the class courts were replaced by courts that were open to all citizens, including the former serfs. The judiciary was separated from the executive branch of government and at higher levels within the hierarchy judges were given both tenure for life and the rights of discretion, of interpreting the law.

The previous inquisitorial practice was blended with adversarial meetings in court, with oral testimony being heard and contested. There were trained prosecutors and the accused had the right to defence counsel. In serious cases there was also an option allowing for the use of jury proceedings.[37]

In the formal sense, these provisions did represent a major breakthrough, but they too were fraught with both problems and limitations. As Solomon rightly notes, although it may not have been obvious at the time "The 1864 reform produced a judicial system that was bound to challenge the unlimited power of the tsar".[38] This is all the more important since, in the words of Thomas Owen, "the tsarist bureaucrats who refashioned Russian political institutions in the 1860s and 1870s carefully avoided imposing constitutional restraints on the autocratic state. The reforms thus demonstrated the government's minimal accommodation to the principle of the rule of law".[39]

A first real test of the new judicial arrangement came in 1878, with the trial of Vera Zasulich. The background was linked to a major demonstration that had been held in front of the Kazan Cathedral in St Petersburg. One of those arrested was a young student who was flogged for having personally insulted the governor of St Petersburg, a certain General Trepov. The incident provoked a prison riot, which was brutally suppressed. This made Zasulich take the law into her own hands, shooting but not killing Trepov.

Making no attempt to escape, Zasulich was arrested and tried in front of a jury, in a court where Russia's most liberal judge presided. Although there could be no doubt whatsoever concerning her guilt, she was acquitted. The prevailing mood was that while murder was wrong in the eyes of the law, if the law was in the hands of evildoers, a revolutionary would have to be guided instead by conscience. The jury accepted that she had been morally right in doing what she had done: "The reason – the nobility of the culprit's motive. . . . it is a crime under the law, but we, the jury, will judge this woman not by the law but by our conscience."[40]

Thus placing morality before the law the jurors provided illustration of a classic problem in the relations between the power and the people. The American founding fathers, for example, glorified individual rebels against state authority. Thomas Jefferson wrote repeatedly on the importance of people asserting "natural" justice against an oppressive state. And many later liberals have taken Russian incidents of the Zasulich kind as inspiration for defence of the individual against the state (e.g. Camus in *Les Justes*).

The other side of the coin, however, is when we end up in a situation of arbitrary assertion of morality by tyrants. Here we enter into serious problems of transparency and predictability. No one in such a situation can really know what the law is, let alone be confident that it will be applied identically today and tomorrow. And when the law ceases to protect rights, individuals are reduced to asking for mercy.

In order to illustrate this problem, Yakovlev refers to a play by Aleksandr Ostrovskii, where a group of merchants placed before the chief of police are offered the following choice: "Well, and how do you want for me to judge you: by the law or by conscience? I have a lot of laws at my hand and every one of them is harsher than another . . . What do you prefer?" Their response was to opt for mercy rather than rights: "Judge us by conscience, not by law, being to us as our father."[41]

Soviet legality

The practice of "Soviet legality" provided many deplorable illustrations of the danger that lurks in placing arbitrary morality before the laws. With the communist party assuming the right to determine morality, courts of law were placed in a situation where in any case that went outside the trivial, prosecutors and judges would first have to obtain an opinion from a relevant party official before they could proceed with a case. The actual trial was then reduced to a ceremony, where the outcome was predetermined. This was sometimes referred to as "telephone justice".

What this implied under Stalin needs no further elaboration, but we might add a particularly nauseating illustration from Khrushchev's rule. Although the example is admittedly extreme, it is nevertheless illustrative of the function of Soviet justice.

The background concerns a directive that was issued towards the end of the 1950s, for the relevant authorities to crack down on a growing trend of speculation in gems and hard currency. The business was highly lucrative and could render long prison terms, but according to the law the death penalty did not apply.

The problem was that the scandals received substantial coverage in the media. Readers were outraged at the stories about the speculators' lives of debauchery and luxury. The result was a flood of indignant letters to the editors, many demanding that the death penalty be imposed.

When Khrushchev was informed of these reactions, he summoned the Soviet prosecutor general, Roman Rudenko, in order to set things straight. When the latter tried to explain that there were no legal possibilities to impose the death penalty, he was subjected to a torrent of vilification: "Khrushchev then spoke the wonderful sentence that sums up the attitude of Soviet power to legality: 'Who's the boss: we or the law? We are masters over the law, not the law over us – so we have to change the law; we have to see to it that it *is* possible to execute these speculators!'"[42]

When Rudenko again tried to explain that this would not help, that the law could not be changed retroactively, Khrushchev argued that this might be the case in bourgeois states but not in the Soviet Union. Thus, on 1 July 1961, on direct command from the top, the death penalty was retroactively introduced for major cases of speculation in hard currency.

Under the new law, the already convicted speculators could be tried again for the same crimes, and this time they were sentenced to death. Rumour has it that the presiding judge found it hard to control his voice when reading these appallingly unjust retroactive sentences.

When Mikhail Gorbachev began talking about transforming Soviet society into a *pravovoe gosudarstvo*, a society based on the rule of law, it is far from clear that he actually understood the full implications of what he was talking about. Judging, not least, from his own actions, he may be better understood as a continuation of the old tradition of rulers, of holders of unaccountable power won in secretive power strife rather than in popular election.

The rule of law in Russia?

As will be shown below, Boris Yeltsin would be keen on having a constitution and a constitutional court, both of which are important formal components in a system that is based on the rule of law. Again, however, his own actions would hardly bespeak any greater degree of understanding of the basic idea of the rule of law, namely that the law should apply to peasants and presidents in equal measure. Simply put, it is *his* constitution, not the constitution of Russia.

Flagrant examples may be quoted where the president has nonchalantly violated his own constitution, and it has become increasingly obvious that he regards himself as a true autocrat. Referring to himself in the third person, as *"gosudar"*, soon gave way to jokingly (?) claiming to be "Boris I" (thus, incidentally, implying that he does not recognize Boris Godunov as a legitimate tsar).[43]

One of many illustrations of the president's claims to autocratic power was provided during a state visit to Norway, at the beginning of April 1996. The background was the case of a Russian environmental activist and formal naval officer by the name of Aleksandr Nikitin, who had gathered information about environmental problems on the Kola Peninsula for the Norwegian environmental organization "Bellona". He had been arrested for treason and was to be prosecuted in a military court. When a Norwegian journalist asked how the court might be influenced, Yeltsin stated with a broad grin that "I stand above the court!" (*Ya vyshe suda*).

The true essence of the problem that faces present-day Russian legal reformers is brought out by Yakovlev, in a comment to the fact that Great Britain lacks a written constitution:

> It would be more exact to say that in this country a statutory constitution was never adopted, but that nonetheless the constitution exists because it is written in the culture, it exists (and this is most

important) in real norms of social behaviour. It is a living law, law as an integral part of a culture. Would it ever be possible to realize something at least relatively close to this in Russia?[44]

The conclusion must be that the stated Russian ambition of establishing the rule of law was something vastly more complicated than the writing of new laws. The latter would be accomplished without too much trouble, under the assistance of numerous Western consultants. But successfully establishing the rule of law would also require a cultural transformation, in the direction, say, of accepting rules and of honouring contracts and agreements. We shall have more to say about this in subsequent chapters.

So much for the Russian quests for democratization and legality, i.e. that of separating the executive from the legislature and the judiciary. Let us now turn to the specific Russian complication that was mentioned above, i.e. that the building of democratic institutions must proceed hand in hand with the separation of the sphere of power from that of money and private enterprise.

Money and banking

In all basic economics teaching, much effort is devoted to explaining the importance of the introduction of money, one of the greatest innovations in economic history. When we turn to look at the transition from a planned to a market-based Russian economy, it is important to bear such teachings in mind. A functioning market economy requires a functioning money economy, and a functioning money economy in turn requires a functioning banking system. This implies that we must consider some very special problems that are related to trust and enforcement.

In a context that is marked by the absence of the rule of law, it is rather obvious that serious banking will be hard to conceive. Accepting paper money is after all a rather strong statement of trust in the issuer, and granting credit is an even stronger statement of trust in the borrower. A stable dictatorship may certainly instil faith in its currency, but a banking system that rests on the use of brute force to redeem loans will not be very successful.

A late beginner

This is not the place to enter into a discussion on the rise of money and banking in the market economies. Suffice it to note that the instruments and institutions of financial markets arrived late in Russia. A state budget of sorts had been introduced by Peter the Great, but it had been kept as a closely guarded state secret. Paper money was introduced under Catherine the Great, but it was not until the mid-nineteenth century that a serious monetization of the Russian economy was begun.

In 1860 a Russian State Bank was founded, to serve as a keystone to a financial system, and in 1862 a proper system of state budgeting was introduced. There were also ambitions to promote private banks and to stabilize the currency, but at first none of these were very successful. In the period from 1860 until 1880 between one-quarter and one-third of all budget expenditure went into servicing the state debt.[45]

Although a late starter, by the turn of the century the Russian money economy could show an impressive track record. Under the direction of Finance Minister Sergei Witte, a tax system had been developed which was so regressive that peasants were forced into marketing food that they would have rightly needed to consume. The slogan of the time was that "We do not eat enough, but we export!" (*Ne doedim, no vyvezem!*)

By exporting this surplus, Witte secured a positive balance of payments, which in turn made it possible, in 1896, to make the rouble convertible into gold. And foreign investment was already rising rapidly, from 97.7 million roubles in 1880, to 214.7 million in 1890 and 911 million by 1900.[46] Russia was definitely forging ahead. The power of this movement was such, moreover, that it would survive well into the 1920s.

When the Bolsheviks came to power, the banks were first in line to be nationalized. Lenin had a rather naïve belief in the role of banks as the real heart of capitalism. If only they could be brought under control, then the whole economy would be under control: "Without big banks socialism would be impossible. The big banks are the state apparatus which we need to bring about socialism, and which we take ready-made from capitalism." The rest would be simple "because capitalism has simplified the work of accounting and control, has reduced it to a comparatively simple system of book-keeping, which any literate person can do".[47]

Once the financial system had been placed under political control, the commissar in charge proceeded to destroy it. The chaotic conditions that were brought about by civil war certainly contributed, as the government resorted to inflationary financing, but there were also voices hailing the destructive effects of high inflation.

In 1920, the system duly collapsed. The Bolshevik state operated with a money-free budget and some began to entertain visions of a money-free society, with distribution of goods and services according to politically determined priorities. Trotskii spoke of organizing labour armies under strict military discipline. Full communism was seen by some to lie just around the corner.

The Kronstadt uprising in February 1921, and the subsequent introduction of Lenin's New Economic Policy, put a brutal end to all such visions. Agriculture recovered quickly and trade between the cities and the countryside was booming. It was a mixed economy – of sorts.

The general confusion over the future course of the revolution was expressed by Nikolai Bukharin, one of the leading economic minds: "We thought that we could, at a blow and swiftly, abolish market relations. Yet it turns out that we shall reach socialism through market relations."[48]

But it was not only agriculture that recovered. The financial system showed an even more remarkable recovery. In 1922 a parallel new currency, the *chervonets*, was introduced with gold backing, and great efforts were made to raise new taxes. In the fiscal year 1923–4 there was a balanced budget. In February 1924, the *chervonets* was made the sole currency, and in 1924–5 the budget actually showed a surplus.

The fact that this could be achieved within the framework of the time is rather important to bear in mind, when we proceed to look at the failures of similar undertakings in the first half of the 1990s.

The monobank system

With the introduction of central planning, which happened with the first five-year plan in 1928, the fate of the financial system was sealed. But it would not be a question of a full return to 1920. The problem of how to create a Soviet financial system had two separate dimensions.

On the one hand, the experiences of War Communism had taught the Bolsheviks that a full suppression of money was not feasible. The distribution problem would quite simply be overwhelming. But allowing full play of the market forces was equally unthinkable. Thus a very special arrangement had to be constructed.

Since consumer goods were to be distributed between the households by money exchange, the households had to be given money, which in turn meant that they had to be paid wages for their labour. This implied that within the system of central planning two quasi markets were created, one for labour and one for consumer goods. The money instrument that was developed to support these transactions (i.e. notes and coins) would be known in Russian as "available roubles" (*nalichnye rubli*). Below we shall use the term "cash roubles".

On the other hand, it was realized that enterprises manufacturing several different products would be impossible to monitor and evaluate unless prices were assigned. It is not difficult to determine whether a hydropower station has delivered the required volume of kwh, but when enterprises manufacture several products of varying quality and specifications, measurement problems are bound to arise.

As soon as products are assigned rouble prices, however, a total rouble production value may be computed, which is easier to track than long lists of quantitative targets for various products. Thus were born the "unavailable roubles" (*beznalichnye rubli*), an artificial accounting unit that will be referred to below as "non-cash" roubles.

The importance of making a distinction between these two spheres of the Soviet monetary system lies in the fact that it was legally impossible to transform non-cash into cash roubles. An enterprise manager, for example, could not decide to cut back on the labour force and use the wage savings to buy a new piece of machinery. Since machinery was not to be purchased, only requisitioned, there was no incentive to save on labour costs: all cash roubles that were delivered from Moscow could be handed over to the workers at no cost to the enterprise.

In addition, all enterprise bank accounts were "earmarked" according to purpose. Thus non-cash roubles could not be substituted for one another (funds designated for investment could not be used to pay suppliers, etc.). The outcome was that (barring the use of bribery) the sphere of production rested exclusively on administrative commands. Thus the official Soviet currency could not function as money – it was not a universal medium of exchange by any stretch of the imagination.

This is where accounting and evaluation problems become relevant. Responsibility for monitoring the output of the enterprises and their consumption of inputs, including labour, must be vested in some organization and this would be the task of the banking system.

At first sight it may seem a bit odd that an economy which refuses, for ideological reasons, to recognize capital as a factor of production, and thus is unable to introduce interest payments as a form of remuneration for the use of capital, nevertheless has a banking system of sorts. This is odd since the primary function of a bank in a market economy is that of channelling capital from savers to investors, and to determine a market rate of return to the savers for this transfer.

If there is no other investor than the state and no other owner than the state (or "the people") it is hard to find any serious market-oriented functions for a bank to fulfil. Although nominally there were several different Soviet banks, the phenomenon as such was normally referred to as a "monobank" system. Its primary function was to monitor the fulfilment by producers of assigned production targets.

The fact that the system also included three specialized banks, namely the Stroibank, which was charged with financing state investments, the Sberbank, which accepted household savings, and the Vneshtorgbank, which handled foreign trade transactions, reflected nothing more than a sectoral division of responsibilities within the same monobank hierarchy. All three were controlled by the state bank, the Gosbank.

For the record, we may note that the foreign trade bank did have a special position. Being charged with conducting business with real enterprises and real banks in the West, it did have to develop market-related skills. Symptomatically, however, this was an exception that was well shielded from the rest of the Soviet economy.

A special position was also taken by the Sberbank. Though it did not fulfil any function of channelling capital from savers to investors, from 1968 onwards it had an important function in financing the state's internal debt. While that arrangement was of a rather primitive nature it did show some early awareness that deficits had to be covered via borrowing. Most importantly, it set the stage for the *de facto* confiscation of citizens' savings that took place when the Yeltsin government, at the beginning of its reforms, forced Sberbank to lend it vast sums of money at ludicrously low interest rates.

In 1987–8 the monobank system did undergo some reform, aiming to produce a two-tier banking system.[49] The Gosbank was transformed into the Central Bank of the Soviet Union, which was charged with conducting monetary policy and maintaining a stable currency, as well as with supervising the growing number of commercial banks and facilitating interbank settlements.

The second tier of the system was made up of a number of specialized banks, *spetsbanki*, which were created out of the old system. By breaking up the Stroibank, three new investment banks were created: the Promstroibank for industrial construction, the Agroprombank for agriculture and the Zhilsotsbank for housing and social purposes. At the same time, the Vneshtorgbank was succeeded by the Vneshekonombank, bearing similar responsibilities.

The true dynamics of change, however, rested not in these reforms of the state sector, but in the growth of new banks, beginning with joint ventures but soon coming to be wholly dominated by domestic commercial banks. The latter process will be discussed further in Chapter 5 below. Here we shall stay with the monobank system, at the core of which we find the Gosbank.

Figure 2.2 provides a highly stylized illustration of the main flows in the production system of the Soviet economy. At the top we find the state planning commission, Gosplan, and the state supply commission, Gossnab, being responsible, respectively, for the issuing of production orders (*zayavki*) and allocation certificates (*naryady*). A hypothetical example will serve to illustrate.

Assume that Enterprise A has manufactured a tractor, which in accordance with plan instructions is shipped off to Enterprise B. Simultaneously, an instruction is sent to the Gosbank's local office A, stating that a tractor worth "x" roubles has been produced and shipped. The non-cash account of Enterprise A is then credited with the relevant amount, and local office B of the Gosbank is instructed to debit the same amount to the non-cash account of Enterprise B.

On the surface it may look as though a "sale" has taken place and that "payment" has been made, but that is only a mirage. What has really

Figure 2.2   Money in the enterprise sector

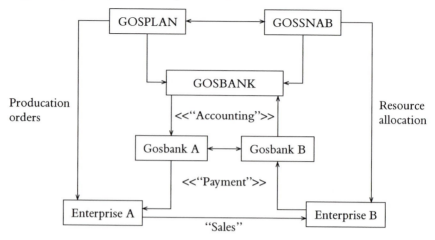

happened is that a product has been moved between two workshops in the same enterprise, i.e. "USSR Inc." Neither of these two workshops has any economic responsibility of their own.

Although Enterprise A may have several tens of thousands of employees, the authority of its manager does not go much beyond that of a workshop foreman. It is all a question of plan fulfilment, never one of independent economic decision making. The real managers, who are in charge of the real "business" operations, are to be found in Moscow.

On the banking side, we may note that the transaction in question has very little in common with what is considered normal banking practices in a market economy. Since the bank is not dealing with legal persons, no screening of credit worthiness is made and evaluation of results involves nothing more than a checking against given plan targets. Notions such as "profit" or "loss" have little if any economic meaning. Nor are there any competing banks. It is a question of essentially money-free monopoly banking, which must be regarded as a rather special phenomenon.

Let us turn now to the other side of the monetary system, that which is related to the consumer sector. At the top of Figure 2.3 we again find Gosplan, which works out balances for the utilization of labour in various enterprises. These balances are then communicated to Gosbank, which makes sure that the relevant local offices have sufficient volumes of notes and coins in order to supply the enterprises with cash roubles for wage payments.

Once the enterprise has paid out, workers have a choice between two options. They may either go to officially designated shops that accept cash roubles in return for goods, or they can take their wages to the local branch of the Sberbank, the Sberkassa. In the former case it is "consumption", in the latter "savings". In both cases the cash roubles are returned to the local Gosbank office from where they are returned to common circulation.

Figure 2.3   Money in the household sector

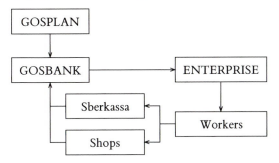

In its simplified form, this circular flow represented a closed system, and as long as central control over the economy functioned all worked according to plan. The central authorities knew roughly how many workers there were and roughly how many cash roubles each was due. Substantial manipulations from the side of enterprises implied that figures were notoriously unreliable, but the system turned over all the same, mainly because there were no financial markets where cash roubles could be subjected to speculative attacks.

Once the Soviet Union began cracking up, however, the financial system ran out of control. Workers demanded more cash roubles, and managers passed their demands on to the money printers in Moscow, who willingly obliged. As we shall see below, the wage spiral was not the only cause of the rapid build-up of a towering monetary overhang, but it did add its fair share.

The fact that this form of virtually uncontrolled monetary expansion would result in repressed inflationary pressure, which in the end would lead to rapid open inflation, with serious real effects, was not something that seems to have been obvious to all. It was, after all, designed to be a centrally planned money-free economic system.

Below we shall return to see what happened when the price system was liberalized, and the transformation from repressed to open inflation was allowed to trigger a process of sustained, high and variable inflation. The main question underlying that discussion will concern whether the failure of the initial attempts at stabilization was due merely to technical shortcomings, or if there were also institutional factors at play, which had been given insufficient attention.

Free enterprise

All of the activities that have been discussed above, in relation to our previous three zones of confrontation, really amount to nothing more than pre-conditions for wealth creation. It is now time to turn to those who are charged with actually transforming available resources into goods and services, i.e. the entrepreneurs.

Looking at Russian entrepreneurship from a historical perspective, there are a couple of facts that stand out. Small has never been beautiful. Nor has private initiative. From its early beginnings, Russian industry has been large scale, state controlled, geared to military needs and driven by impulses from abroad.

From the time of old Muscovy, the autocracy was almost obsessed with imposing state monopolies on all forms of trade that seemed to offer profit. Thus the tsar became the exclusive proprietor of industries and mines, as well as a monopolist in all lucrative trades: "In practice, any product which entered into commerce became the subject of a state monopoly. It is difficult to conceive of a practice more fatal to the entrepreneurial spirit".[50]

In Muscovy, moreover, there were no indigenous industries. The first steps on that road were taken by foreigners (Dutch, Germans and Swedes) coming to Russia in the seventeenth century, acting under permission and license from the tsar.

Most important of all, up until 1861 Russian industry was heavily dependent on the system of serfdom. This, in particular, would condition much of the process of industrialization towards the end of the nineteenth century, when it looked as though Russia was finally about to enter into the community of the industrialized European nations.

The vengeance of serfdom

The pattern for a state controlled serf-based process of industrialization was established already by Peter the Great, when he decided that military needs called for a fundamental transformation of the Russian economy. One might say, as does Marc Raeff, that the real hallmark of Peter's great reforms was the ambition to turn Russia into an "active, creative goal-directed state".[51] And that goal was to mobilize the country for total war. For most of his reign, Russia would indeed be at war, and at the time of his death the foundations of an empire had been laid.

The most immediate need was to raise money, which was done in several ways: church incomes were sequestered, the currency was debased, and a great number of fanciful indirect taxes were introduced, to be completed, in 1719, by the "soul tax". In 1702 a decree was issued inviting foreigners to settle in Russia, promising religious freedom and separate courts of law. But most importantly, the autocracy encouraged the expansion of mining and manufacturing that was needed to support the bellicose ambitions.

While it was true that private ventures accounted for a fair share of the new works, they were highly dependent on state support. The state helped overcome the shortage of capital by providing subsidies and tax exemptions. It alleviated the shortage of labour by assigning state peasants to factory work and by rounding up a variety of orphans, vagabonds and prostitutes for the same purpose, and it offered protective tariffs, to shield against foreign competition, as well as rights to free imports of machinery and raw materials. In short, this was something very different from free and competitive enterprise.

When Catherine the Great issued her Charter of the Nobility, the Russian nobles were technically free to leave the service of the autocracy – only to find that they had nowhere else to go. It was up to them to create from scratch, and that was a task for which they were ill prepared indeed. The Russian nobility had been brought up to spend money, not to create wealth.

Rather than serving to create a vibrant private sector, driven by an entrepreneurial class seeking to maximize its profits, the outcome of Catherine's reforms was at first the creation of a Russian "leisure class". And the top layer of this new class was very wealthy indeed. Some went to live permanently abroad, where they indulged in gambling and conspicuous consumption: "The gambling casinos and spas of Western Europe well knew these free-spending Russian potentates. It is said that Monte Carlo never recovered from the Russian revolution."[52]

While it is obvious that the system of service and serfdom had deplorable moral implications, it was not only a moral dilemma. From an economic point of view, serfdom meant that the wealth of a potential entrepreneurial class was tied up in serfs and estates. There was very little capital and no financial markets, even of a rudimentary nature. As Alec Nove points out, this background had not been conducive to the emergence of capitalism and entrepreneurship:

> The progress of Russian industrialization suffered from relative shortage of capital, as well as from a poorly developed banking system and a generally low standard of commercial morality. The traditional Muscovite merchants, rich and uneducated, were far from being the prototypes of modern capitalism.[53]

Although the reforms of Alexander II, which brought an end to serfdom, did represent an important watershed in Russian history, in the short run the outcome was mixed. The problems that were involved in building an economic system based on private property and free labour were so great that they tended to overshadow the benefits.

To the peasantry, heavy redemption payments made a mockery of their new "freedom", but they were not alone in finding the adjustment difficult. The nobility found their share of trouble. According to Pipes, the "emancipation of serfs was a calamity for the landlords", who were suddenly placed in a situation where they would have to develop economic skills:

To survive one had to be able to calculate the costs of rents and services, and exercise some control over expenditures. Nothing in its background had prepared the dvorianstvo for such responsibilities. Most of them did not know how to count roubles and kopecks, and indeed scorned doing so. It is as if, after long tradition of free living, they were suddenly put on strict allowance. This was the ultimate vengeance of serfdom.[54]

Things certainly did change throughout the course of the nineteenth century, as the legal position of the nobility *vis-à-vis* the autocracy was gradually strengthened. This was particularly important with respect to private property, the very notion of which had been introduced only in 1785. When the young nobles who had taken part in the 1825 Decembrist revolt were punished it was symbolically important that they were not deprived of their property. This was a change in attitude that would remain in force until 1917. While in the last quarter of the century, for example, the authorities showed little leniency with revolutionaries like Lenin (whose elder brother was executed) there was no more talk of confiscating their property.

Although this did represent an important transformation, it was still a process that concerned only the top layers of society, the vast majority of the population still being serfs or newly freed serfs. Towards the end of the nineteenth century, the process had reached the point where in a small number of cities, notably so of course in St Petersburg, there was a small stratum of market-oriented merchants and industrialists.

Whether this small group of an embryonic bourgeoisie would really have been capable of initiating a fundamental and sustainable transformation of Russia – had they been allowed to continue – is a debatable point. It is quite clear that there was an industrial upswing, but it is questionable whether this would have been accompanied by an equally fundamental transformation of social and legal norms, i.e. a genuine institutional transformation.

Addressing the very same question, Nove concludes that "the question of whether Russia would have become a modern industrial state but for the war and the revolution is in essence a meaningless one". Based on simple extrapolation of statistics, the picture would look promising, but this entails both "conjuring out of existence" the complications of the march towards war, and assuming that the autocracy would be able to adjust: "There is no need to assume that everything that happened was inevitable because it happened. But there must surely be a limit to the game of what-might-have-been."[55]

He rests his case with a quote from Alexander Gerschenkron: "Industrialization, the cost of which was largely defrayed by the peasantry, was itself a threat to political stability and thus to the continuation of the policy of industrialization."[56]

Counter-factual speculations aside, it remains a fact that when the experiment was interrupted by the Bolsheviks, Russia was still a predominantly agrarian society, and the Russian countryside was still in the grip of the old *mentalité*.

Pipes finds that "until the beginning of the twentieth century, the concept of private ownership of land was confined to the relatively small upper and middle classes, for the peasantry held land communally and refused to acknowledge it as the legitimate object of private ownership".[57]

But it was not only the peasantry who would remain in the old *mentalité*. Under Bolshevik rule, whatever sense of private property had been established in relation to the means of production would be eradicated, to the point even where the very notion was purged from the Russian mental universe: from an economic perspective the notion of "people's property" is void of all content. What is owned by everyone is the property of no one.

Although the communist system would be dressed in fancy new clothes, its contents would be strikingly similar to the old: there would be neither money, nor markets nor property. And the outcome would not be a great success, at least not economically.

Cannibalistic production

With the introduction of central planning, and the subsequent suppression of all serious scholarship in political economy, the development of the Soviet economy was locked into a pattern of destructive and distorted activities that would last for more than half a century. For all of its outward pretence of optimality, efficiency and long-termism, in practice the Soviet economy was nothing more that a gigantic system of workshops, deprived of all rational economic management.

The best illustration would be to imagine a multinational corporation that is suddenly deprived of its purchasing department, its sales department, its accounting department and all aspects that deal with investment, banking and finance. What is left would correspond to the state owned Soviet "enterprise".

Since orders on what was to be produced, in the multitude of workshops that appeared as "enterprises", were issued by the central planning office – Gosplan – in Moscow, there was no need to invest resources in product planning or product development. Allocation of inputs needed to fulfil the plan targets was also issued by Moscow, by Gossnab, the material supply commission. Thus there was no need for a purchasing department. To complete the picture, Moscow also filled the function of matching suppliers with their "customers", thus making all forms of marketing activity unnecessary.

The common denominator of all these activities was that they represented money-free transactions: enterprises were allocated raw materials and semi-finished goods free of charge and handed over the finished product without financial compensation. The legal system of penalties and rewards was linked exclusively to the fulfilment of assigned production targets. Since money did not appear in any relation to production, there was no need to undertake activities like accounting or seeking cost efficiency.

Summing up, we might say that what was missing in the Soviet enterprise sector was most of that which combines to form modern business administration. There were exceptions, but they were mainly of the kind that serves to confirm the rule. One such was the widespread use of cash roubles for bribery, another was the payment of wages, which was also made in cash roubles.

Given this background, one of the obvious challenges to the class of would-be entrepreneurs that emerged with the demise of the Soviet system was that of retooling the human capital, of developing all the skills that are normally associated with modern business activities. But that was not all. There was another challenge as well, which may be technically less complicated but economically all the more formidable, namely that of restructuring the stock of physical capital.

In Soviet times, producers had been shielded not only from the world market, but also from all forms of domestic consumer influence. There was no marketing and no need to worry about changing tastes. If the consumers did not care for what was produced, they had no other options but abstaining. This shielding of producers was incorporated in a price system that reflected few if any economic realities.

Since the market did not determine prices, there was no way for the system managers to know whether specific production processes were value adding or not. Thus, some industries could consume resources that would have brought a higher price on the world market than did their finished product. In Russian parlance, this was known as "cannibalistic production" (*samoyedskaya produktsiya*).

In a study made at the time of the Soviet break up, Claudia Senik-Leygonie found that 7.7 per cent of Russian industrial production was value reducing in the short run. If longer-term considerations were to be made, say of depreciation of the capital stock, the figure would be a stunning 35.8 per cent.[58]

Studies of this kind pointed at a strong need to revise Western (and official Soviet) figures on the capabilities of the Soviet economy. Such needs had indeed become evident already under Gorbachev, when Soviet economists began producing a set of considerably less impressive figures. In the subsequent Western discussion, the CIA in particular ended up with a bit of egg on its face.

But the implications of the need for revision concerned not only the size of GDP. Even more so it concerned the fact that once the Russian economy was opened up to domestic consumer influence and foreign product competition, much of the old Soviet capital stock would become obsolete more or less overnight. Some of the extractive industries would still have a future, but for the bulk of the manufacturing industries there was no way in which they could count on a profit-making future – without heavy investment.

The core of this problem concerns what Steven Rosefielde has called the infungibility of the Soviet capital stock.[59] In Western industries, the volatilities of fashion dictate to producers that their production lines must be flexible, geared into making rapid changes of style and models. In the Soviet case, consumer influence was relevant only in the production of military hardware. In car manufacturing, for example, assembly lines could turn out the same substandard automobiles year after year, without much bother.

Once the borders were opened up, and domestic producers were subjected to international competition, their inability to adjust was placed in the limelight. The implied need for restructuring also implied a massive need for investment.

This really should have been obvious, and perhaps it was, but in that case it was ignored. The heavy investment needs in turn implied a heavy reliance of industry on the banking sector for finance, which would not be forthcoming. On the contrary, we shall see in the following chapters how the Russian government would effectively crowd out the enterprise sector from the financial market.

The need for a working link between industry and the financial markets was, in turn, conditional upon the legislature being able to produce relevant legislation that was backed up by credible enforcement mechanisms. Not only would there need to be protection of investor rights and procedures for opening bankruptcy proceedings. Even more importantly, there would have to be trust in the currency, such that domestic savers would offer roubles to the banks, rather than put dollars in their mattresses. In all these respects, there would be serious shortcomings.

And that brings us back to where we started, to the point where the Russian government decided to launch an all out offensive in all of the four zones of confrontation that have been indicated above, an offensive which would make a farce of everything that has been said about stable rules and credible enforcement. Did it really have to happen in the way that it did?

In some sense it is certainly true that in the end it was the implosion of the Soviet economy which brought about the collapse of the Soviet Union and the subsequent Russian project of systemic change. The combination of a rapidly deteriorating economic situation, and total political paralysis in seeking to deal with the mounting problems, created a situation where options for great structural change were opened up. This, however, is not the same as to say that what did happen was in any way inevitable.

To those who defend, say, the action that was taken at Belovezh in December 1991 (the second *coup* against Gorbachev), it was an act of historical inevitability. Writing about this problem, Lynn Nelson and Irina Kuzes quote Sergei Vasiliev, a prominent member of the Gaidar team, as saying that "There are some problems which cannot be decided democratically," and go on to add a statement by Gennadii Burbulis, one of Yeltsin's closest advisors at the time, saying that "No one 'invented' the Belovezhskaia pushcha, the CIS. It was an objective historical act".

In response, they quote Grigorii Yavlinskii, the most prominent Russian critic of Yeltsin's reforms, pointing out what the issue is really about: "'Empires fall apart inevitably, unavoidably,' Yavlinskii agreed. 'But because a person must eventually die, 'inevitably, unavoidably', must he, then, be killed?' "[60]

The situation was certainly combustible, but it still needed a spark to set it off. And that spark was Boris Nikolaevich Yeltsin. The following chapters will deal with the various aspects of his crusade.

First, however, we shall take a closer look at Mikhail Gorbachev's time in power, in order to map out the domestic processes that led to the Soviet collapse. And we shall look at the adjustment of the West to the thus drastically altered political landscape.

Notes

1. Pipes, R. 1974. *Russia under the Old Regime.* New York: Charles Scribner, p. xxi.
2. Ibid., p. 23.
3. Offe, C. 1996. *Varieties of Transition: The East European and East German Experience.* Cambridge: Polity Press, p. 31.
4. Pipes 1974, op. cit., p. 19.
5. Kochan, L. and Abraham, R. 1990. *The Making of Modern Russia.* Harmondsworth: Penguin, p. 19. On the *kholopy*, see also Pipes 1974, op. cit., p. 43.
6. A process of discriminating between the sons in drawing up a will had been introduced by the Moscow princes already in the fourteenth century, thus paving the way for a quiet introduction of royal succession via property inheritance (Pipes 1974, op. cit., p. 63).
7. Ibid., p. 46.
8. Ibid., p. 47.
9. Pipes, R. 1994b. Was there private property in Muscovite Russia?, *Slavic Review*, **53**(2), 525.
10. Ibid., p. 526.
11. It should be noted that on this count Muscovy differs fundamentally from Kiev Rus. In Muscovy, settlement was the result of colonization that was organized by the princes, who thus came to regard the land and everything on it as theirs. In Kiev Rus and in its other successor states, such as Novgorod and Lithuania, settlement came first and authority followed. Thus the princes in the latter cases could never aspire to the degree of power and prestige that

would be enjoyed by those in the northeast. Most importantly, this would
have far-reaching consequences for the notion of individual "rights" in the
northeast. (Pipes 1974, op. cit., p. 40.)

12. Pipes 1994b, op. cit., p. 527.
13. Ibid.
14. Ibid., p. 526. All of these provisions would later be incorporated into the law
    code of 1649, the *ulozhenie*.
15. Pipes 1974, op. cit., p. 88.
16. Pipes 1994b, op. cit., p. 529.
17. Layard, R. and Parker, J. 1996. *The Coming Russian Boom: A Guide to New
    Markets and Politics*. New York: The Free Press, p. 13.
18. Pipes 1994b, op. cit., p. 530.
19. Pipes 1974, op. cit., p. 106.
20. Ibid., p. 108.
21. Kochan and Abraham, op. cit., p. 254.
22. Ibid., p. 270.
23. See further Keenan, E. 1986. Muscovite political folkways, *The Russian Review*,
    45, 119–20.
24. Pipes 1974, op. cit., p. 288.
25. Ibid., p. 289.
26. Ibid., pp. 180–81.
27. Ibid., pp. 50–51.
28. Yakovlev, A.M. 1995. The rule-of-law ideal and Russian reality, in Frankowski,
    S. and Stephan, P.B. III (eds), *Legal Reform in Post-Communist Europe: The
    View from Within*. Dordrecht: Martinus Nijhoff, pp. 5–6.
29. Owen, T.C. 1998. Autocracy and the rule of law, in Sachs, J.D. and Pistor,
    K. (eds), *The Rule of Law and Economic Reform in Russia*, Boulder, Colo.:
    Westview Press, pp. 24–5.
30. Yakovlev, op. cit., pp. 6–7.
31. Pipes 1974, op. cit., p. 158.
32. Keenan, op. cit., p. 142.
33. Billington, J.H. 1970. *The Icon and the Axe: An Interpretive History of Russian
    Culture*. New York: Vintage Books, p. 119.
34. Pipes, R. 1995. *Three "Whys" of the Russian Revolution*. New York: Vintage
    Books, p. 17.
35. Pipes 1974, op. cit., p. 290.
36. Solomon, Jr, P.H. 1997. Courts and their reform in Russian history, in
    Solomon, Jr, P.H. (ed.), *Reforming Justice in Russia, 1864–1996: Power, Culture
    and the Limits of Legal Order*. Armonk, NY: M.E. Sharpe, p. 6.
37. See further Bhat, G.N. 1997. The consensual dimension of late Imperial
    Russian criminal procedure: the example of trial by jury, in Solomon, Jr, P.H.
    (ed.), *Reforming Justice in Russia, 1864–1996: Power, Culture and the Limits
    of Legal Order*. Armonk, NY: M.E. Sharpe. One of the most important parts
    of the reform was the transformation of the role of the Russian procuracy,
    which had been charged with supervising the legality of public administration.
    Now it was tasked with supervising the courts and conducting criminal
    proceedings, a role that it would handle with a far greater deal of success
    (Kazantsev, S.M. 1997. The judicial reform of 1864 and the procuracy in Russia,

in Solomon, Jr, P.H. (ed.), *Reforming Justice in Russia, 1864–1996: Power, Culture and the Limits of Legal Order*. Armonk, NY: M.E. Sharpe).

38. Solomon, op. cit., p. 8.
39. Owen, op. cit., p. 26.
40. Yakovlev, op. cit., p. 10.
41. Ibid., p. 9.
42. Simis, K. 1982. *USSR: The Corrupt Society. The Secret World of Soviet Capitalism*. New York: Simon & Schuster, p. 30. It might be noted that Rudenko had been appointed by Stalin, and had served as Soviet prosecutor at the Nuremberg trials. He was thus not to be seen as a closet liberal. The fact that Khrushchev's action was a bit too much even for him is thus rather telling.
43. One of the first occasions where Russia's president spoke of himself as a "tsar" was at a meeting in Rostov in August 1994. When invited also to visit Novocherkassk, and told that "All the tsars came . . .", Yeltsin responded jokingly: "If Nicholas II could come, then Boris I will come". (*Literaturnaya Gazeta*, 24 August 1994.) What may thus have started as a joke would soon enough be transformed into truly autocratic ambitions.
44. Yakovlev, op. cit., p. 19.
45. Kochan and Abraham, op. cit., pp. 194–5.
46. Ibid., p. 227.
47. Nove, A. 1982. *An Economic History of the USSR*. Harmondsworth: Pelican, p. 28.
48. Nove, A. 1974. Some observations on Bukharin and his ideas, in Abramsky, C. and Williams, B.J. (eds), *Essays in Honour of E.H. Carr*. London: Macmillan, p. 188.
49. See further Johnson, J.E. 1994. The Russian banking system: institutional responses to the market transition, *Europe-Asia Studies*, **46**(6), 977–8.
50. Pipes 1974, op. cit., p. 195.
51. See further, Raeff, M. 1976. Imperial Russia: Peter I to Nicholas I; in Auty, R. and Obolensky, D. (eds), *An Introduction to Russian History*, Cambridge: Cambridge University Press, p. 121.
52. Pipes 1974, op. cit., p. 188.
53. Nove 1982, op. cit., p. 17.
54. Pipes 1974, op. cit., p. 190.
55. Nove 1982, op. cit., pp. 43–4.
56. Gerschenkron, A. 1962. *Economic Backwardness in Historical Perspective*. Cambridge: Harvard University Press, p. 130.
57. Pipes, R. 1994a. *Communism: The Vanished Spectre*. Oslo: Universitetsforlaget, p. 15.
58. Senik-Leygonie, C. 1992. The Breakup of the Soviet Union, *Economic Policy*, October, 360.
59. Rosefielde, S. 1998a. *Efficiency and Russia's Economic Recovery Potential to the Year 2000 and Beyond*. Aldershot: Ashgate, ch. 12.
60. Nelson, L.D. & Kuzes, I.Y. 1995b. *Radical Reform in Yeltsin's Russia: Political, Economic and Social Dimensions*. Armonk, NY: M.E. Sharpe, p. 10.

CHAPTER THREE

Prelude under Gorbachev

Looking back at the almost seven years that Mikhail Gorbachev was in power, from March 1985 until December 1991, it is striking to note the sharp contrast that emerged between the respective results of his foreign and domestic policies. While the "new political thinking" marked a radical and successful departure from the old Cold War confrontation between East and West, the parallel attempt to undertake a "perestroika" on the domestic scene turned into a long string of failures.

The main aim of this chapter is to take a closer look at the domestic failures. We shall do so against the background of the image of four "zones of confrontation" that was presented in the previous chapter, all with the purpose of creating a background for better understanding Boris Yeltsin's subsequent "radical" policies of shock therapy and systemic change.

Let us begin, however, by looking at an important dimension of interaction between foreign and domestic policy, an interaction that would contribute its share to the pressures that eventually led to the breakdown of the Soviet system.

The Sinatra doctrine

When Gorbachev made his first overtures to other world leaders, his intentions were regarded with considerable suspicion. This was, after all, in the midst of the era of Western powers standing up to the "Evil Empire". Hawkish advisors to Western leaders warned of a Soviet ruse. Once the West had been lured into disarming, the Soviets would emerge with even bigger and better bombs. Gradually, however, such suspicions were replaced by great expectations and wholehearted admiration.

Gorbachev delivered. The Cold War was put to an end, Central Europe was liberated and Germany united. The machines of war could be scaled down. The prospect of a "Peace Dividend" of substantial dimensions was held up. The Soviet charm offensive was such that hawks in the West began to experience new worries: having lost the Cold War, the Soviet Union was now about to win the peace race.

Unfortunately, the victories that were scored in relations with the West were not without a price at home. To many of the believers in the old system, the new general secretary became an object of increasing hatred, and the slow progress of domestic reform soon meant that whatever initial support he had commanded in various "liberal" circles began to melt away. The anti-alcohol campaign did little to enhance his standing among male Russians, and his way of promoting his wife as a public figure probably added negative sentiments from Russian women.

The contrast that emerged between success abroad and reversals at home was important above all in terms of the effects it would have in the periphery of the Soviet system in Europe. To the peoples in Central Europe, there was a double effect. While Gorbachev's liberal foreign policy created expectations for regaining their own freedom, his increasing unpopularity at home created fears of an imminent reversal. Thus a great sense of urgency developed.

The challenge to Soviet power that emerged from Central Europe was compounded by a contamination effect the Baltic states. Seeing what the Central Europeans could get away with, the Baltic "popular fronts" were radicalized,[1] which in turn fed back into Central Europe. Gorbachev's central power was caught in a situation that might be framed in terms of the "weakness of strength".

With the bulk of the elite units of its armed forces being stationed in Central Europe, the Soviet leadership was undoubtedly in a position where it had sufficient military might to put the house back in order. But the price would have been high. It was not only that there might have been serious armed resistance, above all in Poland. Even worse, the whole forward thrust of the new thinking in foreign policy would have been stopped dead in its tracks. All the investments that had been made in creating an atmosphere of credibility would have been for nothing.

In order to illustrate the crucial importance of Central Europe in the greater game between East and West, we may compare Gorbachev's reformist agenda to that of Nikita Khrushchev, three decades earlier. While their respective motives for doing so may be left aside, we may note that both men set out to deal with the Stalinist past of the Soviet Union. Both chose openness about the past, and both had to witness serious repercussions in Central Europe.

Khrushchev's policy of openness with regard to the atrocities of the Stalinist regime was launched at the twentieth party congress in 1956. In his famous secret speech, held behind closed doors while visiting delegates from communist parties in the West were out, a selection of Stalin's crimes were presented to the stunned audience. (The speech was immediately leaked to and published by American authorities.)

Khrushchev's openness, however, represented no more than a limited thaw. It saw the publication of Solzhenitsyn's *A Day in the Life of Ivan Denisovich*, but stopped short of publishing any of his other works on the camp theme. Most importantly, only a short time after the twentieth congress followed the uprisings in Poland and Hungary, where the latter was quelled by substantial Soviet brutality.

The violent reaction in Central Europe illustrated how precarious the party's hold really was on its vassals, and thus also held up a danger of internal dissent. Khrushchev decided to go all out and restore order by brutal force. The price was paid in terms of a serious deterioration in relations between the Cold War adversaries in NATO. And it would have to be paid in terms of tightening controls at home as well.

Having served as ambassador in Budapest at the time of the Soviet repression, Yurii Andropov went on to lead the KGB in its highly effective ambition of suppressing all signs of Soviet dissent. At the price of economic stagnation and an increasing atomization of the population, the communist party leadership succeeded in prolonging the life of the Soviet system for another three decades.

When Gorbachev came to power he spent his first couple of years doing nothing of substantial importance. Like Khrushchev, he had to devote some energy to purging internal opposition, but this time the task was relatively easy. There was no need to take on and purge any "anti-party group". The remnants of the old gerontocracy could be shifted aside without too much of a struggle.

While the new general secretary was busy securing his own position, limited glasnost was gaining momentum in the media. It began with a rather harmless critique of "stagnation" (*zastoi*) under Brezhnev, proceeded to condemn the "hare-brained" schemes of Khrushchev and finally, after much trepidation, arrived at the Stalin period.

The real turning point came in June 1988, when an extraordinary party conference was held. In sharp contrast to Khrushchev's secret speech, which had been held behind closed doors, this time the session was broadcast on live television. A long line of delegates were allowed to take the stand, from which they gave vent to such harsh criticism that the communist party suffered irreparable damage.

Again, the Central Europeans jumped on the bandwagon. Fearing that the window might soon be slammed shut again, there was a great sense of urgency. Trapped in his own rhetoric of *détente*, Gorbachev was unable to use force. Instead, he allowed the spokesman of the foreign ministry, Gennadii Gerasimov, to introduce he "Sinatra Doctrine". In lieu of the old

"Brezhnev Doctrine", which had been used to defend the 1968 intervention in Prague, all socialist countries would now be allowed to "do it their way".

And so they did. In the autumn of 1989, the communist system in Central Europe collapsed like a series of dominoes. Again it was the Hungarians who started, this time by opening the border to Austria, but now there were no Soviet tanks. Instead, the liberation movement spread back to the Baltic republics, where the popular fronts were raising the stakes and soon began demanding full independence from the Soviet "occupation power".

When we turn to look at the contest for power that would be played out between Mikhail Gorbachev and Boris Yeltsin, it is important to have this context in mind. When Yeltsin finally decided to make his move, Gorbachev would have been reduced in power both by the failures of domestic economic reform and by the consequences of the collapse of the Soviet order as such. By then, his friends in the Western capitals would also be all too willing to forget what Gorbachev had done and to embrace instead his tormentor.

By now, however, we are way ahead of our story. Let us backtrack somewhat, to examine the shift in generations that took place when the last of the old Soviet leaders, the ailing Konstantin Chernenko, died in March 1985. The long and increasingly lethargic Brezhnev era was over. The power of the Soviet gerontocracy was broken, at least formally.

A fresh start for Socialism

When Mikhail Gorbachev came to power he was a breath of fresh air, a new force who set out with great vigour to recapture a position in the world that would be fitting for the Soviet military superpower. There are interesting parallels here with President Ronald Reagan's earlier programme to make America great again, though with one decisive difference: the Soviet economy was in shreds. The latter, however, was a realization that Moscow decision-makers would be slow in coming to terms with.

It was evident that Gorbachev had a strong mandate for renewal, but exactly what this was supposed to involve was not equally clear. Although we may only speculate about his own initial plans and ambitions, with hindsight two main priorities stand out. The communist party must be kept together, and the Soviet Union must be preserved intact. Needless to say, priorities of this type placed serious restrictions on any potential ambitions to introduce reforms in the direction of democracy and market economy.

The heritage from the Brezhnev era was a heavy one. From a social science perspective, we may draw the contours of a mental framework that was less than conducive to reforms seeking to imitate the West. People who had been taught the superiority of central planning, and who had never been allowed to openly dispute or discuss whether there were in fact possible alternatives available, could hardly be expected to have any deeper insights into the workings of a Western style market economy.

When the Soviet leadership could finally be forced into contemplating sweeping market-oriented economic reforms, this heritage from the past presented a serious handicap in terms of human capital. For the younger generation of reformers who gathered around Mikhail Gorbachev, the problems that would soon have to be addressed were still hidden in the dark.

Initially, the new thinking that was associated with glasnost was restricted to some rather painful coming to terms with the crimes of Stalinism. Over time, the process would also come to include a serious questioning of the fundamental principles of the planned economy, but that was not to be until the real seriousness of the economic decline was making itself felt.

The economic reform process may be said to have commenced at the April 1985 plenum of the central committee, where the new general secretary drew up the principles for a programme of socialist renewal. The time had now come to "accelerate economic growth" (*uskorenie tempov rosta*). It was time to "restructure" (*perestroit*) the management and planning functions, and it was especially important to speed up scientific and technical development (*kardinalnoe uskorenie nauchno-tekhnicheskogo progressa*).[2]

Behind these slogans, however, there was not much that could be likened to a serious economic reform programme. Returning to the image of our four zones of confrontation, there would be some movement on all fronts. But it would be progress of a very insignificant order. Gorbachev's reforms were important in terms of preparing the ground for Yeltsin, but given the ideological restrictions that were still in force at the time, they stood little chance of being successful in their own right.

New political bodies were set up, but there was no readiness to engage in real power sharing. A feeble discussion about the rule of law was initiated, but no serious steps were taken to separate the judiciary from the executive. A reform of the old monobank system was implemented, but it was not designed to introduce real money into the economy. Finally, the dominance of state enterprise was relaxed, but the rapid growth of co-operative and quasi-private enterprise was tolerated at best.

When the system finally collapsed, it was still very much Soviet in character. It would break before it bent. And the man who set out to revitalize it would go down with his ship. While all of this is now part of history, and may certainly not be changed, it is hard to resist the temptation of counter-factual history writing, of speculating on possible alternatives.

If the new guard that took over after Chernenko's death had been better versed in the ways in which Western democracies and market economies function, would they then have been able to chart a less painful course in that direction? Or was the Soviet system really doomed to collapse, before something new could be built? We shall find reason to return to this question, once we have taken the story from 1985 up to the present.

Part of the explanation for the failure of Gorbachev's reforms lies in the fact that he failed to exploit his mandate for change, while the situation was still amenable to change. During his first two years in power, he focused exclusively on issues like corruption, nepotism and general lethargy. Logically enough, the policies prescribed followed similar lines. The crucial first two years of perestroika would thus be mainly concerned with discipline and attempts at general shake-ups.

The most prominent feature in this respect was a campaign to reduce the extensive abuse of alcohol that had long marked the male part of the Slav population. Given all that was known about the Russian drinking problems, the ambition as such was certainly a praiseworthy one. Unfortunately, the means chosen would also bring about unintended side effects of a rather serious nature.[3]

The anti-alcohol campaign may be seen as something of an early prototype for the long series of partly unrelated policy measures that made up Gorbachev's reform programme. This is so mostly because it illustrated that unless thoroughly considered and placed in their wider context, even small policy measures may have considerable unwanted consequences.

In addition to intensive propaganda, the anti-alcohol campaign included a series of concrete draconian measures, all of which were intended to make it more expensive and more difficult to get hold of officially produced alcohol. It did not stop at implementing sharp price rises and substantial reductions in production. It also brought serious restrictions in sales.

The number of state stores that sold alcohol was drastically reduced and their opening hours were restricted to just four hours a day, between 4.00pm and 8.00pm. (Wine and beer, though, could be purchased from 2.00pm.) In restaurants, no alcohol could be served before 2.00pm. The fact that the latter restriction applied equally to foreign tourists, who had normally been exempt from many of the everyday hassles afflicting the Soviet citizenry, provides a measure of the high political priority that was assigned to the campaign.

The anti-alcohol campaign was to have a significant albeit short-lived positive influence on public health. These gains, however, were achieved at the expense of a number of negative economic and political consequences, all of which were apparently unforeseen. What is most striking of all, in this respect, is that no one seems to have thought of the implications for the state budget of drastically reducing tax revenues from the extensive state sales of alcohol.

The fact that the budget would be deprived of such an important source of revenue, without any sort of compensatory measures being implemented, presents a good illustration of the strength of the institutional obstacles against market economic thought that permeated the old command system. Herein lies an important part of the fiscal crisis, caused by a rapidly increasing budget deficit, which began to be felt during 1990 and resulted in serious imbalances in 1991.

The mirror image of the rapidly increasing gap in the state's finances was a growing mountain of liquid roubles among the general public, who could no longer find much to buy. As the supply of consumer goods to Soviet rural areas had always been very limited, and as around one-third of the Soviet population lived there, the sale of vodka had come to account for a large part of household expenditure. Radically reduced alcohol sales thus resulted in a rapidly increasing household liquidity. Here the fuse was lit for the "inflation bomb" that would be set off in early 1992.

The positive health effects that were achieved from the rapid and unexpected reduction in the official supply of vodka were soon enough to be outweighed by other and more detrimental intoxicants coming into use. It was hardly a coincidence that the anti-alcohol campaign went hand in hand with the rapid disappearance from the shops of perfumes, deodorants, shoe polish and other products containing solvents. The fact that home brewing, the famed Russian *samogon*, also increased was, however, not only a health problem.

An acute shortage of sugar led to general hoarding phenomena, which, in combination with an increasing rouble surplus, rapidly eroded confidence in the Soviet currency. A vicious circle was created, in which people tried to get rid of their roubles in exchange for just about anything. In an article in the ideologically important journal *Kommunist*, published in the spring of 1989, the economist V. Bogachov stated that "Jewelry, moth-eaten rugs, half useless television sets and household appliances, anything that can be stored has been bought up".[4]

Perhaps the most serious consequence of the temperance campaign, however, was not an economic one. In the struggle to reduce the official production of alcohol, bulldozers were sent to destroy tens of thousands of hectares of vineyards in the southern parts of the country, particularly in Georgia and Moldova.[5] As drunkenness was perceived by the peoples in these republics as a distinctly Russian problem, unknown to the wine cultures of the south, the fact that southern vineyards were being razed to the ground simply because the Russians had alcohol problems could hardly avoid provoking a strong sense of moral outrage.

In his book *The Future Belongs to Freedom*, the then Soviet foreign minister Eduard Shevardnadze, himself a Georgian, describes with great bitterness how this ill-conceived campaign attacked the very roots of the Georgian cultural tradition.[6] Symptomatically enough, both Georgia and Moldova were among the first of the Soviet republics to break with Moscow by proclaiming their sovereignty.[7]

In all fairness, it should be recognized that the first two years of perestroika did involve more than campaigns for discipline and sobriety. There was also a grand attempt to address the notorious problem of poor quality that had become something of a hallmark of Soviet industrial production. Since poor quality was largely the result of poor consumer influence, at least in the civilian sector, a cure should have been sought in strengthening consumer power *vis-à-vis* the producers.

Since this would have meant going the way of the market, the choice actually made can be seen as a manifestation of the strong preferences for control that were associated with the old thinking. "Gospriemka" was the name of an extensive new bureaucracy, consisting of independent government-employed quality controllers. The system was introduced in 1985 and expanded during 1986 to include the majority of the Soviet manufacturing industry.

During the first months of 1987, gospriemka inspectors carried out their tasks with considerable enthusiasm. The new quality controllers rejected products to such an extent that a large part of the Soviet manufacturing industry slid way down into the red in their plan fulfilment reports. As a result, both workers and enterprise managers began losing their bonus payments. Spontaneous strikes broke out and the authorities found themselves under great pressure. Something had to be done.

A rational policy would have been to reduce the output targets to a level that could be achieved without cheating on quality. Such a move, however, would have involved an open admission of the true production capacity of the Soviet economy. Given this dilemma, it was decided instead to put gospriemka on ice.

The really serious outcome of the retreat was that it served to establish expectations for perestroika to be a universal failure. As the first litmus test of dedication of the new policy, gospriemka made it clear to all that the reformers either did not dare or did not have the intention of staying the course. Their credibility was thus given a serious blow, from which it would not recover. Meanwhile, the economy continued to decline.

Time for "radical reforms"

The need for "radical reform" (*radikalnaya reforma*) had been proclaimed by General Secretary Gorbachev already at the February 1986 plenum of the central committee,[8] but at the time the political situation was hardly such that the proclamation could be converted into concrete action. Instead, the main part of 1986 was spent on attempted "democratization", along with various foreign policy moves. At a speech in Vladivostok in July, Gorbachev spoke of opening a window towards Asia and the Pacific Ocean,[9] and later on in the autumn, a summit meeting was held in Reykjavik with President Ronald Reagan.

Here the ground was prepared for the subsequently so successful foreign policy that would lead to Gorbachev being awarded the Nobel Peace Prize. These successes, however, were not without cost. The one-sided focus on foreign policy gave rise to a sharp contrast between domestic and foreign policy that, among other things, would create great ambivalence in the attitudes of the West towards the Soviet reforms. While the general secretary was away on his foreign campaigns, on the domestic front nothing much was happening.

Those domestic policy measures that – in addition to gospriemka – could be said to have had some economic significance, rather tended to raise doubts over the sincerity of the economic reform process as a whole. In May 1986, for example, a decree was adopted concerning "non-labour incomes" (*netrudovye dokhody*).[10] Its purpose was to radically reduce the scope for private market-oriented activities undertaken in the "second economy", and it had considerable negative consequences, particularly for the peasants' desire to sell foodstuffs in the urban kolkhoz markets.

In November, there followed a further decree on individual business activities, which included a list of explicitly permitted private activities.[11] The main emphasis of this decree, however, lay in the restrictions that were established rather than on what was explicitly allowed. In practice, it would have little effect. The logic of the reform policies was still to be found in the realm of control and discipline, rather than in market relations and private initiatives.

In January 1987 it was time for new grand gesture. In a speech before the central committee, Gorbachev launched a strong attack against what he called lingering dogmas from the 1930s.[12] A clear signal was thus given for a radicalization of the reform debate. Throughout the remainder of spring, a number of reform-oriented economists came forward with analyses of the state of the Soviet economy, which further emphasized the need for sweeping reforms.

In the February issue of *Novyi Mir*, the subsequently well known economists Vasilii Selyunin and Grigorii Khanin launched an attack on the prevailing picture of the Soviet economy's performance. According to official statistics, the annual economic growth rate had been a respectable 3.9 per cent during the 1970s, falling marginally to 3.1 per cent in the first half of the 1980s. According to Selyunin and Khanin, however, the correct figures were a mere 1.0 per cent and 0.6 per cent, respectively.[13] This would imply that, after adjustment for a population growth of about 0.8 per cent per year, economic growth had ceased already by the end of the 1970s.

Some months later, Nikolai Shmelyov went on record with an article in the same journal that focused on the human factor. In clearly alarmist terms he sought to warn that further unsuccessful reform attempts would risk depriving the people once and for all of their faith in the future: "If people's expectations are once again (for the umpteenth time) deceived, apathy may well become irreversible."[14]

Many other contributions in the same vein were presented and the effects were not long in being felt. By June the ground had apparently been sufficiently prepared for the party leadership to take the plunge. Addressing the central committee, Gorbachev said that the country was now in a "pre-crisis situation" (*pred-krizisnoe sostoyanie*), and that "radical" reforms were therefore of the utmost necessity.[15] An extensive economic reform package was presented, touching most of the essential parts of the system of state planning.

The core of the new reform package was a law concerning the activities of state enterprises, the contents of which appeared, at first glance, to be radical enough.[16] It was stated that the binding nature of central planning would cease and that enterprises would be allowed to make their own plans. In theory, this meant that the days of central planning were over, but in practice, there was a significant catch.

Alongside the elimination of the old plan targets, a new system of "state orders" (*goszakaz*) was introduced for "strategic goods". With this complement, the choice for the rational enterprise manager must have been clear. While those who accepted state orders could also expect state deliveries of inputs, those who chose to go their own way would also be left to fend for themselves. The reform can thus be said to have harboured the seeds of its own failure.

In addition to the law on state enterprises, the central committee was also presented with nearly a dozen decrees imposing reforms on a broad range of other functions of the centrally planned system. Here, as well, there were significant contradictions and inconsistencies. For example, while being charged with reducing its own bureaucracy, Gosplan was given the added tasks of responsibility for seeing through the current five-year plan *and* of working out the new system of state orders. It is hardly surprising that in practice, *goszakaz* simply came to replace the old system.

While it is easy to criticize the decrees that were actually presented, it is mainly through the list of *missing* reforms that we can best understand why the results were so meagre. There were no concrete measures undertaken that might have served to separate the economy from the sphere of power, i.e. to create autonomous market institutions.

Although the reform stated that enterprises should make their own independent decisions based on a profit motive, nothing was done to create a realistic basis for such decision making. Most importantly, the introduction of market-based pricing was still held to be so explosive that it was postponed. Therefore the very idea of independent enterprises was, in practice, dead in the water. Encouraging enterprises to seek profits in a situation where prices failed to reflect relative scarcities would have been potentially catastrophic.

A similar stumbling block was encountered in relation to the question of recognizing capital as a factor of production. Ideologically, such an acknowledgment was just as sensitive as it was unavoidable for a market-oriented reform. Without markets for capital, it would neither be possible for companies to control their own investments, nor would any market-determined assessments of the risks and rewards of different investment projects be possible. With continued central control over the allocation of capital, the discussion of increased self-determination of enterprise "planning" was hardly to be taken seriously.

The most sacred of the many cows that *ought* to have been brought to slaughter concerned private property in the means of production. Ever since the nationalization of industry in the early 1920s and the collectivization of agriculture in the early 1930s, the Soviet economy had been founded on the principle of the superiority of collective ownership over private ownership.

As we have noted previously, the problem with this restricted form of ownership lies in the fact that what is jointly owned by all, in actual practice is not owned by anyone. Thus there cannot be any incentive for effective resource use (i.e. economy).

Since the system of "people's property" was universal in the entire bloc of socialist economies, it is hardly surprising that privatization was to be a prominent feature in the reforms that were introduced in Poland, Hungary and Czechoslovakia after 1989. Clearly defined property rights are obvious prerequisites for a successful transition to a market economy to be possible.

In the Soviet case, however, the issue of property rights would be surrounded by a strong taboo, not only up until but way beyond the dissolution of the Soviet state. The question of private ownership of agricultural land, in particular, has been hotly disputed. Despite the fact that the *Russian* president, Boris Yeltsin, decided in 1990 that the Russian Federation would allow private property in land, the *Soviet* president, Mikhail Gorbachev, remained an energetic opponent of all such proposals right through to his departure from power.

All told, the Soviet reform process unfolded in a considerably different manner than had been envisioned in the proud declarations on the need for "radical reforms". While it must be recognized that the June 1987 plenum did represent a clear manifestation of the *will* of the political leadership to undertake economic reforms, it should also be noted that this was very much a case of wanting to have the cake and eat it too. Holding on to the old monolithic system of power was hardly compatible with the necessary processes of separation that were outlined in Chapter 2 above.

During the remainder of the summer of 1987 the reform debate maintained a high profile and great expectations were created for imminent progress that very same year. All such hopes, however, culminated in the month of September, which saw the publication of General Secretary Gorbachev's book on the programmes of perestroika and new thinking.[17] While those parts that dealt with foreign policy were daring indeed, what was written about economic reform policies left a great deal to be desired. The signal was clear. The programme had failed and it was now time to look for scapegoats.

In October there followed an important speech in Murmansk, in which the party chief pointed at the country's 18 million bureaucrats as being responsible for the lack of positive results. Together, they formed a "brake mechanism" (*mekhanizm tormozheniya*) that blocked all progress.[18] In November it was time for the seventieth anniversary of the "Great October Revolution", which would subsequently come to be known as the "Great October Catastrophe".

On this important occasion, Gorbachev delivered a speech that was so ambivalent and so full of contradictions that it could only have been the product of many opposing minds. What was particularly striking was that despite all talk about glasnost, he could still only bring himself to mention the Stalinist terror by stating that "thousands of party members had suffered".[19]

A whole two and a half years had been squandered on endless discussions and half-hearted reform attempts. While the new foreign policy was scoring great triumphs abroad, at home dark storm clouds were gathering. The absence of a well thought-out strategy for reform of the "command–administrative" economic system was beginning to make itself known.

Katastroika

During the spring of 1988, the political scene was dominated by power struggles at the top. Conservative circles were mobilizing for a counter-attack and rumours started to circulate about an imminent *coup*. At the same time, it was becoming increasingly obvious that the economic reform package from June 1987 would not be sufficient. The radical reform economists began voicing deep unease about the future.

In the April edition of *Novyi Mir*, Shmelyov published another well received article entitled "New concerns", (*Novye trevogi*) where he speculated over "the conception of our people as docile serfs whom only the whip can induce to work".[20] One month later, Selyunin stated in the same journal that further time wasted would mean that all was lost: "Just look at all the years lost in fruitless discussion, and no changes can be seen. History will not forgive us if we, yet again, squander an opportunity."[21]

Despite the increasingly frequent warnings of an approaching economic catastrophe, the political leadership was in a state of near-total paralysis, still looking for ways to avoid or postpone a decisive step towards a market economy. The only measure of relevance that resulted was a decree about the creation of co-operatives.

Initially very popular in the catering sector, where small family operated co-operative restaurants began to change the townscape, with time the number of registered co-operatives began to grow rapidly in other sectors as well. If that process had been allowed to deepen and widen it might well have achieved a transformation from below of the Russian economy. As we shall see below, however, under Boris Yeltsin's rule the small-scale private sector would be heavily discriminated against.

As the realization grew that perestroika was turning into katastroika, General Secretary Gorbachev shifted the focus of his energy, seeking instead to implement reforms in the political dimension. Again, however, his ambition would stop short of achieving a real separation of power, of establishing functioning institutions of democracy.

In June 1988, the above-mentioned extraordinary party conference was called. While its manifest purpose was to unite the party, its practical result was to definitively alienate the country's intelligentsia from its political leadership. From the rostrum, so many speakers expressed such sharp criticism that for the first time the Soviet "project" as a whole came to be seriously and openly questioned.

Rather than responding to the flood of criticism by seeking to undertake fundamental reforms of the workings of the economic system, Gorbachev chose to compensate by seeking changes in the political system. As was the case in the economic dimension, however, the political reforms would be half-hearted and without much – positive – effect.

In March 1989, elections were held to a new "Congress of People's Deputies", but it was hardly a question of democratic elections. In a process that had many similarities with the semi-democratic Polish elections from the summer of 1989, the election procedures were manipulated in such a way that the communist party could be guaranteed a majority of the seats, and that all of the leading officials in the party and state apparatus would be "voted" in.

After the first session of the newly elected congress, held in June of the same year, it became apparent to the then still optimistic democrats that Mikhail Gorbachev would never willingly agree to share power. During the subsequent autumn, Central Europe was shaken by the "democratic revolutions" that swept away the communist regimes outside the Soviet Union, and thereby indirectly also placed the Soviet colleagues under considerable pressure. The days were now numbered, both for the Soviet communist party and for its general secretary.

In November 1989, a large reform package was worked out within the Soviet Reform Commission whose head was Leonid Abalkin. The essence of this plan was expressed in the following passage: "The reform must meet the challenges of the time, make use of the historical opportunity to demonstrate the strength of the socialist economic system, its ability to assimilate the achievements of modern science and technology, its humanist nature and its creative character."

While Central Europe was paving the way for a transition to market economy, in Moscow they were, thus, still intent on saving the old system. That rearguard action, however, would soon collapse.

In July 1990 the communist party was convened for what would turn out to be its last congress. Before the event there had been great hopes that Mikhail Gorbachev would allow the party to split and thus open the way for a multi-party system. The political divisions were now so great that this seemed to be the obvious path to take.

To the great disappointment of the "democratic forces", however, Gorbachev invested all his prestige and political talent into holding the party together. As his crowning achievement, he also managed to be re-elected as the party's last general secretary. Gorbachev was now both president and general secretary. This feat, however, would prove to be something of a Pyrrhic victory.

While for the country's part, the outcome of the party congress meant that all hopes of a Soviet multi-party system were effectively derailed, for Gorbachev's part it meant that his continued political deeds would be intimately connected with a communist party which, in the wake of the revelations that had been made during glasnost, would be hated by increasingly large parts of the population.

Gorbachev responded by allowing himself to be granted extensive political powers, manifested in the right to rule the country by decree. His authority, however, left a great deal to be desired. Time and again, ultimatums laid down turned out to be idle threats. In the steadily increasing current of presidential decrees, one could find features as "essential" for the further development of the country as a ban on vandalizing Lenin statues. The "Soviet" president was becoming paralyzed, and with him the whole of the central decision making apparatus.

Both power and authority began to slide into the hands of the individual Soviet republics. As a result of this devolution of power, near-chaos came to mark the economic policies of the union authorities. The republics collected taxes, but chose to pass on only part of the revenue to the union authorities, which reacted by allowing the printing presses to work at full steam. The Soviet economy was adrift.

The final chance to undertake a Soviet economic reform programme presented itself in the summer of 1990, when a number of Soviet reform economists were busy working out a concept for a rapid transition to a market economy. The leader of this group was Stanislav Shatalin, who would also lend his name to a plan that was intended to transform the Soviet Union into a market economy in a mere 500 days.

In comparison with the Abalkin plan presented above, whose intention, less than a year before, had been to blow new life into the socialist economy, the Shatalin plan was framed in a radically different ideological context. In itself, the introduction to the published document provided astonishing ideological evidence of how far the radical economists were now prepared to go:

> Mankind has still not suceeded in finding anything more efficient
> than a market economy. The market creates a strong stimulant for
> mankind's self-fulfilment, for an increase in the economic activity

and for rapid technological progress. Its self-regulating mechanisms guarantee the best co-ordination of all the activities of the economic actors, a rational use of the materials, financial and work resources and a balance of the national economy.[22]

It was, however, only as a manifestation of a new ideological departure that this plan was to earn its place in history. On closer inspection, it was obvious that behind the generally applicable formulae, there was far too much of programmatic statements and far too little by way of suggestions for concrete measures. As it was never to be implemented, however, we will not go into further detail, nor into discussions concerning to what extent it might have been warranted to entertain hopes that it could have succeeded.[23]

The important point lies in the political dimension, in the fact that the Shatalin plan did represent a real ambition and a readiness to undertake serious market-oriented economic reforms. As August 1990 unfolded, it also seemed as though a political alliance really was on its way to being formed between Yeltsin and Gorbachev. Moscow was rife with optimism about the future.

Gorbachev, however, chose to distance himself from all such thoughts in September, thus immediately provoking renewed political tensions. A considerably more conservative economic reform plan, authored by Prime Minister Nikolai Ryzhkov, was launched in opposition to the radical Shatalin plan. In many important respects, the two plans were so strongly opposed to each other that a compromise was not even technically possible. Nevertheless, in his own characteristic way, President Gorbachev entrusted yet another economist, Abel Aganbegyan, to seek just such a compromise.

After a few hectic days of rewriting, a rather remarkable mishmash was placed before the Supreme Soviet of the Soviet Union, which decided to reject it. The president himself was charged with the task of presenting yet another revised version. The result, known as the "President's Plan", was a still more watered down product, where precious little more than the general proclamatory parts remained of the earlier proposals. Deprived of almost all concrete content, this plan could finally be approved.

While these manoeuvres were under way, Gorbachev oriented himself ever further towards the conservative Soviet camp. One after another, liberals and democrats were replaced by the "dark forces" that would be responsible for the January 1991 massacres in Riga and Vilnius. The president could have used these events as an excuse to purge the conservative camp and – thereby – to reclaim the leadership of the democratic, reform-oriented camp. Instead, he chose to continue with his endless toeing of the middle line.

The beginning of the endgame came with the failed August *coup*, which in practice would mean the end both for the Soviet Union and for its president. Ironically, the Bolsheviks' rule in Russia thus came to be sandwiched between two *coups* – one in November 1917 (new style) and one in August 1991. The remainder of the autumn was spent on formal winding up and a division of the spoils. By Christmas time it was all over. Yeltsin had won.

Let us now backtrack to see *how* the victory was won, the purpose being not so much to understand how the Soviet state could break up, but to examine the tactics that were used by Boris Yeltsin. In the struggle with Gorbachev we shall see him enter into a game that resembles one of the classics in game theory, namely the "chicken" game. Given that this was a game that would be repeated in many subsequent confrontations, it is all the more important to pick up the early rounds.

"Chicken" game one: Yeltsin vs. Gorbachev

The dissolution of the Soviet Union was a remarkable event, not only because of the speed and the repercussions it had in terms of changing the European security structure. Even more remarkable was the fact that its collapse followed from a head on collision between the Russian republic and the Soviet Union. Putting it more bluntly, it was the result of a bitter struggle between President Yeltsin of Russia and President Gorbachev of the Soviet Union, both residing in and ruling from the same capital – Moscow.

Against this background, it may be of some interest to note that Yeltsin was originally brought to Moscow by Gorbachev, and catapulted into high office at great speed. He was made a member of the party politburo, and was appointed to the prestigious post as party first secretary for Moscow. Since it was the latter appointment that in many ways would condition the confrontations that in the end would lead to the break-up of the union, it forms a good starting point for looking at this process.

Round one: falling out of favour

Appointed with an explicit mandate to clean up corruption and nepotism, Yeltsin went about his task with the same energy and impatience that marked his benefactor. By declaring a private war on political privilege, he at once placed himself on collision course with the old power apparatus in Moscow.

According to the grapevine, he made a habit of travelling on the metro, and of making unannounced visits in stores with empty shelves but well stocked backrooms. Whether this is true or not is beside the point. The important point is that Yeltsin created an aura around his person. He was the protector of the little man. A political bigwig who voluntarily renounced the privileges and struck out at the all-pervasive practice of corruption.

It is hardly surprising that his struggle against the Moscow establishment earned him many bitter enemies. Prominent among the latter was the reportedly clean-living Yegor Ligachev, who at the time was thought to be number two in the power hierarchy. Perhaps it is true that Yeltsin did handle his mandate in an unprofessional manner. Be that as it may. The facts of the matter are that his crusade was brought to a bitter conclusion in the autumn of 1987.

The trigger was Yeltsin's own decision to resign from the politburo. The reason was simple enough. Faced with increasing resistance and feeling that support from Gorbachev was waning, he decided that he had had enough. The problem lay in the timing. It was not only that resignation from the politburo was a provocation in itself. To make the announcement on 21 October 1987, when the central committee had been called to discuss Gorbachev's preparations for the coming celebration of the seventieth anniversary of Great October, was simply outrageous.

In order to minimize the damage, Gorbachev decided to postpone announcing the resignation until after 7 November and limited his reaction to a simple condemnation of Yeltsin's decision. News, however, leaked on 31 October, and the result was as predicted. Speculation about dissent within the top leadership overshadowed the intended glory of the celebration.

Gorbachev's revenge would be fearsome. On 11 November, only four days after the celebration, Yeltsin was hauled out of sickbed in hospital in order to attend a special meeting with the Moscow city party plenum. It was pure inquisition, designed to achieve maximum humiliation. Marshall Goldman even draws a parallel to the show trials of the 1930s:

> As if the accusations, many of them false, had not been enough to break this proud man's spirit, Yeltsin was also forced to acknowledge his shortcomings publicly and to confess that his resignation had detracted from the anniversary ceremonies. This too resembled the confessions of the "wreckers" of the Stalin era, but Yeltsin, unlike them, was not jailed, exiled, or executed. Nonetheless, the ruthlessness of the assault, especially in view of his weakened state, made him determined to seek revenge.[24]

Gorbachev's first impulse was that Yeltsin should be expelled from politics altogether, but after some protests he retreated somewhat and offered his victim a rather unimportant post as minister for the construction industry. In that office the colourful Siberian would linger for 18 months. Despite glasnost, he was a non-person whose name was never mentioned. Some even thought that he might quietly disappear altogether.

As we now know, such fears were unfounded. Yeltsin would make his comeback with a vengeance, and when he did he would give Gorbachev a taste of his own medicine, thus illustrating the old saying that what goes around comes around. Before proceeding to that revenge, there is, however, one aspect of this first round in the struggle that may merit some comment.

In his subsequent career, Boris Yeltsin would make a big issue out of his own strong anti-communism. Is this a credible stance, or is it simply for show, perhaps a useful tool in the Kremlin power struggle?

It is rather obvious that he emerged from the 11 November showdown with strong antipathies towards Gorbachev, who had orchestrated the show. It is also rather obvious that he emerged with strong antipathies towards the communist party, which had executed his public humiliation. In both cases these were feelings that would later result in his exacting a terrible revenge.

But does it also follow that Yeltsin had come to dislike the basic principles upon which the communist party was founded? After all, he had built his own career within this party, professing his loyalty to its ideas and practising its policies. Was he a dissident, perhaps even a closet liberal, already at the time of his arrival in Moscow? Or was he transformed during his time as Moscow party boss? Or is his anti-communism perhaps nothing but a big misunderstanding by Western observers?

Putting the question simply: Is Yeltsin really an anti-communist, or was it simply that he hated the people in the apparat of the communist party? The answer will have some important implications for our understanding of his own attitude and commitment to the implementation of democratic and market-oriented reforms.

Round two: regroup and return

The occasion that broke Yeltsin's political exile was the June 1988 party conference. At first, it had been decided that Yeltsin should not be allowed to attend, but at the last minute party officials from Karelia somehow nominated him. Perhaps Gorbachev had given in to protests. Being allowed to attend was one thing though. Being allowed to speak at the televised proceedings was another. On the very last day of the conference, Yeltsin pushed his way to the rostrum and Gorbachev relented, perhaps to his own later regret.

Facing millions of viewers, Yeltsin not only repeated his old critique of privilege and corruption within the party. In an emotional gesture he also turned to Gorbachev with a question regarding his own political rehabilitation, saying that he wanted to be rehabilitated in his lifetime, rather than wait half a century like Stalin's victims. Gorbachev dismissed the plea with an arrogant gesture, thus adding further to the bitterness of his own would-be rival.

At the time, the party still had sufficient control over the media to guarantee that Yeltsin would disappear quietly back into the shadows. Although Western media were keen on getting interviews, it would be several months before he was given another chance to speak in public to his own people.

His first real step on the way back to power was taken in the spring of 1989, when Gorbachev decided to hold his semi-democratic elections to the new Congress of People's Deputies. A third of the seats were reserved for various important groups and, indirectly, for senior officials like Gorbachev, but in theory the rest were open for anyone who wanted to run. Yeltsin pounced on the opportunity, deciding to stand for a Moscow seat. In spite of determined opposition from the party, he won a landslide 89 per cent of the vote.[25]

The party was now being drawn into a rearguard action, against a man it thought it had dealt with once and for all. And it was losing. Since the 2,250-member congress was to convene only twice yearly, membership did not carry all that much weight. Real power began among the 542 delegates it was to appoint for the Supreme Soviet of the Soviet Union, which was to be more of a sitting parliament.

Having failed to keep Yeltsin out of the congress, the party decided at least to keep him out of the Supreme Soviet. Thus a list was presented which did not contain his name. But the party's grip was no longer total. One of the selected delegates withdrew, specifically to be replaced by Yeltsin. He now had a seat in an important political body, from which he could continue his opposition. The race was on.

During the spring of 1990, Boris Yeltsin emerged once and for all as a serious challenge, not only to Gorbachev personally, but also to the very integrity of the Soviet state. In March of that year, elections were held to the local soviets, elections that were marked by a broad surge of the "democratic forces". In Moscow and Leningrad the subsequently well known radicals Gavriil Popov and Anatolyi Sobchak were elected mayors.

Riding on this wave, Yeltsin decided to run for a parallel seat in the Russian Federation's Congress of People's Deputies. Standing in his hometown of Sverdlovsk/Yekaterinburg, moreover, the outcome was a foregone conclusion. With 84 per cent of the vote, it was nearly as stunning as the Moscow sweep.[26] As in the all-union case, the Russian congress was to elect a Supreme Soviet and again Yeltsin was successful. The party retreated.

The first real showdown came in May, when it was time to elect a chairman of this body, a post that was then known as "president". Seeking to draw a line for his opponent's expanding power base, Gorbachev intervened heavily, calling and addressing a special meeting of the Russian congress. His desperation was shown by the fact that he decided to back Ivan Polozkov, a hard-line conservative who would go on to form the Russian communist party and would also be involved in the August 1991 *coup*.

But Yeltsin was unstoppable. Having been elected chairman of Russia's Supreme Soviet in May, in June 1990 he directed this body to a declaration of sovereignty, which, among other things, asserted that Russian law took precedence over Soviet law. In practice this meant that – barring violence – the game was now over, both for Gorbachev personally and for the union that he so wanted to preserve.

When the Soviet communist party held its last congress in the summer of 1990, Yeltsin was ready to take a decisive step. In the eyes of the public, the party was now deeply compromised, and it was not only among the liberal intelligentsia that it was felt it would have been better to have allowed it to split and disappear.

For Boris Yeltsin, the master tactician, a golden opportunity presented itself. In a dramatic gesture, right before the sitting congress, he marched out and declared that he no longer saw any opportunity to co-operate with this party. His act led to considerable political polarization. Some celebrated his courage and steadfastness, others were embittered about his treachery. The dice were thrown and his political standing was becoming extremely perilous.

As we have noted above, during autumn there was a general deterioration in the political climate. President Gorbachev was moving towards the conservative wing of the party, and the liberal forces were losing heart. Shortly before Christmas, Foreign Minister Eduard Shevardnadze delivered his famous speech, where he announced his own resignation and warned the president that "dark forces" were preparing to take over. Gorbachev seemed shaken, but took no concrete steps in order to head off the waiting storm.

When the "dark forces" finally decided to make their move, with the January 1991 attacks in Vilnius and Riga, Yeltsin was presented with another golden opportunity. As soon as he learned about the massacre in Vilnius, he flew to Tallinn where he met with the leaders of the three Baltic republics. In a joint communiqué they demanded an immediate intervention by the UN.

Yeltsin also took the opportunity to issue an appeal for all Russian troops in the Baltic republics to refrain from using violence against civilians. He even hinted that it might actually become necessary to form a *Russian* army, in order to protect Russia from attacks by Soviet troops.

The implications of this move were dramatic. The Russian president had single-handedly taken on the Soviet Union and the Soviet president. An immediate result was that there emerged a new consensus between Balts and Russians, a sense of standing together against Soviet power, as represented by Gorbachev. Yeltsin also received immediate support from the rejuvenated democratic forces in Russia.

His first move after this challenge was to secure his own power base, something he proceeded to do by striking at Gorbachev's one really weak point: the fact that he had never dared face the people in an open election.

In the spring of 1991, as it was becoming increasingly clear that the Soviet state was on its way to breaking up, a hard-pushed Gorbachev decided to make a desperate final move. In a referendum, the Soviet people were to decide whether they were in favour of "maintaining a renewed Soviet Union". The result of this somewhat remarkable procedure was certainly in the president's favour, but it was another Pyrrhic victory. The decision to hold a referendum revealed another weak point that Yeltsin was quick to exploit.

Via his office as chairman of the Russian Federation's Supreme Soviet, he pushed through a crucial decision. In addition to the referendum on whether one should "maintain a renewed" union, the Russian voters would also be allowed to decide whether they wanted to have a popularly elected Russian president. Here too, the answer was yes, and the ensuing presidential campaign was tough.

As the Soviet president could not run himself, he persuaded Nikolai Ryzhkov, the former Soviet prime minister, to stand. (It was characteristic of Gorbachev's leadership style that the very same Ryzhkov had recently been forced to leave his post, which was given instead to Valentin Pavlov, soon to be the leader of a *coup*. In spite of this, Ryzhkov loyally stood up for his party chief, as candidate for an office that he could not hope to win.[27]) In support of "his" candidate, Gorbachev used a wide range of tactics normally associated with "negative campaigning" in American election campaigns.

Yeltsin answered in kind. In a truly remarkable television appearance on 22 March 1991, he demanded that Gorbachev should resign. In response, the reactionary forces were mobilized for a broad counter-attack. The atmosphere was tense and many analysts were inclined to believe that the hardliners would come out of the battle victorious. At the same time, extensive strikes among the miners threatened the country's economy.

The conflict culminated on 28 March, when the democratic faction of the Supreme Soviet of the Russian Federation organized a gigantic demonstration in Moscow in support of Yeltsin. It was demanded that the Soviet president should resign and that Russia be saved from the communist party. As the demonstration was held despite an express ban from President Gorbachev, the situation was critical, but although many police were commandeered, there was no open violence. At the decisive moment of the chicken game, it was Mikhail Gorbachev who blinked first.[28]

On 2 April, Yeltsin narrowly survived a vote of no confidence in the Russian Supreme Soviet, and on 12 June, he became the first ever popularly elected president of Russia, by 57 per cent of the vote. The result of the election was a victory in two respects: many had expected that no candidate would get more than 50 per cent of the vote, and that a second round would therefore take place between the two foremost candidates.

On 10 July 1991, the self-proclaimed ex-communist Boris Yeltsin took the oath as Russian president and received the blessing of the head of the Russian Orthodox Church, Patriarch Aleksii. The resultant shift in the balance of power was substantial. Yeltsin not only had the upper hand in terms of a stronger democratic legitimacy. In his totally overpowering ambition to get rid of Gorbachev, he was also in a position to use the Russian Federation as an effective battering ram. Mikhail Gorbachev had lost his greatest political showdown.

Round three: going all out

Resting safely on his new power base, Yeltsin immediately proceeded to challenge the communist party that he had parted with under such spectacular circumstances less than a year before. In a move that was reminiscent of Caesar's step across the Rubicon, he issued a decree prohibiting all organized political activity in state workplaces in the Russian Federation. At the same time, he urged the Soviet government to adopt the same measures.

In order to fully comprehend the extent of this challenge, it should be noted that it was the comprehensive organization of party cells, which existed in all workplaces, that formed the organizational base of the party. Without this base, it would not only lose its influence over production. It would also be forced to build up a whole new organization. Yeltsin's decree was thus a death threat to the party as such. By implication, it was thus also a matter of life or death for Yeltsin personally. Lacking courage is not something that this remarkable man will ever be accused of.

Before the decisive G7 meeting in London in July 1991, Yeltsin entered into preliminary negotiations with Lithuania. In the context of the blockade that had been introduced by Gorbachev, following Lithuania's March 1990 unilateral declaration of independence, and the tense relations that had since existed between Moscow and Vilnius, the Russian president's move was highly provocative.

In the evening before President George Bush arrived in Moscow for his last summit meeting with Gorbachev, Yeltsin and the Lithuanian president, Vytautas Landsbergis, signed an agreement of mutual recognition.

For President Bush it must have been somewhat unclear who was really in charge in Moscow, and for the Russian reactionary forces, it was equally obvious that one more week of political wrangling would be sufficient to crush both the communist party and the Soviet Union.

The intention was that on 20 August 1991, nine out of fifteen of the Soviet republics would gather to sign a new and considerably looser union agreement, which in practice would have put an effective end to the union. Faced with this prospect, the reactionaries decided to pre-empt.

In the morning of Monday, 19 August, a self-appointed committee introduced a state of emergency and declared that the Soviet president was no longer capable of upholding his office. On Tuesday, tanks rolled in the streets of Moscow, but the resolve of the junta appeared to be lacking. Boris Yeltsin could lead the resistance from the Moscow "White House", the parliament building of the Russian Federation.

By Wednesday it was all over. After some initial wavering, the military had decided to remain neutral. Boris Yeltsin's great moment had finally arrived. He could begin to collect his rewards and dole out his punishments.

Round four: wrapping up

Mikhail Gorbachev's personal fate was sealed by his apparent difficulty in comprehending what had happened. Upon returning from captivity in the Crimea, he opened his first interview by seeking to exonerate the communist party, and by explaining that the gallant resistance of the people against the junta was a victory for perestroika. There was general concern about the president's apparent lack of contact with political reality.

On 23 August, Yeltsin administered his final humiliation of a victim that by now was already lying down. At a session in the Russian Supreme Soviet, he forced Gorbachev to read aloud the minutes of a Soviet cabinet meeting held at the time of the *coup*. Goldman sees the final revenge being exacted: "He wanted Gorbachev to acknowledge in public that Gorbachev's own appointees had been disloyal. In some sense this was Yeltsin's revenge for the time in 1987 when Yeltsin also had to confess to his failures as the party chief of Moscow."[29]

On the same day, Yeltsin also signed a decree in which the communist party was prohibited on Russian soil until further notice. On 24 August 1991, the Republic of Ukraine declared its complete independence from the Soviet Union, albeit with the addition that the decision must be confirmed in a referendum. On that same day, Gorbachev stepped down from his post as the party's general secretary and declared, in his office as president of the Soviet Union, that the party's property had been nationalized.

Then, on 5 September, the last big decision was taken. The Soviet Congress of People's Deputies voted for the dissolution of the Soviet Union. Now it was just the formal winding up that remained. That, however, would be a rather bizarre process, providing ample illustration of the absence in Russian political culture of such institutions that may step in and take over when the executive power is paralyzed.

An excellent parallel is the speed at which Germany pulled itself together after the collapse of the Weimar regime. Elections were held and a new government was put in place. Not so in Russia.

The paradox in the Soviet collapse rested in the fact that although the country's parliament had voted, in democratic order, to dissolve both itself and the Soviet state, and although the state-bearing communist party had been declared criminal and illegal, Mikhail Gorbachev decided to remain in place as president, and to continue his claims of representing some form of redefined, transformed Soviet Union.

Under "normal" conditions, in a normally functioning constitutional context, the president would have had no choice but to resign. But the

Soviet system was very far from the "normal" Western ideal. At all previous occasions of Soviet power transition, the question had concerned who in the ruling political mafia would be designated as the new Godfather, and for this purpose the routines of the old communist political culture had been sufficient.

In the autumn of 1991, however, entirely new questions were asked and the country that at the time was one of the world's two superpowers lacked the institutions necessary to provide answers. The Soviet Union was quite simply incapable of undertaking a peaceful devolution of government. In practice it would thus be up to the outside world, notably so the United States and Germany, to decide how the Soviet state should be dismantled and who should be recognized as president.

The general conclusion was that Mikhail Gorbachev would have to go, but nobody seemed to know just how that could be achieved. He was apparently bent on remaining in office no matter what happened, and there were no additional parliamentary means at hand – over and above the dissolution of the parliament and the state. Extra-parliamentary means would be needed.

Hence, in the night between 7 and 8 December the leaders of the three Slavic republics, i.e. Boris Yeltsin of Russia, Stanislav Shushkevich of Belarus and Leonid Kravchuk of Ukraine, held a secret meeting in Belovezh, outside Minsk. There they decided to form among themselves a Slavic commonwealth, thus declaring the Soviet Union defunct and Gorbachev without a job.

The *coup* in Belovezh was important not only as a fatal blow to the Soviet state, but also as an illustration of the powerful centrifugal forces that had been unleashed during the "war of laws" between Yeltsin and Gorbachev.

While it might have been logical that the three Baltic republics were not invited, the fact that the three Transcaucasian and the five central Asian republics were kept out represented a more serious problem. It illustrated the power of the regional forces, which in practice had made it impossible to preserve the union.

One who was particularly irate at the clandestine formation of the Slav Commonwealth was President Nursultan Nazarbaev of Kazakhstan. During the previous process of negotiations on the proposed new union charter he had risen to prominence, and no doubt felt that he should have been consulted. (Perhaps this was also part of Yeltsin's reasons for not inviting him.) Belovezh forced the Central Asians to take sides, and they decided to join the new commonwealth.

On 21 December 1991, Alma-Ata, the capital of Kazakhstan, was host to a summit meeting where 11 of the previous 15 Soviet republics agreed to the formation of a "Commonwealth of Independent States", the CIS. Georgia and the three Baltic republics opted to stay out. Although President

100

Gorbachev chose to remain in power until 25 December 1991, that was it for the Soviet Union. Thus it was also time for Russia to step forth, outwardly at least freed from both communism and Soviet power.

For Boris Yeltsin, this would mean moving from destruction to construction. Given the prominence of Russia within the CIS, it would largely be up to him to decide on the future course. An immediate problem was that of Ukraine, where the political leadership was wary of anything that might smack of reintroducing Russian supremacy. Thus the CIS was constructed as a very loose form of co-operation, with a headquarters in more neutral Minsk.

But it was not primarily in relations to the other formerly Soviet republics that Boris Yeltsin's leadership qualities would be put to the test. Having proclaimed his ambition to build democracy, market economy and the rule of law, it would now be up to him not only to protect the creation and enforcement of the new rules, but also to ensure that they were given legitimacy in the eyes of the population. The latter in particular was a real *sine qua non* for the reforms to succeed.

This is the background against which we must view the events that have been depicted above. The most important lesson to be learned concerns Yeltsin's obvious predilection for confrontation as a political style. In a number of key situations, we have witnessed him play the chicken game, i.e. a game where there is no compromise, where one side or the other (or both) must lose. There would also emerge a periodic pattern, where he rises up in times of sharp confrontation and displays great resolve, whereas in times of routine affairs, he leaves the arena and retreats into illness and solitude (perhaps also to find consolation in the bottle).

From an institutional perspective, setting out to create, more or less from scratch, democracy, market economy and the rule of law by the use of confrontational tactics was a project that boded ill for the future. As we shall see in the following chapters, the main outcome would be a disastrous transformation of the economy into a political battlefield, where the president continued to confront his various adversaries (real or imaginary).

Before stepping onto that arena, however, we shall also look at how the outside world came to be drawn into Moscow power politics, in a way that has not been uniquely positive.

Notes

1. See further Gerner, K. and Hedlund, S. 1993. *The Baltic States and the End of the Soviet Empire*. London: Routledge.
2. *Kommunist*, **7**, 1985, 6–7.
3. See further White, S. 1996. *Russia Goes Dry: Alcohol, State and Society*. Cambridge: Cambridge University Press.
4. Bogachov, V. 1989. Eshche ne pozdno, *Kommunist*, **3**, 36.

5. In Moldova alone, the figure was as high as 70,000 hectares (*Literaturnaya Gazeta*, 2 August 1989, p. 12).

6. Shevardnadze, E. 1991. *The Future Belongs to Freedom*. London: Sinclair-Stevenson, pp. 3–4.

7. When the "Commonwealth of Independent States" was created, as a sort of successor to the Russian Empire to follow in the wake of the collapsed Soviet Union, Georgia chose to remain outside (along with the Baltic States). This decision, however, was reversed after the Georgian civil war in 1992, when Russian troops intervened militarily to separate the Georgian and Abkhaz forces.

8. *Kommunist*, **4**, 1986, 29.

9. In his talk (*Literaturnaya Gazeta*, 30 July 1986) he quoted Pushkin's classic poem *The Bronze Horseman*, which all educated Russians would immediately associate with the thoughts that were expressed in Tsar Peter's speech in St Petersburg about opening a window for Russia towards Europe.

10. *Pravda*, 28 May 1986.

11. *Pravda*, 21 November 1986.

12. *Kommunist*, **3**, 1987, 6–11.

13. Selyunin, V. and Khanin, G. 1987. Lukavaya tsifra, *Novyi Mir*, **2**, 194–5.

14. Shmelyov, N. 1987. Avansy i dolgi, *Novyi Mir*, **6**, 146.

15. *Kommunist*, **10**, 1987, 27.

16. The whole reform package is discussed in Schroeder, G. 1987. Anatomy of Gorbachev's economic reform, *Soviet Economy*, **3**(3).

17. Gorbachev, M.S. 1987. *Perestroika i novoe myshlenie dlya nashei strany i dlya vsego mira*, Moscow.

18. *Ekonomicheskaya Gazeta*, **41**, 1987, 3.

19. *Kommunist*, **17**, 1987, 14.

20. Shmelyov, N. 1988. Novye trevogi, *Novyi Mir*, **4**, 164.

21. Selyunin, V. 1988. Istoki, *Novyi Mir*, **5**, 189.

22. *Komsomolskaya Pravda*, 29 September 1990.

23. See further Hewett, E.A. 1990. The new Soviet plan, *Foreign Affairs*, **69**(5).

24. Goldman, M. 1996. *Lost Opportunity: What has Made Economic Reform in Russia so Difficult?*. New York: Norton, p. 38.

25. Ibid., p. 43.

26. Ibid., p. 44.

27. One is easily reminded here of how, during a visit to the United States, Khrushchev claimed that Foreign Minister Andrei Gromyko was so obedient that, if requested, he would let his pants fall and sit on a block of ice. A similar pattern was displayed by Yeltsin at a press conference in October 1995, when he suddenly let it be known that Foreign Minister Andrei Kozyrev had been dismissed, only to have him reinstated on the following day (if only for a couple of months).

28. The demonstration took place in Moscow's Manezh Square, which would subsequently be transformed into a mall of sorts, on top of a three-storey underground shopping galleria. Rumour in Moscow has it that President Yeltsin ordered this transformation, lest someone else pull off a similar demonstration against himself.

29. Goldman, op. cit., p. 50.

CHAPTER FOUR

The West gets involved

Relations between Russia and the West have a long history of complications, at times even of deep mutual suspicion and hostility. Looking at the most recent series of divisions that have been provoked, both among Russians and among Westerners, concerning the potential merits of Russia's post-Soviet path of development, we can see familiar mental structures emerging that have deep historical roots.

On the Russian side, we have one camp that may be loosely said to represent the classic pattern of "Westernizers" (*zapadniki*). In the nineteenth century, these were people seeking to bring their country closer to the West. As the Russian nineteenth century philosopher Pyotr Chaadaev noted, in a highly provocative clarion call, Russia had missed out on the fundamental transformations that had taken place in Western Europe, such as the Renaissance and Enlightenment. To him and his friends the only solution was an immediate *rapprochement* with the West, and with Catholicism![1] Today his followers are enthusiastic supporters of reforms that seek once again to re-model Russia after a Western pattern.

In sharp opposition to the present-day neo-liberal Russian reformers we find the equally classic camp of "slavophiles", whose stand in the nineteenth century debate was that nothing good came from the West. According to them, Russia was a *sui generis*, wedged between Europe and Asia, and must act on this realization and seek to find her own way. Today these are the people who struggle hard against ongoing attempts to introduce the Western way of life in the land of Rus.

Even a cursory reading of the Russian press will tell you that there is certainly no love lost between these two camps. Yet, their present struggle is somewhat different from that which was waged a century ago. In order to pre-empt possible objections, it should be recognized that the historical parallel is deficient in one important respect. In the nineteenth century debate, both camps shared the same negative attitudes to Western materialism.

Even ardent *zapadniki* would have shied away from the very thought of imitating Western society as a whole. What they were after was the sadly lacking notion of individual rights, of reforming the autocracy and introducing constitutionalism. Whether science, rationality and liberal values really could have been successfully emulated without importing the rest of the Western way is beside the point.

The difference between then and now lies in the present division of the Russian scene into what might be loosely called "communists" and "liberals". There is a great deal of continuity between the slavophiles and the communists, in the sense of rejecting the basic building blocks of democracy and market economy (notably, individual rights and private property). Yet, the current neo-liberals go much further in their embrace of the West than the *zapadniki* ever have. Thus the current confrontation over the merits of "systemic change" is of an even more fundamental nature than that which shook the nineteenth century.

One might even argue that while both the slavophiles and *zapadniki* of old were debating concepts that had been imported from the West, neither side had a very good grasp of what those concepts really meant, nor of how Western societies really functioned. Ironically, that seems to be as true today as it was in the nineteenth century.

In equal measure, Western opinions have fallen into two camps, which at times have also appeared to be mutually exclusive. On one side we have the Western enthusiasts, being firmly convinced that out from under the Soviet rubble a Pushkin-style Russia will emerge, one that is ready, able and willing to embrace the Western way of life. On the other side of the fence, we have the sceptics, doubting – at times – that Russia will ever be able to change.

Neither of these latter two camps has any direct correspondence with the Russian side. Even if some of the enthusiasts gladly refer to nineteenth century Russians clamouring for Western influences, they will not be equally ready to recognize the limits that were placed on such calls. Viewed from this perspective, the alliance that has been formed between Western enthusiasts and Russian neo-liberal reformers, often known as the "young reform economists", is an ahistorical phenomenon with little chance of finding any fertile Russian soil for their visions.

Similarly, the Western sceptics are a world apart from the Russian slavophiles in the normative sense. While the latter argue that Russia should refrain from emulating the West because it is wrong, the former argue that Russia will not emulate the West because it is inherently incapable of doing so. It is hard indeed to find any form of common ground between these two camps.

Given that the divisions outlined above, between four essentially different camps, have influenced, perhaps even greatly influenced, policy making both inside Russia and in Western capitals pondering how to deal with "the new Russia", it may be of some interest to take a closer look at the historical roots of the respective Russian belief systems that provoked the initial rift.

After all, if we are to accept that history matters, it does so not in terms of forests that have been felled, railways that have been built or mountains that have been climbed. The impact of the past on the present is transmitted via the memory of the past, and is thus susceptible to the various ways in which this memory may be manipulated.

It is worth noting, for example, that the "return to history" has been one of the most prominent, and at times also one of the most dangerous, aspects of the post-communist re-orientation of Eastern Europe and the former Soviet Union. In the extreme, selecting and rewriting the history of one ethnic group has served to rationalize the horrors of "ethnic cleansing".

Stating that "history matters" is simple enough, yet even at this level it remains controversial. Since history must always be a question of subjective interpretation, there can be no such thing as *the* Russian history. To slavophiles and *zapadniki*, for example, a given succession of Russian historical "facts" will have radically different interpretations and thus also radically different implications for what the Russia of today should do. Similarly, Western enthusiasts and sceptics will draw very different conclusions from the very same observations.

Explaining *how* history matters is therefore a matter of considerable complication, one that is logically bound to be controversial. In the following, we shall approach the issue from the economic point of view, seeking to establish how decisions made in the past will influence decisions that are made in the present. This is the realm of thinking in terms of path dependence and historical lock-in effects, which will be pursued at length below.

Bearing these questions and complications in mind, let us now proceed to look at the background. Simply put, what is the importance of the Russian past for the present debates on Russian policy choices?

Russian roots

Setting out to find the true roots of the Russian institutional matrix would be a rather fruitless endeavour. No matter how far back we go, it may always be argued that even at that early time "history matters", such that we must look even deeper. In the end, we would run out of recorded history and that would be that. Ambitions will thus have to be satisfied when and if we have found some defining characteristics that may be linked to current complications in the institutional structure.

In his classical study of Russian cultural history – *The Icon and the Axe* – James Billington finds that "As one looks at the history of Russian culture, it may be helpful to think of the forces rather than the forms behind it.

Three in particular – the natural surroundings, the Christian heritage, and the Western contacts of Russia – hover bigger than life . . . These forces seem capable of weaving their own strange web of crisis and creativity out of the efforts of men."[2] Let us pursue this line of thinking.

The harshness of nature

When we set out to explain how the harshness of nature conditioned the lives of the early Slav settlers, it should be noted that we are referring here not to the famed black soils of present-day Ukraine, but to the harsh and inhospitable environment that lies to the north.

When the old Kiev Rus disintegrated, it gave way to three distinctly different regions. In the west and the southwest were lands that would come to be dominated by Poland–Lithuania, in the north lands that would form the Principality of Novgorod, and in the northeast lands that would come to be dominated by the Principality of Moscow. All talk about the harshness of nature refers to the latter two.

To Billington, the impact of nature is noticeable above all in the symbolism of Russian imagination: "The underground world of the mythological 'damp mother earth' has beckoned in many forms from the first monastery in the caves of Kiev to the present-day shrine of the mummified Lenin and the gilded catacombs of the Moscow subway."[3] To others, there are more concrete implications.

Devoting a whole chapter of his study on *Russia under the Old Regime* to the natural conditions, Richard Pipes underlines that when the eastern Slavs arrived in the area that would become Muscovy, the peoples who were already living there – Finns and Turks – were engaged in farming only as a supplementary occupation. In the forest they relied on hunting and fishing, in the steppe on livestock breeding.

Although the area was "uniquely ill suited for farming", the ancient Russians persisted in their traditional pastoral habits and they would pay a heavy price for doing so: "Their heavy reliance on farming under adverse natural conditions is perhaps the single most basic cause of the problems underlying Russian history."[4]

Edward Keenan takes a similar approach to the importance of nature, in a classic article about Russian political culture:

> When, toward the end of the first millennium of the Christian era, the last great pre-modern migrations on the Eurasian continent ended, the East Slavs, like the last non-loser in a game of "Musical Chairs", found themselves with the last choice – with land in the northeastern margins of Europe that, to put it rather plainly, no one else seems to have wanted.[5]

In contrast to many others, who underscore how the harshness of nature led to a number of negative influences on the early Russian society, Keenan emphasizes the remarkable resilience of the solution that was found. His point is that the survival, and even vigour and demographic vitality of the Slavs was assured by "a remarkably congruent and tenacious set of practices and attitudes."[6]

Orthodox Christianity

Turning to the second dimension of Russia's institutional heritage, that of Orthodoxy, we may recall from above how Boris Yeltsin, when inaugurated as the first popularly elected Russian president ever, received a blessing by the head of the Russian Orthodox Church, Patriarch Aleksii. The symbolism was not merely that of demonstrating a clean break with the proclaimed atheism of the recent communist past. Even more so, it was an act that demonstrated continuity with a much deeper past, a past when Orthodoxy was the very foundation of Russian society.

As Billington underlines, it was not only that Orthodox Christianity "created the first distinctively Russian culture and provided the basic forms of artistic expression and the framework of belief for modern Russia". The Orthodox Church also "played a key role in infecting Russia with the essentially Byzantine idea that there is a special dignity and destiny for an Orthodox society and but one true answer to controversies arising within it".[7]

The roots of this Christian influence in turn go back to the old Roman world, i.e. to times before the arrival of Slav settlers to what would be the land of Rus.

Shortly after the adoption of Christianity by Emperor Constantine, the Roman Empire was split in two. Formally, it happened with the death of Emperor Theodosius, in 395, but in reality this was mere confirmation of a process of division between East and West that had been going on for some time.

One half was a rather short-lived West Rome, which would be repeatedly overrun by assorted Barbarians and would finally succumb in 476, when the last emperor was retired. The other was a much longer-lived East Rome, which would be known as Byzantium and would be around for centuries, until it was finally overrun by the Turks, in 1453, never to be heard of again.

The main dimension of rivalry between these two halves of old Rome was that of religion. Friction within the Christian Church led to increasing hostility between the Pope in Rome and the Patriarch in Constantinople. Mission from the respective sides was regarded with increasing suspicion and hostility by the other. In 1054, tensions came to a head. Differences over the nature of the Holy Trinity led to a clean and lasting break. Mutual excommunications were issued by the Pope and by the Patriarch.

For the land of Rus this was a fateful event. Having adopted Christianity from Constantinople, as late as 988, the future Russians would now be locked into the world of a declining Eastern Church, subjected to increasing pressure from the advancing Turks.

At the time of the split, however, Russia was still not a player in the game. On the contrary, as we have noted above, 1054 was also the year, by pure coincidence, when Grand Prince Yaroslav died, an event which marked the beginning of the decline and the eventual eclipse of Kiev Rus. Secular power over the land of Rus shifted to the Moscow area.

For the Church, this implied a need to follow, but at first it was not clear which of the many tiny warring principalities would emerge as the winner. At the time, the main battle stood between Tver and Moscow. Preferring to tread gently, in 1299 the Metropolitan of Kiev moved his see to more neutral Vladimir. After the abortive uprising of Tver in 1327, however, the Metropolitan moved to Moscow, which became and would remain to this day a holy city, the centre of the Russian Orthodox Church.

To the Church, the Mongol Yoke was a golden era. Taking little interest in the religious practices of the Russians, the Mongols rested content with demanding that the Orthodox Church should offer prayers for the Muslim khan and his family. In return, churches and monasteries were granted exemption from the taxes and tributes. Always ready to protect its growing wealth, the Church would keep a permanent representation at Sarai, and it would be a loyal supporter of all claims made by Moscow in its future ambitions to "gather the lands".

While the shift from Kiev to Moscow brought the Church many favours under the protection of the khans, it would also come to share in the growing isolation of Rus. The crusades, in particular, served to push Rus out of the orbit of the Mediterranean world, thus stretching the bonds of Russian clerics who were dependent on Constantinople for religious leadership. By the mid-fifteenth century, the growing isolation of Muscovy from the rest of Europe reached a critical point.

Faced with increasing Turkish pressure on Constantinople, the leaders of the Eastern Church approached their Western competitors with a plea for help against the mutual enemy. The issue was discussed at the Council of Florence, in 1437–9, and the final outcome was that help was promised in return for recognition of the supremacy of the Pope over the Christian Church as a whole.

When Muscovy's delegate to the Council of Florence, Metropolitan Isidore, returned home, he brought a distressing message. The Orthodox world had succumbed to the Papist forces. It was not only those churches that felt an immediate threat from Islam, such as the Greeks, that had fallen. Even the Orthodox Church of Lithuania had crossed to the enemy camp.

Rejecting the union out of hand, the Russian Orthodox Church effectively broke off its relations with Constantinople. The Grand Princes of

Moscow assumed the right to appoint their own Metropolitans, beginning by driving into exile the Greek Metropolitan Isidore, who had approved the decisions taken at Florence. At a Russian Church Council in 1448, he was replaced by a native Russian. Shortly afterwards, as Constantinople was overrun anyway, the Russian Church saw this as God's revenge on Byzantium and as confirmation that it had acted correctly in refusing the Florentine union.[8] Thus all links between Russian Orthodoxy and the remainder of Christianity were severed.

Muscovy now began to cultivate a self-image of being the last defender of the true faith. A prominent illustration of such claims may be found in a famous letter to Grand Prince Vasilii III, written in 1511 by a monk from Pskov by the name of Philoteus. The message was that there had been one Rome (that of Peter) which had fallen to heresy (Catholicism). Then there had been a second Rome (that of Constantine), which had also fallen (at Florence). Now there was a third Rome (Moscow), which was still standing, and there would be no fourth.

The notion of Moscow as the "Third Rome", i.e. as the true heir to the original Rome and thus the only remaining defender of the true faith, was prompted by the fates of the Serbian and Bulgarian kingdoms at the hands of the Turks, and by Khan Akhmed's attack on Moscow in 1480. There were real fears that the Orthodox world as a whole might succumb.

Placing this view in the context of Muscovy being surrounded by Muslim Mongols in the East and by Catholic Polish–Lithuanians in the West, we have an early version of the encirclement theme that would come to be so prominent in Soviet foreign policy.

Towards the end of the sixteenth century, in the midst of the "Time of Troubles", the shrewd Boris Godunov succeeded in luring the Patriarch of Constantinople into visiting Moscow, where he was forced, in 1589, to create a Patriarchate of Moscow and All Russia. This move had the dual effect of strengthening the Russian Orthodox Church, by averting the danger of influence from the Islamic powers that controlled Constantinople, and of reinforcing Moscow's claim to the status of a Third Rome.

By then, however, the strength of the Church had already begun to erode. The tsars found various indirect ways of infringing on the exemption rights of Church property, and in the mid-seventeenth century there followed the violent convulsions that were associated with Patriarch Nikon's liturgical reforms.[9] By the early eighteenth century the autocracy was ready for a final confrontation.

When Peter the Great embarked on his Great Embassy to the West, in 1697, it was the first time ever that a Russian tsar had travelled abroad, and it was the first time that a Russian tsar would seek to undertake a true "systemic change" at home. Upon his return, which was prompted by news of an uprising, Peter immediately proceeded to transform Russia into a modern European state.

Symbolism always being important in the Russian context, he started his project by making some rather powerful statements to his subjects. One was that of forcing his boyars to shave off their beards and to adopt Western dress (Dutch or Austrian). This was not merely an attempt at transforming the appearance of his entourage. Beards being an important feature of icon art, it was in fact a calculated assault on a vital part of old Russian culture.

Another attack on the old ways was directed at the political culture. In support of his Table of Ranks, which rested on placing merit before heritage, Peter also "conducted several gross travesties of the marriage ceremony that was so central to the older political system – he had his court dwarfs married, conducted a marriage in a palace of ice, etc."[10]

But it was the third message that contained the real heresy. Already in 1696 Peter began to restrict the rights of the clergy to dispose of incomes from Church properties, and he started organizing parties – known as "The Most Drunken Synod" – where he and his friends ridiculed priests and Church rituals. When Patriarch Adrian died, in 1700, he was not replaced. The Church instead was placed under secular authority and was forced to surrender all its incomes in return for regular salaries to the clergy.

In 1721, a general charter was issued that formally abolished the office of the Patriarch and introduced instead a sort of ministry of religion, known as "The Most Holy Synod". In 1762, Peter III completed the process by having all Church land expropriated. This assault was met by silent submission from the Church. As Pipes notes, "No Church in Christendom allowed itself to be secularized as graciously as the Russian".[11]

For all his symbolic statements, however, the reforms that were implemented by Peter the Great had little lasting impact on the institutional design of Russian society. A few important exceptions, such as the Table of Ranks and the Senate, did survive until the end of tsardom, but in principle the *status quo ante* Peter had been already restored by 1730.

Relations with the West

Peter's drive for greater modernity did, however, plant the seeds for new social classes to emerge, and thus also led to lasting divisions below the surface. Such tensions were heightened under Catherine the Great, who made a valiant attempt to introduce Enlightenment in Russia. The combined result was that of bringing to the surface an old Russian ambivalence.

As Billington has it, "Few problems have disturbed the Russians more than the nature of their relationship to the West. . . . It was rather like a trauma of adolescence. . . . Propelled by the very momentum of growth, Muscovy suddenly found itself thrust into a world it was not equipped to understand."[12]

At the core of the problem lies the fact that out of the three great Russian cities, it was only Kiev and Novgorod that had relations to the West. To Muscovy, the former was soon reduced to memory but the latter turned into a serious ideological adversary. After his crushing of Novgorod, Ivan the Great came to exhibit "some of the same obsessive fear of the West that was to recur under Ivan IV and Stalin".[13]

These observations are important in the sense that they point at internal explanations to Russian isolationism. Keenan rightly warns against being taken in by what he calls the "deprivation hypothesis", i.e. all those developments in Western Europe that Russia opted to stay out of: "The deprivation hypothesis has little explanatory power with regard to the political culture that *did* arise in Muscovy, nor does it address the question of why that culture was – despite features that Westerners might consider unattractive or 'deficient' – so effective and, apparently, so admirably suited to Muscovy's needs."[14]

The main importance of the story about the harshness of nature is that it led to the creation of an institutional arrangement that was successful in sustaining life, if not progress, and the relevance of the story about religion lies in the creation of a self-image which is strongly opposed to any *rapprochement* with the West. Both stories are admirably suited to interpretation in terms of path dependence. We shall have reason to return to that later on.

It was only with the Napoleonic wars that Russia entered into serious contact with Western society and Western culture. At the subsequent Congress of Vienna, where the new map of Europe was drawn up, the Russian tsar played an important role. Russia had finally assumed the position of a major player in European politics, a position it would retain up until the present.

Domestically, however, the opening up to the West was fraught with complication. While the tsar retreated from his early "liberal" ideas, under the surface dissent was brewing. The first open manifestation of the social tensions came with the Decembrist revolt in 1825. Although the *coup* as such was something of an unevent, it did leave a lasting imprint on the new tsar and thus influenced the autocracy for the coming three decades.

The remainder of the nineteenth century would be marked by an autocracy that was becoming less and less able to understand and deal with the changing social patterns. The reforms of Alexander II were certainly important, but it was too little, too late. In the final decades of the century, terrorism came to dominate the political landscape. The country was drifting towards a cataclysm that the autocracy perceived as inevitable.

The latter impression was expressed in the slogan of "Orthodoxy, Autocracy and Nationality", which was coined by Count Uvarov, the Minister of Education under Nicholas I. The stance of the autocracy was to serve as an "ideological dam", postponing rather than seeking to avoid the inevitable. Said Uvarov: "If I can succeed in delaying for fifty years the kind of future that theories are brewing for Russia, I shall have performed my duty and shall die in peace."[15] Uvarov succeeded, but the autocracy did not, at least not under the Romanovs.

When the Bolsheviks took power and embarked on their own very particular quest for modernity, it was a quest that initially met with great admiration in a crisis-ridden West. There were many "political pilgrims" who travelled to the Soviet Union in order to see the future.[16] Some had the intelligence not to be deceived, and a few even the honesty to go back home and tell the truth about, say, the great famine in the early 1930s. But most were enthusiasts.

With the Cold War, hostility between Russia and the West reached an historical peak. Massive resources were devoted to the arms race, and even Western society underwent ugly transformations, such as the McCarthy witch-hunts. Towards the end, President Reagan could officially agitate against the "Evil Empire". Then Gorbachev stepped in to deliver us all.

Although the conclusion of the military confrontation in the Cold War was real enough, it remains to be asked whether the new friendship that emerged between East and West really was tantamount to saying that Russia wanted to be *like* the West, in all respects?

That would be the one really important question facing decision-makers in the post-Soviet environment. As we shall see below, the main thrust of the ambitions by the West to help in Russia's post-Soviet reconstruction would rest on a belief that Russian society, relieved of all its communist trappings, basically worked in the same way as societies in the West, and thus would be both willing and able to implement a speedy transition.

This attitude was given a powerful illustration at a World Bank seminar, held in Bangkok in October 1991, at the annual meeting of the World Bank and the IMF. One of the speakers at this seminar was Lawrence Summers, who was then chief economist at the Bank. He used the occasion to voice a strong belief in the general applicability of economic laws: "Spread the truth – the laws of economics are like the laws of engineering. One set of laws works everywhere."[17]

Given that this occurred at a time that was a critical juncture on the Russian scene, his statement would be oft repeated, as a sort of clarion call for shock therapy. In February 1992, for example, the very same was proclaimed by Pyotr Aven, who was then Russian minister for foreign economic relations: "There are no special countries from the point of view of economists. If economics is a science, with its own laws – all countries and all economic stabilization plans are the same."[18]

So much for all the work that had been done in institutional economics. Among the Russian reformers, all institutions were taken to be the same. If you need a constitution – just copy one from abroad. If you need a monetary policy – have one off the shelf. The consequences of acting on such grossly mistaken beliefs have only just begun to emerge.[19]

Let us turn now to see how the direction of Western policy was transformed, from that of helping to reform the Soviet Union, to placing Russia first. This policy transformation would be in many ways revealing.

Reforming the Soviet economy

From our above account of Gorbachev's time in power we may recall how the Soviet political leadership showed itself to be incapable of questioning in earnest the foundations of the Soviet economic system. The few changes that were implemented were either short-lived (*gospriemka*) or marred by such inherent contradictions that in practice they never had any real chance of working (*goszakaz*).

It was rather obvious from the course of events that no serious policy analysis had ever been undertaken, i.e. an analysis of what effects and side-effects different reform measures might bring about (the anti-alcohol campaign is an excellent example here). The ideological fences were still too narrow to allow an objective assessment. Thus the result. Gorbachev's economic policies bring to mind Napoleon's classic maxim, "*On s'engage, et puis on voit*".

There was a deceptive superficial trend, in the sense that the economic reform rhetoric gradually came to incorporate a number of fundamental concepts that are associated with the market economy. But beyond the rhetoric there was no serious discussion concerning which conditions would be necessary for setting up a working Russian market economy.

The main part of the struggle for the market economy would be waged on the ideological level, and it was in this struggle that the Westernizers scored a great victory. In this simple fact we may find an important part of the explanation as to why the whole project as such would come to end in dismal failure.

The ideological triumph of the market economy over the planned economy created unwarranted expectations for rapid progress in making the ambitions come true. The overwhelming enthusiasm of the reformers tended to obscure the fact that under perestroika both the pre-conditions for institutional change – formal as well as informal – and the accumulation of human capital – chiefly in the form of relevant economic knowledge – had been greatly neglected.

This was unfortunate not only in the sense that the necessary pre-conditions for a transition to market economy were largely absent. As Marshall Goldman puts it, "Russia simply wasn't ready".[20] Even more detrimental was the fact that unrealistic expectations were created on both sides. On the Russian side, the reformers forged ahead believing not only that the transition would be fairly easy, but also that the West would stand by, ready to lend a helping hand. On the Western side, however, it was believed that the transformation of Russia into a copy of the West could be quickly achieved, without much help being needed.

As a result of these asymmetric expectations, the Western world was to become involved in the Russian reform process in a way that had no previous parallel in international economic relations. In the first half of the 1990s, both individual consultants and major international organizations would devote a considerable amount of time and money to a massive international effort to help Russia along its chosen path.

There would be a veritable trek of Western economists travelling to Moscow with a variety of miracle remedies. Some would be invited, others would come on their own initiative. Some would be Nobel Prize winners, like Wassily Leontief and Milton Friedman, others would be less well known. All certainly had a mission, but since economists seldom tend to agree on what should be done, the outcome was hardly surprising: "Since much of the advice was contradictory and applicable only for already-existing market economies, the Soviets were often confused."[21]

Against the background of all the attention that would later come to be focused on Boris Yeltsin and his Russian reform programme, it is important to note that the commitment of the West to help out in some way had already been made towards the end of Mikhail Gorbachev's time in power.

At the "Group of Seven" (G7) economic summit meeting in Houston in July 1990, the World Bank and the IMF were charged, along with the OECD and the then only just started European Bank for Reconstruction and Development (EBRD), with compiling a report on the Soviet economy. The mandate was to "undertake a detailed study of the Soviet economy, make recommendations for its reform, and establish the criteria under which Western economic assistance could effectively support such reforms".[22] ("The West" will henceforth be defined as the G7, with the possible exclusion of a reluctant Japan.)

Given the high political and organizational level at which this study was commissioned and undertaken, it is striking to note the contrasts that would emerge between its recommendations presented, in December 1990, and those actual policies that would be decided on by the Russian side in the autumn of 1991, and which would subsequently be held up by the same Western partners as the supreme wisdom of "transition economics", whatever that might be.

The list of such contrasts is so long that only a few salient illustrations can be given here. Throughout, the emphasis is on the need for comprehensive reform, i.e. the diametric opposite to the narrow focus of shock therapy. The following passage sums it up: "Short run stabilization needs to be complemented by a determined beginning of structural reform in the fiscal, monetary and external areas, as well as systemic reforms, affecting, for instance, ownership arrangements, enterprise management, prices and the labour market."[23]

Looking at more detailed issues, the following is said with respect to stabilization policy: "In the short run this should be supported by an incomes policy which would set both a floor for social reasons and a ceiling on the growth of incomes. Given the weaknesses in other control instruments, incomes policy seems indispensable at least for the transition."[24] To date, it has been hard indeed to identify anything that even looks like a thought-out Russian incomes policy.

Against the background of all the troubles that would come to plague the budget sphere, once the days of easy inflationary financing were brought to an end, we may recall another recommendation: "The tax administration will require extensive reorganization and an overhaul of procedures to adapt it to a market economy. Substantial reforms of the budgetary process, which to date has been tied closely to the plan, will also be required."[25] Serious tax reform would be considered only in the autumn of 1997, after heavy prodding from the IMF.

With regard to the (abortive) assault on the natural monopolies that was finally launched in 1997, the following recommendation is relevant: "Steps should be taken to create and maintain competitive markets. If the transition to a market economy is going to succeed, existing barriers to competition, including monopolies, must be broken down, and new enterprises and products encouraged."[26]

The issue of privatization naturally looms large, as a necessary precondition for establishing a functioning market economy, and there is no question that "security of private property must be assured from the outset in order to encourage private initiative".[27] But establishing private property is not tantamount to the rapid mass give-aways that would be Russia's choice. On the contrary: "This will involve procedures for ownership reform, demonopolization, and the enforcement of a hard budget constraint on enterprises that continue under state ownership."[28]

Most importantly, privatization, like all other policies, must be worked out in such a fashion that costs and benefits of alternative approaches are carefully balanced:

> To strike a balance between the desirability of moving rapidly and the practical impossibility of doing so effectively on a large scale, it is necessary to use a flexible approach . . . The need for revenues to help cover some of the costs associated with the economic reform – among them the cost of restructuring potentially viable enterprises, of cleaning up the balance sheets of banks, and beginning to catch up on the backlog of necessary infrastructure investments – argues for sales rather than give-aways. However, there may well be advantages to giving away some shares in some of the larger enterprises.[29]

Finally, we have the question of how to deal with the monetary overhang. Here it is said that "A monetary reform would be the most sure and effective instrument, and it could distinguish between the assets of households and those of enterprises".[30] But it is also recognized that there are some important political issues involved. Since this issue really goes to the heart of Russian shock therapy, we shall find reason to return to it at length below.

In sum, as we shall see in the following chapters, the "young reform economists" who gathered around Boris Yeltsin in the autumn of 1991 would embark on a programme of slash and burn reforms that derived little if any inspiration from the work that had been undertaken by the IMF and its sister organizations. Yet, the latter were soon to be found among the most ardent supporters of the shock therapy approach.

Part of the explanation for this development may be found in one of several groups of Russian and Western economists that were formed in the final years of Gorbachev's rule, seeking to work out recommendations for the formulation of a Soviet economic reform programme.

The group in question was formed in 1991, with Harvard University as its base.[31] From the Russian side it was joined by a young economist by the name of Grigorii Yavlinskii, who would later go on to form his own political party – Yabloko – and to be a serious candidate in the 1996 presidential election. From the American side, it was led by two political scientists, Graham Allison and Robert Blackwill, but it also included the economists Jeffrey Sachs, a previous economic advisor to the governments of Bolivia and Poland, and Stanley Fischer, who had similar experience from Israel.[32]

Within the framework of this group, a programme for economic reform was worked out, together with recommendations for massive economic support from the West. At first the project went under the name of "Grand Bargain", but later it would be known as the "Window of Opportunity" (in Russian: *shans na soglasie*). The group's suggestions were presented on 29 June 1991, only days before the crucial G7 economic summit meeting in London.

The Harvard group, however, was marred by strong internal conflicts, which concerned the involvement of the West in particular. Allison and Sachs came to differ seriously over the question of economic aid. While Sachs publicly emphasized the significance of gigantic amounts of support, to the tune of $30–50 billion annually over five years, Allison believed that it would be counter-productive to promote the involvement of the West in this manner.

Thus it was obvious already early on that the "Grand Bargain" according to Sachs was not really the same thing as that according to Allison. Already within the Harvard group, Sachs formulated what would later come to be a recurring theme in discussions concerning the Russian economic reforms, namely that the optimal strategy is shock therapy coupled with a massive economic support from the West. Despite intense lobbying, however, the Harvard group would fail to win support for its ideas.

When the G7 finally met for its London summit, the world had changed. During the first half of 1991, contacts between Washington and Moscow had intensified. The Gulf War was over and the United States directed a great deal of attention towards developments in the Soviet Union. According to Jack Matlock, US ambassador to Moscow in 1987–91, the American–Soviet relationship took on an "unprecedented intensity".[33]

The Soviet Union was on its way to splitting up and American beliefs in Gorbachev were faltering, to the point where even Gorbachev himself felt the growing doubts. At a meeting with Ambassador Matlock on 7 May 1991, the Soviet president gave a long monologue, where he noted that President Bush had "reassessed" the relationship.

When Bush learned about Gorbachev's unease, frantic attempts were made to reassure him about continued US confidence. On 8 May, the day after the meeting between Gorbachev and Matlock, Bush received the Estonian, Latvian and Lithuanian leaders. Instead of using this meeting to express support for the Balts' struggle for freedom, he chose to pay homage to Gorbachev. Matlock expresses great surprise over this: "Implausibly, indeed incredibly, he used their visit to heap public praise on Gorbachev."[34]

This reassurance, however, did not extend beyond words. At the end of May, Lady Thatcher came to Moscow as Gorbachev's personal guest. After dinner at the Gorbachevs, Thatcher met Matlock. She was very explicit and urged that the USA should invite Gorbachev to the upcoming G7 meeting. Matlock recalls her plea: "'Please get a message to my friend George,' she requested, 'We've got to help Mikhail. Of course, you Americans can't and shouldn't have to do it all yourselves, but George will have to lead the effort, just as he did with Kuwait.'"[35]

On 11 June, Gorbachev went to Oslo to receive his Nobel Peace Prize. By then, however, he had already passed the peak of his political career. In the West, preparations were under way for a world without Gorbachev, perhaps even without the Soviet Union. Although he did eventually receive an invitation to join the G7 leaders in London, it was not an invitation to participate as a member of the group, merely to be a guest at the ceremonies after the formal session. And it would be John Major, not George Bush who issued the invitation.

It was the time that passed between these two economic summit meetings – between Houston 1990 and London 1991 – that was really formative for the subsequent policy of the West towards post-Soviet Russia. In Houston, there was a broad agreement that help of some kind should be extended, and much work went into thinking about how that could be done. A year later, in London, Western leaders would still express worry about the deteriorating condition of the Soviet economy, but their willingness to lend a hand had dissipated.

One may certainly question the wisdom of this about-face. Goldman, for example, asks the intriguing question of what might have happened if the events of the subsequent month had been known in advance. Would the G7 then still have refused support? Would there indeed have been an August *coup* in Moscow, if Gorbachev had returned with billions of dollars in support?[36]

For those who criticize the cool attitude that was shown in London, one possible and rather paradoxical development might be taken into account. By agreeing to a massive package of aid, in support of a programme to reform the Soviet economy, the G7 would have intervened rather decisively in Moscow power plays. Such an action might conceivably have saved both Gorbachev and the Soviet Union, at least for some time. Would that have been a change for the better or for the worse?

Be that as it may. We know what did happen. The Soviet Union fell apart, as did the Harvard group. Yavlinskii was sidelined and Sachs went it alone, with shock therapy but without the massive economic aid that he claimed to be a necessary pre-condition for success.

Although it was becoming increasingly clear that the West was about to change sides in the Soviet power struggle, the London summit was no decisive moment. Even in the wake of the failed August *coup*, there would remain substantial ambivalence in the West, making it possible for Gorbachev to hold on to power for another few months.

It was not until December 1991, when the writing was really on the wall, that *The Economist* could definitively distance itself completely from Gorbachev: "However unappetizing it may be for America and Western Europe, the truth is that the greatest threat to security lies in the attempts to preserve the relics of the collapsed Soviet system – attempts which are led by the most cherished of all the system's relics, Gorbachev himself."[37]

While the West was busy being puzzled, the men around Boris Yeltsin were busy working out a strategy for Russia's post-Soviet existence. Given the context of a Soviet Union that may have been crumbling but was still intact, and ruled in a vague sort of way by President Gorbachev, the various groups that were seeking Yeltsin's favour differed on the issue of what should be done with the union.

While Yavlinskii and his team continued to work under the assumption that the centralized Soviet structures would be somehow preserved, there was another group which pushed a strategy of "Russia first". The leader of this group was Yegor Gaidar, a young economist who had served as economic editor to two vital communist party publications, first *Kommunist* and then *Pravda*. To the surprise of many, and not the least himself, he would be chosen by Yeltsin as the point man for Russia's economic reform.

With this choice, Yeltsin put an effective end to all talk about reforming the Soviet economy. It was now a whole new ballgame, with new players and new rules. It is hardly surprising that the West would be slow in realizing and adapting to this transformation.

Russia first

For some reason or other, Yeltsin left Moscow on 24 September, not to return until 10 October 1991. Needless to say, this absence added to the general confusion of post-*coup* developments. After his return, however, the president displayed typical energy, setting out to organize his own administration and looking for a concept for economic reform. (We shall return to the details of that search in the following chapter.)

The decision to push ahead with truly radical reforms was made public on 28 October. In his "state-of-the-federation" speech before the fifth session of the Russian Congress of People's Deputies, Yeltsin announced that Russia would now become a "normal country", that it intended to introduce democracy and a market economy.

With the benefit of hindsight, we may see the importance of this speech – Russia's project of "systemic change" had been launched – but at the time there were few Western observers who realized the importance of the moment.

One of the few was Jeffrey Sachs, who gives voice to the subsequent bitterness of the Western economic advisors at what they would call the West's "betrayal" of Russia: "I woke up on 29 October – the day after Yeltsin's speech – [expecting to see] red, white and blue banners around the *Financial Times*, with Western leaders praising the speech and saying that a new day had dawned in international collaboration."[38]

There are good reasons, however, that may help explain why the proclamation did not receive the attention it might well have deserved. The context within which Yeltsin made his play was that of a decaying Soviet Union, which was still ruled by President Gorbachev. If nothing else, international law still demanded that the Soviet leader be shown some respect. At the time, moreover, it was far from clear what the outcome would be. Despite the failed August *coup*, many Western observers were still loath to accept the notion that the Soviet Union might break up.

During the autumn of 1991, Western leaders had two overriding priorities in dealing with the Soviet break-up. One was to make sure that the Soviet nuclear arsenal be transferred to Russian hands, in order to prevent nuclear proliferation, and the other to secure a continued servicing of the Soviet foreign debt. No doubt there were those recalling how, after the Bolshevik *coup*, Lenin had repudiated Russia's tsarist foreign debt.

Thus an arduous process of negotiations was set in motion, at a time when Russia's reformers probably could have put their time to better use in tending to the country's domestic economic troubles. It is understandable that this caused great resentment on the Russian side.

In one of his articles on the "betrayal", Sachs lashes out at how "the G-7 governments disgracefully pressed the Russian government to continue servicing the Soviet foreign debt, at a time when the G-7 should have been working hard to provide the new government with fiscal breathing space".[39]

A similar sense of anger is displayed by Richard Layard, another of the more prominent foreign economic advisors to the Russian government, when he (and co-author John Parker) speaks of how the West sent in the "debt collectors". He noted how the negotiations "involved Gaidar for hour after hour when he was trying to construct his reform plan," and added a rather serious practical complication.

By insisting that servicing of the debt should continue until a rescheduling could be worked out, the West pushed Russia into a position where its dollar reserves ran out. By mid-December payments were unilaterally suspended: "This incompetent outcome, which blocked the dollar accounts of many Russian and foreign firms, was the first notable failure of the reform government, and it was due directly to Western advice and pressure."[40]

While this line of criticism may have some justification, it should be noted that in the overall picture of Western attitudes to the Russian "transition", it represents a mere technicality. The realm of the real "betrayal" was that of failing to put up tens of billions of Western tax dollars in support. Once we move into this dimension, the issue at hand becomes considerably more complicated.

One part of the problem concerns whether massive economic assistance was actually motivated in the first place. One might question the absorption capacity, and one might ask why a country that had been running quite substantial trade surpluses should be in need of balance of payment support in the first place. Most importantly, the volume of capital flight from Russia indicates a serious lack of confidence in the reform process. The problem would thus seem to rest on the Russian rather than the Western side.

This line of reasoning will not be pursued any further. We know what did happen, and we know that there is in this dimension a problem of far greater importance than that of insufficient dollars, namely the allocation of responsibility for dealing with Russia's needs. Given that Russia was no traditional Third World aid recipient – economically or politically – it should have been dealt with – from day one – as a very special case. The failure to do so would prove to be a recipe for major trouble.

The decisive turning point came on 6 December 1991, when President Yeltsin asked the G7 for a stabilization fund, intended to support the rouble. Rather than agreeing to deal with Russia on a bilateral basis, under a special arrangement, the G7 governments decided to shift the burden onto the shoulders of the IMF. Layard and Parker rightly criticize this move:

That was a fatal step, for the IMF is an organization with its own procedures and criteria, which quite naturally it wished to apply to Russia as to other countries. The basic issue for the IMF was: Did Russia qualify for an IMF loan using the standard criteria? Unless specifically instructed to do so by its shareholders (the G7) the IMF was not going to take into account Russia's critical role in world politics.[41]

The decision by the G7 to place the IMF in charge of helping Russia is certainly explicable in the sense of distorting the vision of the taxpayers who would have to foot the bill. If it was actually going to be a question of aid in the amounts mentioned by Sachs, governments would have a hard time gathering the necessary political support. Better then to do it indirectly via the IMF. There was also the added complication of sour relations between Russia and Japan over the Kurile Islands. Another reason, therefore, for not getting Japanese taxpayers directly involved.

While the IMF solution might thus have been politically expedient at the time, it would soon turn out to harbour a string of added complications. One such concerned the very rationale of this organization. Since its conception at Bretton Woods in 1944, the IMF had been the world's financial policeman. It had functioned on the basis of credibility. Once an IMF team had given its stamp of approval for a country in crisis, other creditors would feel safe. Now that was set to change.

Accepting responsibility for Russia not only meant moving into an area where the Fund had little expertise and experience of its own. It also meant taking on a debtor that would not gladly accept the strong-arm tactics used by the IMF in its relations with its traditional borrowers.

We might, for example, recall warnings issued in public in the spring of 1994, by the former Russian finance minister Boris Fyodorov, that the credits would never be repaid: "There are too many people in senior positions in the Russian government who think it patriotic to take as many loans as possible and then quietly plot to obtain debt forgiveness and debt reductions."[42]

But the process had already been set in motion, and could not be stopped. As pressures grew, and accusations of betrayal started flying in the air, it was rather logical that the IMF would succumb and begin to consider what was "politically correct" in the capitals of the G7 countries.

Another complication was linked to the fact that the IMF was on the prowl for a new mission. Its way of handling the debt crises in the Third World had not been a success, and the number of its critics was growing rapidly. Further funding was by no means secure.

With the fall of communism, a whole new arena was opened up. By agreeing to shoulder the main responsibility for a post-socialist reconstruction effort, the IMF would once again be placed in the limelight, and its chairman, Michel Camdessus, would be one of the world's top leaders.

In both of these dimensions we find obvious problems of moral hazard, of temptations to abandon sound financial considerations and venture instead into the domain of very high level politics. Such problems would be exacerbated by a conscious Russian strategy of presenting Boris Yeltsin as the only reliable force of "good" on the Russian scene.

The essence of this strategy is captured by Bruce Clark, who went from being Moscow correspondent for *The Times* to becoming diplomatic correspondent for *Financial Times*:

> At that time, the smugness that descended on the Western world in the aftermath of its Cold and Gulf War victories was still very much intact; it was still assumed that a Russia which was prosperous, as the West defined prosperity, would be a force for good in the world, as the West defined goodness. The Yeltsin administration would have been foolish if it had not capitalized on that sentiment for all it was worth. If Yeltsin was the repository of all the world's hope for "goodness" in Russia, it followed that helping his administration, and forgiving it any minor peccadilloes, was an overwhelming political imperative.[43]

When President Bill Clinton met Yeltsin at the summit meeting in Vancouver in April 1993, and when, some months later, the G7 held its own economic summit meeting in Tokyo, it was already obvious what kind of political games were now being played. Both the IMF and the G7 governments were adapting themselves to a new set of rules – rules, moreover, that were being laid down by the Russians.

We may think of the adjustment as a three-stage process. In the first stage, from Houston 1990 to London 1991, a transformation occurred from betting on Gorbachev and a preserved Soviet Union to thinking in terms of disintegration of the Soviet Union. In the second stage, lasting from the August *coup* through much of 1992, there is confusion as to what the post-Soviet world will actually look like, and in the third stage, which is taking shape in 1993, the policy of "Russia first" is taking root.

Clark summarizes the essence of the new game: "Somewhere in the course of these frantic discussions, it came to be accepted by everyone that for reasons of historical necessity, Russia must be given a uniquely privileged sort of treatment by the International Monetary Fund and the World Bank."[44]

What this meant, in plain language, was that political considerations must be allowed to override the rules and practices that had been IMF standards for decades. What type of pressure was applied is a bit unclear – perhaps the IMF did not need too much prodding – but the outcome is all the more obvious. Russia would be more or less exempt from all the rules and sanctions that were rigorously enforced in all other cases of countries turning to the IMF for assistance. To some, the transformation was baffling:

For the bankers and economists who worked at those institutions and had spent a lifetime schooling unruly nations in the ways of financial rectitude, it was a bemusing experience, at once comical and exasperating, to watch Russia's leaders cheerfully rewrite the rules of the capitalist club before they had even joined. High-flying bureaucrats, used to laying down the law in every semi-bankrupt finance ministry in the world, found to their astonishment that Russian officialdom treated them with condescension: the condescension of borrowers who know that their banker has no real choice, because the political cost of meanness is even higher than the financial risk of profligacy.[45]

The true reasons for this about-face will remain a matter for speculation. In some quarters, there was likely to be a significant amount of *naiveté*, of an expectation that soft terms for Russia really would lead to positive results, that the Russian economy would rapidly recover and that in the slightly longer term one would actually be able to recover all the billions that were granted in credit, perhaps even with interest.

In other circles, it is equally likely that pure cynicism prevailed, i.e. that it was fully appreciated that the soft credits would neither be repaid nor perhaps even have the promised effects, but that the short-term political gains in the relationship to the Kremlin could be worth some tens of billions of dollars. This becomes even more likely if we realize that the global availability of aid and credit to the needy – if anything – has been decreased. It is thus – *de facto* – other poor countries that – indirectly – have paid the price for aid to Russia.

No matter how we choose to interpret the decision to give Russia a uniquely privileged treatment, there can be little doubt as to the potentially negative long-term consequences of this decision. At the bottom lies the vital issue of credibility, both for the leading governments in the West and for the international financial institutions.

In the former case, a situation has been created where Russia's political leaders and bureaucratic elite have been used to soft terms, expecting that the bill will always be picked up by the West and that taking a threatening stance is a practicable way of solving any negotiation problems. The events that followed upon the 17 August, 1998 devaluation of the rouble illustrate how difficult it will be to achieve an effective break in this pattern of behaviour.

In the latter case, we may anticipate considerable fallout effects, where other countries that are dependent upon credit from the IMF and the World Bank start referring to the special considerations that Russia has received and begin demanding equally soft terms for themselves. The strict discipline that had been upheld in previous distribution of credit may thus have received a serious knock, one that could have been avoided altogether if the G7 governments had assumed direct responsibility for the "special regime".

Most serious of all, however, is the fact that the very basis of the project as such, i.e. that the economic assistance given to Russia would be meaningful, has not been satisfied. There are good reasons for this outcome, reasons that are not primarily linked to insufficient support but to an insufficient realization in the West of what the transformation of the political game between East and West really implied. Expectations were that the quick fix would work.

Once the communist monopoly on power had been broken, and no obstacles remained in the way of private ownership, free pricing and other vital components of a working market economy, it was generally believed that a rapid "normalization" would indeed follow. The Russian economy would be integrated in the world economy and the enormous Russian market would be opened up to Western interests. The need for economic and technical assistance might certainly be massive, but it would be of a highly transitional nature. This was the context of the political reorientation.

Reorienting international relations

Perhaps the most fascinating aspect of the processes that have been outlined above concerns how, when and why the West decided to change horses, to push Mikhail Gorbachev aside and to give its full backing instead to Boris Yeltsin. Given the deep antagonism that the two Russian presidents had demonstrated for each other, the decision was a very delicate one. And it would determine the shape and content of the post-communist security structure in Europe.

Gorbachev's grand ambitions for a revitalization of the Soviet system had acted as a catalyst for many diverse processes. On the Soviet scene, as we have seen in the previous chapter, it sparked debates about the degree of decay in the Soviet system and about what steps would be necessary in order to find a cure. Nothing more needs to be said about that.

In the West, however, the entry of Gorbachev had led not only to polarization in the views about Moscow's intentions and abilities. Even more strikingly, it had started a Western quest for "heroes" to support. While Gorbachev was still in power, he was very much the focus of admiration, being designated by *Time Magazine* as "Man of the Decade". Those were the easy days.

Facing Gorbachev

At first, the Western response to Gorbachev was one of hesitation and suspicion. As we have noted above, many influential voices warned that the new openness and the "new thinking" in foreign policy might be no more than a ruse. At the very least, one could not be sure that even if he

Figure 4.1 Facing Gorbachev

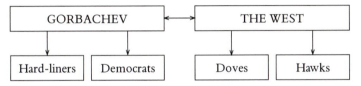

actually *were* sincere, Gorbachev would also succeed in delivering. At the same time, others argued that the opportunity must be seized and that Gorbachev must be given a chance.

Needless to say, this split in Western opinions was matched by a split on the Soviet side, with some coming out as strong supporters for the new policy and others doing their best to stop it. What developed was a simple two-level co-operative game, where Gorbachev and the Western leaders were engaged in supporting each other in their respective attempts to deal with domestic opposition. The general outline is presented very loosely in Figure 4.1.

There is nothing remarkable about this game. The stakes were easily defined. Both sides stood to gain from arms reductions, the Soviet side perhaps more so in economic terms. If we accept that the purpose of defence spending was to achieve military parity, it follows that the Soviet side, with its smaller GDP, would have to spend a much greater proportion of its resources than did NATO. Layard and Parker quote a ratio of 7:1.[46]

For the West, the tricky side was to deal with fears of a Soviet ruse. For Gorbachev, the problem was that of defending political concessions in giving up its hegemony in Eastern Europe, i.e. the "Sinatra Doctrine". For a few crucial years the game was successful and Gorbachev became a hero in the West. Then he started to buckle under domestic pressure, and the West began to sway.

Analytically it is obvious that the transfer of Western favour from Gorbachev to Yeltsin was not merely a question of supporting a new player in an old game. After all, one of the reasons why the West had so stubbornly supported Gorbachev up until the very last moments was that he was seen as the guarantor of maintaining the integrity of the Soviet state.

As a last grand gesture of such support, we may recall President George Bush's infamous speech in Kiev – the "Chicken Kiev" speech – where he warned against Ukrainian separatism. That was only days before the August 1991 *coup*.

Transferring favour to Yeltsin meant backing the very man who had done more than any other to bring about the collapse of the Soviet state. This was a man who had been regarded as a drunkard, whose visit to the United States was described as one long series of drinks, who when in Paris was not even admitted to the Elysée Palace, etc.

Figure 4.2   Facing Yeltsin

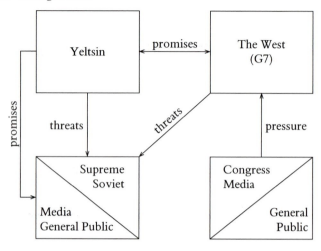

Facing Yeltsin

When the West decided to back Yeltsin rather than Gorbachev, it was thus not simply changing its favourite. It was, in fact, entering into a whole new game, with a completely new set of rules and stakes. Since Russia claimed that it was now bent on becoming a Western-style democratic and market-oriented society, to the point even where Yeltsin, in December 1991, told a Washington audience that he wanted to seek full NATO membership, the issue was no longer a military one.

What Yeltsin promised was not only the transformation of Russian society, which was no mean prize in itself, but even more so the final ideological triumph of the Western way of life. As Francis Fukuyama had envisioned, history would finally come to an end. This was something different altogether and it led to a substantial rearrangement of forces on the Western side. Figure 4.2 provides another loose summary.

The only real similarity between this game and the one that was played with Gorbachev lies in its two-level character. Like Gorbachev, Yeltsin was in a position where he needed Western support to deal with domestic opposition, but in stark contrast to Gorbachev's eternal manoeuvring Yeltsin opted for a consistent policy of confrontation. This would have important consequences both at home and in relations with the West.

In the previous chapter we saw him take on both Gorbachev and the Soviet Union, in a game of "chicken" that could well have led to far greater bloodshed than actually did occur. In the following chapters, we shall see that tactic repeated both in his struggle with the opposition in the legislature and in his campaign for presidential re-election. These "chicken" games are presented not in order to elicit sympathies for one of the sides, but to show how the institutional design has been conducive to such confrontation.

Most importantly, in contrast to its experiences under Gorbachev, the West was now confronted with clear-cut alternatives. Where Gorbachev had insisted on being treated as an equal, maintaining that the Soviet state needed co-operation with the West but was in no way dependent on help, Boris Yeltsin has not balked at coming as a beggar, one, moreover, who at times has gone about his asking in a rather aggressive manner.

Yeltsin's message to the West has been similar to the "chicken" games he has played out at home. And it has been played out in a way that is reminiscent of one of Thomas Schelling's classic illustrations of bargaining behaviour: "The sophisticated negotiator may find it difficult to seem as obstinate as a truly obstinate man. If a man knocks at a door and says that he will stab himself on the porch unless given $10, he is more likely to get the $10 if his eyes are bloodshot."[47]

Throughout the post-Soviet period, Russian foreign policy has rested on a skilful manipulation of the "greater evil". Demands have been linked not to direct threats, but to thinly veiled indirect threats of what might happen if insufficient Western support were to result in other "forces" coming to power.

Foreign Minister Andrei Kozyrev's classic performance of "shock diplomacy", at the December 1992 meeting of the CSCE in Stockholm, is a case in point.[48] The Western refusal to see and acknowledge the horrors in Chechnya is a reflection from the receiving end.

Under Gorbachev, a strategy of "Support me or else . . ." would not have been credible. Under Yeltsin it has. That in itself says something important about the transition from Soviet to post-Soviet Russia.

Looking at the outcome of Western relations to Gorbachev's Soviet Union and to Yeltsin's Russia, we may also find a further important point of difference. While Gorbachev delivered his end of the bargain, it is not even clear what it is that Yeltsin has promised to deliver. In the former case, Central Europe was allowed to break free, the Warsaw Pact was dismantled, Germany united and arms control agreements were signed. In the latter, Yeltsin has promised to transform Russia into a "normal society", based on the Western way of life. To date, however, there has not been any consensus on what that meant, far less as to its success.

Different games – different pay offs

The most obvious difference between the two games lies in the different nature of the respective pay offs, and in the consequent problems of monitoring success. The game with Gorbachev concerned arms reduction. It was comparatively easy to monitor the missiles, and the Pentagon was always ready to act as enforcer. In the game with Yeltsin it was unclear

Figure 4.3   Different games – different pay offs

	Gorbachev	**Yeltsin**
Prize	Arms Reduction	Systemic Change
Monitoring	Missiles	Monetary Policy
Enforcer	Pentagon	IMF

what the real pay off was to be, it was difficult to monitor progress, and it was perhaps most difficult of all to see who would act as enforcer. Figure 4.3 illustrates.

While debates on the progress of negotiation with Gorbachev were clear-cut – trust or not trust in promises to destroy x number of missiles – debates on progress in the game with Yeltsin have been confusing at best. The abundant use of metaphors about jumping abysses in one or several leaps, of dentists extracting teeth at a slow or a fast pace, of amputating a leg bit by bit or of turning aquaria into fish soup and the like have hardly helped clarify the real issues at hand.[49]

The use of such metaphors must be seen against the background of the parallel understanding that there was no theory at hand which could explain how the systemic change should be implemented. By prescribing "shock therapy", it would be possible to rapidly undertake something that had never been done before.[50] It is thus not surprising that the criteria for evaluation have also tended to be rather odd.

When, for example, the Russian privatization programme is hailed as a success because it has been the "fastest in human history",[51] one is led to wonder what kind of economic theory has been used in order to derive that conclusion. Has anyone ever derived proof for the optimal speed of privatization? Simply stating that everything should be done as quickly as possible is sheer nonsense, since it hinges on how you define "possible".[52]

It is problems of this kind that explain why to date it has not even been possible to reach a reasonable consensus on whether the Russian economic reform programme has been a resounding success or one of the worst disasters in history. Against this background it is hardly surprising that there has also been a great deal of debate as to the merits of Western involvement in this process.

Has the West been an invaluable support in promoting irreversible reforms, as President Yeltsin has told IMF chairman Michel Camdessus on his frequent Moscow visits? Or has the Western involvement been a giant CIA–IMF conspiracy, aimed at achieving the final extermination of the Russian people, as some of the most chauvinist parts of the Russian press would have us believe?

The specific role of the IMF in supporting Russia's attempts at financial stabilization will be discussed further in the following chapter. Before proceeding to that discussion, it may, however, be worthwhile to direct some interest at the highly personal nature of the relations that have emerged between Western governments and international organizations on the one hand, and the leading Russian reformers on the other.

If asked, any respectable international organization – like the IMF or the USAID – would profess that they deal only with governments, not with individuals. If reality corresponds to this principle, two conclusions follow logically. First, changes on senior posts in the Russian government will in no way affect decisions or policy formulation in such organizations, and secondly, the Russian government will in turn have no reason to consider possible financial reprisals when making such appointments.

This is certainly as it should be, but has it also really been the case? Let us conclude this chapter by taking a closer look at the issue of Western attitudes and relations to some of the leading actors in the Russian reform process.

A question of moral hazard

Looking back at the way in which the Russian reform process has been portrayed in Western media, and in statements by Western leaders, we may find a striking pattern of not only compulsive optimism about the future but also of a consistent practice of heaping praise on a select number of "heroes" in the Moscow power game.

The highly frequent use of words like "brilliant" and "outstanding" may be understandable in writings by people who in one way or another have been personally involved in the process, but the fact that even more detached observers, or indeed representatives of international financial and aid organizations, have been prone to the same practice of devotion is a bit more puzzling.

The main question, of course, is if all of this really matters. Has the hero worship merely been a quaint ingredient in the new partnership between Russia and the West – a way of being nice to our new Russian friends – or is it perhaps a more sombre phenomenon, one which has had a negative impact on the Russian reform process?

The point of the following discussion is not to set the picture straight, whatever that might imply, by heaping compensatory sleaze on those Russians who have been designated as the heroes of the West. As Moscow infighting intensifies, the Russians will sort that out themselves, without any assistance from abroad being needed.

An issue that seems to be of far greater importance is that of potential moral hazard, perhaps even of major dimensions, in relations between Western leaders and their new Russian friends. Let us begin by looking at the case of Boris Yeltsin, the true Superman of Russian reform. Is he really a "democratic lightning rod for society"?[53]

Boris Nikolaevich Yeltsin

While Mikhail Gorbachev was still the number one hero, there was little restraint in Western portrayals of Yeltsin as a drunkard and a generally irresponsible figure, but once Gorbachev was gone all such criticisms were rapidly forgotten. Western leaders began heaping praise on Boris Yeltsin in a way that at times, notably so when the butchery in Chechnya was at its peak, took on an air of distinct immorality. There lies an obvious danger in this attitude.

To begin with, there can be little doubt that the personal leadership style of President Yeltsin has been moving steadily in the direction of traditional Russian autocracy. His own increasing preference for speaking about himself in the third person, of calling himself *"gosudar"* or even "tsar" are clear indications that this is a process that few in Moscow even bother to camouflage.

An important consequence is that – like the tsars of old – Tsar Boris must always remain aloof. He will never condescend to enter into the political fray, not even at times when the process of reform is under serious threat. Like a stern father he will intervene only to take his government to task. Ministers are reprimanded, scolded and replaced, at times even on live television and without prior warning. While the power of the tsar is always unaccountable, his boyars must never feel any security of tenure in their posts.

Diplomatic courtesy may certainly explain part of the striking readiness by most prominent Western leaders to accept this form of political retrogression as consistent with the proclaimed Russian ambition of building democracy and a pluralistic society. Yet, even diplomacy must have its boundaries, where excessive praise and an excessive readiness to turn a blind eye become a problem.

Assuming that Western actors are truthful when they say that promoting democracy in Russia is in the best interest of the West, we must seriously question if their refusals to utter even a hint of criticism against the Russian leadership actually represents a rational policy.

If, for example, we were to compare the readiness – not to say eagerness – of the West to criticize Russian economic policy, to the point even of making thinly veiled threats should a variety of recommendations not be followed, the utter silence with respect to the continuing degradation of power is all the more remarkable. It is hard to avoid concluding that by remaining silent the West has helped reinforce the Russian return to autocracy and unaccountable power.

If this had been a question solely of turning a blind eye to what the tsar himself is up to, it might still have been possible to write off as overdoing the courtesy bit. But it has definitely not been a question merely of placing Yeltsin's personal autocratic ways beyond reproach. Looking at the equally obvious trend of increasing corruption and even criminality at the very centre of power, we may find an identically hazardous pattern of looking for heroes in precisely those spots where some of the main culprits are to be found.

Viktor Stepanovich Chernomyrdin

Take the case of Viktor Chernomyrdin, the successful former manager of Russian gas giant Gazprom, who went on to become prime minister of Russia. When the IMF was about to give up on Russia in the spring of 1994, it was Chernomyrdin who took IMF chairman Michel Camdessus for a weekend of successful hunting and socializing. From that day on he would be the darling of the West, a man who represented stability and business-like professionalism. Did it matter then if his hands were not clean?

The case against Chernomyrdin is primarily related to his departure from Gazprom, and the subsequent "privatization" of his old empire. Since no legal case has been made, it is difficult to know the actual truth, but the allegations of misconduct are serious enough. In an article with the somewhat provocative title "Is Chernomyrdin a crook?", Peter Reddaway refers to three high level Russian sources.[54]

The first is the former finance minister Boris Fyodorov, who went on record in March 1995 with charges that senior Gazprom managers had received 1 to 5 per cent of the privatized company's stock. Assuming a market value of $120 billion that came to a handy sum. If and when, moreover, Russia finally achieves stability and Gazprom reserves are valued without heavy discount, the total value might come to $700 billion, making it the largest company in the world. According to Fyodorov, this privatization deal represented "the biggest robbery of the century, perhaps of human history".[55]

In a speech two months later, he followed up by alleging that Chernomyrdin personally had received one per cent of the stocks, making him one of the ten richest men in Russia. Vladimir Polevanov, a former deputy prime minister and head of the GKI, the state property commission, supported this charge. In a televised interview he said that dummies had been placed among the listed Gazprom stockholders and that government members had been allowed to profit from Gazprom. About a month later the assault was carried further by Yurii Skokov, a long time heavyweight insider, who described Chernomyrdin as "the chief mafioso of the country".

In addition to the privatization deal there have also been accusations of misuse of Gazprom funds, for instance to build a *dacha* for Chernomyrdin junior or to finance the prime minister's own political party, "Our Home is Russia". It should be noted that these and other stories do not emanate from people who are friendly to the prime minister, but it is also important to note, as Reddaway does, that none of them has been sued for libel. The question, then, is if it really matters much.

The danger of moral hazard derives from the ambition of Western leaders to present Chernomyrdin as a hero. It is a fact, for example, that when tax collection became a major problem, Gazprom was to be found in the major league of tax dodgers. Its sheer size meant that this had a noticeable direct effect on tax collection, and its political importance implied that it had important indirect effects on the same, by setting a bad example for others to follow.

For the IMF, poor tax collection would soon become a dominant issue in its relations with Moscow, and there would be no reluctance to direct harsh criticism against the fact that enterprises like Gazprom were not paying their taxes. Assuming, however, that Chernomyrdin was extending political protection to his old friends, thus negating all pressure from the outside, the IMF had placed itself in an impossible situation. Simultaneously holding Chernomyrdin up as a hero and questioning his honour in protecting crooks would be difficult. Thus Gazprom could continue generating ill-gotten gains for its protectors.

In addition, one might point at some possible negative fallout in Russian domestic politics. When it comes to the point where major opposition newspapers can argue, with a ring of truth to it, that senior Russian government members are nothing but tools for executing the will of the IMF, the Western involvement in Russian politics has been taken one very large step too far. We quoted one illustration of this in a previous chapter, and there is certainly more of the same to be found.

To the examples of Yeltsin and Chernomyrdin we may add a long list of other prominent Russians, who at one time or another have been the subjects of Western admiration and praise. A common denominator for most of these is that they have been part of that rather odd media phenomenon which is known as "young reform economists".

In this category, none has received more consistent praise, more invitations to chair and take part in international conferences, or – indeed – more funding, than Anatolyi Chubais. He would thus seem to offer an ideal illustration of the problem at hand.

Anatolyi Borisovich Chubais

Chubais received his first appointment as "reformer" in November 1991, when he was appointed to head the GKI. In June 1992 his political position was strengthened further by an appointment to deputy premiership. His main claim to fame relates to the privatization programme, but he is also credited with being a highly successful promoter at large of the process of bringing the market economy to Russia. Does it matter then if his hands are not clean?

Although a variety of rumours and allegations had been around for a long time, it would not be until the autumn of 1997 that the honour and integrity of Chubais began to be questioned openly and in earnest. In Western media it was again Reddaway who began asking some very pointed questions, urging the readers of *Washington Post* to "Beware the Russian reformer".[56]

His article reflected a growing wave of criticism in Russian media, where increasing antagonism among the country's financial elites had led to vicious mud slinging. Chubais at first had the upper hand, succeeding in early November to convince President Yeltsin that he must fire one of Chubais' main enemies, tycoon Boris Berezovskii, from the latter's post in the Russian security council. This, however, would prove to be a truly Pyrrhic victory.

Berezovskii's counter-offensive reached its peak a week later, when Aleksandr Minkin, an independent investigative journalist, revealed that Chubais and four other prominent economists had been given advance royalties of $90,000 each for a book on the history of Russian privatization, a book moreover that might not even be written.

The scandal concerned not only the size of the royalty, which was sensational in its own right, but also the fact that it was paid by the Segodnya publishing house, which was owned by Oneksimbank, which was one of the greatest winners in the privatizations that had been arranged by Chubais.

In response to this scandal, Yeltsin fired three of the authors *in spe* (a fourth had already been fired in a similar scandal) but left Chubais in place. The reason given was that firing Chubais might "destabilize the government and damage the economy". The real reason is captured in an angry article by Matt Taibbi, in the Moscow newspaper *The Exile*:

> Obviously, Chubais stayed in office because Russia was afraid of a negative Western reaction to his firing. And who's responsible for the West's reaction? The West. Who kept Anatoly Chubais in office? We did. We held Russians hostage by communicating to them, in a thousand different ways, that we'll disinvest from their country if they don't keep their corrupt, thieving minister at the highest echelons of power.[57]

In order to prove his point, Taibbi first called IMF spokeswoman Kathleen White in Moscow, and asked the relevant question: "If Anatoly Chubais is fired for non-policy reasons, will that affect the IMF's decision on whether or not to give out the next tranche of its $10 billion loan?" The obvious answer was that the IMF deals with policy, not with people. A similar question posed to Catherine Sylvester, a US embassy spokeswoman, received a similar answer with respect to USAID policy.

Having thus put two of the most relevant financial organizations on record, Taibbi could go on to conclude precisely that which was formulated as a question above, namely that there is a discrepancy between the standards that the IMF and USAID *should* adhere to, according to their own rules, and those that have been actually practised in quiet backroom dealings. Again there is obvious danger here.

In the wake of the book royalty scandal there were many other unsavoury stories that suddenly emerged, or re-emerged. In an attempt to exonerate himself, Chubais claimed that 95 per cent of the royalty would be given to a charity, the "Centre for the Defense of Private Property". This led not only to questions about the very existence of this organization, but also to the resurfacing of an old story that had been carried by *Izvestiya* in the previous summer.

In the latter case, Chubais had received, in early 1996, a $3 million interest free loan from Stolichnyi Bank, another great winner in the privatization process. The money was paid out to the very same "Centre for the Defense of Private Property", which invested it in treasury bills. The profit from this operation – $300,000 – was paid into Chubais' personal bank account. Stolichnyi would subsequently be allowed to take over Agroprombank at a knockdown price.

Two other illustrations will serve to show that Chubais had abused his position not only for personal gain but also to corrupt the domestic political process and to deceive the IMF about the Russian commitment to its contractual undertakings.

The first case originates in the spring of 1996, when all the "reformist" forces were mobilized to secure that Yeltsin was re-elected. Having been fired by Yeltsin in January, because of another financial scandal, which we shall return to in Chapter 7 below, in March Chubais was recalled to head the committee to re-elect. This was a mission that he would carry to a successful completion, but not without getting his hands dirty – again.

According to the law, campaign spending could not exceed $2.9 million, a figure that in all likelihood represents no more than a percentage of what would actually be spent. There was thus a great need for slush funds, and this, as all Americans are well aware, always carries its risks. In Moscow, the scandal burst on the night of 19 June, which was shortly *before* the election.

As had been the case in the US Watergate affair, the story began with a couple of subordinates who were caught in the act. This time it was not a burglary, but a Xerox box filled with half a million dollars in cash, which was carried out of the main government building by two men close to Chubais. The sequel, however, was not a simple cover-up.

Rather than hunker down and disavow his men, Chubais went on an immediate offensive, in the form of a highly successful media campaign. The arrest of the men who had been caught carrying the illicit funds was presented as a conspiracy by "dark forces" in the opposite political camp. The money had quite simply been planted on them.

The result was that the following day President Yeltsin could be per-suaded to fire General Aleksandr Korzhakov, who had been the head of his own security force, together with the head of the FSB, Mikhail Barsukov, and the head of the Interior Ministry.

In Western media, this *coup* was presented not as a triumph of the true crooks over some of their political adversaries, but as a welcome decision by the president to purge some remaining hard-liners from his administra-tion. The course of reform was thus seen to be strengthened. In the after-noon of 20 June, Chubais could tell a press conference that it had been "one of the traditional elements in traditional provocations of the KGB/Soviet type, of which we've had very great experience in our country".[58]

When the truth came out, it again bore some resemblance to Watergate. On 15 November, a Moscow newspaper, the *Moskovskii Komsomolets*, could publish a transcript of a secret tape recording, made two days after the press conference, where Chubais and a few others were discussing the affair. Here it transpired, among other things, that the president had been warned of the danger that 15–20 people a day could be caught carrying sports bags filled with money out of the campaign headquarters.

Chubais not only responded to this new information by flatly denying that the conversation had ever taken place. According to other reports, prompted by the new scandal, he had also rounded up sufficient support to warn the leading media out of pursuing the original story.

The importance of truly independent media was given further illustra-tion when the same investigative journalist who broke the book scandal, *Novaya Gazeta's* Aleksandr Minkin, reported another scandal involving Chubais. This time it was the IMF that was set up. Charged with improving Russian tax collection, the first deputy prime minister did not hesitate to use dirty tricks.

By rigging an auction of treasury bills, Chubais contrived to send a total of 45 trillion roubles of the state's money on a long journey through the financial system. Beginning in accounts of various local authorities, it found its way to special accounts set up for major industrial tax defaulters, from which it could be returned to the state – and be counted as tax revenue, thus pleasing the IMF.

Minkin provides the following rationale: "The reason for this massive movement of money was to convince the IMF inspectors that Chubais is getting Russia's revenue problems in hand, that tax collection is starting to pick up, and that he should be rewarded with more IMF money. As you may know, the government survives mainly on IMF money."[59]

Although none of the stories that have been retold here (and there are many more) were in any way news to the community of Russia watchers, it was the book scandal that finally made the cup run over. In *The New York Times*, a long-standing fan of Chubais, an explicit demand was made for his resignation:

Anatolyi Chubais is both the agent and enemy of Russian reform. Without Mr. Chubais' wily advice and determination to shed communist economics, Boris Yeltsin might not have brought Russia so far along the road to democracy and free markets. But Mr. Chubais, Mr. Yeltsin's top economic and political advisor, has also condoned unseemly dealings between the Kremlin and Russian businessmen. Even by the raw standards of Russian politics, he has now disgraced himself and ought to vacate his post as First Deputy Premier.[60]

But why?

The really interesting question is why it had taken so long for Chubais' Western supporters to wise up. Reddaway provides an answer that actually makes the thing look even worse:

The West for the most part ignored the charges that began in 1993; it tended to see privatization as a success. In early 1995, when Russia approached the IMF for a major loan, Western governments were receptive. Significantly, though, in granting a loan of $6.4 billion, the IMF insisted, as one of its main, although unpublicized conditions, that economic policy must be run in 1995 by Chubais.[61]

If this is true, it was thus not merely a question of turning a blind eye, but of actively intervening to force the Russians to retain in such an important position a man of such dubious morality. Was this really in the best interest of the West – or indeed of Russia? The only reasonable explanation must depart from good intentions, from an initial belief that supporting the "young reform economists" would actually be in the best interest of both Russia and the West.

While subsequent developments would provide ample and regrettable illustrations of the old saying about the road to hell being paved with good intentions, there is also some bureaucratic logic in the fact that the agencies which set out on this path would show great reluctance in recognizing and coming to terms with their mistakes.

There is plenty of evidence to support a view which says that Chubais was actually created by the West. The main mechanism was the links that were formed, early on, between Harvard University's Institute for International Development, often known simply as the "Harvard Project", and the group around Chubais, presented by Janine Wedel as the "St Petersburg Clan".

In a hard-hitting article about the way in which American aid flows to Russia came to be controlled by these two centres of power, Wedel notes that "between 1992 and May 1997, the Harvard Project received $43.4 million from USAID in noncompetitive grants". On the Russian side, the aid pipeline was hooked up to the "Russian Privatization Center", which was firmly controlled by the Petersburgers: "The centre received more than $41 million from USAID, millions of dollars more in grants from G-7 countries, and loans from both the World Bank ($59 million) and the European Bank for Reconstruction and Development ($43 million) to be repaid by the Russian government."[62]

When interviewed, responsible American officials will not deny that there was a policy of deliberate favouritism. Asked, for example, if the USAID had propelled Chubais to power, the agency's assistant administrator, Thomas Dine, stated bluntly "As an observer, I would say yes". And in a February 1997 interview, the rationale for supporting Chubais was laid out as follows, by Ambassador Richard Morningstar, the US Undersecretary of State who was co-ordinating assistance to the former Soviet Union:

> If we hadn't been there to provide funding to Chubais, could we have won the battle to carry out privatization? Probably not. When you're talking about a few hundred million dollars (the annual average of bilateral, non-military aid to Russia in recent years), you're not going to change the country, but you can provide targeted assistance to help Chubais.[63]

The way in which the programme to help Russia was set up presents an almost textbook-like case of moral hazard. From the very beginning, it was made clear that "The West wanted to see new faces and to hear 'new' ideas, but from its own ideological mold". Dine, again, spells out the rationale: "We will not waste US taxpayers dollars to provide . . . assistance where reformers do not, or cannot, flourish".[64]

To the Russian political leadership, in search of support for its new programme, this implied that it would have to come up with a set of young, market-oriented economists who were fluent in English and untainted by the old system. And so it did. These "young reform economists", moreover, would have to be given extensive undemocratic powers. Walter Coles, another USAID official, sums up the outcome: "If we needed a decree, Chubais didn't have to go through the bureaucracy."[65]

Thus the West promoted the creation of a Russian clique, which would successfully monopolize all incoming aid and block the efforts of other potential Russian reformers. Wedel points at the crucial impact on Russia's fledgling democracy:

> Did the strategy of focusing largely on one group further the aid community's stated goal of establishing the transparent, nonaligned institutions so critical to the development of democracy and a stable

economy for this world power in transition? . . . Ironically, far from helping to separate the political and economic spheres, US aid has instead reinforced their interdependency.[66]

And it was not only on the Russian side that this pattern prevailed. The way in which the "Harvard Project" was favoured did not stop at awarding noncompetitive grants. By virtue of their Russian contacts, the Harvard people were also placed in the unique situation of being at the same time a recipient of aid and a monitor of other aid recipients. This unfortunate outcome was pointed out in a GAO review, finding that the Harvard Project had "served in an oversight role for a substantial portion of the Russian assistance program" and that the project had "substantial control of the US assistance program".[67]

The moral hazard that is involved here may be given two concrete illustrations. In January 1996, when Chubais had been fired by Yeltsin for involvement in a variety of scandals, he was immediately taken on board by the Harvard Project, which provided a grant of $14,400 to tide him over. The signal to the Russian side, that Chubais will remain our man, could hardly have been made stronger.

Then, in late May 1997, it was discovered that two of the Americans who had been involved in the Harvard Project – Andrei Shleifer and Jonathan Hay – had succumbed to the temptation of "when in Rome, do like a Roman". Revelations of various abuses of aid money, including speculation on the Russian securities market and allowing the wife of Mr Hay to conduct private investment business from aid-sponsored facilities in Moscow, led to a decision by USAID to discontinue its links with the Harvard Project.

As a result, Harvard University lost $14 million in scheduled additional funding and Andrei Shleifer was fired from the project. The fact that a Harvard economics professor had allowed himself to be drawn into dealings of this kind produced a major scandal in American academic circles. But the real scandal, of course, was the way in which the whole programme had been set up – from the very beginning. If you go about asking for trouble, you are likely to get it!

With this we shall conclude the framework presentation and turn to look at the economics of the Russian economic reform programme, or, more properly, at that which would be paraded as economics.

Notes

1. Chaadaev's "Philosophical Letter" was published in 1836, in the Moscow journal *Telescope*. It provoked uproar and resulted in his being officially declared insane and placed under house arrest.

2. Billington, J.H. 1970. *The Icon and the Axe: An Interpretive History of Russian Culture*. New York: Vintage Books, p. ix.
3. Ibid., pp. ix–x.
4. Pipes, R. 1974. *Russia under the Old Regime*. New York: Charles Scribner, p. 5.
5. Keenan, E. 1986. Muscovite political folkways, *Russian Review*, **45**, 121.
6. Ibid., 122.
7. Billington, op. cit., p. x.
8. Ibid., p. 57.
9. On the broader context, see ibid., pp. 121–62.
10. Keenan, op. cit., p. 160.
11. Pipes 1974, op. cit., p. 240.
12. Billington, op. cit., p. 78.
13. Ibid., p. 84.
14. Keenan, op. cit., p. 119.
15. Kochan, L. and Abraham, R. 1990. *The Making of Modern Russia*. Harmondsworth: Penguin, p. 161.
16. Hollander, P. 1981. *Political Pilgrims – Travels of Western Intellectuals to the Soviet Union, China and Cuba 1928–78*. Oxford: Oxford University Press.
17. Quoted by Keegan, W. 1993. *The Specter of Capitalism: The Future of the World Economy after the Fall of Communism*. London: Vintage, p. 109.
18. Quoted by Goldman, M. 1996. *Lost Opportunity: What has made Economic Reform in Russia so Difficult?*. New York: Norton, p. 106.
19. The fundamental problem with this belief in "economic laws" is that it assumes out of existence the role of history and accumulated experience, which has been perhaps the most important of all factors determining the transformation of the former socialist economies of Eastern Europe. Jozef van Brabant rightly notes that "Unlike legal principles (with their normative laws) or objective findings (as in physics), an economic law can exist only through human activity". (van Brabant, J.M. 1998. *The Political Economy of Transition: Coming to Grips with History and Methodology*. London: Routledge, p. 27.) This observation comes close to the heart of the argument that will be pursued in subsequent chapters of this book.
20. Goldman, M. 1999. Can you get there from here: what must Russia do to become a normal market economy?, unpublished.
21. Goldman 1996, op. cit., p. 79.
22. IMF *et al.* 1990. *The Economy of the USSR*. Washington, DC: The World Bank, p. 1. In addition to the original report, the work also resulted in a three-volume compilation of background papers analyzing in great detail the various aspects of the problem at hand. (IMF *et al.* 1991. *A Study of the Soviet Economy* (vols. 1–3). Paris: OECD.)
23. IMF *et al.* 1990, op. cit., p. 19.
24. Ibid., p. 2.
25. Ibid., p. 20.
26. Ibid., p. 17.
27. Ibid.
28. Ibid., p. 26.
29. Ibid., pp. 26–7.
30. Ibid., p. 22.

31. Another prominent group that deserves mention in this context was formed within the International Institute for Applied Systems Analysis (IIASA) outside Vienna. The IIASA group was initiated in 1989 by the Russian economist Stanislav Shatalin, who was Gorbachev's advisor at the time. In March 1990, Merton Peck was named as its leader. In December 1990, a short policy memorandum was presented to Gorbachev. (See further Peck, M. and Richardson, T.J. (eds) 1991. *What is to be Done? Proposals for the Soviet Transition to the Market*. New Haven: Yale University Press.)

32. Goldman 1996, op. cit., pp. 80–84, summarizes the story around this group and provides references to some of its main publications.

33. Matlock, J.F. 1995. *Autopsy on an Empire*. New York: Random House, p. 523.

34. Ibid., p. 528.

35. Ibid., p. 537.

36. Goldman 1996, op. cit., p. 84.

37. *The Economist*, 14 December 1991, p. 16.

38. Sachs, J. 1994b. Life in the economic emergency room, in Williamson, J. (ed.), *The Political Economy of Policy Reform*. Washington, DC: Institute for International Economics, p. 517. (Red, white and blue are the colours of the Russian flag.)

39. Sachs, J. 1994a. Betrayal, *The New Republic*, 31 January, p. 15.

40. Layard, R. and Parker, J. 1996. *The Coming Russian Boom: A Guide to New Markets and Politics*. New York: The Free Press, p. 84.

41. Ibid., p. 87.

42. His warning about the "dangers of Western gullibility" was published in *Financial Times* on 28 March 1994 and in *The New York Times* on 1 April 1994. Michael Waller reports being told by Fyodorov, in an interview, that Chernomyrdin was one of the people he had in mind. (Waller, J.M. 1997. Author's rebuttal to the Department of State, *Demokratizatsiya*, 5(1), 120.)

43. Clark, B. 1995. *An Empire's New Clothes: The End of Russia's Liberal Dream*. London: Vintage, pp. 208–9.

44. Ibid., p. 209.

45. Ibid.

46. Layard and Parker, op. cit., p. 48.

47. Schelling, T. 1980. *The Strategy of Conflict*. Cambridge, Mass.: Harvard University Press, p. 22.

48. The speech is replicated in Layard and Parker, op. cit., p. 271.

49. In a scathing critique of this practice, Jozef van Brabant notes that "The euphemisms embraced . . . ranging from turning omelets into eggs and *bouillabaisse* or its variants back into fish, though perhaps amusing, have been neither appetizing nor very illuminating." (van Brabant, J.M. 1998. *The Political Economy of Transition: Coming to Grips with History and Methodology*. London: Routledge, p. 130.)

50. It may perhaps be worth pointing out that the original meaning of "shock therapy" refers to the use of electrical shocks for the treatment of psychiatric disorders, including depression. In psychiatry, it would be replaced by tranquillizers. In economics, the application of this term is bizarre in the extreme. (See further ibid., pp. 102–8.)

51. Much quoted statement by Richard Layard, in *Financial Times*, 6 October 1993.

52. The present author's irritation at the sloppy use of the notion of speed is shared by van Brabant: "The international organizations continue to advocate *ad nauseam* that speedy and comprehensive action pays off . . . But it is not mentioned that the recovery and growth attained in the early starters have not led to a marked improvement in average output and wealth prevailing before the transformation. Poland is an exception. But even in 1996 it only marginally exceeded 1978 output levels." (van Brabant, op. cit., p. 126.)

53. Lipton, D. and Sachs, J. 1992. *Prospects for Russia's economic reforms*, Brookings Papers on Economic Activity, No. 2, p. 255.

54. Reddaway, P. 1995. Is Chernomyrdin a crook?, *Post-Soviet Prospects*, **3**(8).

55. *Izvestiya*, 21 March 1995.

56. Reddaway, P. 1997a. Beware the Russian reformer, *Washington Post*, 24 August 1997.

57. *The Exile*, 20 November 1997.

58. Reddaway, P. 1997c. Questions about Russia's "Dream Team", *Post-Soviet Prospects*, **5**(5), p. 2.

59. Quoted by Fred Weir, on web-site *Johnson's Russia List*, 10 December 1997.

60. *The New York Times*, 19 November 1997.

61. Reddaway, 1997c, op. cit., p. 1.

62. Wedel, J.R. 1997. Cliques, clans and aid to Russia, *Transitions*, **4**(2), 66, 68–9. See also Wedel, J.R. 1998. *Collision and Collusion: The Strange Case of Western Aid to Eastern Europe 1989–98*. New York: St Martin's. The latter text regrettably came to the present author's attention only as these pages were going to the printer.

63. Wedel 1997, op. cit., p. 70.

64. Ibid., p. 66.

65. Ibid., p. 68.

66. Ibid., pp. 67, 71.

67. Ibid., p. 69.

III

The reform programme

CHAPTER FIVE

Financial destabilization

The opening signal for shock therapy to commence was given on 2 January 1992, with the announcement of a sweeping liberalization of the previously state controlled prices. As such, there was certainly nothing wrong with this move. Freedom for the market to determine prices was one of the very necessary conditions for a functioning Russian market economy to be established. The problem was that a number of supporting measures would also have needed to be implemented, above all so in the political sphere. And that, as we shall see below, was where the programme went seriously wrong.

In the following chapters much will be said about the role of credibility. Given this focus, there is one feature in the early stage of shock therapy which may be worth emphasizing at this point. In their strongly monetarist rhetoric, the Russian reformers kept repeating the crucial importance of achieving rapid stabilization of the economy. Against this background it is rather striking that one of their main initial shortcomings would be registered in precisely this dimension. By failing to contain the initial pulse of inflationary pressure that was released by price liberalization, the Russian government was simply bound to run into serious credibility problems.

In his 28 October address, President Yeltsin had promised that by the autumn of 1992 "there will be economic stabilization and a gradual improvement in people's lives".[1] That was not to be. Instead, a process of very high and variable inflation led to a rapid erosion of real incomes and to a destruction of the pre-conditions for normal business activities. Thus, the legitimacy of the reform programme as a whole was seriously undermined.

But how, then, may we explain the initial failures of stabilization? Was it merely a question of bad luck, of unexpectedly tough political opposition, or perhaps indeed even of a "betrayal" by the West, as some of the leading Western advisors would argue? Closer inspection will show that it was none of the above.

144

In this and in the following two chapters we shall map out a course of events which in the main may be explained only by factors that were endogenous to the political process at the top, i.e. consequences of the way in which the Russian president was to set and enforce his priorities. Let us begin by looking at the political context in which the decision to implement shock therapy was taken.

A shocking decision

The events that unfolded in the time between the failed August 1991 *coup* and the actual launching of Russia's economic reform programme, in January 1992, are crucial in the sense that they would be so obviously formative for subsequent developments. This was the "window of opportunity", when the course for future policy could have been charted in a variety of directions. The frequently heard argument, that what was done was the only thing that *could* be done, is valid only in the normative sense of accepting that all alternatives were inferior.

From an analytical point of view, the period at hand is of interest mainly because it serves to reveal some of the core preferences of the new political leadership that was now being formed to rule over the future of Russia. And the pattern of behaviour that emerged was clearly marked by a triumph of politics over economics. From the very outset, the leading actors that took part in shaping the structure of the economic reform programme, and in building support for it to be launched, revealed preferences that had little indeed to do with economics.[2]

It is easy, for example, to agree with the following statement by Lynn Nelson and Irina Kuzes: "Whereas analysts often justify Yeltsin's consolidation of power as the reforms continued by arguing that presidential power was serving economic reform, we find strong evidence that the reality was quite different – that the kind of economic reform approach that was initiated under Yeltsin placed economics in the service of his political agenda."[3]

The pivotal point in this argument concerns constituency building. In a normal, democratic political setting, this is one of the most important functions of politics. Russia in the autumn of 1991 was certainly neither normal nor democratic, and it would be easy to say that no matter how hard it had tried, no constituency of sufficient size could have been found to support the radical reforms that were then envisioned. Yet, this is perhaps too easy a way out, one that smacks a bit more of apologetics than of serious analysis.

In a scathing critique of the way in which the Russian reformers went about their business, Nelson and Kuzes make an important point with respect to the formulation of policy: "It is no justification for shock therapy advocates, however, that their theory did not mesh well with constraints that prevailed in Russia. A key to effective policy is to anticipate such impediments, rather than to use them as excuses in the aftermath of policy misjudgments."[4]

The case for the defence at this point would be something along the lines of what Yegor Gaidar had to say in an August 1992 article: "When it is pointed out what Russia was lacking at the end of last year that was needed to create an effective market economy, I want to, not disagree, but add to the list. . . . But there was no – absolutely no – time to sit around and wait while all of these preconditions were created. The choice was very clear."[5]

In support of their own critique of the shock therapists, Nelson and Kuzes quote similar arguments from Pereira, Maravall and Przeworski, whose discussion on the post-communist transition underlines a rather obvious point, namely that if economic reforms are to proceed under democratic conditions, there must be sustained political support:

> They continue, "A sound economic strategy is a strategy that addresses itself explicitly to the issue of whether reforms will be supported as the costs set in," rather than trying to excuse the loss of support for reforms as an effect of irresponsible populism. This "typical argument of economists," they maintain, "is just bad economics".[6]

While *ex post* rationalizations are certainly not specific to the Russian reform process, there is one important point here that should be brought out. At first impression, the issue would seem to concern whether or not there was sufficient time to engage in constituency building. Since we cannot go back and try again, that question will never have an answer. And, to repeat what has been said above, perhaps it does not matter much any more.

The real crux of the matter concerns whether constituency building was even *attempted*. And that is something altogether different, because it says something important about the overriding political priorities of the country's government. Let us return to see how the men who gathered around Boris Yeltsin came to be imbued with their crusading mentality.

As we may recall from our previous account, in the aftermath of the failed August *coup*, at the time when his authority was at its peak, Boris Yeltsin chose to leave Moscow for a crucial couple of weeks. Leaving the reasons for this little excursion aside, we may also recall that upon his return he displayed great energy. But in which direction? This is where we may find much of the key to understanding the subsequent developments.

First steps

On 10 October 1991, Boris Yeltsin was a president in search of an economic reform programme. On the table he had the remnants of the "Window of

Opportunity" programme, which had been worked out within the Harvard group, and the odds were that this would indeed form the platform of the government's new policy. The latter interpretation was supported by the fact that one of the members of the four-man commission that had been appointed to manage the post-*coup* transition was Grigorii Yavlinskii, one of the main architects of the Harvard project. His transitional mandate was to propose a new comprehensive economic reform programme.

To most of those involved, including Graham Allison, it seemed logical that Yeltsin would draw on all the work that had already been done.[7] But that was not to be. According to Yavlinskii, the president did ask him if he was ready to do the job, but the terms could not be agreed. Again according to Yavlinskii, the reason was that Yeltsin and his closest circle had set such political priorities that successful economic reform would not be possible: "It was necessary to choose – either these political goals, or economics. Then there was a discovery. Another person [Gaidar] came, and said, 'I'll do it'."[8]

The interesting dimension of this decision making process is concerned not so much with the background of Yegor Gaidar, or with the potential merits of Yavlinskii's competing programme. The main importance lies in the very speed of events. From 10 October until 28 October, the president of the Russian Federation had a mere 18 days in which to decide on how one of the most important reforms in Russian history should be implemented.

The rise of Gaidar to prominence was made possible by Gennadii Burbulis, one of Yeltsin's closest aides at the time. Having met Gaidar during the August days, he had become impressed by the concept of "Russia first" and arranged for him to be secluded at an official government dacha in the Moscow suburb of Arkhangelskoe. There Anatolyi Chubais and a few others joined him.[9]

It would take this small group of very young economists no more than a couple of weeks in which to work out how to implement something that had never been done before. And it would take the president no more than a couple of days in which to decide that theirs was indeed the best proposal. When Yeltsin delivered his big speech on 28 October, it incorporated much of what the Gaidar team had proposed.

Yet, there was even more still to be decided. At a meeting on 4 November, Burbulis proposed that Yeltsin should create a special group within the government, which would be charged with working out a programme for the first steps that needed to be taken. The group was to be headed by Gaidar, a choice that at first did not find the president's favour: "Who is this? What are you proposing? What are you suggesting? Yeltsin was seriously annoyed, and threw the proposal across the table."[10] Two days later, however, Gaidar had been appointed deputy prime minister and finance minister. And that was that.

Having seen this process unfold, one is inclined to join Marshall Goldman in wondering "just how deep [Yeltsin's] understanding of or commitment to the market was". There is also a striking parallel to the crucial negotiations in the late summer of 1990, when the fate of the Shatalin "500-day program" was being decided:

> During the intense meetings . . . Yeltsin was off in Siberia meeting his constituents. Upon his return to Moscow he immediately moved to push the Shatalin plan forward, if need be in Russia alone. However, some of the participants in the discussions suspected that Yeltsin had not even bothered to read much of the program.[11]

To Yeltsin it was all really just a question of power, personal power. In 1990 he was ready to use the Shatalin plan as a battering ram against Gorbachev, and in 1991 he was equally ready to use Gaidar's plan to finish off the job. The crucial distinction between Yavlinskii and Gaidar was concerned not with economics, but with the fact that while Yavlinskii worked on the premiss that some form of union structures would be preserved, Gaidar offered "Russia first".

Parallel agendas

With his decision to back Gaidar, Yeltsin clearly demonstrated that there were two parallel agendas being pursued, one that was designed to further his own personal power and another that focused on the economic aspects of reform. This interpretation has two important implications, which would be brought out by subsequent events. One concerns the president's personal ranking of the two agendas, and the other their respective audiences. Let us begin by looking at the political agenda.

The choice of "Russia first" certainly had serious merit in its own. Given all the centrifugal forces that had been unleashed by the Soviet break-up, the prospects for a weakened centre in Moscow to enforce its will across the territory of the old union as a whole must have looked bleak indeed. And uniformly enforcing a programme of sweeping reforms in Russia, Central Asia and the Caucasus probably would have been a hopeless undertaking from the very start.

The point here, therefore, is not to question the choice as such, but to examine the implications for the personal power of President Boris Yeltsin and for his personal relations with major Western leaders. What might have been rational from the economic policy point of view would also have important consequences for the relations between the "new Russia" and the West. And, as we may recall from above, the latter would not be uniquely positive.

To Boris Yeltsin, "Russia first" implied a clean break not only with the communist past but also with the other former Soviet republics. Although there would be some showboating on the side within the new "Commonwealth of Independent States", Yeltsin made it very clear that Russia was now the self-appointed leader, for others to follow, and that in Russia he was the boss, for others to obey.

The president's striving for personal power was clearly reflected at the October session of the Russian Congress of People's Deputies, where the announcement of the reform programme was made. Here Yeltsin succeeded not only in having himself appointed to the parallel post of prime minister, but also in securing a right to rule the country by decree for a year.

Speed appears to have been of paramount importance. Where the "Grand Bargain" had envisioned a drawn-out transformation that would have lasted until 1997, Gaidar was ordered – and accepted – to have the whole thing finished in six months. Yavlinskii is far from alone in maintaining that from the point of view of economics, this was an impossibility.

It is here that the ranking of the two agendas is brought out. If the president had been genuinely concerned about the fate of his economic reforms, a logical first move would have been to provide an unambiguous political backing for the reformers. Instead, however, he was to pursue the classic policy of *divide et impera*. In order to balance the reformers, he decided to retain several of the pre-*coup* ministers, notably so hard-liners Yurii Skokov, Oleg Lobov and Mikhail Malei.

It may be argued that he was forced to make that choice, that going further in support of Gaidar and his team might have jeopardized the project as a whole, but given the political context at the time, that argument carries little weight. There are few cases in history where a political leader has been able to enjoy such undisputed political authority as did Yeltsin in the aftermath of the failed August *coup*. His decisions must thus be accepted as conditioned by preference rather than political necessity.

The president had made his choice. Rather than engage in constituency building, in support of the economic reform programme, his domestic political agenda would be geared into securing autocracy, and his tactics would be based on seeking confrontation, thus achieving the elimination of potential rivals for power.

In retrospect we may conclude that from the president's personal point of view, this agenda has met with resounding success. The near decade that passed between the public humiliation of Boris Yeltsin at the hands of the communist party, in the autumn of 1987, and his presidential re-election victory over communist party leader Gennadii Zyuganov, in the summer of 1996, represents a truly remarkable political come-back.

To the country, however, it has not been without cost. An obvious implication of the president's priority for the political agenda was that he would abandon the "young reform economists" to fight their own battles.

During the crucial first months of shock therapy, Gaidar was elevated merely to the status of deputy prime minister, and when he was eventually promoted, in June 1992, it was only to the rank of acting prime minister.

Looking back, it is apparent that throughout the course of reform the president has consistently arranged matters so that the advocates of reform would find themselves in an unclear and, to some extent, undefined state. Logically, the credibility of their economic policies would be undermined to a corresponding extent.

At first, however, the reformers – and their foreign advisors – could sense nothing but optimism. They believed themselves to be at war with the old system, a war, moreover, in which they thought that they had the explicit support of the president. Thus began a peculiar "kamikaze" process, the details of which will be discussed further below. For the moment we shall rest content with noting that the main result of the president's choice was that of placing the economic reformers in a position of isolation and conflict. Thus they also came to be possessed of a distinct feeling of "us against them".

If we accept that this outcome was indeed the result of a deliberate choice by the president, made from day one, we must also refute the commonly held belief that being faced with growing resistance from various "dark forces" Yeltsin – like Gorbachev before him – was gradually *forced* to give up his original friends and his original politics. The events that were played out in the weeks following the August *coup* offer little support for the latter interpretation.

If we consider his extremely skilful gradual dismantling of the communist party, and his final ruthless treatment of the defeated Gorbachev, there really cannot be much doubt that in September 1991 Boris Yeltsin was the undisputed leader, the winner who could dictate his conditions and set the agenda for the future. And so he did – with well known results.

Logically, we must then also accept that he could have pushed through all that which he would later claim that the Supreme Soviet was blocking. He could have called for free and universal elections to a democratic parliament, and he could have called a constituent assembly to give Russia a democratic constitution. But he chose not to do any of this.

Rather than announce new elections or summon a constituent assembly, he had himself vested with power to rule the country by decree, and then proceeded to pursue a strategy of confrontation *vis-à-vis* the Supreme Soviet. The difference between the two options is not insignificant.

One of the most important conclusions that must be drawn from these events is that being anti-communist is not necessarily the same as being pro-democracy and pro-market economy. Boris Yeltsin's struggle against the communist party is considerably easier to explain if it is considered from a perspective of personal antipathies, than if it is seen as the result of a persuasion that Russia's economic and political system ought to be built on classical liberal values.

We will find further support for this interpretation below, when we consider the bloody battle for the Russian parliament building, the White House, that took place at the beginning of October 1993.

Accepting that Yeltsin placed his highest priority on the power agenda, we should not forget that he did have an economic reform agenda as well. The space, however, that was left for the latter would be constrained indeed. Since the president was bent on pursuing confrontation in his relations to the country's legislature, there was only one direction left in which the reformers could turn for support. And that is where the West enters the picture.

From our previous discussion of the problems of moral hazard, we may recall that an ideologically triumphant West made it clear from the beginning what type of policies and policy-makers it would be ready to support. Reading these signals correctly, Yeltsin surrounded himself with people who would go down well in Washington: young economists who were fluent in English and well versed in the jargon of financial markets and high politics.

Needless to say, this choice could only serve to further aggravate his confrontation with the legislature. People in the democratic camp, who had supported Yeltsin in the past and might have entertained visions of being invited to join in the process of designing the country's political future, were now being ignored. Perhaps this outcome was not entirely disagreeable to the president, who could present himself – successfully – as the lone champion of reform.

Recalling our previous classification of attitudes into four different "camps", we may see how tenuous the coalition was that was forged to support the economic reform programme. On one side, there was a small group of Russian neo-liberal economists, with little correspondence between either current Russian democrats or traditional Russian Westernizers. On the other, an equally small group of enthusiastic Western economic advisors could be found who at first would also work in isolation. As a constituency to support radical reform, this coalition was weak indeed.

On the Russian side, it would only be a matter of weeks, if not days, before it started cracking up, as the government was forced into making concessions, and on the Western side, it would not be until after the December 1993 election, which brought communists and nationalists to the fore, that genuine concern over the future of Russia would be translated into serious economic support.

The conclusion of this argument is that at the time when a "window of opportunity" for radical reforms to be undertaken might indeed still have been open, the president and his reformers blankly refused to seek domestic support, to the point even of deliberately keeping their economic programme a secret.

It is a rather strange and revealing fact, for example, that the very first document which was produced by the Russian government, in order to set out its economic priorities, was presented only in February 1992. And then it was addressed not to the country's citizens or lawmakers but to the IMF. As Nelson and Kuzes conclude, "the Gaidar team was working to generate international support for the Russian government's economic policy, rather than to build political constituencies at home."[12]

One of the main effects of the "kamikaze" choice was that for the first crucial months of reforms, the economic dimension of the reform process was consciously withheld from the realm of serious debate. In October, Yavlinskii would give vent to his frustration: "There were guesses concerning the inappropriateness of the [government's] proposed economic path . . . but the government did not announce [the main features of its] program until July. How could one judge what they were going to do?"[13]

Placing themselves in a situation of war with the economy, and with the legislature, it is rather logical that the Russian reformers would come to show little interest indeed in listening to complaints from "the enemy". And here their foreign advisors supported them. The distinctive lack of empathy that marked the first phase of shock therapy was illustrated in an early interview given by Jeffrey Sachs to *Financial Times*: "Professor Sachs dismissed the tide of complaints against the vastly increased prices and taxes levied on enterprise as 'yak, yak, yak'."[14]

Another implication of the government's decision to opt for confrontation was that all those who felt that they had a grievance, and there were bound to be many, would have to take their complaints elsewhere. And this is where the Supreme Soviet enters the picture. Being forced to stand idly by as the government engaged in destroying all remnants of the old system, it soon came to regret the extensive powers it had granted the president. As a result, it would become a willing subject of intense lobbying by the country's "red directors".

When Yeltsin embarked on his reform programme, he began by asking for trouble. And he would be richly rewarded. Before we proceed to look at the details of the various policy struggles, it might, however, be a good idea to take a closer look at the magnitude of the macroeconomic imbalances that Russia inherited from the Soviet Union. This is important for the very simple reason that subsequent attempts at economic stabilization would serve to define one of the main political battlefields.

The scope of the problem

For reasons that will soon be explained, during the course of 1991 the monetary authorities in Moscow succeeded in creating no less than 137.3 billion roubles, which may be compared to an accumulated total of 133.8 billion roubles created between 1961 and 1990.[15] During a single year, they thus managed to print more money than in the preceding three decades put together.[16]

Under normal circumstances, this would have led to massive inflation, but since Soviet prices were still under state control, they could not move in response to monetary expansion. Instead, a severe inflationary pressure was created. The notion of an "inflationary overhang" conjures up the image of a large overhanging crest of snow, ready at any time to start an avalanche. And so it was. There was a mountain of liquid roubles waiting for the state-controlled prices to be set free.[17]

One of the reasons for this development is linked to the growth in wages during the last year of the Soviet state. The workers demanded higher wages and the general dissolution of Soviet state institutions eroded effective control over such demands. Nor did enterprises find any reason to resist. To them, wages were no cost. If wages were increased, they would automatically receive more cash roubles from above. All demands for higher wages could thus be met by resorting to the printing presses, apparently without cost to anyone.

Another, and considerably more important reason behind the reckless monetary policy was linked to the increasingly bitter struggle that took place between Soviet president Mikhail Gorbachev and Russian president Boris Yeltsin. During the autumn of 1990, Yeltsin had begun offering significant favours to all that were prepared to join his camp: lower taxes, higher wages and pensions, and higher subsidies. As it was not possible to finance this open-handed policy within the budget of the Russian Federation, more money had to be created. And this is where the real root of the problem may be found.

Under the old Soviet system the state bank, Gosbank, was subdivided into a number of branches for the different republics. As part of the "war of laws", which would lead to the dissolution of the Soviet Union, Yeltsin moved to take control over the Russian Federation branch, which would subsequently be transformed into the Central Bank of Russia. It was this step that made it possible to finance the political campaign whose purpose was to put Russia before the Soviet Union (that is to say, Yeltsin before Gorbachev). In 1991, the Russian Federation ran a budget deficit that was equivalent to 31.9 per cent of its GDP.[18]

According to the Russian economist Andrei Illarionov, this fiscal war was a seriously contributing factor to the dissolution of the Soviet Union:

> The populist macroeconomic policy of the Russian government dealt a fatal blow to the financial and monetary system of the USSR, and thence to its political structures. From an economic perspective, the USSR was finished not in December 1991, when the Belovezh accords were signed, and M. Gorbachev was forced to resign, nor in September, when the Union parliament was dissolved, but in April 1991, when the weapon of financial destabilization was trained upon the Union authorities.[19]

Currency reform and incomes policy?

When the reformers set out to create a market economy, dealing with the rouble overhang really *ought* to have been the first order of the day. By implementing a currency reform, and by introducing some form of credibility enhancing anchor for subsequent stabilization policy, the necessary pre-conditions could have been met for a successful liberalization of prices.

Politically it could perhaps have been difficult, above all so since it would have been thus made clear to the Russian people that a large part of their (fictitious) wealth was being confiscated. But against the background of how the other components of economic policy were formulated, it is difficult to believe that the reformers were prepared to make such considerations.

From an economic point of view, there are many good arguments that *ought* to have spoken for a currency reform. To begin with, such a choice would have made it possible to introduce a post-Soviet stabilization policy without the burden of a gross imbalance between the real and monetary sectors of the economy. It would still have been necessary to address all those problems that are related to credibility and expectations, but it remains striking that the reformers failed to clear away the Soviet rouble overhang.

Perhaps even more important is the fact that a currency reform would have allowed for a more equitable distribution profile, in the form of graduated rights to change old money for new. Savings up to a certain level could, for example, have been converted at a ratio of 1:10, then, up to the next level, at 1:100, and so on. Simply put, a currency reform would have been a sensible political investment.

There were good previous examples of what could have been done (viz. Germany in 1923 or Israel in 1985), and the possibility of doing so even in a post-Soviet environment was demonstrated in 1992, when Estonia – despite many warnings about the likely consequences – introduced its currency reform. During a transition period of merely three days, from 20 June to 22 June, the Estonian Kroon was substituted for the Soviet/Russian rouble, which ceased to be legal tender. The reform was well planned, including strict monitoring of all major bank transfers in order to prevent a massive inflow of roubles to Estonian bank accounts. Limits on the right to change were set at a maximum of 1,500 roubles, to be exchanged between 26 June and 30 June, at the rate of 1 kroon per 10 roubles. Between 26 June and 30 June, larger amounts could be converted at the rate of 1 kroon to 50 roubles.[20]

A currency reform, however, was not the only missing element in the Russian reform strategy. If we recall from above the study of the Soviet economy that was commissioned by the G7 at its 1990 economic summit meeting in Houston, the *leitmotif* of the subsequently presented findings was that a successful transition from the old system required a comprehensive approach: "Clearly, a lasting solution to the problem requires the implementation of fiscal, monetary and incomes policies capable of checking the current income streams fueling the overhang."[21]

The question of incomes policy is of particular importance here, for the simple reason that an exaggerated belief in one-shot inflation as a means of reducing the inflationary overhang may create considerable additional problems. The report is very clear on this point: "In summary, relying on price increases to eliminate the overhang may involve a lengthy and potentially disruptive adjustment process. Other, non-inflationary, ways to deal with the problem should also be considered."[22]

By now, that conclusion has become textbook knowledge. In her book on *The Economics of Transition*, for example, Marie Lavigne states that "Stabilization policy implies a package of measures, which are linked with the beginning of a structural reform". She presents a five point package and provides illustrations of the different approaches to incomes policy that were chosen by Poland, Hungary and the Czech republic.[23]

Why none of this was done in the Russian case is not entirely clear. In another textbook on the economic transition from socialism, Daniel Gros and Alfred Steinherr point out that monetary reform could have been a solution, but then conclude that "this path was not used for political reasons".[24] The "political" reasons in question were linked to a Russian desire of maintaining control, by way of the rouble, over the other former Soviet republics.

Another possibility is that Moscow quite simply bowed to heavy international pressure in favour of maintaining the rouble zone. Perhaps Gaidar and others are correct when they claim that the economic situation at the time was indeed so desperate that there really was no time for sophistication. The latter view is supported by Illarionov:

> The enormous budget deficit, the absence of currency reserves, the bankruptcy of the foreign trade bank, the collapse of administrative trade, the real threat of hunger in the major cities were only a few characteristics of the economic situation in which the Gaidar government found itself. Under those circumstances, abstaining from immediate and complete price liberalization would have threatened the country with unpredictable consequences.[25]

Whatever the reasons, however, it is important to recognize that the Russian choice was extreme, not only in comparison with all previous historical experience but also with regard to other transition economies, notably so those in Central Europe. The Russian approach was one of "cold turkey". Prices were liberalized without any supporting policies and the reformers retreated into their "kamikaze" attitude of non-communication with the nascent market economy.

Table 5.1 Russian inflation rates, 1992–7*

	1992	1993	1994	1995	1996	1997
Annual Average	1,526.5	874.3	307.2	197.5	47.7	14.7
End of Year	2,508.8	840.1	204.7	131.3	21.8	11.0

* The difference between the two rows in the table is purely technical. One measures the change between two years in annual average inflation rates, the other the change in prices from the end of one year to the end of the next. When the monthly inflation rate is constant, the two will coincide.
Source: EBRD 1998. *Transition Report Update*, London: EBRD, p. 63.

Inflation and seigniorage

The results of this policy choice would not be long in coming. As may be seen from Table 5.1, a process of high and protracted inflation was triggered, which at times would even border on hyperinflation.

The immediate losers were those who had some money saved in the bank; inflation rapidly eroded the value of those savings. Then followed all those who lived on fixed wages or state transfers, such as pensions. As inflation surged ahead, they were forced to see the real value of their incomes dropping.

A more important category of losers was future generations, as the real sector of the economy adjusted its behaviour and expectations. High inflation led to a drastic shortening of the time horizon, serving to destroy long-term contracting, and to a serious erosion of government credibility, eroding the basis for further reforms.[26] The loss, over five years, of three-quarters of the previous investment volume is but one indication of the real costs of this process. What this in turn will imply for the long term development of the Russian economy will depend on technology and human capital development, both being sectors where the prospects appear gloomy indeed.

Turning now to the winners, i.e. to those who succeeded in reaping the gains from high inflation, one actor looms larger than any other, and that is the Russian government, as represented by the Central Bank. We are dealing here with a very special form of revenue, known as seigniorage, which is made up of two components. One is the issuing of coins and banknotes, which represent an interest free loan made by the holders to the issuer, and the other is reserves held by commercial banks in zero interest accounts in the Central Bank. Together, these two components make up what is known as the monetary base. During the first two to three years of high inflation, government revenues from this source were substantial indeed.

In 1992, cash in circulation increased from 184 billion roubles to 1,716 billion roubles. The increase was equal to about 8.5 per cent of GDP, or close to total direct tax revenue. Add to this an increase in commercial bank reserves of 2,100 billion roubles, corresponding to 13 per cent of GDP, and we get a total seigniorage revenue of 21.5 per cent of GDP, which was larger than the sum total of all direct and indirect tax revenue. In 1993, the cash component of seigniorage remained about the same, at 7.6 per cent of GDP, but the total fell by almost half, to 12 per cent of GDP, as commercial banks reduced their reserves in the Central Bank.[27]

Noting that seigniorage remained substantial even in 1993, we may conclude that inflation was good business indeed for the Russian government. In order to show just how good, Gros and Steinherr compare to Brazil in 1991, when prices increased sevenfold, which was close to the Russian situation in 1992. During that time, however, cash increased by merely 1.6 per cent of GDP and the total monetary base (i.e. total seigniorage revenue) by 3.7 per cent of GDP.[28]

The position of the commercial banks was also one of net gain, although not on a scale remotely comparable to the government. In 1992, they received cheap credits (at negative real interest) from the Central Bank corresponding to 15.5 per cent of GDP, which was 2.5 percentage points more than their own zero interest reserves in the Central Bank.[29]

With both the government and the commercial banks thus being on the winning side, and with enterprises still being largely barred from using cash roubles,[30] there remained only two categories of losers, namely wage earners and savers. During 1992, the former paid an inflation tax of about 10–15 per cent, and people having accounts in Sberbank, the state savings bank, were expropriated to the tune of 6.6 per cent of GDP.[31]

Perhaps it would not be too far off the mark to suspect that the chief recipient of these gains, i.e. the government, was possessed of a certain reluctance to engage in serious inflation fighting.

To those who succeeded in building fortunes by speculation in the currency market, we may also add those who were in positions to engage in rent seeking, exploiting a wide range of opportunities created by incomplete price liberalization (primarily in the energy sector). The combined result of these processes was the creation of a powerful coalition of entrepreneurial and bureaucratic elites. This is where real power in Russia would be vested.

Three games

In the following we shall investigate how the new rules that were set by President Yeltsin created a situation where the reforming part of the Russian government was engaged in playing highly illustrative games of confrontation with two of the most important actors in the domestic reform process, namely the enterprise sector and the Central Bank, and how the very same reformers succeeded in enticing the IMF into providing collusive foreign support for its domestic battles.

Let us begin with the group of enterprise managers, whose task it would be to restructure the economy and bring it onto a trajectory of rapid high-tech growth. What was the response of the old "red directors" to the change in the rules of the game that was signalled by price liberalization?

Government vs. enterprises

Going beyond the simple rhetoric of proposing liberalization, stabilization and privatization, recommendations that are sweeping to the point of being both empty and uncontroversial, the real challenge that was implied by "shock therapy" was that a new, uncompromising market regime should be imposed on the old state enterprises.

Speaking with János Kornai, the notorious "soft budget constraint" was now to be replaced by hard and effective financial constraints on enterprise decision making. Thus the old practice of bargaining and *blat*, so conducive to the growth of such political dependencies that produce hierarchies, would be replaced by marketing, cost efficiency and horizontal relations typical of the market economy. Simply put, commands were to be replaced by contracts.

The means by which this transition from plan to market was to be achieved was to cut all direct links between the state budget and state industry (not yet privatized). Deprived of state orders, and of the implicit state guarantee that all losses would be covered by subsidies, enterprise managers would be placed in a situation of "sink or swim", and for those who proved unable to swim there would be no pardon.

Given the high degree of militarization of the old Soviet economy, there was an obvious first target for the assault. Gaidar recalls how he was engaged in conversation with an old-time bureaucrat about the possibility of undertaking drastic budget cuts:

> He told me it was absolutely impossible. I said that it was possible, and that the problem was not one of economic possibility but of political will. He said: "That's fine; try to cut military procurement by 30%." I decided not to cut it by 30% but by 70%. I knew that it was a unique moment in history when such an act would be possible.[32]

The representatives of the old system were still in such a state of shock, following the destruction of the Soviet system, that constituencies which would otherwise have been formed to resist all serious attempts at cutting the budget could now be almost entirely left out of the picture. But this was certainly not a situation that could be expected to last – thus the great haste.

The decision by the reformers to work in isolation, and to refuse all attempts at communication, was a deliberate move, no doubt designed to prolong the state of shock. In an interview with *The Economist*, in the spring of 1992, Gaidar clarified his own attitude: "Generally we say: it's your business. That creates a barrier which is very difficult to get over. The structure that linked enterprises and government has been destroyed."[33]

This was the logic that may help explain the "kamikaze" posture of the reformers. For shock therapy to succeed, it was quite simply necessary for the government to make itself unavailable to demands for continued soft credits and for soft rules in general. At least, so it was seen from the side of the government. But how did it look from the other side of the playing table?

Even if industrial leaders had been skilled market analysts, which most can be safely assumed not to have been, it would not have been possible for them to ascertain what the real objectives of government policy were. Yavlinskii was certainly not alone in complaining about this. Nothing was said about crucial macroeconomic variables that could have been used as anchors, such as the exchange rate or the interest rate. Nor was there a clearly formulated incomes policy.

If the Russian government did have any anchor at all for its new reform policies, it would be this: that the essence of shock therapy was its uncompromising nature. Under no conditions would there be negotiations about further soft credits or indeed bailouts of inefficient firms. Since government credibility was linked to the shock as such, it was not possible for actors in the nascent market to measure the progress of the reforms. Thus, it was hardly likely that there would be any credibility at all.

As Barry Ickes and Randi Ryterman pointed out, already in the autumn of 1992, the decision by enterprise managers to cease paying their bills was a rational one:

> To a large extent, the growth in arrears reflects the contradictions in the reform process. That is, the arrears have risen precisely because many enterprise directors did not believe that the program's calls for hard budget constraints were credible. As they continued to behave as if it were business as usual, the arrears have materialized as the outcome.[34]

When the government ceased to make payments, a financial avalanche of secondary non-payments was set in motion. Enterprises that received no payment from the government were unable to pay their suppliers, who in turn were unable to meet their obligations, etc. With no effective sanctions being available, such as bankruptcy, with no functioning financial markets in existence and with a serious lack of credibility for the programme as such, enterprises had powerful incentives to create a financial system of their own, by resorting to the use of mutual zero interest credits, i.e. non-payments.

Table 5.2   Growth of inter-enterprise debt, 1992
(Billion current roubles, beginning of each month)

January	39
February	140
March	390
April	780
May	1,420
June	2,150
July	3,200

Source: Ekonomika i Zhizn, **30**, 1992, p. 11.

From Table 5.2 we can see that after the first six months of systemic change, Russian enterprises had succeeded in accumulating a mountain of mutual debt which, according to one observer, "attained truly epic proportions".[35]

From a strictly economic perspective, however, this problem seemed far worse than it really was. As Gros and Steinherr point out, discussion at the time was marked by a bit of confusion between stock and flow. While the accumulation of debt is a stock variable, GDP is a flow. Under zero inflation, comparing the stock of debt to the rate of GDP flow at a certain point in time is no problem, but under high inflation the outcome may get seriously distorted.

In the Russian case, GDP in July 1992 was compared to debt that had been accumulated from January onwards, i.e. during a period when prices were rising rapidly indeed. The outcome of that comparison was the image of a mountain of debt that by 1 July had increased almost a hundredfold, to reach about 80 per cent of GDP.[36] If, however, the stock of debt had been compared instead to the *annualized* rate of GDP in July, debt would have corresponded to merely 20 per cent of GDP, which is considerably less alarming.[37]

A better way of looking at the economic seriousness of the non-payments problem would have been to compare, month by month, how many months of production could be covered by the outstanding debt.

From this perspective, the Russian situation was at its worst in June 1992, when arrears reached a peak of three months worth of production. Thereafter it improved steadily, to reach its initial January 1992 value of one month by mid-1993. This development may be compared to that of Czechoslovakia, where arrears grew to reach a peak of 4.5 months after one year, without provoking any crisis.[38]

The reason for the latter is simple. In all market economies it is stand-ard practice for suppliers to extend trade credits to their customers, often 90 days. If the Russian development had been understood as normalization in this sense, it would not have provoked a crisis. But the problem of Russian inter-enterprise arrears was not primarily an economic one. It lay instead in the political – or institutional – dimension, in the creation of serious conflict over how the problem should be handled.

The best outcome for all concerned would have been to institute the use of trade credit under the rule of law, clearly specifying obligations and enforcement mechanisms. Thus a major step towards normalized enterprise behaviour and working financial markets could have been taken. As it turned out, however, each of the actors concerned pursued individual strategies that led to collective disaster. Directors proceeded to make unregulated non-payment a standard business practice, the Central Bank proceeded to issue credit that could only produce inflation, and the government retreated to an easy dependence on seigniorage revenue.

One might advance technical reasons for this outcome. Perhaps it was not so wise to decree overnight the introduction of hard budget constraints in an economic system where the very notion of bankruptcy was little known, and where the necessary legislation was lacking. But the problem was much more than a simple technical oversight. It actually represented an institutional shortcoming of the first magnitude. We may usefully recall the central message of Douglass North's theory of institutions, namely that it is the combination of rules, norms and mechanisms of enforcement that determine economic performance.

In the Russian case, the rules of the game were changed easily enough, but in the absence of a credible mechanism of enforcement, there was no way of making the new rules stick. As the game was repeated, moreover, the new rules entered into predictable conflict with the old norms (and old knowledge), thus serving to undermine the legitimacy of the formal rules.

For the bulk of Russian industry, the end result would in effect be a retreat to primitive barter. And the problem of non-payments would come to be endemic, with disastrous consequences for the tax system in particular. According to some calculations, reported by Nikolai Shmelyov in a 1997 article, for every government rouble that is not paid out, additional non-payments of 6–7 roubles are generated throughout the economy.[39]

For the first few months of 1992, the "young reform economists" seem to have been lulled into a feeling of success. The feared popular uprising did not happen, and seigniorage revenue was rolling in. Once, however, that the problem of non-payments had been noted, which seems to have been only in late April, the reaction was one of near panic.

A sharp discussion arose on how it should be dealt with. Strong conservative interests demanded massive credits be issued, which would make it possible for enterprises to pay their debts. Such demands were supported by the Central Bank, which declared itself ready to go as far as one trillion roubles.[40] Needless to say, the impact of such a credit expansion on the financial system would have been devastating.

At first, the government succeeded in blocking that proposal. Appointed by Yegor Gaidar to deal with this mess, the new Central Bank chairman Viktor Gerashchenko chose a rather innovative approach. All outstanding debt was frozen as of 1 July, 1992 and a process of netting out was initiated. The charm of accounting being that if all items are included correctly the sum will have to come to zero, it followed that if only all bills could be traced, the problem could thus be "solved".[41]

On 11 December, 1992 Interfax could announce that the process had been completed. All debts had been netted out, save a minor amount of 181 billion roubles, which would be covered by new credits. On first impression, it would thus seem that the problem had indeed been solved, and that Russia was now ready for market economy.

Already on the following day, however, the cynics were proven right. ITAR–TASS reported that following the July freeze of old debt, Russian enterprises had succeeded in building a new mountain of mutual debts of three trillion roubles.

The failure of the government to enforce its new rules provides an eminent illustration of one of the central tenets of North's theory of institutional change: "Since it is the norms that provide legitimacy for the rules, revolutionary change is never as revolutionary as its advocates wish, and performance will be different than predicted."[42]

As we shall see below, the problem of non-payments was not to be a temporary one. Thus, it cannot be explained as the result of initial technical policy shortcomings, such as lacking legislation. Before proceeding with these issues, however, let us look at the other two of the three games that were mentioned above.

Government vs. Central Bank

While seeking to impose a hard market regime on the enterprise sector, the Russian government was also involved in playing a game with the Central Bank, a game which was intimately linked to the first and would serve to compound the damage done by the spreading practice of non-payments.

During the spring of 1992, rapid inflation had done the job that could have been done – more equitably – by a currency reform. During the first four months, with a recorded inflation of 653.3 per cent, the relation of M2 to GDP fell by a factor of 5.1, from 76.5 per cent to 15.1 per cent.[43]

The implication was that by the beginning of May, the monetary overhang that had been accumulated under Soviet rule had been practically eliminated. This could have been the starting point for a period of successful stabilization. Instead, it would prove to be the start of what Vladimir Gligorov has called a process of "gradual shock therapy".[44]

The proponents of shock therapy are correct in pointing out that, in sharp contrast to political statements made at the time, the Russian government did not adhere to the austerity it preached. Far from it. While professing to the world that it was pursuing an austere monetary policy, the government was in actual fact very lax in giving in to a variety of demands.

Already on 18 January, two weeks after the start of the reforms, it signed an agreement with the miners which went clearly outside the budget limits, and the following months would see more such deals. Beginning in February, Moscow also added to its financial obligations by providing credits to the other governments in the "rouble zone". The latter increased from 1.2 per cent of GDP in February, to 8.4 per cent of GDP in May.[45]

But this does not imply that the reform policy as such was without guilt in the actual outcome. What proved to be really devastating was a combination of the worst of two possible worlds: repeated attempts at austerity followed by lavish credit expansion. Illarionov divides Russian stabilization policy during the first three years into no less than eight separate phases, of three to seven months duration.[46]

A crucial role in bringing about this highly disruptive pendulum movement was played by the Central Bank, operating via the rapidly emerging commercial banking sector.

By the end of 1991, there were more than 2,000 commercial banks in the Soviet Union. About 1,500 of these were in Russia, with 500 just in Moscow.[47] Few of these, however, were banks in the normal understanding of the word.

In the years immediately before the Soviet break-up there had been an accelerated process of proliferation. While the 1988 Law on Cooperatives stimulated the growth of new commercial banks, the old structures also found private banking to be an attractive undertaking. Local branches of the *spetsbanki* set up their own operations by means of share issues, and many enterprises set up their own "pocket banks".

As William Tompson notes, the driving force behind these developments was that of rule evasion: "creating one's own bank was, in the circumstances of the time, a way of softening one's budget constraint and escaping policy makers' attempts to impose market discipline on firms."[48]

When the Gaidar government embarked on its programme of shock therapy, this banking structure would prove to be a real stumbling block. With about four-fifths of all Russian commercial banks having been set up by one or more state enterprises,[49] the Central Bank had an excellent back door via which subsidies to industry could be continued. The "pocket banks" applied for credits at subsidized rates from the Central Bank and then passed the money on to their owners.

At the outset of reforms, the government had moved to prevent the Central Bank from stepping in where it pulled out. In January 1992, the re-finance rate was increased from 5 per cent to 20 per cent (in April, there was a further increase to 80 per cent), and the growth of Central Bank lending to the commercial banks was capped at 15 per cent for the first quarter. The latter limit, however, was broken already at the beginning of February, and by the end of the first quarter lending had increased by as much as 125 per cent. For the first five months of 1992, total credits to the commercial banks amounted to 8.7 per cent of GDP.[50] Then it went from bad to worse.

After having "solved" the problem of inter-enterprise debt, Viktor Gerashchenko addressed himself to the problem of money supply. Correctly noting that the real value of money balances had fallen sharply, he decided that it was up to the Central Bank to guarantee that there was enough money in the economy to cover inflation.

Hence, credits to the commercial banks took a substantial leap, increasing by 15 per cent of monthly GDP in July and by 31 per cent of monthly GDP in August 1992. (Credits to other governments in the rouble zone added another 5.5 per cent of GDP.) Taken together, total Central Bank lending grew by 40 per cent in June, by 49 per cent in July, and 56 per cent in August. During these three months, the deficit of the consolidated budget amounted to 28.8 per cent.[51]

In 1992 as a whole, the Central Bank issued credits to the Ministry of Finance and to the commercial banks corresponding to, respectively, 13.4 per cent and 13.8 per cent of GDP.[52] The difference between this and the old Soviet practice of automatic *ex post* coverage by the Gosbank of all financial deficits was not all that great, and definitely not in line with the clean break implied by shock therapy. We may safely assume, therefore, that in the eyes of enterprise managers the credibility of the reformers was proportionately eroded.

While the massive credit expansion that was undertaken by the Central Bank in the summer of 1992 wreaked serious havoc on the government's avowed policy of stabilization, it was well received indeed by the opposition. In December 1992, the Supreme Soviet decided to give Gerashchenko an award for his "substantial contributions to the stabilization of the economy of the Russian Federation".[53]

Subsequently, Jeffrey Sachs would deride the very same Gerashchenko as the "worst governor of a central bank of a major country in history",[54] and following the rouble crisis in October 1994 Yeltsin did fire him. (In the autumn of 1998, however, he would be back at his post.)

In order to understand how the government and the Central Bank could end up pulling in such different directions, it is important to note that the latter was placed under the authority of the Supreme Soviet, which was less than enthusiastic about the government's reform policy. The Bank could thus act as an important executive instrument of the political opposition. Gerashchenko bluntly stated that "the structure we have now when our Central Bank is accountable to Parliament is rational and expedient".[55] The executive branch of government had quite simply been cut out of the loop.

Against this background, one is inclined to believe that Yavlinskii is sincere when he claims that one of his conditions for accepting Yeltsin's offer of heading the economic reform effort had been that he should be allowed to control who was appointed to head the Central Bank. Making sure that the Bank and the government would pull in the same direction would have been a smart move.

As it turned out, however, controversy over the direction of monetary policy would be at the heart of the tug-of-war between the president and the Supreme Soviet that would reach its climax in October 1993, with the shelling of the White House in Moscow.

From an analytical point of view, it is interesting to note that even this bloody event failed to alter any of the basic strategies pursued. As we shall see below, many of the same moves that have been described above would be repeated in the coming years. The problem was therefore not fully explicable in terms of political opposition or simple dislike of the market economy.

Government vs. IMF

Before proceeding to the second phase of systemic change – that of low inflation – we must complete the initial picture by looking at the third game that was played by the Russian government, this time a co-operative, or even collusive, game with the IMF. Here it was not only the credibility of the Russian side that was at stake. From our previous account we may recall how the IMF, being once conceived as the world's financial policeman, was pushed into an unfortunate role of accepting direct responsibility for supporting the Russian reforms.

At first this came about reluctantly. Russia was not a member of the IMF and thus not eligible for emergency assistance. Initially, moreover, the discussion was mostly focused on providing a $6 billion stabilization fund for the rouble. (This was patterned on the $1 billion stabilization fund that was granted by the G7 to Poland late in 1989, in order to support the zloty.) Maintaining its traditional strict standards, it was not until July 1992, when Russia became a member, that the IMF granted a first credit of $1 billion.

Then, in 1993, a "Systemic Transformation Facility" was invented, in order to facilitate lending to post-communist economies on more lenient terms. In May 1993, the IMF reached an agreement with Russian representatives on a programme of stabilization, and on 1 July Russia received a first tranche of $1.5 billion under the STF.

Implementation, however, went wrong from the start, and the second tranche of another $1.5 billion, which was due to be released in the autumn, was withheld. Russia had failed to live up to even the less stringent conditions of the STF. According to a senior IMF official, "The May 1993 program went

Table 5.3 Official financial assistance to Russia ($ bn.)

	1992	1993
IMF	1.0	1.5
World Bank	0	0.6
Export Credits	12.5	5.5
Western Government Grants	1.5	0.5
Total	15.0	8.1
Corresponding Headline Offer	(24.0)	(28.0)

Source: Layard, R. and Parker, J. 1996. *The Coming Russian Boom: A Guide to New Markets and Politics.* New York: The Free Press, p. 90.

off track because it was not followed; and it was not adhered to because major political forces within the country refused to live by its provisions. The government was not able to protect the program from those who wanted to derail it."[56]

During the period when traditional IMF rules were still being enforced, there would thus be little money available. From Table 5.3 we may see that in 1992–3 Russia received a total of no more than $3.1 billion in untied credits from the IMF and the World Bank.

It would not be until April 1994 that the second tranche of the STF was released, and then it was not because of improved Russian performance. The reason was a little hunting expedition undertaken by IMF managing director Michel Camdessus and Russian prime minister Viktor Chernomyrdin. We have mentioned this above, in relation to our discussion of how the West was drawn into the Russian orbit, and it may now be time to return to this dimension. Games of moral hazard would be played on both sides, and in both cases the outcomes would be negative.

Returning to Table 5.3, we see a bottom line of "Headline Offers". This is the caption used by Richard Layard and John Parker to capture hollow promises of financial assistance, made by the G7 on two occasions when President Yeltsin seemed to be under serious threat from the domestic opposition.

The first occasion was linked to the April 1992 session of the Russian Congress of People's Deputies, which promised to offer a showdown between the reformers and their opponents. In order to strengthen the hand of the former, on the day before the congress opened the G7 made a public offer of a $24 billion package, including $6 billion to stabilize the rouble, once the Russian government was ready to fix the exchange rate.

The second occasion arrived in the run-up to the crucial referendum that was held in April 1993 (more about the politics below). On 3 April,

Presidents Clinton and Yeltsin met in Vancouver and ten days later, in Tokyo, the G7 promised to put up a total of $28 billion (plus $15 billion in phantom debt relief).

Turning to look at the reality, we find that very few of these promises were made good in hard cash. Of the $24 billion promised in 1992, only $15 billion arrived, and of that sum $12.5 billion was export credits made available by Western governments to Western firms wanting to sell their goods in Russia. In 1993, as can be seen from Table 5.3, it was even worse. The talk about a stabilization fund for the rouble would remain just that, talk, for the simple reason that stabilization, as we have seen above, was nowhere within reach.

Layard and Parker are justifiably upset about these discrepancies between promises and actual deliveries, but perhaps not for the right reasons. If we look at the sums involved, it may be noted that if the full amounts had indeed been delivered, in hard cash, the former would have been equal to 30 per cent of Russian GDP in 1992, and the latter would have been greater than total Russian imports in 1993. Is it really reasonable to criticize Western taxpayers for not putting up funds of that magnitude, to a Russian government that enjoyed such low credibility?

A considerably more justifiable critique is found by Gros and Steinherr, when they conclude that, "it is apparent that the total amounts announced to the press were used mainly for propaganda purposes".[57] Making promises of this kind, which no one intended to keep, but which were bound to be believed by at least some parts of the Russian population, was shortsighted Western expedience. In the longer term it may have serious Russian fallout effects indeed.

The turning point in the IMF's relations with Russia arrived with the disastrous December 1993 election, which brought communists and nationalists to the fore. When the duly reshuffled Chernomyrdin government began 1994 by stating that the period of "market romanticism" was over, the foreign economic advisors decided to jump ship and to unleash a torrent of harsh criticism against the IMF – for having failed to lend a helping hand. Jeffrey Sachs' classic article about the "Betrayal" was perhaps the harshest, but it was not alone.[58]

At the beginning of February, Michel Camdessus responded angrily to the accusations of being too insensitive in its dealings with Russia or too strict in the conditions it imposed: " 'We are the scapegoat', he complained, insisting that if the international community wanted to 'give unconditional aid to Russia, the money should come from bilateral grants'."[59] The IMF had a charter to follow and member states whose interests must be safeguarded. That stance, however, was soon to change.

After the April hunting expedition the above-mentioned $1.5 billion tranche was released, and from then on IMF involvement in Russia grew increasingly enthusiastic. In April 1995 there followed a $6.5 billion credit, and in March 1996, in the midst of the presidential election race, a three-year $10.1 billion "Extended Fund Facility" credit was agreed, representing the second largest credit ever granted by the Fund (after Mexico but before the Asian crisis).

The question that needs to be answered here is not whether all this lending was undertaken according to traditional IMF standards. That had been excluded from the start. The crucial point concerns whether it was undertaken even according to the purposely lax standards that had been created for Russia? Let us begin by listening to a Russian voice, commenting on the involvement of the IMF.

One of the casualties of the December 1993 election was the Russian finance minister Boris Fyodorov, who chose to resign in January 1994, and then went on to become a serious critic of the way in which relations between Russia and the West were evolving.

In late March 1994 he lashed out at the plans that were under way to give Russia more soft aid: "Is it not clear that the West is being used to bury the remnants of the reforms? . . . Is it not clear that anti-Western and nationalist attitudes are becoming more and more prevalent? . . . The sooner this money is handed over, the sooner we shall see a change in policy – in the wrong direction."

Notwithstanding such critique, on 20 April 1994, the IMF released the second tranche of $1.5 billion under the STF. At first it went well. By late June, all the agreed targets had been met. Then it collapsed. In the third quarter, Central Bank credit to the government surged, as a number of special interest groups were lobbying for handouts. At first the government tried to counter the inflationary pressure by running down international reserves, but on 11 October 1994, that strategy ran into a brick wall. "Black Tuesday" saw the rouble fall by more than 20 per cent against the dollar.

According to the same IMF official who was quoted above, the latter crisis

> . . . reflected a rational reaction of market participants, by now well informed, quick to move, and aware of the lagged but predictable effects of monetary expansion on inflation and exchange rates. It was a rational reaction to bad macro-economic policies, and particularly to an unsustainable fiscal deficit, and the appropriate response should have been to correct those policies.[60]

The latter conclusion reflects the core of the problem. If the whole point of the exercise was to enforce hard rules in the Russian economy, and the IMF chose to support that effort not only by offering soft rules, but also by repeatedly giving absolution for breaking even the soft rules, there was bound to be problems.

The soft rules that were introduced by the IMF for Russia have also been subjected to harsh criticism from Marshall Goldman, who points at serious moral hazard in two directions. On the one hand: "The wrong message is transmitted when the Russians come to perceive that credit terms can be stretched. Given that they already tend to treat credit obligations lightly, there is a danger that they will not learn how important such obligations are and that capital flight will continue."

And on the other:

> There is also a strong likelihood that, once such concessions have been made, some Western advisers will seek to obtain even more concessions – after all since an exception was made once, why can't it be made again? A problem here is that some Western advisors have come to act more as advocates than as analysts. Once they give advice, they tend to have a vested interest in that reform and therefore are reluctant to be critical of the results.[61]

These really are textbook illustrations of the problem of moral hazard, and it would not be long before reality proved that the warnings had been justified. In the first months of 1995, the IMF was involved in lengthy negotiations on the new twelve-month standby arrangement for $6.5 billion. When agreement was finally reached, the Russian side had pledged to block further direct Central Bank financing of the deficit, to bring monthly inflation down to one per cent in the second half of the year, and to liberalize further the foreign trade regime, notably so with respect to oil. None of these commitments would be honoured.

The game with the Central Bank will be discussed in greater detail in the following chapter. Here we shall merely point at the tricks that were played with respect to inflation.

In the first quarter of 1995, while negotiations were under way, money supply, measured as M2, increased by an average of 1 per cent per month. Given that monthly inflation in January 1995 was running at 17.8 per cent, that was austere enough. Then the agreement with the IMF was signed, and in April M2 was free to increase by no less than 25 per cent. As a result, the average increase in M2 for the first four months of the year rose to 4–6 per cent.[62] Cash alone increased in April by 6.8 trillion roubles, which may be compared to the previous record of December 1994, when 4.5 trillion roubles had been created.[63]

In the autumn of 1995, Dmitri Tulin, Executive Director of the IMF Russian office, responded to criticism of the Fund's Russia policy in a rather interesting way. He begins by acknowledging that "Russia has failed so far to accomplish any of the stabilization programs agreed with the Fund". Then, however, he goes on to state that this "places the Fund's critics in an awkward tactical position, since in such a case any unbiased observer would be inclined to attribute Russia's unsatisfactory economic performance to noncompliance with the Fund's policy recommendations, rather than to the deficiencies of these recommendations".[64]

This defence is striking in two ways. It seeks to reduce important criticism to simple tactical debating points, and it maintains that all fault rests with the Russians, rather than with the IMF. The fact that the Fund had been consciously playing along with Moscow in a game of systematic rule evasion seems to be of no consequence. As long as no criticism is directed at the *technical* quality of the advice offered, whether or not it is actually implemented is an exclusively Russian problem.

From a bureaucratic point of view it was at the same time logical and regrettable that none of the tricks employed by Moscow were chastised by the IMF, which was being drawn into a relationship of increasing mutual dependence with the Russian government. In a 1996 article in *The Institutional Investor*, David Fairlamb opens with a striking characterization of this relationship – "They're as intimate as lovers in a classic Russian novel" – and then proceeds to point out the inherent dangers:

> The relationship between the world's financial policeman and its biggest debtor after Mexico is now so cozy that it has become a tad unwholesome. So anxious are the Russians to please the Fund that they often agree to unrealistic financial targets that are impossible to meet. So keen is the Fund to help Russia that it often turns a blind eye when its supposedly stringent lending conditions are infringed on. . . . It doesn't take a Tolstoy to see the potential for tragedy, or at least melodrama, in this situation.[65]

With this, we shall leave the IMF – for the moment. The combined result of the three games that have been outlined above, all taking place under a cloud of high inflation, was one of confusion. In the short term, there were many seeming winners. Primarily, these were located in a banking sector that was thriving on the redistribution of wealth, but it was not only a question of banks getting rich.

While enterprise directors were busy stripping the assets of their "privatized" companies, the government was coasting along on easy seigniorage revenue, and the Central Bank was priding itself on being the only force that could prevent a total collapse of the old Soviet industries. It would seem, therefore, that all the main actors involved had good short-term reasons to be pleased, even more so given that the bulk of the costs would only have to be paid later on – and by others.

All good things, however, must come to an end. By the end of 1995, the IMF had finally managed to put an effective brake on the Russian printing presses. Inflation came down and the rouble was stabilized – both in a relative sense of course. So, what next?

In the following chapter we shall proceed to look at how the major actors adjusted their strategies to the new rules of the game that were implied by low inflation. First, however, we shall conclude this chapter by looking at the second of Boris Yeltsin's three big "chicken" games, this time being played against Ruslan Khasbulatov and the opposition in the Supreme Soviet. The importance of this illustration is vitally linked to issues like credibility, and to the intended shift from commands to contracts.

"Chicken" game two: Yeltsin vs. Khasbulatov

One of the most striking features in the games that have been described above is the way in which the president remains aloof, preferring not to intervene even in battles that would decide the fate of his own economic reforms. It was up to Gaidar and his team to wage their own battles, both against enterprise managers, who sought to prevent hard budget constraints from being imposed, against the Supreme Soviet, which took every chance of obstructing, and against the Central Bank, which effectively cancelled out every attempt at austerity.

The time has now come to look in somewhat greater detail at Yeltsin's way of consistently allowing his own personal power agenda to take precedence before the economic agenda, which was designed to promote market reforms. Symptomatically, we shall see that the only times when the president did intervene in politics was when his own personal power was challenged. This is also well in line with suspicions advanced above, of his not even having bothered to read much of the economic reform documents.

Round one: white knight

Before proceeding to look at the political struggles that would be played out over the question of economic reform, and which would culminate in the cataclysm of October 1993, it may be useful to recapitulate briefly some of the events that followed in the aftermath of the failed *coup* in August 1991.

Standing on top of the famous tank outside the Moscow White House, Boris Yeltsin was the undisputed hero, who could have gotten away with pretty much anything. The president could have called elections to a new parliament and he could have called a constituent assembly. It may be argued that neither would have been very successful, but that is beside the point.

The point is that he chose not even to *attempt* any of this, preferring instead to invest his political capital exclusively in securing his own power. We may recall the public humiliation that he administered to Gorbachev, and his crushing of the communist party. And then he chose to disappear from Moscow.

After his return, Yeltsin displayed considerable administrative energy, hand-picking a government consisting of young market-oriented economists and starting to build new bureaucratic structures around his own position, structures that would soon swell to a size that was even larger than the old Soviet ones.

But none of this was really designed to support the economic reforms. Yeltsin had himself appointed prime minister, and then largely withdrew from his own reform programme, allowing the three games that have been described above to be played out, all to the detriment of the Russian economy.

Round two: growing opposition

The first showdown between the reformers and the opposition took place at the sixth session of the Congress of People's Deputies, which was held in April 1992. The delegates took the offensive from the start, preparing a vote of no confidence in the government and a resolution where the president would be asked to resign from his parallel post as prime minister.

In the days before the congress, Yeltsin had tried to reach out by moving some of his most controversial ministers to other positions, but the gesture had not paid off. The opening confrontations illustrated how small the scope was for compromise and negotiation.

The great day for the congress was 13 April 1992. Subjected to harsh criticism, the government offered to resign but the offer was immediately branded as attempted blackmail. When the Speaker, Ruslan Khasbulatov, compared the government members to "urchins in pink pants", the government as a whole rose and left the hall in protest. Khasbulatov immediately adjourned the tumultuous session and bargaining in the wings was begun.

It was symptomatic that the opposition consistently directed its attacks at the government rather than at the president, whose popular standing was still fairly strong. By refraining from making the confrontation all out, however, it also deprived itself of the chance of victory in a showdown.

On 14 April 1992, the conservative block failed to secure enough votes for a resolution that would have granted the Supreme Soviet control over all public appointments, and on 15 April the government received formal support for a continuation of the economic reform policy. On 21 April, Yeltsin concluded the congress with a triumphant speech, declaring that the conservative counter-attack had been beaten off and that the strategic reform course would be maintained.

In reality, however, the president had been forced to make considerable concessions and there were divided minds as to the value of his "victory". The sixth session of the Russian Congress of People's Deputies had provided a rather depressing performance of what the country's nascent democracy was capable of. Expectations for its upcoming seventh session were not bright.

Towards the beginning of autumn 1992 it was becoming clear that Moscow had undergone a considerable change of political climate. The "red-brown" coalition of old-style communists and neo-fascists was coming out into the open. A "National Salvation Front" was formed, the purpose of which was said to be to stop the "Jewish plunder of Moscow".

Unpleasant as this was, the real threat to the government's reform policy emanated not from the street but from forces gathering around Arkadii Volskii, the forceful chairman of the Russian entrepreneurial association. Demands were made for continued subsidies to the state owned enterprises – particularly so for those in the military-industrial complex – and for an easing of the burdens that were placed on the population.

To the president, a hard choice was offered. While refusing these demands would provoke a political crisis, conceding them would imply giving up on the reform policy. In order to gain more time, he proposed to the Supreme Soviet that the communist-dominated Congress of People's Deputies should not be called until March. That proposal, however, was turned down and it was decided that the congress should convene on 1 December 1992, the very day when the president's right to rule by decree would expire.

On 13 November, the Supreme Soviet adopted a law depriving the president of his right to appoint government ministers, but since Yeltsin still had his special presidential powers he could refuse to sign this law. The attempt, however, was a serious warning of brewing discontent.

Following intense negotiations, it seemed that a compromise might be in the offing but at the very last moment it all collapsed. On 27 November, Gaidar declared that the opposition's economic proposals were in many ways unacceptable. In consequence, the government had to make its own proposal, which was duly voted down by the Supreme Soviet.

Round three: full confrontation

When the Congress of People's Deputies met for its long-awaited seventh session, the latent confrontation between the president and the Supreme Soviet was brought to a first real boiling point. The event was stormy, showing a distinct lack of both democratic tradition and democratic institutions. Again, the opposition opened by launching an immediate attack. The first speaker to take the stand started out by demanding that the president be impeached – a tactic that would be put to repeated later use.

The controversies that were played out during the session concerned two main issues: the position of acting prime minister Yegor Gaidar and the powers that were to be vested in the president. On his own, Gaidar did not stand much chance of survival. At the beginning of the congress he did give a speech in defence of the reforms, but it failed to leave much of an impression.

173

The offensive from the congress included calling for a radical realignment of the economic reform policy, and a refusal to even vote on Gaidar's candidacy for prime minister. It peaked when Yeltsin narrowly escaped a constitutional amendment, which would have seriously limited his own powers.

Again attempting to seek a compromise, the president offered the congress a right to appoint the four "power" ministers, i.e. the ministers of defence, security, the interior and foreign affairs. The offer was accepted and the constitution duly amended. In exchange, the president's choice of prime minister – Yegor Gaidar – would be confirmed, but then the compromise was suddenly forgotten. Speaker Khasbulatov called for a closed vote and Gaidar was defeated.

On 10 December 1992, Yeltsin delivered a sharply worded speech where he accused the delegates of conducting a creeping *coup*. He said that the very walls were blushing at all the curses, fistfights and insults that had shamed the country as a whole, and demanded that the congress should call a referendum, to be held in January 1993. The question: "Who do you think should lead the country out of the crisis – the president or the congress?" The president, however, had no authority of his own to call a referendum and the congress was certainly not about to help.

Thus, no resolution to the crisis seemed within reach. The confrontation was turning into gridlock. Rumours were spreading of a pending military *coup*, which forced the "power" ministers to announce that there was no threat to democracy from their side.

Upon leaving the congress, Yeltsin had himself driven in a black limousine to an auto factory where he delivered a televised speech to the workers, appealing to the people to gather the one million signatures necessary to call a referendum. In response, the congress voted in favour of an amendment to the (1978) constitution, which would preclude the holding of referenda on questions regarding dissolution of the highest organs of power.

At this point, the president of the Constitutional Court, Valerii Zorkin, intervened. After tough negotiations with Yeltsin and Khasbulatov – negotiations that were held under the threat of impeachment – he managed to force a compromise. It was agreed that the congress should select three candidates for the post of prime minister. From among those three, Yeltsin would choose one who would then have to be approved by the congress.

In addition, it was also agreed that a referendum should be held on 11 April 1993. The people would then be allowed to vote on a proposed new constitution, where it would be decided if real power should be vested in the president or the parliament.

On 14 December 1992 the agreed vote on the selection of prime minister was held. Although Yegor Gaidar had just barely managed to qualify among the three top candidates selected by the congress, the president chose to let him go. Viktor Chernomyrdin, then minister for the gas industry, was chosen instead. Gaidar's year in power was over. But Yeltsin's struggle against the legislature had only just begun.

Round four: to the brink

The political scene in 1993 would come to be dominated by an increasingly bitter struggle between Boris Yeltsin and Ruslan Khasbulatov. At the focus of this struggle was the question of whether or not a referendum was actually to be held, and if so, how the questions were to be formulated. As an alternative to a referendum, it was proposed that new elections should be held, either for the parliament or the president, or both. It was a power struggle, pure and simple, which had little indeed to do with economics.

Much of the quarrel between the two sides was handled via the media or personal intermediaries, but there were also attempts at personal negotiations. On 11 February 1993, Yeltsin and Khasbulatov met for a frosty and fruitless discussion. Four days later the president characteristically announced – in the midst of a constitutional crisis – that he intended to withdraw to his dacha outside Moscow for a 12-day vacation. On the following day, however, he returned to Moscow for a 20-minute talk with Khasbulatov.

On 3 March, a group of high-ranking officers demanded that the president should bring the destructive power struggle to an end. Many took this as an ominous sign that the military might after all be about to interfere in politics. And perhaps this implicit threat was decisive: on 5 March it was decided that the Congress of People's Deputies should be called for an extra session, to decide whether Russia should be led by the president or by parliament.

When the session began, on 10 March, the debate again opened in style, by defeating a motion that the Russian state emblem should be freed from the Marxist slogan "Proletarians in all countries – unite." But the real confrontation arrived when Speaker Khasbulatov described how at the previous meeting of the congress, the Devil himself (i.e. the president), had persuaded the delegates into an impossible compromise. In a new round of voting, everything that had then been negotiated was annulled, and a new attempt at reaching a settlement was relegated to a committee.

In the balance hung not only Yeltsin's own pet project, the referendum that was planned for 11 April. On the table were also a number of restrictions on the president's power, including a right for the Supreme Soviet to veto presidential decrees. In the earlier compromise, these proposals had been frozen. Now they were reopened.

On its last day, the congress voted against the holding of a referendum, which was held to be dangerous under the prevailing conditions. The president was warned against seeking on his own to push through an unconstitutional referendum. Driving the point home, money already set aside for the referendum was allocated instead to the construction of housing for Russian officers returning from postings in the Baltic republics and in Central Europe.

Right after the congress Yeltsin began hinting that the only remaining way out of the country's political crisis was presidential rule, i.e. in reality a *coup d'état*. The president did have the right to impose emergency rule, but according to the (1978) constitution such a decision must be confirmed by parliament within 24 hours. And there was not much hope of gaining such confirmation.

On 20 March, the conflict was brought to a head. In a 25-minute pre-recorded televised address, Yeltsin declared that the Supreme Soviet would be dissolved. Russia would be governed by a "special regime" until 25 April, when a "vote of confidence" would be held. He also issued a decree placing the Kremlin guard under the president's personal command, and called on the military not to allow itself to be drawn into the political game. Weapons were handed out to members of the government.

In an immediate response to the president's announcement, Vice President Aleksandr Rutskoi spoke of an inexcusable *coup*, and Valerii Zorkin talked about introducing impeachment procedures. On the following day, both the Supreme Soviet and the Constitutional Court did convene, but the feared eruption failed to materialize – this time. Instead it was agreed that a referendum would indeed be held, on 25 April.

In a sense, this was a success for Yeltsin. But Khasbulatov also managed to take a few steps forwards. Instead of a clearly formulated question about power, which could have resolved the political crisis, the Supreme Soviet had secured that in addition to the question of confidence in the president and his policies, questions would also be added on the holding of early elections to both parliament and the presidency. Most importantly, it also managed to classify these latter questions as constitutional issues, which demanded a majority of all *possible votes* rather than of *votes cast*.

At first glance, the outcome of the referendum was a clear victory for Yeltsin. The turn-out was high and the majority of those who voted did express confidence, both in the president and in his reform policies, the latter being something of a surprise. Crucially, however, the question of early elections to parliament came to nothing. Although 65 per cent of those who voted did answer yes, this only corresponded to 41.5 per cent of the *possible* votes. Thus the issue that the referendum was really intended to solve, namely the deadlock between president and parliament ended in a draw. So, confrontation was to continue.

Round five: battle for the White House

When the new political season was opened, following the summer recess, the president was faced with three distinctly threatening developments, two of which were directly concerned with his own personal power. In the Supreme Soviet, delegates were regrouping for a new attack. Having failed – narrowly – in the spring to impeach the president, there were moves under way to abolish the presidency altogether, via a constitutional amendment.

In a parallel process, the Constitutional Court under Valerii Zorkin was moving ever closer to the opposition in the Supreme Soviet, and might perhaps proceed to declare that the December 1991 decision to dissolve the Soviet Union had been illegal. While the full range of potential implications of such a decision was quite unpredictable, the danger to the Russian president was clear and present.

In the third of the three developments, it was the Russian economy that was at stake. In August the Supreme Soviet had voted for an amendment to the budget that would greatly increase spending and thus wreak havoc on both inflation and the currency.

In sum, the stage was set for a further showdown. The official – and politically correct – version of the events that were to follow is that Yeltsin in the end was forced into a situation where he had no option but to use minimal violence, in order to avoid widespread bloodshed. Consequently, all blame could be put on the opposition. It is a comfortable version, above all because it made it possible for Western leaders to continue their support for Yeltsin.

If the West had been forced to recognize that the Russian president had *deliberately* lured his political opponents into a trap, that he had *deliberately* provoked a crisis from which the only way out was a bloodbath, including tank fire against the country's parliament – perhaps the most important symbol of democracy – it would have been difficult to avoid a fundamental policy reappraisal. This obviously was a bit too much to ask.

Unfortunately, there is a great deal of evidence which supports this unpleasant argument, namely that it was indeed a question of a trap, of a cynical political power game aimed at crushing once and for all the political opposition that was beginning to form around Speaker Khasbulatov and Vice President Rutskoi.

Although it will never be possible to produce evidence that events actually happened in this way, it is possible to construct a chain of circumstantial evidence that has a great deal to say about Yeltsin's power preferences.[66]

The first link in this chain is connected to the president's general political conduct during the period after the turbulent December 1992 meeting of the Congress of People's Deputies. As president, Yeltsin had the main responsibility for seeing to it that a compromise could be reached. Failing this, there would always be a final democratic escape in the form of resignation. We have certainly seen a number of compromise attempts, but it remains a fact that most were suggested by third parties and that none was successful.

Writing about the October crisis, Archie Brown maintains that in the end "Yeltsin had no alternative but to reply to force with force," but he also recognizes that it was "a notable failure of coalition-building on Yeltsin's part to turn the parliamentary majority he could command, however precariously, in 1990–91 into a determined opposition".[67]

Brown was writing in the aftermath of the crisis. With the benefit of another few years of hindsight, it is quite obvious that neither compromise nor resignation was ever really on the president's agenda. Each time when a settlement began to take shape, which might have impaired his own power, he made some move that destroyed all basis of possible agreement. Compromise under duress, moreover, is something essentially different from democratic constituency building.

The most striking example is the political crisis in March 1993, when Yeltsin declared his intention of dissolving the Supreme Soviet and of introducing a state of emergency, i.e. exactly what he would come to do in September. Whether he really had intended to run the course in March, or if it was just a matter of political skirmishing, we will never know. (If the former was indeed the case, it is evident that the ground had not yet been properly prepared.)

The next link in the chain concerns the events that were played out at the end of August and the beginning of September 1993. On 19 August, i.e. on the second anniversary of the previous *coup*, Yeltsin laid out his intentions of making sure that elections to a new parliament were held before the end of the year: "It will cover about two and a half months . . . Part of August – I call it the artillery preparation – then September, the crucial month, then October and probably part of November."[68]

The first person to be informed of the president's plans was Viktor Ilyushin, a loyal apparatchik who had been with Yeltsin since his time as party leader in Sverdlovsk: "In a phrase that spoke volumes about Russian attitudes to law," he was told to "prepare a proper juridical basis" in order to defend "an action whose illegality was absolutely plain."[69]

On 12 September 1993, the power ministers were informed, i.e. the minister of defence, Pavel Grachev, the interior minister, Viktor Yerin, and the security minister, Nikolai Golushko, as well as the foreign minister, Andrei Kozyrev.

On 16 September, Yeltsin made a visit to the Dzerzhinskii Division, formerly a classic KGB division, which had been transferred to the interior ministry under Yerin. Given that the latter was close to the president and considered to be completely trustworthy, military support in the event of disturbances was thus secured. The artillery was in place.

On 19 September, Moscow hospitals were warned that large numbers of casualties could be expected, and in the evening of 21 September, Yeltsin was ready to complete the project that he had started in March. In a second television broadcast, he informed the Russian people that he had dissolved the Supreme Soviet. New elections would be held in December.

Again, the response from the opposition was swift and forceful. Only hours after Yeltsin's declaration, hundreds of delegates gathered for an emergency meeting in the White House, where they voted to impeach the president. Once Vice President Rutskoi had taken the oath as new president of Russia, they also proceeded to name a number of ministers of their own, notably so a new minister for defence, which would force the military to take sides.

As a result of this open rebellion, the Moscow White House was transformed into a besieged fortress of sorts, which attracted a riffraff of generally dissatisfied opposition groups. There were extreme nationalists and Russian Nazis, supported by armed groups made up of a mixture of mercenaries and regular soldiers. The situation rapidly intensified.

On 24 September, Moscow mayor Yurii Luzhkov, who was loyal to Yeltsin, ordered the supply of electricity and hot water to the White House to be turned off. Assisted by Yerin, he also had the building surrounded by paramilitary police forces. Thousands of riot police were brought into town from the province. The confrontation was now complete, and considerable unease began to spread.

While the battle of words sharpened, it was becoming clear that the outcome was far from obvious. Many maintained that legality must take precedence, that the president might be right in principle, but that the means he was using were unlawful. Across the country, the opposition was beginning to win sympathies.

On 29 September, Vitalii Mukha, the governor of Novosibirsk, called a meeting of representatives of the 14 Siberian regions. A threat was issued, saying that unless the siege of the White House was brought to an end, they would break off relations with Russia and proclaim a republic of their own.

On 30 September, even Patriarch Aleksii, the head of the Orthodox Church, intervened. Representatives of both sides were invited to a meeting at the Danilov Monastery. The discussion focused on what would come to be known as the "zero solution", i.e. that simultaneous elections should be held for both parliament and presidency. Speaking for the armed forces, Defence Minister Grachev recommended that this suggestion be accepted, and in a telephone conversation with Valerii Zorkin on the morning of 3 October, even Prime Minister Chernomyrdin is said to have expressed sympathy for this plan.

On 5 October, the Russian Federation Council, consisting of the heads of all of Russia's 89 republics and regions, was due to convene in Moscow. It was generally thought that this meeting would put great pressure on Yeltsin to accept a compromise. Before that could happen, however, all hopes of a peaceful solution were dashed. On 3 October 1993, tanks were back in the streets of Moscow.

Looking at this course of events, it is hard to escape an impression that Boris Yeltsin had decided that the confrontation must be brought to a head, once and for all and at any cost. This is also a view that is explicitly suggested by Bruce Clark:

The army was, in fact, one of many institutions agitating for a compromise in the few days before the final clash. The fact that a compromise was very much in the air provides the political context for the final upheaval. It helps to explain why Yeltsin's hardest men so desperately needed to bring the stand-off to a confrontational head, in which all talk of meeting in the middle would be brushed aside.[70]

When Clark specifies what an eleventh hour compromise would have involved, he also points his finger at the real weak spot in Yeltsin's defence: "For the strategists in the presidential camp, that sort of 'reasonable' outcome would spell disaster. It would seem clear that the crisis had been provoked by Yeltsin and resolved by the moderation of his opponents."[71]

The strongest link in the chain of circumstantial evidence concerns the decisive hours when the crisis was being transformed into a bloodbath. A prominent figure among those who were seeking to achieve a compromise was Oleg Rumyantsev, a lawyer and a social democrat, who had been involved for three years in working out a draft for a new Russian constitution.

Together with Zorkin and some prominent spokesmen for the Federation Council, among others, he had spent the last few days working intensively on a compromise proposal that would involve the Federation Council assuming power pending simultaneous elections to parliament and the presidency.

In the afternoon of 3 October, Rumyantsev came to the White House to meet Rutskoi. Moments after they had started talking, the building came under sniper fire. Rutskoi lost his composure and ordered a fateful counterattack. Clark sees the trap: "If only Rutskoi had shown a bit more intelligence and self-restraint, and simply kept the situation under control until the Federation Council meeting had taken place, victory would have been his. But . . . the Vice President gobbled up the bait – hook, line and sinker."[72]

The events that followed form the final link in the chain. Despite the blockade of the White House, supporters of both ultra-communists and openly fascist parties had somehow managed to gain entrance. From our perspective, the reason is easy to understand. When Rutskoi gave his signal to attack, it was mainly these unsavoury characters that would charge out of the building. Thus the impression of Yeltsin as the champion of good was given a real boost.

When the rebels finally did launch their attack, it also proved surprisingly easy for them to break through the blockade. The police handed over their weapons and allowed themselves to be chased away without great resistance. Adding to their sense of victory, the rebels discovered a number of abandoned vehicles with the ignition keys still inserted. Led by hard-line general Albert Makashov, they boarded these vehicles and headed off to storm the state television station at Ostankino.

The most dramatic hours of the uprising were played out when the rebels entered the ground floor of the television station, and the country's many millions of viewers could see the broadcasts being interrupted, the latter reportedly at the direct request of the Prime Minister Chernomyrdin. The whole thing was a well-orchestrated play, which from the president's point of view had already been sufficiently bloody. Both cameramen and reserve studios were available, but broadcasting the events that followed would not have been in Yeltsin's best interest.

When Makashov's rebels arrived, there were practically no defenders in sight, not even regular police. What no one seemed to know at that time, however, was that since 21 September, there had been about thirty ordinary policemen inside the building, along with about the same number of elite soldiers from the semi-secret Vityaz Force. The latter was a special unit within the Dzerzhinskii Division whose normal task it was to quickly and efficiently (without too many questions being asked) crush prison revolts or race riots in Central Asia.

When fighting broke out, the forces were highly uneven. According to subsequent information from Defence Minister Grachev, about 100 armed and 4,000 unarmed aggressors were pitted against 400 well prepared special troops from the interior ministry, who were also getting speedy reinforcements.

The real danger was over in ten minutes, but the shooting continued throughout the night. The area between the two television station buildings became a bloody battlefield, where heavily armed special troops were spraying bullets over rebels, journalists and innocent bystanders alike. When it was all over, 61 people had been killed. There was only one "defender" among them, and he had been killed by a grenade.[73]

One week after the bloodbath, *Moscow News* quoted an anonymous Russian intelligence officer, who was said to have participated in Soviet-inspired *coups* and military provocations in Latin America and Indochina. He claimed that the 6,000 OMON riot police who had been available could easily have stopped the 10,000 largely unarmed demonstrators who broke through the weakened cordon around the White House on that Sunday afternoon.

The fact that the demonstration was not stopped points to a policy decision by the mayor and the interior minister, to refrain from intervening. Concerning the vehicles and buses that were "thoughtfully" left behind for the rebels, the anonymous officer has the following to say: "Motor vehicles with ignition keys 'abandoned in a panic' are a trick used by special forces in banana republics."[74]

Wrapping up

Much more could be added to strengthen the conspiracy theory, such as the mysterious reduction of the paramilitary forces around the White House that occurred on 2 October, but this will have to do for now. The facts are there, and it is difficult indeed to see the president as the victim, as the one who was seeking compromise but was forced into using violence. Accepting a version of October 1993 that places Boris Yeltsin in the role of seeking confrontation is even easier if we look at subsequent events.

No matter what degree of trust one chooses to put in the alternative version of the October events, it is an indisputable fact that – yet again – Yeltsin's victory was absolute. He was the strong "tsar" who – with a determined fatherly intervention – had saved the country from chaos and civil war. Almost all of his enemies were in jail and the population was in a state of fearful bewilderment.

The tsar was *"groznyi"* in the real meaning of the word, i.e. not just "terrible", but a combination of impressive and fearsome – "awesome" in all senses of the word. Adding to this image, rumours soon began to spread that there had been a tremendous number of deaths, that piles of bodies had been carted off in underground tunnels.

The parallel with the events of August 1991 lies close at hand. For a couple of months after the 1993 battle for the White House, Yeltsin had almost absolute authority. He could have used this opportunity to compose almost whatever government he chose and to launch pretty well whatever political programme he wanted. Again, however, he chose to completely disregard coalition building. This choice reveals a great deal about his overriding priorities.

While the West was busy speculating about the outcome of the election to the new state Duma that was to be held on 12 December, Yeltsin vested all his political capital and administrative capacity in the preparation of a greatly revised proposal for a new constitution, which would be the object of a referendum alongside the Duma election.

Russia's political map was now being redrawn from the bottom up. The compromise product that had been hammered out in long drawn-out negotiations over the previous months was simply thrown out. The bulk of the concessions that had been made by the federal centre, in order to gain acceptance from republics and regions, were withdrawn. The final proposal was to be an essentially different product, with a considerably stronger position for the central power.

Recalling our previous presentation of two parallel agendas, it was symptomatic that in the weeks leading up to the Duma election and the referendum on the constitution, the president would largely ignore the one that related to the economic reforms while jealously hovering over his own personal power agenda.

It is an interesting fact, for example, that one of the rare occasions on which the president did intervene in the election campaign was provoked by some critical remarks that had been made regarding the proposed constitution. On 26 November, all political party leaders were called to a meeting in the Kremlin, where they were informed that any further attacks of this kind would lead to the loss of all free television time for the offending party.

The message was clear. The political parties could play their games, and the president would take care of his. When the election campaign was nearing its end, and a variety of different opinion polls showed that political extremism was on the rise, it was also symptomatic that Yeltsin refused in any way to interfere. Some powerful statements from his side might certainly have provided a boost for the democratic parties, but maybe that was not in his own best interest.

There remained only one problem, namely to ensure that sufficient numbers of voters would turn up at the ballot boxes for the referendum to be valid. For this purpose, Yeltsin began expressing concerns that a rejection of the proposed constitution would cast the country into a bloody civil war.

In the end, however, it seems that not even this was enough. In a study of what went on during the night after the election, the Russian scholar Aleksandr Sobyanin has documented considerable election fraud. Realizing that fewer than 50 per cent had actually turned out to vote, which would imply that the referendum was invalid and the country without a democratic constitution, a total of no less than nine million "extra" votes were added.

If we accept that Sobyanin is right,[75] an interesting extra complication followed, in the sense that there was a parallel Duma election. Extra votes that were added in the referendum would thus have to be allocated to political parties as well, and here some intriguing patterns emerged.

According to Sobyanin's study, six million extra votes were given to Vladimir Zhirinovskii's "liberal democratic" party (LDP), meaning that the LDP's share of the party votes increased from 13 per cent to 23 per cent. Of the remainder, 1.8 million votes went to Gennadii Zyuganov's communist party and a further 2.7 million votes to a couple of communist support parties. Most intriguing of all, however, is the fact that Yegor Gaidar's democratic party, "Russia's Choice", was deprived of about two million votes.[76]

Adding to this conspiracy theory, we may also note that the fraudulent support seemingly given to the LDP during the election night, had a striking parallel in the allocation of political air time during the election race.

Russian state television had decided that each of the political parties running would be allocated three hours of advertising time free of charge, and an option to purchase a further eleven hours. To "Russia's Choice", which had strong support from the new class of bankers, securing the maximum 14 hours presented no problem. The fact, however, that the LDP managed to get the same amount of time, against diffuse promises of paying later, is a bit more difficult to explain.

Summing up the argument, if Sobyanin is indeed right, it would mean that the 1993 Duma election was manipulated so that the ultranationalists were given a big boost, the communists a small boost and the democrats were robbed of a good deal of the support they had actually gotten in the election. Does this make sense?

From the president's point of view, as we have presented it above, it most certainly does. The final outcome of the story has two separate dimensions, both of which were favourable to his personal power agenda.

Most importantly, Yeltsin now had a constitution that while irreproachably democratic, in reality made him an extraordinarily strong president. There were provisions included for making amendments, but in all important respects such complicated procedures were prescribed that in practice it cannot be changed. The possibility of impeachment was also included, but again after such complicated procedures that it is unlikely indeed to occur.

Yeltsin's personal power agenda had thus been firmly based on constitutional guarantees, including a paragraph that explicitly acknowledges the role of the president as the guarantor of the constitution. His own subsequent predilection for referring to this role provides further evidence that he had come to see himself as a true autocrat, in good old Russian tradition.

In the second dimension, the outcome of the election to the new state Duma provided the president with an excuse for clearing the remaining "democratic forces" out of the way. The main Russian reform economists – Yegor Gaidar, Boris Fyodorov and Vladimir Shumeiko – were forced to leave the government.

The only important figures left from the old reform team were the privatization minister, Anatolyi Chubais, and the minister of foreign affairs, Andrei Kozyrev. By now, the latter had been reduced to complete insignificance in Russian domestic politics, and he would soon have outlived his usefulness on the foreign scene as well. As we shall see in subsequent chapters, however, Chubais would still have several major parts to play.

Before concluding this chapter, we shall return once more to the involvement of the West in Russian domestic politics. From above we may recall how the IMF decided to withhold the second tranche of the "Systemic Transformation Facility", that was due in the autumn of 1993. The political process that led up to that decision has a great deal of relevance to the story that has been told above.

The first storm clouds began to gather in late August, when the IMF organized a seminar in Moscow. Here the message was spelled out, clear and simple. If the Russian president were to agree to the budget amendments that had just been passed by the Supreme Soviet, the Fund would stop all further financial support.[77]

In mid-September, pressure was increased, as the IMF warned that the second tranche of the STF would not be released until Russia "returned to the path of reform". Suddenly, there were several high-ranking US officials going to bat. On 13 September 1993, US Treasury Secretary Lloyd Bentsen warned that "There has been slowing down in some areas. That is certainly a concern." On the following day, the under secretary for foreign affairs at the treasury department, Lawrence Summers, arrived in Moscow, having only just told the US Foreign Relations Committee that "The battle for economic reform in Russia has now entered a new and critical phase in which many of Russia's accomplishments on the economic front are being put at risk. The momentum for Russian reform must be reinvigorated and intensified to ensure sustained multilateral support." On 15 September, Jeffrey Sachs also joined in, by saying that the drift in the Russian government was "dreadful" and that "things are dead in the water".[78]

On 16 September, Yeltsin told soldiers at the Dzerzhinskii Division (!) that Yegor Gaidar was back in the government, having been appointed first deputy prime minister. This, however, was not enough. On 20 September, *The New York Times* quoted a senior IMF official, saying that the Fund was unhappy with recent "backtracking" on reforms, but that "Moscow might receive the loan by the end of the year if it displayed a strong and renewed commitment to reform."

On 21 September, the Russian president dissolved the country's parliament and triggered a crisis that would culminate in the bloodbath on 3 October. That, seemingly, was finally enough. In the spring of 1994, relations between Moscow and the IMF would start improving, soon to blossom into a full-scale love story.

What, then, may we conclude from these events? Was it by pure coincidence that the two chains of events coincided? Or was the IMF indeed instrumental in bringing the crisis to a head? Only Yeltsin himself can give a proper answer to that question, but doubts will always remain, as to the wisdom of this heavy Western involvement in Russia's domestic politics.

In defence of the IMF it might certainly be argued that it is unreasonable to accuse the Fund of being at the same time too lenient and too insistent in its relations with Moscow. That line of defence, however, would only serve to befuddle the basic issue, which is that the IMF should never have been involved in the first place.

Layard and Parker, for example, are quite correct in pointing out that charging the IMF with helping Russia was a strategic mistake, for the simple reason that conflicts of interest and rule violations were simply bound to arise. We may rest the case by agreeing with Marshall Goldman in pointing out that the IMF itself may in the end also turn out to be a victim: "To use the International Monetary Fund for this purpose undercuts the IMF's credibility and its work elsewhere in the world."[79]

Let us now proceed to look at the second act in the drama, namely that of playing for money and power under conditions of low rather than high inflation.

Notes

1. Quoted by Nelson, L.D. and Kuzes, I. Y. 1995b. *Radical Reform in Yeltsin's Russia: Political, Economic and Social Dimensions*. Armonk, NY: M. E. Sharpe, p. 3.

2. The following comment, by Jozef van Brabant, is highly relevant here: ". . . many of the errors committed to date could have been avoided or minimized if those under fire had better understood what was at stake and formulated their concrete strategy accordingly. Not only that, wielding the economic ax to settle intrinsically ideological and political battles is not usually the most fruitful option. Alas, economists are not good at configuring the tradeoff." (van Brabant, J.M. 1998. *The Political Economy of Transition: Coming to Grips with History and Methodology*. London: Routledge, p. 101.)

3. Nelson and Kuzes 1995b, op. cit., p. 19.

4. Ibid., p. 93.

5. Ibid., p. 16.

6. Ibid., pp. 93–4.

7. The preface to the published version of the programme is dated in September 1991, i.e. after the putsch. (Allison, G. and Yavlinsky, G. 1991. *Window of Opportunity: The Grand Bargain for Democracy in the Soviet Union*. New York: Pantheon Books.)

8. Nelson and Kuzes, op. cit., p. 21.

9. See further Goldman, M. 1996. *Lost Opportunity: What has Made Economic Reform in Russia so Difficult?* New York: Norton, pp. 89–90.

10. Nelson and Kuzes, op. cit., p. 17.

11. Goldman, op. cit., p. 95.

12. Nelson and Kuzes, op. cit., p. 18.

13. Ibid., p. 41.

14. *Financial Times*, 16 January 1992.

15. *Ekonomika i Zhizn*, **10**, 1992, 9.

16. We should note that there was a prehistory of slowly growing imbalances, from 1961 onwards, and of a serious deterioration during the Gorbachev years (Illarionov, A. 1995. Popytki provedeniya politiki finansovoi stabilizatsii v SSSR i v Rossii, *Voprosy Ekonomiki*, **7**, 4–6). Thus recognizing that the Soviet regime had added its share to the build-up of inflationary pressure does not, however, change the fact that it was events during 1991 that made the situation explosive.

17. We should note that this is a phenomenon that is particular to the centrally planned economy. It is not due to forced savings in the sense that there is absolutely nothing to buy. It arises because households keep money for reasons that do not exist in a market environment, namely for the eventuality that desirable goods might suddenly appear. With market liberalization that behaviour also ceases to be rational. See further van Brabant, op. cit., pp. 147–9.

18. Illarionov 1995, op. cit., p. 7.

19. Ibid., p. 8.

20. Lainela, S. and Sutela, P. 1994. *The Baltic Economies in Transition*. Helsinki: The Bank of Finland, p. 45. Estonia also opted for a currency board solution, which despite early warnings from abroad turned out to be quite successful.

On the merits and pitfalls of this type of approach, see further van Brabant, op. cit., pp. 157–66.

21. IMF *et al.* 1991. *A Study of the Soviet Economy* (vol. 1). Paris: OECD, p. 396.
22. Ibid.
23. Lavigne, M. 1995. *The Economics of Transition: From Socialist Economy to Market Economy*. London: Macmillan, pp. 114–15.
24. Gros, D. and Steinherr, A. 1995. *Winds of Change: Economic Transition in Central and Eastern Europe*. London: Longman, p. 383.
25. Illarionov 1995, op. cit., p. 9.
26. See further Hedlund, S. and Sundström, N. 1996b. The Russian economy after systemic change, *Europe-Asia Studies*, **48**(6), 895–6.
27. Gros and Steinherr, op. cit., pp. 430–31.
28. Ibid., p. 431. The figures are taken from Fischer, S. 1982. Seigniorage and the case for national money, *Journal of Political Economy*, **90**(2).
29. Gros and Steinherr, op. cit., p. 432.
30. The technical detail of maintaining the distinction between cash and non-cash roubles is presented in ibid., pp. 388–90.
31. Ibid., pp. 431–2.
32. Gaidar, Y. 1995. Russian reform, in Gaidar, Y. and Pöhl, K.O., *Russian Reform/International Money*. Cambridge, Mass.: MIT Press, p. 30.
33. *The Economist*, 25 April 1992, p. 20.
34. Ickes, B.W. and Ryterman, R. 1992. The interenterprise arrears crisis in Russia, *Post-Soviet Affairs*, **8**(4), 333.
35. Rostowski, J. 1993. The inter-enterprise debt explosion in the former Soviet Union: causes, consequences, cures, *Communist Economies & Economic Transformation*, **5**(2), 131.
36. The same was reported in the international press. See, e.g., *The Economist*, 30 January 1993, p. 81.
37. Gros and Steinherr, op. cit., pp. 162–5, 427–30.
38. Ibid., p. 428.
39. Shmelyov, N. 1997. Neplachezhy – problema nomer odin rossiiskoi ekonomiki, *Voprosy Ekonomiki*, **4**, 27.
40. *Moscow News*, **24**, 1992, p. 4.
41. On the technical design of this operation, see Rostowski, op. cit., pp. 139–40 and *passim*.
42. North, D. 1995. Economic performance through time, *The American Economic Review*, **84**(3), 366.
43. Illarionov 1995, op. cit., p. 9.
44. Gligorov, V. 1995. Gradual shock therapy, *East European Politics and Societies*, **9**(1).
45. Illarionov 1995, op. cit., p. 9. See also Ickes and Ryterman, op. cit., pp. 348–51.
46. Illarionov 1995, op. cit., pp. 28–9.
47. Ickes and Ryterman, op. cit., p. 340.
48. Tompson, W. 1997. Old habits die hard: fiscal imperatives, state regulation and the role of Russia's banks, *Europe-Asia Studies*, **49**(7), 1161.
49. Johnson, J.E. 1994. The Russian banking system: institutional responses to the market transition, *Europe-Asia Studies*, **46**(6), 979.

50. Illarionov 1995, op. cit., p. 9.
51. Ibid., p. 10.
52. Gros and Steinherr, op. cit., p. 430.
53. *Vedomosti verkhovnogo soveta RF*, No. 1, 1993, Art. 51. (I am indebted to Stefan Gullgren for drawing my attention to this little gem.)
54. *The Economist*, 6 August 1994, p. 71.
55. Johnson, op. cit., p. 980.
56. Hernández-Catá, E. 1995. Russia and the IMF: the political economy of macro-stabilization, *Problems of Post-Communism*, **42**(3), 24.
57. Gros and Steinherr, op. cit., p. 433.
58. E.g. *Financial Times*, 11 January 1994, and *The New Republic*, 31 January 1994.
59. *Financial Times*, 2 February 1994.
60. Hernández-Catá, op. cit., pp. 25–6.
61. Goldman, op. cit., pp. 223–4.
62. Belyakov, G. *et al.* 1995. Poterya tempa pri potere kachestva, *Kommersant*, 23 May, p. 53.
63. Vasilchuk, Y. 1995. Razogrev ekonomiki stavit krest na popytke finansovoi stabilizatsii, *Finansovye Izvestiya*, 20 June.
64. Tulin, D. 1995. The IMF and the World Bank prevents what?, *Transition*, **6**(9–10), 12.
65. Fairlamb, D. 1996. When love's too blind, *Institutional Investor*, September, p. 21.
66. The details of this story are laid out in Clark, B. 1995. *An Empire's New Clothes: The End of Russia's Liberal Dream*. London: Vintage, chs 11–12.
67. Brown, A. 1993. The October crisis of 1993: context and implications, *Post-Soviet Affairs*, **9**(3), 183–4.
68. Clark, op. cit., p. 234.
69. Ibid., p. 238.
70. Ibid., p. 258.
71. Ibid., p. 260.
72. Ibid.
73. Ibid., p. 247.
74. Ibid., p. 253.
75. Sobyanin's allegations have been investigated by Filippov, M. and Ordeshook, P.C. 1997. Who stole what in Russia's December 1993 elections?, *Demokratizatsiya*, **5**(1), who conclude that the evidence is so problematic that fraud can be neither proven nor dismissed.
76. Clark, op. cit., pp. 277–8.
77. Nelson and Kuzes, op. cit., p. 25.
78. Quotes from ibid., p. 148.
79. Goldman, op. cit., p. 224.

CHAPTER SIX

Banks, bonds and surrogate money

The basic dilemma of Russian economic policy during the post-Soviet years has been, and continues to be, that the winners do not find it rational to share their spoils by engaging in the payment of any serious amounts of taxes, customs or other contributions to the budget. At a cursory glance, it is easy to interpret this development as a manifestation of the classic prisoners' dilemma. If others do not pay their taxes, I have little to gain from making a contribution on my own, and little to fear in the way of getting caught should I decide not to pay. Thus a negative self-reinforcing spiral is established.

The gravity of the situation can hardly be overestimated. The longer it continues, the more serious will be the damage that is done to the very foundations of the Russian state. If actors are locked into a stable equilibrium, where it is both rational and acceptable to ignore taxes, the state will lose its ability to provide even those services which are normally associated with the nightwatchman state, i.e. a system of laws and law enforcement. So, what – if anything – can be done?

Finding a cure logically requires that we first undertake a thorough examination of the disease, and here we at once run into serious trouble. Making the diagnosis of a prisoners' dilemma is easy enough, but understanding how the process got started in the first place is not quite as easy.

The prisoners' dilemma is after all a threat that applies to all regimes seeking to elicit payments from below, be it citizens or members in a club of some sort. Nevertheless, practical experience tells us that in all of those real life situations where the threat is indeed present, it is still very infrequently that it is triggered. The very existence of stable Western societies shows that there are strong countervailing forces at work. So, why then has Russia been hit so hard?

The answer to this question has two separate dimensions, one being tied to the purely technical detail of the Soviet economic system and its dismantling, the other having deeper historical roots, in institutional factors such as rule obedience and common trust. Rephrasing the answer somewhat, the former may be said to represent the formal rules and the latter the informal norms of the institutional matrix. Leaving the latter for discussion in Chapter 8, we shall proceed here to look at the development of the formal rules, and at the practical consequences of the associated failure to raise sufficient taxes.

Budgets and deficits

When the Soviet order was imposed, all taxes were abolished. It was, after all, supposed to be a money-free command economy, and the state (or the people) as the sole proprietor of all productive assets was in no way dependent on raising taxes. Although the words were used, and budget transfers of sorts were indeed made, neither taxes nor subsidies were designed to have the functions they have in a market environment. It was chiefly a matter of an *ex post* reshuffling of the books, within the single enterprise of "USSR Inc."

Behind the façade, however, the hybrid monetary system that did exist – in the form of cash and non-cash roubles – soon began to create problems, in the form of growing imbalances.

Over the years 1961–85, the annual rate of growth in money supply (M2) was about 10 per cent. Meanwhile, the rate of growth in nominal GDP was shrinking. Thus, the degree of monetization of the economy (M2/GDP) grew, from 22.8 per cent in 1961, to 44.2 per cent in 1980 and 52.6 per cent in 1984.[1]

At first, the consequences of this development were noticeable primarily in the household sphere, where the increasing supply of cash roubles created open inflation in the black and kolkhoz markets, as well as repressed inflation in the form of longer and longer lines in front of the state shops. Towards the end of the Brezhnev era, however, the use of non-cash roubles in the enterprise sphere was adding its share of problems. Still, in official Soviet circles macroeconomic phenomena such as budget deficits and inflationary pressures were receiving little or no attention.[2]

When Mikhail Gorbachev launched his perestroika, the Soviet budget came under serious pressure from two sides. On the revenue side the anti-alcohol campaign led to shortfalls in the collection of turnover taxes, and on the expenditure side the policy of "speeding up" (*uskorenie*) led to increased expenditure on retooling industry. In 1985, the consolidated budget went into the red for the first time in the post-war period.

From Table 6.1 we can see how the initial drop in revenue and the rapid growth in expenditure combined to produce a four-fold growth in the

Table 6.1 Soviet budget deficits, 1985–91 (Billion roubles, 1991: Russian Federation)

	1985	1986	1987	1988	1989	1990	1991
Revenue	367.7	366.0	360.1	365.1	384.9	410.1	316.4
Expenditure	386.0	415.5	429.3	445.9	465.1	485.6	731.5
Deficit	−18.3	−49.6	−69.2	−80.8	−80.2	−75.5	−415.1
% of GDP	−2.4	−6.2	−8.4	−9.2	−8.5	−7.9	−31.9

Source: Illarionov, A. 1995. Popytki provedeniya politiki finansovoi stabilizatsii v SSSR i v Rossii, *Voprosy Ekonomiki*, **7**, 23.

deficit between 1985 and 1988, but also how the situation in 1989–90 showed some improvement. Most importantly, however, we can see how events in 1991 produced a situation where – in the Russian Federation – the deficit spiralled completely out of hand, setting the stage for the drawn-out process of inflation that has been recorded above.

Returning to the latter part of the 1980s, Gorbachev's government decided to cover the growing deficits by way of credits from Gosbank SSSR, the Soviet state bank. Having increased by merely 2.8 per cent of GDP in 1986, in 1990 the growth of Gosbank credits was equal to 14.1 per cent of GDP. As a result, the annual rate of growth in money supply (M2) increased in 1987–90 to 14.1–15.8 per cent. As a measure of the growing inflationary overhang, the ratio of M2 to GDP increased from 52.6 per cent in 1984, to 67.7 per cent in December 1990.[3]

Given that Soviet prices were still state controlled, these inflationary pressures could not be translated directly into open inflation, but below the surface dangerous cracks were opening up. The pressure on the black and kolkhoz markets was increasing rapidly, and shelves in the state stores were being emptied. Although the writing was thus on the wall, through to the end of 1990 the Soviet government under Nikolai Ryzhkov remained passive, seemingly incapable of bringing itself to take remedial action.

At the beginning of 1991, Valentin Pavlov was appointed to lead a new government, which immediately undertook a 50 per cent increase in producer prices. This at once reduced the ratio of M2 to GDP from 67.6 to 56.9 per cent. There was also a new turnover tax of 5 per cent, and a rather odd currency reform, the withdrawal of all old 50 and 100 rouble banknotes. At first, consumer prices were left unchanged, implying a tremendous need for subsidies to producers, but on 2 April a 55 per cent increase in consumer prices followed, bringing the M2/GDP ratio down to 51.0 per cent.[4]

Although Pavlov's actions fell far short of a true market-oriented reform, they did succeed in bringing about a short-term easing of the inflationary overhang. But that was to be a temporary victory. In April, the fiscal war between Mikhail Gorbachev and Boris Yeltsin kicked in. During

May–December 1991, the average monthly growth in money supply (M2) increased to 8.1 per cent and by the end of the year M2/GDP had reached the record level of 76.5 per cent.[5] Although the system was now beginning to break down, prices still remained fixed.

The real watershed came with Boris Yeltsin's programme for systemic change. Once it was decided to liberalize and privatize large parts of the Russian economy, the rules of the game underwent a fundamental transformation. Given that the bulk of previous budget revenue had been incomes from state enterprises, the need for a new tax system suddenly took on the utmost importance.

We may recall here, from Chapter 4 above, one of the conclusions that was reached by the IMF *et al.* study on how to reform the Soviet economy: "The tax administration will require extensive reorganization and an overhaul of procedures to adapt it to a market economy. Substantial reforms of the budgetary process, which to date has been tied closely to the plan, will also be required."[6]

With the attempted transition to market economy, the creation of a functioning system of taxes and subsidies suddenly became an absolute necessity for the very running of the state, no matter what the level of ambition, be it a welfare state or a pure nightwatchman state.

At first, the failure to achieve this transformation of the way in which the state raised revenue to cover its basic functions may be put down to the fact that the technical skills necessary were largely absent. That, however, was a fairly trivial problem of retooling and retraining, which merits no further comment.

Remaining on the purely technical level, there is a related and fairly simple additional reason for the subsequent troubles of Russian tax collection. Given that a new tax system would have to be built from scratch, it was rather likely that substantial inefficiencies would develop, at least initially. If we combine this with the conditions of high inflation that marked the first years of Russian economic reform, we have the makings of another well known negative spiral.

In a situation of high inflation, where the government succeeds in raising taxes only with a certain time lag, the real value of tax collection will be eroded and the government will be tempted into further inflationary financing, thus exacerbating the problem. In the economics literature, this is known as the "Olivera-Tanzi effect".[7]

As will be shown below, however, the main shortcomings of the Russian tax system would be the result of factors of far greater importance than these purely technical ones, factors that were endogenous to the political process at the very heart of the system. Before proceeding to explanations, however, the gravity of the problem may be reflected in a few statistics.

Measured in relation to GDP, taxes paid into the federal budget (in money form) dropped from 16.6 per cent in 1992, to 12.4 per cent in 1993,

11.5 per cent in 1994, 9.4 per cent in 1995 and a low of merely 5 per cent in the first six months of 1996 (which was the time of the presidential election campaign).[8] This, moreover, took place within the framework of a drastically shrinking GDP, implying that the real crunch on the expenditure side was of a much greater magnitude than is implied by the revenue statistics given here.

In the end, however, a budget will – by logical necessity – always have to balance. Being faced with serious shortfalls on the revenue side, the Russian government resorted to a policy of aggressive sequestration of practically all kinds of budget obligations, from investments to wage and pension payments.

An IMF official who was involved in the process describes how it got started: "In the last months of 1993, [finance minister] Fyodorov used the only weapon that remained in his arsenal: he simply refused to pay. The policy of aggressive sequestration continued in the first half of 1994 and, coupled with a restrained monetary policy . . . it helped to achieve a significant albeit temporary reduction in inflation."[9]

This *ad hoc* way of running the budget, which in reality had started in the first weeks of the Gaidar government, would have a number of detrimental effects, notably so in the creation of a chronic arrears crisis, which we shall have repeated reasons to return to below, both in this and in the following chapter.

An important contributing factor, making it possible for the finance ministry to rely on "aggressive sequestration", may be found in the constant political turmoil that has surrounded the process of getting federal budgets approved by the Duma.

While the budgets for 1992 and 1993 were approved only after the end of the respective fiscal years, the 1994 budget was approved in June of that year, i.e. halfway through its implementation. Showing some improvement, the budget for 1995 was approved in February and the budget for 1996 at the end of December 1995. Then it went from bad to worse. While the president signed the budget for 1997 in February of that year, it had already broken down after the first quarter, not to be heard of again, and in 1998 the budget was lost in the general economic collapse.

If we accept that stable and transparent rules of the game are necessary for a positive development in the real sector of the economy, we may begin to appreciate the real gravity of the budget battles. The problem has two main dimensions. On the one hand, aggressive sequestration creates unpredictability in that sphere of the economy which depends on payments out of the budget, notably so in enterprises working under state contracts. On the other, the absence of a stable budget aggravates the already serious problem of a plethora of punitive and inconsistent taxes. A vicious spiral is established where firms that are hunted by an aggressive tax police invest more and more in tax evasion, thus enhancing the aggressiveness of the tax police and the consequences for those who do get caught.

One of the main reasons behind this deplorable process may be found in the patterns of confrontation that were presented in the previous chapter. The essence of shock therapy was not to seek consensus and stable rules, but to ram through an economic reform programme that was deemed at the very outset, by the reformers themselves, to stand no chance of finding a majority constituency. Given that approval of the budget was the only arena where the Duma had any real chance of fighting back, it should have been obvious from the start that this would indeed become the main battlefield.

In order to fully appreciate the damage that would be done to the economy we shall leave for a moment the Kremlin perspective and look instead at the evolution of post-Soviet fiscal relations between the federal centre and the periphery. This takes us into the field of what is known in the economics literature as fiscal federalism.

Pekka Sutela underlines why this topic is so important: "Stabilization policy . . . presupposes both central money creation, recourse to well-defined revenue sources by the centre, and limitations on both national and subnational budgetary deficits."[10]

Putting it more bluntly, in the absence of a working federal agreement we may predict serious regional problems in terms of the creation of various forms of quasi money, of constant struggles over the assignment of taxes and expenditure, and of attempts to shift deficits between different levels in the budget hierarchy. This also is precisely what would happen – and indeed is still happening.

Fiscal federalism

While formally a union, in actual practice the Soviet state was unitary and highly centralized. It was only with the "war of laws" of the late 1980s that previously decorative institutional arrangements in the various republics acquired political significance, and then of a mainly centrifugal nature. Republican legislatures began issuing laws and declarations of sovereignty that eventually led to the collapse of the union.

Embarking on its post-Soviet path of building democracy and market economy, Russia had to deal with the fallout of this process. Itself being a nominal federation, the pre-conditions for a repeat performance were in place, and momentum in that direction had been built up as the subjects of the Russian federation were goaded by the Soviet authorities to break off from the Russian centre. Politically as well as economically the Yeltsin administration was thus faced with the task of finding a working federal arrangement.

In theory, there were good prospects for running parallel processes of democratization and federalization. There are plenty of previous examples where federalism has shown itself to be a superior constitutional arrangement. Sutela holds up the positive experience, "Historically, federalism has proved to be among the most stable and most enduring of polities," but he also warns that "it does seem to require a political environment conducive to popular government and traditions of political co-operation and self-restraint".[11]

The catch, in the Russian case, is that federalism represents a contractual arrangement and thus hinges for its success upon actors who are willing to prefer rules to confrontation. In what was said in the previous chapter, about the games that were played at the centre, we have seen the very opposite, i.e. weak enforcement and a high level of rule aversion, emerge as defining characteristics.

But this was not the only threat to the prospects for establishing a working system of Russian federalism. The context of the Soviet break-up and of the institutional arrangements that were inherited by the Russian Federation added further fuel to the fire.

In contrast to the Soviet Union, which at the time of its death consisted of 15 republics of formally equal status, the Russian Federation is made up of 89 federation subjects (if Chechnya is included), which are grouped into categories of different status. There are 21 ethnically defined republics (including Chechnya), 55 Russian regions (*oblasts* and *krais*), plus 11 autonomous regions (*okrugs*) located within the krais, and two cities – Moscow and St Petersburg – "of federal rank". The new federation charters that were approved in March 1992 explicitly recognized this rather complicated constitutional arrangement.

In the first couple of years after the Soviet break-up, there emerged in the Russian Federation a clear difference between territorially defined regions and ethnically defined republics. While the former were content with seeking to gain as much economic and legal autonomy as possible, many of the latter had outspoken ambitions of seeking political autonomy or even full independence. The most extreme case was Chechnya, which also provided the most tragic manifestation of the struggle between centre and periphery.

In 1993, these various centrifugal forces were making heavy inroads into the ongoing work on drafting a new Russian constitution. As we may recall from above, the draft that existed towards the end of summer provided for a considerable devolution of power. Following the October events, however, considerable redrafting was undertaken, making the final version that was put to a referendum on 12 December 1993 a more centralized product.

These observations, however, concern only the *formal* rules that make up but one part of the picture. Throughout, the real trouble has rested in the dimension of enforcement, where bilateral bargaining has systematically served to preclude the emergence of clear-cut rules. The underlying tensions are best reflected in the complicated budget procedures.

In the literature on fiscal federalism, some of the standard criteria are efficiency, equity, transparency and simplicity, i.e. the arrangement should support a rational fiscal policy, it should be consistent with national goals on income distribution, it should rest on objective, stable and non-negotiable criteria, and it should be simple, so as not to invite complicated rule evasion.

Looking back at the track record of Russian fiscal policy from 1992 onwards, we may see rather clearly how the confrontations that were played out between the Central Bank and the Ministry of Finance at the central level were replicated in similar patterns of confrontation between the different levels in the budget hierarchy. In that process, all of the above criteria have been violated.

The Russian federal arrangement was grossly inefficient from the start, most obviously so on the revenue side, where shortfalls in tax revenue were to become chronic. Whether it is in tune with national goals on income distribution is hard to say, since it is hard to identify such goals, but it is obvious that the regional income differentials will have some rather unpleasant consequences, both for national growth prospects and for the political cohesion of the federation.

All of this may be derived from a gross violation of the principle of transparency. Instead of resting on objective and non-negotiable rules, the basis for Russian federalism has degenerated into a steady stream of bilateral negotiations where the outcomes have reflected the strength of the respective actors, rather than considerations of federal needs. This process is diametrically opposed to the principle of *salus publica suprema lex est.*

The present-day social contract in Russia has been portrayed by Stephen Holmes as an "exchange of unaccountable power for untaxable wealth".[12] In many ways precisely this pattern may also be identified in the regional dimension. Peter Reddaway offers the following portrayal:

> Centre-region relations are fraught with political and economic tensions, and the federal government is usually in the weaker position. The ten or so economically strong regions and republics can, with skillful leadership, almost dictate their terms to Moscow. They sell temporary political support in return for less temporary tax concessions, which are then written into a treaty between the region and Moscow.[13]

In all fairness, this rather deplorable outcome must be seen within the highly specific context of the rapid Soviet disintegration. In the first round of its regional game, the Russian government was burdened with the legacy of this process. As we have seen above, in his struggle against Mikhail Gorbachev, Boris Yeltsin had called upon the Soviet republics to take all the power they could handle, the obvious aim being to free his Russia from Gorbachev's Soviet power, and in response, Gorbachev had issued the same call to the constituent parts of the Russian Federation.

Once the Soviet Union was gone, the main challenge to the Russian central authorities was to prevent a repetition of the Soviet break-up within the Russian Federation. With the *de facto* exception of Chechnya, this ambition seems by now to have been formally met. In terms of international law, the Russian Federation is a sustainable and legitimate state.

The price for this success, however, has not only been paid in blood on the killing fields of Chechnya. It has also been paid in terms of a serious erosion of the pre-conditions for building a working contract of fiscal federalism. Sutela explicitly recognizes that in contrast to previous examples of constructive federation building, Russia has found herself in a defensive position:

> The original purpose of federalism was therefore either nation-building or the joining of forces for common defense. Either way, federalism was a way of creating cohesion. In the Russian case, however, federalism is now more appropriately viewed as an attempt to contain at least some of the obvious threats to cohesion.[14]

Seeking to meet the dual goals of preventing further demands for full independence from the federation and of securing political support for his own regime, Boris Yeltsin has been ready and willing to enter into a string of bilateral negotiations with the various federation subjects. The results of these negotiations have been a steady growth in the number of bilateral power-sharing treaties between the centre and the federation subjects.

At first, bargaining took place between the centre and the republics and the outcomes were mostly informal, but over time the regions were being included as well and formal treaties were signed. The first case was in February 1994, when Moscow concluded a formal treaty with Tatarstan, which according to its own constitution was a sovereign state. In the spring of 1996, which was marked by the presidential election campaign, the process snowballed and presently treaties have been signed with well over half of the subjects of federation.

Most of these are within the limits of the federal law, but there are cases where arrangements have been agreed that are in violation of both federal and constitutional law.[15] In Tatarstan, for example, Moscow has granted such far-reaching concessions that the situation is approaching *de facto* independence, but in many other cases minor concessions on taxes and subsidies have been sufficient.

At first sight, one might be lured into viewing this process as a positive way of enhancing stability, which also is the official policy line. In a speech towards the end of October 1997, for example, President Yeltsin referred to the revenue sharing and policy provisions of these treaties as a "fundamentally new constitutional instrument", which is necessary to prevent "a weak rag state in which everyone is out for himself."[16]

Somewhat ironically, however, this has very little to do with constitutional choice, or with constitutionalism in general. In actual fact, it represents the very opposite and can thus hardly fail to have seriously detrimental consequences for the constitutional process as such. Not to mention the impact on fiscal discipline in general.

Noting that the "rules, agreements, and laws themselves remain highly unstable, excessively complicated, and often contradictory", the OECD emphasizes the latter:

> The presence of a high degree of discretion and uncertainty not only leads to wasteful rent-seeking activities, associated with the continual necessity to lobby and pressure higher levels of government for more advantageous conditions and allocations. It also perpetuates the common perception that revenue-sharing rules and transfers are "soft" and can adjust on a regular basis to reflect particular budgetary situations. This dampens the incentives for officials at lower levels of government to behave in a fiscally responsible manner.[17]

In order to make sense out of this extra-constitutional bargaining process we must recognize that the motives are not primarily economic, but rather political. The winners are, on the one hand, Boris Yeltsin who secures – governor by governor and president by president – support for his own power as president of Russia, and, on the other, the regional and republican leaders who find themselves in a situation where everyone truly *is* out for himself. The price for these achievements, however, is paid in terms of moving ever farther away from the pre-conditions for creating a functioning federal agreement, meeting the criteria outlined above.

Comparing this Russian outcome to the textbook ideal of fiscal federalism, Sutela finds cause to question in which direction the process is moving:

> The ideal, however, is so far from contemporary Russian reality that one is left wondering whether Russia, as it withdraws from a unitary state, will really see federalism as its destination, or whether federalism will only prove a way station along the road of further devolution towards something still unknown.[18]

The only real solution to this problem would have been a firm commitment to a credible tax system, including the federal dimension, but that was an undertaking which would not even be proposed until the spring of 1997, and which foundered completely in the crisis of 1998. As a result of this failure, the Russian government came to find itself in a situation of steadily shrinking budget revenues, where the question of the resultant deficit simply had to become a constant irritant in its relations with the IMF.

It is against this background that we must view the changes in the rules of the game that accompanied moving from high to low inflation.

A market for state securities

Being barred from creating new money, the Russian government set out to look for another short-term non-solution to the problem of the persisting budget deficits. The choice was to embark instead on a path of borrowing, from domestic as well as external sources. Thus was born the Russian market for state securities, an innovation the implications of which would be far-reaching indeed.

In principle, the sale of state securities was nothing new to Moscow. After repudiating the old tsarist debt, the Soviet government soon began issuing domestic bonds, albeit under a somewhat different regime. Citizens were attracted into buying not by high money yields but by the prospect that upon maturity they might, say, be allowed to purchase a car.

After the Soviet break-up, the new Russian government began issuing domestic bonds (ovvzs), which were denominated in hard currency. Often known as "MinFins" or "taiga bonds", these securities grew rapidly, from an outstanding stock of 3.3 trillion roubles by the end of 1992 to 35.3 trillion roubles by the end of 1995.[19]

Although an important source of revenue, these bonds would not have any real impact on the way in which the domestic money game was played. It was the introduction of rouble denominated domestic debt instruments that would radically alter the rules of the game and thus the money-making strategies.

The first three-month treasury bills (GKO – *gosudarstvennye kratkosrochnye obligatsii*) were introduced already in May 1993, and in October six-month T-bills followed. In spite of the early start, however, it would take some time before this addition to the financial markets could assume any significant role. The turning point arrived in June 1995, when bonds (OFZ– *obligatsii federalnogo zaima*) with a quarterly coupon were introduced.[20]

The reason why the securities market was so slow in developing may be derived from Table 6.2. Throughout 1994 we can see a rather peculiar pattern of monthly inflation rates first coming down and then beginning to

Table 6.2 Monthly inflation rates, 1994–5

	Jan.	Feb.	Mar.	April	May	June	July	Aug.	Sept.	Oct.	Nov.	Dec.
1994	17.9	10.7	7.4	8.5	6.9	6.0	5.3	4.6	7.7	11.8	14.2	16.4
1995	17.8	11.0	8.9	8.5	7.9	6.7	5.4	4.6	4.5	4.7	4.5	3.2

Source: Monthly issues of *Ekonomika i Zhizn* 1994/5.

Table 6.3 Russian financial markets, 1995–6
(Percentage shares, January–January)

	1995	1996
Currency market	44.3	6.0
Interbank credits	35.3	13.1
State securities	20.4	80.9

Source: Illarionov, A. 1996a. Upushchennyi shans,
Voprosy Ekonomiki, **3**, p. 98.

rise again. The reasons behind this pattern are linked to the games that were played with the IMF over the "Systemic Transformation Facility". Without repeating the details of that process, we can note that while inflation remained high, inflationary financing was easier than borrowing. In the spring of 1995, however, austerity was beginning to take serious root and by summer the period of high inflation was over.

If we proceed to look at Table 6.3, we may see that this change of monetary regime – from high to low inflation – did produce a radical reorientation of money-making strategies. During 1995, operations on the currency market plummeted, while state securities increased to claim a stunning 80.9 per cent of total turnover on the financial markets. At the beginning of 1996, Russia's financial infrastructure was completely dominated by the government.

While the pay off matrix had been changed, most notably so in terms of a drastic reduction in government seigniorage revenue and in the scope for banks to speculate in the currency market, the predatory nature of the games had not changed. Those who had already made fortunes via speculation in the currency market – chiefly the banks – began moving their capital into the securities market, where yields were rising rapidly. The impact on the Russian economy of this transformation would be every bit as destructive as under the previous regime of high inflation.

At first, however, 1995 did appear to be the decisive year, when stabilization could have been successfully accomplished.[21] On paper at least, all the necessary conditions were met. On 10 March, the State Duma passed a budget law that called for a substantial reduction in the budget deficit for 1995. And in order to provide credibility for that call, it barred the Central Bank from issuing further direct credit to the government. It was in support of this move that the IMF granted the $6.5 billion credit, which would make it possible to finance the lion's share of the remaining deficit in a non-inflationary way.

On casual inspection, it would seem that there was considerable success, and that 1995 was indeed the year of turnaround. While federal budget revenues remained at the same level as in 1994 (13.4 per cent of GDP), federal budget expenditure was cut by a third, from 24.6 per cent to 17.1 per cent of GDP. As a result, the federal budget deficit was reduced from 11.2 per cent of GDP in 1994, to an acceptable 3.7 per cent in 1995.[22]

The impression of a turnaround was also supported by a number of other indicators, notably so by the decisive break with the past pattern of high and variable inflation. As monthly inflation was brought down during the year, from 17.8 per cent to merely 3.2 per cent, the currency could also be successfully stabilized. On 6 July, a "rouble corridor" was introduced, which in essence provided a sort of crawling peg regime.

A further sign of health was that the Central Bank increased its foreign exchange holdings more than eight-fold, bringing its gross reserves by the end of the year to $17 billion, and its net reserves to $7.8 billion. Finally, at the beginning of summer, there were also signs that even the real sector might be turning around. In June, industrial production was 2 per cent higher than in May.

Riding on this wave of optimism, in October the OECD published its first ever country report on Russia. It painted a rosy picture indeed of the Russian economy, talking about a turnaround and holding up a promise of a possible 1996 real GDP growth of up to 10 per cent.[23] Regrettably, however, Russian reality would fail to live up to these expectations.

The problem that very few seemed willing at the time to recognize is indicated by the Russian economist Andrei Illarionov:

> However, the most important instrument in cutting government expenditure was not reforms in those sectors where the introduction of new legal and economic rules and procedures were needed, but a resolute reduction of financing for a variety of budget items, coupled to a withholding of disbursement of already agreed expenditures. Naturally, such a policy provoked a highly negative reaction from all recipients of funds from the budget. But most importantly – it failed to assure stability and continuity in case of changes in the country's political climate.[24]

It is only by reorienting our attention from *what* was achieved to *how* it was achieved that we may gain a better understanding of why 1995 did not turn out to be the year of breakthrough for the Russian economy. On closer inspection, we will find that the main fault lies in the same dimension as it did in 1992–4. The government proceeded to play according to its new rules, without being able to come up with effective mechanisms of enforcement, and without even *trying* to influence the old norm systems. The financial sphere again provides an ideal illustration.

When the Duma passed its budget law, there were good reasons indeed to rein in the government's access to easy sources of (inflationary) financing. During the first quarter of 1995, the Central Bank provided 3.5 trillion

Table 6.4 Credits to the federal budget, 1993–6 (Per cent of total tax receipts, 1996: first half)

	1992	1993	1994	1995	1996
Total credits	116.0	32.3	21.5	38.9	68.7
★ State securities	0.0	0.9	9.8	17.3	37.3
★ External credits	116.0	31.4	11.7	21.6	31.4
IMF	8.6	7.3	4.7	17.3	14.3
Governments, banks	107.4	24.1	6.9	4.3	17.1

Source: Illarionov, A. 1996b. Bremya gosudarstva, *Voprosy Ekonomiki*, **9**, p. 9.

roubles in straight credits to the Ministry of Finance, which added a further 4.3 trillion roubles of its own by issuing promissory notes (*kaznacheiskie obyazatelstva*, or simply KO).[25]

We shall have more to say about the latter financial instruments in a moment; here we shall merely point at their overall importance. According to figures presented by the Russian Institute for Economic Analysis, money supply (M2) in the first quarter increased by on average 4 per cent per month if KO are excluded, and by 5.4 per cent if KO is included.[26] This rather significant difference indicated the beginning of a practice of monetary rule evasion, which in 1996–7 would come to assume an explosive pattern.

By the summer of 1995, however, the issuing of KO had been stopped. In July, the federal budget showed a deficit corresponding to merely 1.5 per cent of monthly GDP, and in August there was even a surplus. As a result, credits granted by the Central Bank in the first quarter could be repaid. And the issuing of new KO, which had long been a bone of contention in relations with the IMF, could be cut to a point where from August onwards repayments began to exceed new issues.[27]

With both these channels of soft credit being closed, and with federal budget expenditure being trimmed to a point that was clearly acceptable to the IMF, the Russian government would indeed seem to have been on the right tracks. What then was it that went wrong? Table 6.4 provides part of the answer.

There is one pattern here that sets Russia apart from all other former socialist economies, namely the heavy initial dependence on external credits. In spite of all that has been said above, about the severe criticism that was directed at the IMF in particular for not providing sufficient economic assistance, Table 6.4 shows that in 1992, foreign credits corresponded to 116 per cent of Russian tax revenue. Measured in relation to GDP, we get a figure of 19.2 per cent.[28]

It remains a fact that much of the external credits that are shown in the table represented phantom aid, but this is a point that has been made previously. Here we shall note that domestic borrowing was nil in 1992 and remained insignificant in 1993. It was only in 1994 that it began assuming any real importance, and in 1995 that real growth began to set in. In the spring of 1996, it overshadowed even the massive amounts that were offered by the IMF and other foreign creditors, in order to support Boris Yeltsin's re-election bid (more about that below).

Although certainly impressive, it is not the rapid growth as such of domestic borrowing that is of interest here. The real damage to the economy would be done as a result of the way in which the Russian government decided to operate its borrowing. If we accept that on the domestic scene it was basically only the commercial banks, which had grown fat during the years of high inflation, that had sufficient loanable funds, it follows that we are approaching a situation of very intimate links between the government and the banks, links that would produce serious distortions.

An obvious way of avoiding much future trouble would have been to allow foreign actors to enter the market. That would have been the collectively rational solution, in the sense that it would have precluded yields from rising to their subsequent astronomical levels. From the individually rational perspective of the major Russian banks, however, there was all to be gained from blocking the entry of foreigners. And in this endeavour the Russian bankers prevailed.

When the Russian government finally did allow external investors to take part in T-bill auctions, which happened in early February 1996, their participation was surrounded by complicated rules restricting the rights to convert rouble gains into hard currency. The effective outcome of these restrictions was that the return to foreign investments in GKOS was capped at 19 per cent. Nevertheless, during 1996 non-residents did purchase $3.5 billion in GKOS ($5.6 billion if OFZS are included),[29] and by mid-1997 they were estimated to hold $15 billion of GKOS, representing 25 per cent of the entire stock.[30]

With the market thus becoming more or less monopolized by the big Russian banks, the Russian government – willingly – entered into a vicious spiral where larger and larger issues of securities – at higher and higher yields – were made. One reason behind this development was that all receipts from the sales of securities went straight into an expanding black hole in the budget, meaning that no money was available for yield payments.

Thus, allowing domestic actors to effectively monopolize lending to the Russian government was only part of the story. Of equal importance is the fact that the rapidly increasing cost of servicing the domestic debt was handled as a separate item, which was not counted as government expenditure: "From the beginning of 1996, government expenditure on servicing this type of debt has in practice not been included on the federal budget expenditure side. The treasury balances all turnover on the GKO market, including income from new issues designed to redeem old ones."[31]

This observation has some relevance to our previous account of the games that have been played with the IMF. If debt service had been properly accounted for, the reported budget deficit would have been much higher than was tolerable to the IMF. At the end of 1996, for example, the budget deficit was 3.5 per cent of GDP according to Russian Finance Ministry definitions – with GKO payments included it would have been 7.7 per cent.[32] (Both the IMF and others, such as the OCED, do report deficit figures also including debt service, but it is the lower ones that figure in most "political" contexts.)

As a result of these arrangements, domestic borrowing by the Russian government came to rest on a rather innovative approach, whereby ever larger issues of new securities were made in order not only to redeem old issues but also to cover the rapidly rising yields.

The situation was aggravated by the fact that the lion's share of the securities market was three-month treasury bills. The growing importance of six-month GKOS, and the introduction of OFZS, did serve to bring about a reduction in the share of three-month GKOS during 1995, from 70.5 per cent to 59.5 per cent,[33] but even the latter figure indicates a serious problem in debt management.[34]

During the course of 1995, the monthly expenditure needed to redeem mature paper grew from 2.2 trillion roubles to 13.8 trillion roubles. The outcome for 1995 as a whole was that new securities (GKO and OFZ) worth a total of 160 trillion roubles were issued, thus bringing the size of the domestic debt from 88.4 trillion roubles to 202.9 trillion roubles.[35] By international standards, the relation of debt to GDP was still very low (below 20 per cent), but the rapid growth was a clear sign of trouble ahead.

Although it was becoming increasingly obvious, at least to outside observers, that this kind of borrowing went far beyond any form of macroeconomic rationality, the system had acquired a life of its own, one, moreover, that to a narrow circle of actors was profitable indeed. In the very short term, the government was winning and the banks were winning. But the financial system was suffering – badly.

In the spring of 1996, when annual inflation was about 40 per cent, the securities market reached clearly absurd proportions. Following a peak of about 130 per cent at the end of 1995, annualized yields to maturity on three- and six-month GKOS fell below 100 per cent at the beginning of January and to around 60 per cent at the end of the month. That level was then maintained until mid-March, when it began rising again. At the beginning of April it passed 90 per cent and by mid-May it had reached 150 per cent. It would remain within that range until after the presidential election, when it fell back to more modest levels.

Longer-term OFZ bonds, with fixed coupons, showed an even more dramatic rise in yields, as increased sales of state securities put a downward pressure on prices. At the beginning of April the OFZS passed 100 per cent.

By the end of April the 500 per cent level had been reached and on 21 May prices had been so depressed that the annualized yield to maturity was pushed up to touch 600 per cent! By mid-July it had fallen back to below 150 per cent and it would then continue down.[36]

The volume of funds rolling into the treasury was staggering. During March alone, the government raised 18 trillion roubles on the securities market, which was about twice the planned volume. In April, the volume fell off somewhat, but yields continued to rise. No price seemed to be too high to finance a presidential re-election campaign the costs of which may have run into billions of dollars.

Although it was becoming increasingly clear that this could not go on for much longer, finding a cure was not so easy. While a sharp reduction in yields would force a wave of bankruptcies among the banks, which had become dependent for their very existence on revenue from the securities market, maintaining the pyramid game would force everything else out of the financial markets, making an eventual crash inevitable.

It is hardly surprising that this development generated expectations for wide ranging nationalizations to take place. As this would play an important role in the presidential election campaign, we shall have reason to return to it below. Here the time has come to look at the role of the Central Bank.

The role of the Central Bank

As had been the case in 1992–4, in 1995 the commercial banks were again to be found on the winning side, reaping considerable gains from the government's economic policy. But this time they would not be allowed to keep their entire windfall profits. The reason was that the role of the Central Bank also underwent a fundamental change.

After having been part of the government apparatus and relied upon to provide direct credits to the budget, in 1995 the Bank assumed a more independent stance. One reason was the budget law. Between 1994 and 1995, the overall growth in Central Bank lending fell from 201 per cent to 49 per cent. As a result, the share of straight government credits fell from 69.2 per cent to 19.1 per cent of total Central Bank lending.[37]

This decoupling of the Central Bank from the government could have led to the creation of an independent Central Bank, charged solely with monitoring interest rates and money supply, much as has been the trend in the European Union. Instead, however, it led to the creation of an even more formidable opponent to the government's quest for stabilization.

First of all, it should be noted that the budget law far from terminated the role of the Central Bank as creditor to the government. It simply acquired a new form, operating instead via the secondary market for state securities. Between January and November, such operations increased

Table 6.5 Central Bank re-finance rates, 1995

	Re-finance Rate	Inflation
January	200	17.8
May	195	7.9
June	180	6.7
October	170	4.7
December	160	3.2

Sources: Illarionov, A. 1996a. Upushchennyi shans, *Voprosy Ekonomiki*, **3**, p. 93, monthly issues of *Ekonomika i Zhizn*, 1995.

five-fold, from 0.15 per cent to 0.72 per cent of GDP. In the latter month alone, the Central Bank bought 3.8 trillion roubles worth of state securities, corresponding to 2.1 per cent of that month's GDP. Adding that the budget deficit for that month amounted to 4.2 per cent, it follows that the Central Bank covered half of the government's budget deficit.[38]

Since operating via the secondary market is more costly than providing straight credits, the outcome of the budget law in this respect was a considerable increase in the cost of government debt management. But that was not all. By allowing the Central Bank to operate under no clear rules on what it should and should not do, the stage was set for further trouble.

One rather destructive policy was pursued *vis-à-vis* the commercial banks, which had built great fortunes during the years of high inflation and currency speculation. In order to deal with the rouble crisis that erupted at the beginning of January 1995, the Central Bank raised its re-finance rate to 200 per cent. There was nothing to be said about this intervention as such, but all the more to be said about the fact, as shown in Table 6.5, that the subsequent fall in inflation was met only by token reductions in the re-finance rate.

To the high real re-finance rate, which soon enough proved to be forbidding for the commercial banks, the Central Bank also added substantial increases in reserve requirements. The consequent results were drastic. In March, Central Bank credit to the commercial banks accounted for a little over 2 per cent of GDP. By May it had fallen to 0.6 per cent, and by June it was practically zero.[39]

For the commercial banks, life was now becoming difficult – in spite of the high revenues obtained from the securities market. With low inflation and a stable rouble putting an effective end to the easy speculative gains that had been made during 1992–4, the high re-finance rate and the high reserve requirements added burdens that proved overwhelming. The crisis that rocked the Moscow inter-bank market on 23–24 August must thus be blamed at least in part on the Central Bank.[40]

But the Bank did not use its freedom only to depress the banking sector. It also engaged in foreign exchange operations that would add their share of destructive effects.

During its January 1995 defence of the rouble, the Central Bank used up $1.7 billion of its reserves. Then it suddenly changed tack, embarking instead on a course that aimed to depress the rouble. In so doing, it again set a straight collision course with both the government and the IMF.

Market interventions caused the rouble to fall against the dollar by 11.3 per cent in February, by 13.3 per cent in March and by 5.5 per cent in April. The Central Bank was selling roubles and the commercial banks were selling dollars. (During February and March, the latter sold about $2 billion.) During the second quarter, the Central Bank bought $6.2 billion. In May, when the Bank spent 13.4 trillion roubles (11 per cent of GDP) to buy $2.6 billion, the rouble plunged to a record low of 5,130 roubles to the dollar. The result was a substantial increase in the growth of money supply (M2) – from 3.3 per cent per month during the first quarter, to 13.5 per cent per month during the second quarter.[41]

According to the agreement with the IMF, by 1 July, 1995 the Central Bank should have held $1.9 billion in reserves. It actually held $7.4 billion. The difference had been bought at the expense of creating 25 trillion extra roubles, causing an increase in monthly inflation of 3–4 percentage points.[42] This is where we may find one of the most important explanations as to why 1995 did not prove to be the year of turnaround.

The use of money surrogates

The basic reasoning behind the games that were played in and around the securities market was linked to the government's new way of covering the deficit in its budget. In the previous chapter we saw how revenue shortfalls could be successfully covered by inflationary financing, but with inflation coming down that road was now to be closed.

For a while, rapidly shrinking seigniorage revenue could be replaced by income from the sales of securities. At first impression, there were winners all around. The commercial banks were happy enough to take part, in order to compensate for their own loss of revenue from the currency market, and the Central Bank, as we have seen above, also managed to secure for itself a winning position.

At the other side of the table, enterprise managers found that money which should have gone to paying wages could be used (with impunity) to buy high yield GKOs instead. While this temptation must have been generally difficult to resist, some of the "red directors" probably found additional benefit in the fact that non-payment of wages would provoke worker discontent with the government's reform policies. In the latter case there would thus be a double gain from buying GKOs.

But to the government, borrowing money was far from enough. It would also resort to the use of a variety of money surrogates, and in a big way.[43] In the previous chapter we mentioned *en passant* how the Ministry of Finance began, in 1994, to issue a sort of promissory note, known as KO. The reason behind this move was the growing volume of outstanding mutual debts.

The issuing of KO provided the government with an easy way of offering extra-budgetary credits and subsidies to a variety of local actors. But soon enough there would also be a price to pay in terms of a multiplier effect. Being faced with the government's parallel policy of aggressive sequestration, local authorities were not slow to follow the example of resorting to the use of money surrogates. And once they had begun issuing their own KO, in order to pay debts to local enterprises, it followed that they themselves in return had to accept KO as payment in lieu of taxes, thus aggravating the problem.

In the summer of 1995 the IMF succeeded in putting a temporary brake on the practice of issuing money surrogates, but when it returned, towards the end of the year, it did so with a vengeance. Given the disastrous effects that this would have for tax collection, we may be justified in taking a brief look at the background. As was the case with the securities market, there is a pre-history from the Soviet days.

The use of money surrogates, then known as *vekselya*, for commercial credit purposes was regulated by a decree from the Supreme Soviet of the RSFSR in June 1991, and in October 1993 a presidential decree permitted the transformation of inter-enterprise arrears into *veksel* credits, explicitly allowing both secondary trading and mutual cancellation. Generally lax regulation, however, led to a proliferation of *veksel* issues that soon went beyond the control of central authorities.[44]

Vekselya have been issued by banks and enterprises, as well as by federal and local authorities. In the latter cases, it has quite simply been a question of resorting to payment of outstanding bills by the use of quasi money such as promissory notes, but in the case of banks, there has been a higher degree of sophistication. Banks have issued *vekselya* both as an instrument of savings, offering investors an interesting new market, and as a credit instrument (the credit being offered as a *veksel* rather than in hard cash).

While recognizing a variety of negative effects of this proliferation of money surrogates, the OECD rightly underlines that – given the rules of the game – the banks did develop considerable sophistication: "In addition to offering a simple but useful means of clearing accounts, the practice of using *vekselya* to finance an entire cycle of production is an impressive financial innovation."[45]

The story, in the latter case, derives from the fact that by granting credit to a producing enterprise, a commercial bank runs the risk of being pulled into the general morass of non-payments. Granting the credit in the form of a *veksel* offers a way out of this problem.

The first step is to give cash credit to the producer, which starts the process. Then a *veksel* credit is granted to the firm that will realize the final sale of the product. These money surrogates are then passed on upstream and finally reach the original producer, which uses them to repay the cash credit. The only weak point is that the bank must make sure that the final sale can be made good in hard cash, which may then be used to repay the *veksel* credit. All other aspects of the production cycle are under its firm control.

Having thus recognized that there are indeed positive innovations involved in this game, we must underline that this is a very partial offset of all the negative features. There are two major reasons which may drive an enterprise into the use of money surrogates, both being symptoms of serious systemic malfunctions.

In the first case, enterprises actually prefer money surrogates to hard cash: "Enterprises prefer to accept *vekselya*, which they can use to purchase goods from other enterprises, as opposed to money, which might be taken by tax collectors when it passes through the banking system."[46] The image here is one of banks and enterprises creating a parallel monetary system, which lies outside the realm of tax inspection, and thus renders the future of the tax system rather uncertain.

In the second case, money surrogates are preferred not to money but to barter, which grew from less than 10 per cent of all industrial sales in 1992–3 to well over 40 per cent in 1997.[47] Enterprises may either issue their own *vekselya*, which is done primarily by the big infrastructure enterprises and utility providers, or they may use bank *vekselya*. The former are highly illiquid and very risky, at times even redeemable only in the products of the issuer. Here the image is one of a serious degradation of the Russian monetary system as such.

Which of the two reasons is more important is not entirely clear, but the OECD is probably correct in concluding that "the enormous increase in barter and money surrogates in 1996 would appear to be linked more with growing liquidity and payment problems, mounting fiscal difficulties for all budgets, and the particular advantages to regional administrations discussed above."[48]

Irrespective of reason, the proliferation of barter, mutual offsets (*vzaimozachety*) and money surrogates has wreaked serious havoc on the Russian reform programme as such. Ickes, Murrell and Ryterman find that the "increasing incidence of barter and other non-monetary media of exchange points, in fact, to a *re-demonetization* of the Russian economy," the point being that while the Soviet policy was to demonetize the economy, achieving re-monetization was an important task of market-oriented reform. Thus: "The trend to barter is a serious reversal of market reform."[49]

The end result has been not only a return to the necessarily personal relations of the barter economy, and thus to an erosion of the attempt at introducing the stable and transparent rules that make up the foundation of a working market economy. Even worse, perhaps, is the moral hazard that is involved in allowing local authorities to avoid monetary discipline by issuing their own money surrogates, in the belief that failure will lead to a bailout by the federal government. We shall have reason to return to these aspects at greater length in Chapter 8 below.

During the presidential re-election campaign in the spring of 1996, the Russian government resorted to so many tricks of surrogate financing that the volume of money surrogates in circulation was threatening the financial system as such. In June, for example, a full 10 trillion out of a total of 18 trillion roubles collected in taxes were money surrogates.[50]

During the first half of 1996, banks issued 20 trillion roubles worth of *vekselya*, and enterprises added a further seven trillion roubles. Another innovation, used by the government to pay its bills, was "treasury tax exemptions" (*kaznacheiskie nalogovye osvobozhdeniya*, or KNO), which soon enough were returned to the treasury. In June alone, the latter form of paper accounted for 30 per cent of total tax payments. By that month, it could also be noted that federal tax arrears had risen to 59 trillion roubles.[51]

Having witnessed this degradation of the Russian monetary system, it is of some importance to note that the main reason behind the payment crisis was endogenous to the Russian government's policy making. It was not primarily a question of *refusals* to pay taxes, but of conscious government actions designed to *allow* tax breaks and/or tax deferrals.

As had been the case in the struggle between Yeltsin and Gorbachev, Yeltsin's struggle against communist leader Gennadii Zyuganov (and the war in Chechnya) required substantial handouts from the budget, handouts that could not be even remotely covered by current revenues. Thus the plethora of quasi money.

Given that actions taken by the government via the budget will have substantial multiplier effects for the remainder of the economy, the impact of this practice was of quite some magnitude. In a 1997 article about the problem of non-payments, Nikolai Shmelyov expresses concern that the disease may well turn out to be chronic:

> In the process, there is widespread use of "mutual amnesty" of debts, natural exchange (barter), tax exemptions and lobbying to obtain tax privileges, all forms of quasi money, artificial reduction of output, etc. . . . Step by step the permanent crisis of non-payments is transforming the Russian economy into something of the highest order of deformity, which in the longer term is unfit for life.[52]

The fact that this deplorable outcome was largely the result of conscious actions taken by the federal government is illustrated in Table 6.6. If we begin with taxes paid in money form, add taxes paid in money surrogates,

Table 6.6 Federal budget revenue, 1992–6 (Per cent of GDP, 1996: first six months)

	1992	1993	1994	1995	1996
1. Taxes in money form	16.6	12.4	11.5	9.4	5.0
2. Taxes in money surrogates				0.9	2.7
3. Total taxes (1+2)	16.6	12.4	11.5	10.3	7.7
4. Unpaid taxes (5+6)			1.0	1.4	2.5
5. Tax deferrals			0.8	0.8	1.0
6. Non-payments			0.2	0.6	1.5
7. Tax exemptions					2.3
8. Possible taxes (3+4+7)	16.6	12.4	12.5	11.7	12.5
9. Difference (8–1)			1.0	2.3	7.5
10. Per cent of total taxes (9:3)			8.7	22.3	97.4

Source: Illarionov, A. 1996b. Bremya gosudarstva, *Voprosy Ekonomiki*, **9**, 6.

unpaid taxes (non-payments and deferrals) and tax exemptions, we arrive at a figure of "possible taxes" for the first half of 1996 (i.e. the presidential race) which is about the same as in 1993–4 and actually a little higher than in 1995.

Taking a closer look at the table, we find that the practice of making tax deferrals began in 1994, and that in 1995 the payment of taxes in money surrogates was added, but the proportions were still manageable. It was in the spring of 1996 that the situation went completely out of hand: money surrogates trebled and very substantial tax exemptions were made.

The main lesson to be drawn concerns the driving force behind this deplorable development. Of the difference between rows one and eight, corresponding to 7.5 per cent of GDP, it was only non-payments (1.5 per cent of GDP) that were exogenous to the government's own decision making process. We may conclude, therefore, that the Russian government willingly sacrificed tax discipline in order to gain more leeway for the political campaign.

By July 1996, when Boris Yeltsin had been successfully re-elected, the IMF finally deemed it necessary to demonstrate its dissatisfaction with the poor performance of the Russian tax system. A monthly tranche of the $10.1 billion credit agreed in March was withheld.

There were good reasons for taking this action, but those reasons had been around since the very day when the credit was granted. The long delay in prompting the Russian government to improve tax collection provides yet another illustration of the problems of moral hazard that have been discussed above.

So much for the financial developments during 1995–6. Let us now return to the political agenda, to look at the chain of events that were to provide the real driving force behind the degradation of the financial system. Again we shall see a president who is inclined towards confrontation, who is ready to place his own personal power ambitions before the needs of the economy – seemingly at any cost.

"Chicken" game three: Yeltsin vs. Zyuganov

Where 1995 had been a year of great – if unwarranted – expectations for the Russian economy, the first half of 1996 would turn out to be a time of great trepidation, when the fate of the reform process as a whole was seen to hang in the balance. The reason for this mood change was entirely linked to the question of whether Boris Yeltsin would be able to secure a second term as president, or if he would be forced to hand over power to the communists.

At the beginning of the year, the prospects were not good. With the Chechen war dragging on, the president was trailing in the opinion polls, to the extent even of being almost unthinkable as a candidate for a second presidential term. In the words of Anatolyi Chubais, his popularity rating was "lower than grass".[53] The ensuing election campaign was remarkable in the sense that coming from a seemingly hopeless position, Boris Yeltsin went on to win the re-election, but then fell back again, within weeks, to a position of hopelessly low approval ratings.

In the following pages we shall look at the strategy that served to bring about this strange outcome. In so doing, we shall bear in mind what the confrontational tactics have meant not only for the budget but also for the process of fiscal federalism and constitutionalism in general. Seeking to establish stable and transparent rules of the game, which are backed up by legitimate mechanisms of enforcement, is clearly incompatible with a president who is bent on playing "chicken" games.

In the following chapter we shall see further illustrations of this type of leadership, which will be shown to have further detrimental effects for the officially envisioned movement towards democracy, market economy and the rule of law. Before proceeding to the real confrontation we shall, however, note that as in the case of the game with Khasbulatov, there was a build-up phase that started some time before the actual game.

Round one: build-up

In the aftermath of the shelling of the Moscow White House, Boris Yeltsin repeated more or less the same pattern of behaviour that he had displayed after the previous stand-off around the same building. With the opposition being both beaten and discredited, he had a tremendous opportunity of setting the agenda, of pushing ahead with further measures that might have strengthened his reforms. Instead, he chose to retreat from the daily fray of politics and to intervene only in cases where his own personal power agenda was threatened.

Symbolically, this may be represented by the two issues that were to be taken to the people on 12 December 1993, namely the election to the new Duma and the referendum on the new constitution. In the previous chapter we saw how the president largely ignored the former, while keeping a close eye indeed on the latter.

In the two years that passed between the 1993 and 1995 Duma elections, economic policy went through a great many changes, causing both markets and foreign observers to vacillate between euphoria and despair. In the present chapter we have charted the course of attempted macro-stabilization, which had quite a few ups and downs.

We might also have brought into the picture the programme of mass privatization, which was both launched and completed during this period, and we might have mentioned the war in Chechnya, which started on 11 December 1994, and was to drag on beyond the re-election of Boris Yeltsin.

For the purpose at hand, however, the most important observation concerns the president's continued refusal to engage in any form of serious constituency building. When the time for the December 1995 election was drawing near, Russia's political landscape was an amorphous mess of political clubs and splinter organizations, most of which (with the notable exception of the communists) refused to call themselves "party". Many were simply one-man shows, organizations designed to propel their leader into a position where he could patronize his clients.

When the election campaign started, there were a total of 252 groups of various kinds that sought to be registered as official contenders. Of these no fewer than 43 succeeded in securing the 100,000 signatures that were necessary. It was hardly surprising that Moscow street humour talked about "taxi parties"; they were large enough for 3–4 people, they were running around the capital at random, and passengers could choose to get on or off at will. More seriously, Richard Sakwa has portrayed the situation as one of "proto-parties". The election campaign was to be about men (and to some small extent women) rather than about ideas and political platforms.

While the president himself persisted in his refusal to get involved in election politics, preferring to hover icon-like over the petty squabbles of the politicians, he did talk his prime minister, Viktor Chernomyrdin, into forming a political party of his own. Patrimonially named "Our Home is Russia" (*Nash dom – Rossiya*), it soon came to be known as the "party of power" or simply "Our Home is Gazprom" (*Nash dom – Gazprom*), reflecting the fact that Chernomyrdin had once headed the powerful gas giant and could certainly be assumed to have strong remaining links in that direction.

In sharp contrast to the 1993 election, where there had been a large number of "parties" which to a greater or lesser extent were associated with the president's reform programme, now there was one and only one that was directly associated with the top echelons of power. Thus there would also be a direct test offered of the popularity of the government's reform policies, and that test would not be a favourable one.

Of the 43 parties that were running, only four would make it past the post in the party election (there was a minimum five per cent vote limit). The unrivalled winner was Gennadii Zyuganov's communist party, which got 22.3 per cent of the vote. Then followed Vladimir Zhirinovskii's oddly named "Liberal Democratic Party" with 11.2 per cent, and in only third place was Chernomyrdin's party with 10.1 per cent of the vote. The fourth party to make it into the Duma was Grigorii Yavlinskii's liberal "Yabloko", with merely 6.9 per cent.

Taken as an opinion poll, the December election could be seen as a powerful signal regarding the president's chances in the coming presidential election. Looking only at the party election, which covered half of the 450 seats (the remainder being one-man constituencies), he would have to conclude that around 90 per cent of the electorate had voted against the government's reform policies, and now there would not be sufficient time for him to disassociate himself from that failure.

Adding that only two-thirds of those eligible had actually turned out to vote, and that only 10 per cent of that smaller group had supported the government party, he might have arrived at a figure of no more than 6.6 per cent active support from the Russian population as a whole, were he to continue on the same course as before.

Although early opinion polls confirmed precisely this picture, it seems highly unlikely that Boris Yeltsin would have allowed himself to be greatly influenced by such democratic trivia. Since he could under no circumstances be expected to turn to the communists for support, an all-out confrontation was all that remained. And that, as we know, is what the president does best. The spring of 1996 would thus come to be dominated by a historical trial of strength between Yeltsin and the communists.

The strategy to re-elect would rest on three distinctly separate legs, which, although they did overlap considerably, will be presented below as further consecutive rounds in the game: a) pre-empting the communists, b) securing support from the West, and c) promising the moon to the Russian population. Let us begin with the communists.

Round two: pre-empt the communists

The first step taken by the president on his road to re-election was to clear out of the government the last remnants of the democratic and market-oriented "forces" who had once formed the basis of his own reform programme. The time had now finally come to sacrifice Foreign Minister Andrei Kozyrev, who was replaced by the old KGB-man Yevgenii Primakov, and to let the massively unpopular Anatolyi Chubais quietly disappear into the wings, for a while at least.

With these people out of the way, the communist opposition was left without any clear human targets to attack. They decided instead to concentrate their efforts on two concrete political issues which must have been truly heartfelt, namely the dissolution of the Soviet Union and the privatization of the large state owned enterprises. In so doing, however, they invited Boris Yeltsin to an interesting poker game. Correctly handled, both of these issues could be expected to attract a large number of voters, but in both instances it would be Yeltsin rather than Zyuganov who cashed in the winnings.

Beginning with the former question, we may note that in its last vote before being dissolved for the December 1995 election, the 1993 Duma had narrowly defeated a proposition to declare the dissolution of the Soviet Union – through the Belovezh accords – an illegal act. The margin had been only a few votes.

At the beginning of 1996, the newly elected Duma was pre-occupied with a hostage crisis in Chechnya, but on 15 March they gathered for a new vote on the illegality of the Belovezh accords. This time an overwhelming majority carried the vote – 250 against 98. The strength of the majority sent a shock wave through the former Soviet republics in "the near abroad", where it was realized what might happen if the communists were returned to power in Russia.

Yeltsin's reaction to this challenge was marked by the same tactical dexterity that he had displayed in previous encounters. In public he condemned the Duma's action, holding himself up as the only guarantee against a return to the old system, but on the sly he launched his own project for a re-establishment of a Russian Empire. On 2 April 1996, there was a grand unveiling of a new "Commonwealth of Sovereign Republics" (*Soobshchestvo Suverennykh Respublik*).

The first two members of the new commonwealth were Belarus and the Russian Federation, but Yeltsin declared that it would be open to others as well. With time it was conceivable that even Bulgaria and the Baltic republics might be included. The beauty of it all was manifested not only in the fact that the abbreviation of the new construct recalled memories of the Soviet Union – from sssr to ssr – but also that it was formulated so that further members could be included without the name needing to be changed. Soviet nostalgics no longer needed to vote for Zyuganov.

Turning to the communist programme of undoing much of what Anatolyi Chubais had achieved via mass privatization, Zyuganov's concrete promises had been to re-nationalize the banks and 200 of the largest privatized enterprises. In a deft countermove, Yeltsin appointed a commission that was charged with formulating a comprehensive nationalization decree. The commission was led by Aleksandr Kazakov, the head of the GKI, which had been at the core of the privatization effort.

In the media it was hinted that a "strong man" from the president's immediate vicinity was moving in the background, and in April the security council initiated a search for the culprits behind the mess in the market for state securities. Its report concluded that the process of escalating yields must be stopped, and nationalization was explicitly mentioned as a possible way out. Thus, the communist threat/promise of sweeping re-nationalization had also been emasculated.

Round three: secure the West

While one part of the campaign was thus busy pushing the communists out of the way, another was equally busy seeking to generate the greatest possible political and financial support from the West. Here the main obstacle was the ongoing war in Chechnya, which had produced strong reactions in Western media and might even force Western political leaders to re-evaluate their Russia policy.

In order to fend off all such threats, the campaign managers successfully mobilized the spectre of a return to the old communist system. The tycoon-controlled media were flooded with powerful anti-communist propaganda, ranging from documentary coverage of the Stalinist crimes in the past to ominous messages about what would happen to Russian democracy and freedom of speech in the event of a communist victory.

The rather strange fact that this campaign sought to secure office in democratic Russia for the only (politically) surviving member of the communist party politburo, seems to have caused no unease.

Amidst a barrage of criticism against the brutality of the conflict in Chechnya, the large Western powers gradually fell in behind Boris Yeltsin. While the humanitarian organization *"Médecins sans frontières"* officially announced that the conflict was the worst in which they had ever been involved, the West chose to turn a blind eye and to begin contributing suitable support to Yeltsin's campaign coffers. Perhaps the deciding moment arrived in March, when Anatolyi Chubais was brought back to head the committee to re-elect.

The first to go to bat for Yeltsin against the communists was the IMF, with the massive $10.1 billion credit that was granted in March. No great secret was made of the fact that the aim was political, i.e. to save Yeltsin by contributing to the financing of his election handouts. Although he was subjected to heavy criticism from the media, including accusations of contributing to the financing of the war in Chechnya, IMF managing director Michel Camdessus laconically explained that it would have been "immoral" not to have helped out.[54]

The IMF, however, was far from being alone. In March, Russia received $2.4 billion in foreign bilateral credits from Germany and France,[55] and in April the "Paris Club" of Western creditor governments agreed to a massive rescheduling of Russia's foreign debt (more about the latter in the following chapter). The West had made its choice. Although there was much unease about Chechnya, and perhaps also about other aspects of Yeltsin's behaviour, in comparison with Zyuganov he appeared to be the lesser of two evils.

But Chechnya was a problem not only in Russia's relations with the West. It also cast serious shadows over the president in the eyes of the Russian population. Once he had made it clear that he did intend to stand in the election campaign, Yeltsin repeatedly recognized this problem, saying that unless he managed to bring an end to the war he would have no chance of winning the confidence of the voters.

Thus, on 31 March he presented a peace plan that envisioned a gradual troop withdrawal and negotiations on a peace agreement – possibly even with the Chechen leader Dzhokhar Dudaev himself. In order to maximize the political impact of this initiative, the presentation was made in a live broadcast, aired on all the three main television channels, both state and private, and in the presence of their respective news anchor persons.

The president's own concern about the matter at hand was brought home by the fact that during the interview he could be seen cleaning his fingernails with a pencil. That is hardly the behaviour of a man who is going through a major crisis. Nor did the behaviour of the three specially invited journalists give much grounds for concern. Even Yevgenii Kiselyov, the news anchor man of the private television station NTV, who had previously been a harsh critic of the Russian army's behaviour in Chechnya, could now be seen to adopt a mild tone. (Perhaps this was partly induced by his being included in the president's campaign staff.)

In all fairness, it should be recognized that the Russian mass media did face a serious dilemma here. By continuing their critical scrutiny of President Yeltsin they could have stood up for the freedom and independence of the press, but in so doing they might also have risked contributing to an election victory for the communists. And the latter outcome might have brought an end to the free press and to the nascent Russian democracy in general.

Right or wrong, in electing to back Yeltsin they proceeded to introduce a form of self-censorship. Given this virtual elimination of serious media scrutiny, it was hardly surprising that – despite the president's peace plan and despite his guarantees that the conflict was now over – the war in Chechnya could continue unabated well beyond the election.

Nor did the Western governments seem intent on saying much about the conflict. When the members of the G7 gathered for their 19–20 April summit meeting in Moscow, President Bill Clinton seized the opportunity to give Yeltsin a clear signal that the war was an internal Russian affair. He maintained that Chechnya was a part of Russia, which had no right whatsoever to break away, and even went so far as to declare that the United

States once had also fought a bloody civil war, in order to prevent a break-up of *its* union.

In the evening of Sunday, 21 April, Dudaev was murdered. According to sources in the Russian ministry of the interior, signals intelligence had succeeded in monitoring a discussion via satellite telephone between him and his peace negotiator in Moscow. Homing in on this signal, which emanated from a field somewhere in Chechnya, a Russian fighter aircraft could guide a missile right onto its target. Russia's "Public Enemy Number One" was dead, killed – most likely – by direct order of President Yeltsin, only a couple of days after President Clinton's visit to Moscow.[56]

When Western leaders gathered in Moscow on 9 May, to commemorate the 50th anniversary of the victory over Nazism, Yeltsin was given a clear and final indication that his actions in Chechnya were not to be allowed to disturb the good relationship with the West.

Both in Russia and in the West the celebration was controversial in the extreme. Many questioned the morality of participating in a military display in Red Square while a bloody civil war was in full swing in Chechnya. Open letters from a number of leading European intellectuals were published in several Western newspapers, including the French *Le Monde*. Without doubt, these protests made some impression, at least on the French president François Mitterand who showed his disapproval by absenting himself from the parade in Red Square, arriving only for the evening reception.

President Clinton, however, had no such qualms. As a sort of moral fig leaf, a promise was secured that the only troops parading on Red Square would be veterans from the Second World War. (The real victory parade was held at a huge victory monument, specially constructed on the outskirts of Moscow.) Despite such express promises, however, on the following day several Moscow newspapers reported that Russian soldiers straight from Chechnya had indeed taken part, parading right under the very nose of Clinton on the honorary stand. The signal could hardly have been clearer.

Round four: promises, promises

In the increasing torrent of opinion polls, it was now becoming clear that Yeltsin was well on his way to a victory. Having been hopelessly behind at the beginning of the year, by April he was running solidly in second place behind Zyuganov. The real reason for this recovery, however, was related not so much to the political steps that have been outlined above, as to the generous distribution of election handouts.

In order to ensure sufficient votes to be able to win in an open election, Yeltsin did not hesitate to use the same tactics that he had used in his struggle against Gorbachev in 1991, i.e. to promise everything to everyone, without the slightest regard for how the bills would be paid. The great difference between 1991 and 1996 lay in the fact that in 1996 he no longer had free access to the printing presses. The result instead was thus those developments in the market for state securities and in the use of money surrogates that have been described above.

The list of various campaign promises was a long one, ranging from the babushka who was given an automobile to regional leaders securing massive economic concessions from the federal centre. At every point where Yeltsin appeared on his campaign trail he had some goodies to hand out.

To mention but one part of this campaign, which would have important sequels in 1997–8, the question of wage arrears came into focus. Here was an issue where votes were very obviously at stake. Thus the arrears must be cleared out of the way, and the government was given a deadline to do so no later than 31 March. And so it happened. At least, if one is satisfied merely with cosmetic changes.

Once the deadline was passed, the government announced that a total of 7.8 trillion roubles had been transferred to the regions. Of this amount, however, a full 4.7 trillion roubles was unbudgeted three-month interest free credits, which according to the budget law would have to be recovered by the end of the year. While that was most unlikely to happen, the maturity date fell after the presidential election, which was all that mattered at the time. It might also be added that the amount as such was inadequate. During the first quarter of 1996, total wage arrears had increased from 20 to 25 trillion roubles.[57]

The problem had thus only been painted over. But for the moment that was quite enough. The re-election campaign was about to succeed.

Last round: victory – with a little help

In the first round of the elections, victory seemed to be within reach: Yeltsin came in first, with 35.3 per cent of the votes, and Zyuganov second, with 33 per cent. Since neither had won an absolute majority there would, however, have to be a second round of elections in July, and in the run-up to that election neither Yeltsin nor Zyuganov would play the leading role.

For a brief period of time, centre stage would belong to the stern paratroop general Aleksandr Lebed, who had come in third in the first round, with close to 14.5 per cent of the votes. Although some have argued that Lebed had been brought on board well in advance of the first round,[58] and that Yeltsin's victory was thus predetermined, to casual observers the balance of power seemed to rest in his hands. Outwardly, there were many attempts made by both sides to woo the general, but again it was Yeltsin who emerged as the winner.

In exchange for his support in the second round, Lebed not only managed to secure an appointment to head Yeltsin's security council (*sovet bezopasnost*). He also succeeded in producing a dismissal of the unpopular minister of defence, General Pavel Grachev. When Yeltsin explained, at a photo-op in the Kremlin, that he had now seen his future successor it looked as though Russia might be entering into a Yeltsin–Lebed era.

This situation, however, would not last for long. Accepting as his first mission to bring about an end to the war in Chechnya, Lebed entered into negotiations which by early autumn had succeed in producing an agreement not about peace but at least about a cessation of hostilities.[59] His reward for this achievement was measured in rapidly rising approval rates in public opinion polls. But that also proved to be his undoing.

In keeping with his style of refusing to tolerate any political figures of stature in his surroundings, Yeltsin would soon fire the general. On the day after being dismissed, Lebed's approval rates went sky-high, indicating a dangerous future rival to the president. After having kept a low profile for most of 1997, in the spring of 1998 he would be back in the race again. (More on that count below.)

Gaming records

Summing up the results of the three "chicken" games that have been presented above, there are some salient features which have a great deal of bearing on the problems of path dependence and multiple equilibria. They will be given some further (bloodless) illustration in the following chapter, which takes our account past the fall of the Chernomyrdin and Kiriyenko governments in March and August 1998, but in essence the patterns have already been clarified. Since this will be important background material for our theoretical analysis in Chapters 8 and 9, it might be useful to sum up at this point.

In the first game, which took place in 1990–91, Boris Yeltsin drove Russia into a head on collision with Mikhail Gorbachev and the Soviet Union. There were many attempts made – by others – to achieve a compromise, but neither side would listen. After several months of steadily increasing pressure, at times nearing a blowout, the final showdown came with a Big Bang in August 1991. The Soviet Union was destroyed and Yeltsin followed up his victory by humiliating Gorbachev and by prohibiting the communist party.

How close a call it really was will never be known, but the mere fact that tanks were rolling in the streets of Moscow should be sufficient to indicate that a full scale civil war could have resulted. If the armed forces had indeed been drawn into the conflict – on opposing sides – there would have been little left to prevent major bloodshed.

Having played for stakes of this magnitude, Yeltsin withdrew from the stage. By thus failing to cash in on the opportunities for reform, he also revealed some of his own priorities: power comes first and economic reform comes second, if even that.

In the second game, which was played out in 1993, Yeltsin drove his confrontation with the Supreme Soviet to another point of explosion. Again there were many attempts made by third parties to achieve a compromise, and again neither side in the conflict was ready to flinch. Again there were tanks rolling in the streets in Moscow, and again the world was left to wonder how close the call had really been. Perhaps the second time was more dangerous than the first, but that is beside the point.

The striking similarity lies in the fact that Yeltsin again decided to withdraw after the event. Again he refused to get himself involved in supporting such political parties that might have provided a solid constituency for entrenching the market-oriented reforms. The only exception was one that confirms the rule, namely the proposed constitution, which was directly linked to the president's own personal power agenda.

In the third game, taking place in the spring of 1996, Yeltsin emerged from a seemingly hopeless position in the opinion polls to take on communist party leader Zyuganov in a total confrontation, with many hints of pending civil war and other disasters in case the communists should win the election. Again Yeltsin emerged victorious and again he vanished after the event.

One real difference was that this time the opposition did flinch. The communists could have made a big issue out of poverty, illness and other problems afflicting the poor but never really did so. Towards the end of his campaign, Zyuganov struck an almost conciliatory note. Maybe this was simply owing to the fact that he is no Lenin, but one may equally well suspect that he feared what might happen if the masses were to be truly agitated, a fear that Yeltsin obviously did not share.

Given that the president had already shown himself willing, on at least two occasions, to go all the way – even up to the point of having tanks in the streets (not to mention Chechnya) perhaps the communists were quite simply intimidated into flinching.

In a final contrast, this time the reason for Yeltsin's disappearance cannot be the subject of speculation. Shortly before the first round of the election he had a heart attack, a fact which at the time was kept a closely guarded secret. But during the autumn it became increasingly obvious that the president's health was failing, and eventually he had to own up to the fact. In November he underwent quintuple heart bypass surgery.

From a medical point of view the operation was successful, but politically the president's long absence from power would have serious consequences for the running of the country. Those developments, and the turn to the bright side that followed once he did recover, will be the subject of discussion in the following chapter.

Notes

1. Illarionov, A. 1995. Popytki provedeniya politiki finansovoi stabilizatsii v SSSR i v Rossii, *Voprosy Ekonomiki*, **7**, 5.
2. The *émigré* Soviet economist Igor Birman does, however, prove that there were at least some who saw the trouble that was brewing. Based on work published in the West, which showed how forced savings had led to repressed inflation in the form of a mass of excess money in the hands of the population, he issued severe warnings about a deep financial crisis the consequences of which could be extremely serious. (E.g. Birman, I. 1980. The financial crisis in the USSR, *Soviet Studies*, **22**(1).)
3. Illarionov 1995, op. cit., p. 6.
4. Ibid., pp. 6–7.
5. Ibid., p. 7.
6. IMF *et al.* 1990. *The Economy of the USSR*. Washington, DC: The World Bank, p. 20.
7. On the Russian case, see further Hedlund, S. and Sundström, N. 1996b. The Russian economy after systemic change, *Europe-Asia Studies*, **48**(6), 909–10.
8. Illarionov, A. 1996b. Bremya gosudarstva, *Voprosy Ekonomiki*, **9**, 6. It should be noted that there is a major difference between the federal budget and the consolidated budget, which includes budgets at lower levels. Measured in relation to GDP, taxes paid into the latter have been considerably higher, on par with US levels both lower than in Western Europe. Our focus on the federal budget is due to its political importance.
9. Hernández-Catá, E. 1995. Russia and the IMF: the political economy of macro-stabilization, *Problems of Post-Communism*, **42**(3), 24.
10. Sutela, P. 1996. Fiscal federalism in Russia, in Dallago, B. and Mittone, L. (eds), *Economic Institutions, Markets and Competition: Centralization and Decentralization in the Transformation of Economic Systems*. Cheltenham: Edward Elgar, p. 153.
11. Ibid., pp. 152–3.
12. Holmes, S. 1997. When less state means less freedom, *Transitions*, **4**(4), 74.
13. Reddaway, P. 1997b. Possible scenarios for Russia's future, *Problems of Post-Communism*, **44**(5), 41.
14. Sutela, op. cit., p. 151.
15. See further OECD 1997, *Russian Federation 1997*. Paris: OECD, pp. 186–99.
16. Helmer, J. 1997. Russia: regions pressure Kremlin into policy shift – an analysis, *Johnson's Russia List*, 4 November.
17. OECD 1997, op. cit, p. 197.
18. Sutela, op. cit., p. 153.
19. OECD 1997, op. cit., p. 62.
20. For definitions and data on this "emerging market", see further ibid., pp. 61–2.
21. See further Illarionov, A. 1996a. Upushchennyi shans, *Voprosy Ekonomiki*, **3**, 85–6.
22. If we look at the consolidated budget, including local budgets, expenditure was cut from 42.2 to 31.6 per cent of GDP, resulting in a deficit reduction from 10.8 to 4.0 per cent of GDP, while if extra-budgetary expenditure is included,

expenditure fell from 52.9 to 38.5 per cent, and the deficit from 11.9 to 3.8 per cent (ibid., p. 89).

23. OECD 1995. *The Russian Federation*. Paris: OECD, p. 23.
24. Illarionov 1996a, op. cit., p. 89.
25. Ibid., p. 90.
26. IEA 1995. Tendentsii ekonomicheskogo razvitiya Rossii, *Voprosy Ekonomiki*, **6**, 131.
27. Illarionov 1996a, op. cit., p. 89.
28. Illarionov 1996b, op. cit., p. 9.
29. Rutland, P. 1997a. Another year lost for the economy, *Transitions*, **3**(2), p. 79.
30. See further OECD 1997, op. cit., p. 70.
31. Khakamada, I. 1997. Gosudarstvennyi dolg: struktura i upravlenie, *Voprosy Ekonomiki*, **4**, p. 76. One argument that has been used by the Russian side, in order to justify this practice, is that zero coupon T-bills do not pay any interest, but that argument is hardly applicable to the OFZs. For more detail on definitions and measurement problems in relation to the Russian budget deficit, see OECD 1997, op. cit., pp. 55–6.
32. Rutland, op. cit., p. 79.
33. Illarionov 1996a, op. cit., p. 91.
34. The trend towards a lengthening of the average maturity of the GKO/OFZ debt would continue, from 111 days at the end of 1995, to 149 at the end of 1996, and 270 in mid-1997 (OECD 1997, op. cit., p. 61).
35. Illarionov 1996a, op. cit., pp. 90–91.
36. See further, current issues of *Kommersant*, and Goskomstat 1998, *Rossiiskii statisticheskii ezhegodnik: ofitsialnoe izdanie 1997*. Moscow: Goskomstat Rossii, pp. 524–5. The record for *auctions* of state securities was set on 13 June, only days before the election, when a six-month GKO was sold at 240 per cent! (*Finansovye Izvestiya*, 21 August 1997.)
37. Illarionov 1996a, op. cit., p. 92. Measured in relation to GDP, there was a drop in total lending from 12.7 to 3.9 per cent.
38. Ibid., p. 93.
39. Ibid., pp. 93–4.
40. In the wake of this crisis, there were several hundred bank failures, including two major ones, namely Tveruniversalbank and Natsionalnyi Kredit. (See further OECD 1997, op. cit., p. 82.)
41. Illarionov 1996a, op. cit., p. 95.
42. Ibid., p. 96.
43. In Russian, money and money surrogates are known, respectively, as "living" (*zhivye*) and "dead" (*mertvye*) money.
44. OECD 1997, op. cit., p. 172 and Annex II, *passim*.
45. Ibid., p. 108.
46. Ickes, B. W., Murrell, P. and Ryterman, R. 1997. End of the tunnel? The effects of financial stabilization in Russia, *Post-Soviet Affairs*, **13**(2), 124.
47. OECD 1997, op. cit., p. 116.
48. Ibid., p. 119.
49. Ickes, Murrell and Ryterman, op. cit., 126.
50. Illarionov 1996b, op. cit., p. 7.
51. Rutland, op. cit., p. 79.

52. Shmelyov, op. cit., pp. 28–9, 32.
53. Quoted by Rutland, P. 1998. A flawed democracy, *Current History*, **97**, October, 315.
54. See further Waller, J. M. 1997. Author's rebuttal to the department of State, *Demokratizatsiya*, **5**(1), 119–20.
55. OECD 1997, op. cit., p. 69.
56. Scholars at the International Institute for Strategic Studies in London corroborate that this version of the events is credible (*New Europe*, 28 April – 4 May 1996).
57. *The Moscow Times*, 1 April 1998.
58. According to Rutland 1998, op. cit., p. 316, "There is strong evidence to suggest that Lebed was co-ordinating his campaign with Yeltsin's people even before the first round." See also Shlapentokh, V. 1997. *Bonjour*, Stagnation: Russia's Next Years, *Europe-Asia Studies*, **49**(5), 867.
59. Lebed was appointed secretary of Yeltsin's Security Council on 18 June and presidential representative for Chechnya on 10 August. The Khasavyurt agreement was signed on 31 August, between Lebed and Chechen Chief of Staff Aslan Maskhadov. Russian troops began pulling out on 8 September and on 3 October a more formal agreement was signed between Prime Minister Viktor Chernomyrdin and acting Chechen President Zelimkhan Yandarbiev. Lebed was fired on 17 October. (See further Rutland, P. 1996. A fragile peace, *Transitions*, **2**(23).)

CHAPTER SEVEN

Russia under the new regime

Once Boris Yeltsin had been successfully re-elected as president of Russia, his new government, which was announced on 15 August 1996, had to begin an immediate process of damage control. The first step was to cancel or postpone the bulk of all those lavish election promises that had been made in practically all directions. This was done by a special presidential decree, scrapping more than 50 normative acts on socio-economic improvements.[1]

Step number two was to make peace with the IMF, by seeking to address the rapidly growing problems of tax collection. At stake was not only the monthly tranche of the $10.1 billion credit that had been withheld in July. If the tax problems could not be credibly resolved, perhaps the IMF would be forced into a painful reappraisal of its relations with Russia. And the omens were bad. In September, tax revenue had fallen by a further 29 per cent, compared to August, to end at merely 45 per cent of the projected level.[2] Drastic action of some sort was needed. And it was imminent.

At the beginning of October, it was announced that a special commission, to be headed by Viktor Chernomyrdin and Anatolyi Chubais, was to be formed to deal with those who refused to pay their taxes. In order to drive home the punitive message, the new commission was given a name – "Temporary Extraordinary Committee" (*Vremennaya chrezvychainaya kommissiya*) – which in abbreviation closely resembled that of Feliks Dzerzhinskii's once dreaded "Cheka", the precursor to the KGB.

Although the much publicized drive of the new "temporary" Cheka did succeed in more than trebling tax collection between September and December (from 8.1 trillion to 25 trillion roubles), the total for 1996 came to only 81.1 per cent of projected revenue. The payment system as a whole was in dire straits. By the end of the year, federal tax arrears had risen to 61 trillion roubles and inter-enterprise debt stood at 490 trillion roubles, or 25 per cent of GDP. (The latter was up from 15 per cent of GDP at the end of 1995.)[3]

In early February 1997, *Gosnalogsluzhba*, the central tax authority, painted a gloomy picture of the situation, stating that "the tax base is shrinking at catastrophic speed".[4] And it was set to get worse.

Tax revenue for the first quarter stopped at merely 59.3 per cent of what had been envisioned in the (wildly unrealistic) federal budget for 1997. By the end of March, federal tax arrears had grown by a further 16 per cent, to reach 69.7 trillion roubles. *Finansovye Izvestiya's* commentator laconically concluded that "The government acknowledges that so far it has not succeeded in turning the tense situation of payments of taxes and fees to the budget".[5]

It was in the midst of all the doom and gloom that surrounded this financial mess that Boris Yeltsin suddenly returned to the Kremlin, seemingly restored to his old good health and vigour. Having miraculously survived the five-way heart bypass operation in November 1996 and a bout of double pneumonia in January 1997, the president not only was back on his feet. He returned to the Kremlin with a vengeance, ready to reassert his power and to put an effective end to all talk about his health.

The "dream team" takes over

On 17 March a government reshuffle was announced, which at once sent waves of optimism through the community of Russia watchers. The main reason was that the two leading figures of the new team – Anatolyi Chubais and Boris Nemtsov – both had impeccable records as liberal market-oriented economists. While Chubais had won his spurs as head of the great privatization programme, Nemtsov had won great praise for his successful local level market reforms while serving as governor in Nizhnii Novgorod.

The appointment of this new regime did seem to mark a significant change in the president's leadership style. In sharp contrast to his 1991 appointment of Yegor Gaidar, the architect of shock therapy who was never made more than acting prime minister, and never really got the president's full backing, this time Yeltsin offered unconditional support to his new men.

Although Russian reactions to this move were mixed, to say the least, both Western leaders and the international financial markets reacted with jubilation. To name but one example, the deputy secretary of the US Treasury, Lawrence Summers, proclaimed that Russia now had a "reenergized presidency and an economic dream team".[6]

Good economic fundamentals?

The optimism that was engendered by this radically new political landscape was given further impetus by the fact that much of the economic groundwork for success already seemed to be in place. Inflation had been brought within reasonable control (22 per cent for 1996, compared to 2,509 per cent for 1992), the rouble had been stabilized, and interest rates had been brought down, from the three-digit range that prevailed in the spring of 1996 to below 30 per cent in the spring of 1997.

Faith in the long term had also been entrenched by two massive debt reschedulings that were agreed in 1996 and 1997. Acting under the impression that the Russian economy was finally on the right tracks, creditors agreed to allow a temporary breathing space, granting a six-year grace period when only interest would be paid. For the "Paris Club" of 18 creditor nations, agreement on a principal of $38 billion was reached in April 1996 – the largest rescheduling undertaken in its 40 years of existence. For the "London Club" of nearly 600 commercial creditors, a deal concerning a principal of $33 billion was concluded in October 1997 (following a preliminary agreement in November 1995). As a result, the average maturity of Russian debt was extended to 20 years (from four years in 1993).[7]

For the first time since Lenin repudiated tsarist foreign debt, these operations placed Russia in a position of commercial creditworthiness. In October 1996, Russia received credit ratings from both Moody's and Standard & Poor's, implying that the doors were now open for the Russian government to venture into the Eurobond market.[8] The first – highly successful – $1 billion issue was made in November 1996 (for five years at 9.25 per cent). In March 1997 followed an equally successful DM 2 billion Eurobond (for seven years at 9.0 per cent), and in June there was a further $2 billion issue (for ten years at 10.0 per cent).[9]

In addition to the federal government, the cities of Moscow, St Petersburg and Nizhnii Novgorod were given the green light to issue Eurobonds of their own, as were regions and even single companies, notably so giants like Lukoil and Gazprom. All of this, which was believed at the time to be followed by further upgrades of the credit ratings, provided an air of optimism and credibility.[10]

The impression of a turnaround was also supported by the Moscow stock exchange. Having more than doubled in 1996, in the first half of 1997 it outperformed all other exchanges in the world. Partly this could be explained by a rapidly increasing international demand for Russian stock, meeting a weak supply of credible Russian companies. Nevertheless, it did represent an impressive growth and expectations were created for further spectacular gains.

Finally, as the crowning piece of evidence for the defence of the Russian success story, at the beginning of 1997 Goskomstat reported positive GDP growth for the first time since 1989 (albeit only by 0.1 per cent).[11] The worst would thus indeed seem to be over. Regrettably, however, there was not much real substance in any of these signs of apparent success.

On the latter count, we may note that positive GDP growth was arrived at by means of a Soviet-style statistical manipulation. By clandestinely revising upwards the estimate of the contribution of the shadow economy, from 20 per cent to 25 per cent of GDP, a continued fall in production could be made to look like an upturn.

There is certainly nothing wrong, as such, in revising the estimate of the size of the unreported sector, but it is a bit odd to make such a large adjustment at once, and, moreover, it is completely unacceptable to do so without due notification. Once found out, the Goskomstat was rightly subjected to heavy criticism and duly retreated.[12] For the first six months of 1997, a further decline in GDP of 0.2 per cent was recorded.[13]

Concerning the remainder of the positive signs reported above, truth cannot be questioned but a number of qualifications deserve to be added, namely: (a) that inflation had been brought down at the cost of a massive accumulation of non-payments in all directions, (b) that the reduction in interest rates was accompanied by a further decline in investment, (c) that the boom on the stock exchange concerned a handful of companies only, with a total capitalization that was in the same league as Motorola, and (d) that virtually all foreign lending went straight into the black hole in the federal budget.[14]

Nevertheless, there did remain some grounds on which to claim that the reform process so far had been a great success, albeit of a special kind, grounds which provided support for hopes that the process of further reform would stay on course. These hopes would last for just about another year.

New men – new tasks

Once in charge, the "dream team" was forced to address two issues of great importance. One was placed on the desk of Boris Nemtsov, who set out to effect a restructuring of the country's natural monopolies. Great expectations were attached to this mission. He had, after all, shown great results in Nizhnii Novgorod. On 23 March he launched his offensive, by declaring that achieving a reduction in the rates charged by Gazprom and power utility UES would be a top priority.

Taking on politically well-connected giants like these was, however, a task of a different magnitude altogether from running the local politics of Nizhnii Novgorod. Gazprom was the country's largest hard currency earner and UES had accounted for about 15 per cent of all taxes collected in the past two months. Officially recognizing what he was up against, Nemtsov followed in the steps of Yegor Gaidar by referring to his task as a "kamikaze" mission.[15]

The IMF sought to exploit the position, by hinting that breaking up Gazprom into smaller units might be a good idea, but that was rejected out of hand by both Nemtsov and other cabinet members. The struggle instead was limited to restructuring, to the payment of taxes and to the exercise of government control over the company. The latter in particular was harshly contested. While the government technically held a 40 per cent stake in Gazprom, it had signed over 35 per cent for management by the company, which in practice meant its powerful chairman, Rem Vyakhirev.

Although Nemtsov's position would be strengthened in the following month, by his appointment to the parallel portfolio of minister for the oil and gas industry, his was still a losing cause. By mid-May it was clear that Vyakhirev and Gazprom had prevailed, as had the other natural monopolies. The assault by the young reformer had been easily beaten back by the old guard. Gazprom in particular would continue to be a major headache for the tax collectors.

Compared to the troubles that were faced by Nemtsov, the task that was undertaken by Anatolyi Chubais would be of an even higher magnitude of difficulty. His mission was to deal with the financial crisis, and by early April this had become an acute problem.

In the budget law for 1997 it had been stipulated that if tax revenue during any quarter were to fall below 90 per cent of target, the government would have to submit a revised budget. As noted above, tax collection for the first quarter fell below 60 per cent. Thus the revision clause in the budget law was triggered. Massive spending cuts would have to be made.

In early May the government submitted a new budget, which included a total cut in spending of 108 trillion roubles. Across the board, that would come to 20 per cent, but given that some items would be protected, others, such as support to agriculture, would have to be slashed in half. Needless to say, the opposition in the Duma found that a hard pill to swallow.

Meanwhile, the total of outstanding unpaid wages had grown to a stunning 50 trillion roubles. Noting that the government accounted for merely one-fifth of this sum, the remainder being owed by enterprises, we may conclude that the problem of non-payments had become endemic to the economy as a whole.[16]

The response from the Duma was to suggest a massive printing of money. According to a proposal made by Viktor Ilyukhin, the chairman of the Duma security committee (!), a total of 330 trillion roubles should be created. According to Central Bank chairman Sergei Dubinin, that would lead to more than a doubling of M2 and most likely trigger hyperinflation.[17]

The following month was marked by increased tensions between the government and the Duma, but eventually the latter seemed to give in, perhaps prompted by thinly veiled threats of dissolution and new elections.

On 11 June, the Duma voted to reject the proposed doubling of the money supply, and on 19 June, it voted to back a proposed draft tax code. As part of a compromise, the deputies were allowed until after summer to come up with proposals for revisions, after the bill had passed a first reading. (A second reading was scheduled for 1 November 1997.)

The main ambition of the proposed tax reform was to make life easier for business. The number of taxes was to be slashed and the total tax burden reduced, from 35.1 to 32.4 per cent of GDP. The consequences for the budget were estimated at a loss of revenue in the range of 73–75 trillion roubles. Hopes expressed by Deputy Finance Minister Sergei Shatalov were that "enterprises will retain these funds and use them primarily for investment".[18]

On 23 June 1997, however, the Duma voted to reject the sequestration bill, and on the following day, Chubais threatened that the government might have to implement further reforms on its own. When politics went into summer recess, the question of the budget remained in limbo. The new government had failed in one of its most important tasks, that of introducing stable and transparent rules. Thus, *ad hoc* would have to continue as the guiding principle of fiscal policy.

At first glance it looked as though tax collection during the second quarter of the year had indeed improved substantially. Following the dismal first quarter, the government could show a figure for tax collection in the first half of 1997 that was brought up to 85 per cent of plan. Of this sum, however, more than half (69 out of 120 trillion roubles) was "dead" money, i.e. various money surrogates.[19]

Even worse, the second quarter improvement was due primarily to the fact that after several months of increasing political pressure, Gazprom had finally been forced to cough up its overdue taxes.[20] It was with the help of this money that the government succeeded in complying with a direct order from the president, that all outstanding pension arrears should be paid by 1 July.[21]

This *ad hoc* way of covering holes in the budget was further illustrated in August, when First Deputy Finance Minister Vladimir Petrov admitted at a press conference that revenue from selling a 25 per cent stake in Svyazinvest and a 40 per cent stake in Tyumen oil would be used to pay six trillion roubles of back wages to the military, police and scientific workers.[22]

At the same time, tax collection was reported to have fallen back down to merely 62 per cent of plan. When reprimanded by President Yeltsin for its poor August tax collection, the Gosnalogsluzhba retorted acidly that "There are no more Gazproms in the country!"[23]

In spite of this progressing erosion of the very foundations for a sound fiscal policy, the Russian government kept up a profile of optimism about the future. At the beginning of August, a currency "reform" was announced by Central Bank chairman Sergei Dubinin. Although it entailed no more than a denomination – striking three zeros – Dubinin used the occasion to announce that the period of economic stagnation was over, and that Russia was now about to enter a period of sustained economic growth.

That optimism, however, was soon to run into a veritable brick wall. During the remainder of autumn, two strings of events would be played out, both of which would wreak serious havoc on the prospects for a continued improvement of Russian economic performance. The first was a series of political scandals, involving several of the leading reformers, and the second was the financial crisis in Asia.

By the end of March 1998, the "dream team" would be out of government. Whether that was because of fallout from the political and financial crises, or if it was simply the result of a whim on the part of the president, remains a matter of some speculation. There were certainly shortcomings in government performance, most notably so in the continuing failure to pay wages on time, but that cannot be automatically linked to the downfall of the cabinet as a whole. Compelling reasons were also linked to the persons of Chubais and Chernomyrdin.

We shall return to the latter in a moment. First, however, there are some good reasons to look at the fiscal track record of the Chubais–Nemtsov government. One such is the simple one that credit should be given where credit is due. More importantly, however, the period from March 1997 to March 1998 provides some important insights into the nature of the problems that bedevil Russian tax collection.

Comparing track records

The frequent government reshuffles that have marked Russia's post-Soviet existence provide ample opportunity for a comparative study of how different "teams" have performed. Although Prime Minister Viktor Chernomyrdin remained at his post from the beginning of 1993 until March 1998, the posts of deputy premier (with responsibility for finance) and of finance minister have had several occupants. Their respective track records have been usefully compared by Russian economist Andrei Illarionov. Table 7.1 reflects his breakdown of federal budget revenues by thus determined periods.

Several interesting patterns emerge. The first is the superficial one of drastic revenue falls in periods III and V, and of significant improvement in period IV. Closer inspection shows total tax revenue falling from 12.0 per cent of GDP in period I, to merely 8.7 per cent of GDP in period III, which covers the presidential election campaign. After the re-election of Yeltsin, his new government succeeded in raising tax revenue to 12.5 per cent of GDP, whereas the "dream team" under Chubais allowed it to fall back to 8.6 per cent.

Illarionov's point, which at once places Anatolyi Chubais in a better light, is that the improvement in period IV was the result of an explosive growth in the issuing of tax deferrals (KNO) and other money surrogates. Between periods III and IV, the share of money surrogates in total tax revenue increased from one-sixth to nearly half, or from 1.5 per cent to 5.2 per cent of GDP, leading to a serious degradation of the Russian payment system.

Table 7.1 Federal budget revenue, 1994–7 (Average over the period, % of GDP)

Period	I	II	III	IV	V
Deputy Premier	Shokhin	Chubais	Kadannikov	Potanin/ Livshits	Chubais
Finance Minister	Dubinin	Panskov	Panskov	Livshits	Chubais
Time	Feb.–Dec. 1994	Jan.–Dec. 1995	Jan.–Aug. 1996	Sept. 1996– Mar. 1997	April–Nov. 1997
Money and money surrogates:					
All revenue	12.1	12.1	10.3	13.0	10.6
tax revenue	12.0	10.5	8.7	12.5	8.6
non-tax revenue	0.1	1.6	1.7	0.6	2.1
Money:					
All revenue	12.0	10.9	8.8	7.8	9.9
tax revenue	11.8	9.9	7.1	7.2	7.9
non-tax revenue	0.1	0.9	1.7	0.6	2.1
Money surrogates:					
Tax revenue	0.1	1.2	1.5	5.2	0.7
Relative shares, %					
Money	99.0	88.7	82.3	58.0	91.7
Money surrogates	1.0	11.3	17.7	42.0	8.3

Source: Illarionov, A. 1998. Effektivnost byudzhetnoi politiki v Rossii v 1994–1997 godakh, *Voprosy Ekonomiki*, **2**, 24.

By drastically curtailing this "surrogatization" of the federal budget, the Chubais government removed a source of largely fictitious revenue, while increasing the collection of sound revenues. Between periods III and V, the collection of taxes in money form increased from 7.1 per cent to 7.9 per cent of GDP (which was better than in period IV) and the collection of non-tax income increased from 1.7 per cent to 2.1 per cent of GDP. The last row in Table 7.1 brings home the real achievement of the "dream team": the share of money surrogates in total tax revenue was cut from 42.0 to 8.3 per cent, thus providing a sounder foundation for future fiscal policy.

With the further aim of mapping out the achievements of the respective government teams, Illarionov proceeds to adjust the figures in Table 7.1 for seasonal influences. According to this new set of data, period IV stands out as the worst of all five in terms of total budget revenue, bringing in merely 9.0 (rather than 13.0) per cent of GDP, while all other periods still recorded more than 10.0 per cent. Looking simply at the collection of taxes in money form, a record low of 6.9 per cent of GDP was reached, which was even worse than during the preceding election campaign, when, as Illarionov puts it, the whole country had "gone on tax holidays".[24]

Turning to look at the budget expenditure side, Illarionov finds similar patterns. While periods II, III and V were marked by fiscal austerity, reducing expenditure from 23.2 per cent of GDP in period I, to 18.0 per cent of GDP in period III and 16.0 per cent of GDP in period V, period IV brought a drastic increase, to 21.1 per cent of GDP. At the same time, however, period IV also brought a drastic increase in public sector wage arrears, from 6.1 to 11.3 trillion roubles, which is rather striking. In stark contrast, period V achieved a sharp reduction in *both* expenditure *and* wage arrears, the latter falling back to 4.9 trillion roubles.[25]

Bringing the two sides together, a look at budget deficits in the respective periods confirms the patterns outlined above. From a high of 11.1 per cent of GDP in period I, in period II Chubais managed a reduction to 5.3 per cent. It is hardly surprising that it grew again during the election campaign, to reach 7.7 per cent, but again it is striking to note that nothing was done to curb that development after the election. On the contrary, in period IV the deficit was allowed to increase to 8.0 per cent, and in the budget for 1997 a further growth to 12.6 per cent was envisioned. In period V, Chubais reimposed austerity, bringing the deficit back down to 5.3 per cent of GDP. Thus a financial catastrophe was narrowly averted.[26]

The most important policy decision made to this end was to bring an abrupt halt to government borrowing. While government debt to the Central Bank had grown by 1.35 per cent of GDP in period III, and by 1.45 per cent of GDP in period IV, in period V it actually *declined* by 0.06 per cent of GDP. Public sector debt (GKO and OFZ) was also brought down slightly, from a high of 13.2 per cent of GDP in July 1997 to 12.6 per cent in November 1997. The government thus succeeded not only in bringing interest rates down – real annual yields on GKO/OFZ fell from 76.6 per cent in period III to 12.0 per cent in period IV – but also in shifting the pattern of commercial bank credits. Between periods IV and V the government's share fell from 76.9 per cent to 34.7 per cent, thus making room for private sector investors.[27]

The conclusion that must be reached from this account consists of two parts. On the one hand, it is clear that from March 1997 onwards Anatolyi Chubais did deliver a badly needed leadership in dealing with the financial crisis. From this perspective, it was certainly deplorable that President Yeltsin began already towards the end of 1997 to withdraw his political support, and that in March 1998 the "dream team" was thrown out.

On the other hand, however, as we may recall from Chapter 4 above, the very same Chubais had also demonstrated serious problems in keeping his hands clean. The combination of making enemies via tough economic policies and via corrupt ways of going about that business would in the end prove to be his own undoing. In the early autumn of 1997, his past was beginning to catch up.

Political scandals

Before proceeding to look at the detail of the various political scandals that contributed to the downfall of the Chubais administration, it may be of some use to say a few words about the background of increasingly intimate relations between the Russian government and the country's financial elites. The point here is to illustrate that the open scandals which erupted in the late summer and autumn of 1997 were the result not of various wrongdoings *per se*, but of the fact that owing to changes in the rules of the money-making game the leading oligarchs were beginning to fall out among themselves.

As political infighting was becoming public, and accusations were flying through the air, the Russian public suddenly became aware of things that had been going on behind the façade for quite some time. The bankers had been in cahoots with corrupt officials to such an extent that massive private fortunes had been built in record time. Access to political power over matters like privatization and federal budget disbursements had become a *sine qua non* for wealth accumulation. (We shall return to the pure mechanics of this process in a moment.)

In the spring of 1996, it was time for the banker-barons to return the favours. Faced with the distinct possibility of a communist election victory, they realized that something would have to be done. And, as we may recall from our previous chapter, so it was.

At a meeting in Davos, the "group of seven" top bankers decided that Yeltsin's campaign must be supported, to the tune of hundreds of millions of dollars.[28] The leading media (under their control) followed the example, tuning down all criticism of the president (most notably so with respect to the war in Chechnya) and engaging instead in a powerful anti-communist drive.

As it turned out, this massive mobilization of both money and media support was successful. But it would not be without a price. Once Yeltsin had been successfully re-elected, it was payback time in the other direction. Several new privatization deals were concluded, and some of the tycoons were offered important political posts. The best example of the latter is Boris Berezovskii, who was offered the post of secretary in Yeltsin's then powerful security council.

Serious questions were now being asked, about how far the process of political patronage would be taken. Writing about this problem in the summer of 1997, *The Economist* pointed at grave worries "that the bankers would exact a license to run the country for their own benefit". It was certainly logical to expect that they would want something in return:

> Many Russians suspect that businessmen turn politicians for less high-minded reasons. And few would quarrel with the injudicious observation of Mikhail Khodorkovsky, president of the Menatep

financial and oil empire (and another member of the group of seven), that politics is the most profitable business in Russia today.[29]

Typically, however, once the president was back in the Kremlin, his new government went about asserting itself against its own benefactors. Nemtsov's private struggles with Gazprom and the other giants was a case in point, but the real challenge lay in declarations by Chubais, that for the bankers the good times were over.

Speaking at a congress of the Association of Russian Banks in April 1997, he announced that they could no longer expect to profit from high yields on state securities, or from other government favours: "For banks there remains only one path; investment in the real sector. Those who are late to realize this will lose, and those who do not realize it will perish financially."[30]

This was a challenge, head on, to the existing structures of power. The battles that raged in the summer and early autumn of 1997, over the privatization of Tyumen oil, Svyazinvest and Norilsk Nikel, provided ample illustration of the fact that there had been two radical changes in the rules of the game: on the one hand, compared to the previous handouts of property, the government would henceforth insist on extracting more reasonable prices for the stakes it handed over, and, on the other, it would do so by picking favourites among the rival clans.

The trigger for the subsequent war of the tycoons was linked to the sale of a 25 per cent stake in the national telecommunications holding company Svyazinvest, which had been formed in 1994. In June 1997, Chubais announced that he wanted an open and fair auction, which went against the expectations of the bankers, that it would be yet another rigged deal at rock bottom prices.

At stake, however, was not only the question of how the spoils should be divided among the elites. It was also stated that in contrast to previous privatization deals, emphasis would now be placed on finding "strategic investors" who would be willing to supply both capital and know-how for the restructuring of Russian industry. The government's narrow interest in raising as much revenue as possible for the budget would have to take second place.

On 30 June 1997, an agreement was reached between the federal property fund and the fuel and energy ministry, on the holding of special auctions to sell off large blocks of shares in six major oil companies, including Tyumen Oil.[31] Although the agreement had quite a lot to say about safeguarding that established rules were followed, it would not work out in quite that way. Yet, it was not in the oil industry but around the privatization of Svyazinvest that the real battle would be joined.

In order to secure the participation of a strategic investor, the process was divided into two phases. In the first, a blocking stake of 25 per cent plus one share would be auctioned off. Here both foreign and Russian tenders would be accepted. In the second round, 25 per cent minus one share would be sold to Russian investors only. The starting bid was set at $1.18 billion.[32] As the closing day was drawing near, however, it was becoming increasingly clear that the outcome would not be the – officially – anticipated one.

On 25 July, the state property committee, GKI, announced the winning bid. Technically, it had been tendered by a Cyprus-registered firm called "Mastkom", but it was no secret that the real winner was Oneksimbank, headed by Vladimir Potanin. At $1.87 billion the winning bid was only marginally better than the $1.72 billion that had been offered by the losing consortium.[33]

Amid all of the accusations of rigging and favouritism that immediately started flying, supported by media outlets that were controlled by the losing side, there was one rather important point. The initially stated ambition of securing a strategic investor had failed. Although Svyazinvest was in serious need of a partner, the winning side included none of the international telecom giants (presumably not because of a lack of interest). And, as one commentator rightly pointed out, once a blocking stake of 25 per cent plus one share had been sold, attempting in a second round to attract a strategic investor with a stake of 25 per cent minus one share would be rather pointless.[34]

Adding further fuel to the fire, on 5 August it was announced that Oneksimbank had emerged as the winner also in the sale of a 38 per cent stake in Norilsk Nikel. This outcome had been surrounded by a legal battle up until the very last moment, where the London-based metals firm Trans World Group had sought to secure, at the very highest political level, that the auction be put off. In contrast to the Svyazinvest deal, the price here was also deemed to be scandalously low.

With an estimated 35 per cent of the world's nickel deposits, according to analysts quoted by *Financial Times*, Norilsk Nikel should have been valued at more than $1.4 billion, implying that Oneksimbank should have paid at least $530 million. Other sources, quoted by AFP, gave figures in the $545–750 million range. The winning bid was merely $251 million.[35] It was hardly surprising that the Oneksimbank attracted considerable wrath from the losers.

The first victim of the ensuing "bankers' war" was Alfred Kokh, a close ally of Anatolyi Chubais. As deputy prime minister and head of the GKI, he had been in an excellent position to influence the Svyazinvest deal, and other deals as well for that matter. The instrument that was used to bring him down was a leak to the media, saying that he had accepted a $100,000 advance royalty for a book to be written.

The scandal was given plenty of coverage in media that were controlled by the losing side. On 13 August, Kokh was forced to resign, and on

1 October, Moscow prosecutors announced that they would begin criminal proceedings against him.[36]

To what extent the losing side in the Svyazinvest deal was right in their accusations is hard to tell. Many Western observers seemed to agree that the price was fair, at least in comparison to the Norilsk Nikel deal, and maybe also that it was indeed the highest bidder who had won.

On the Russian side, Chubais came out in a powerful defence of his companion, but in so doing he did not have the support of the president. In a televised comment to Kokh's resignation, Yeltsin stated that "The scandal around Svyazinvest and Norilsk Nikel is connected to the fact that some banks are likely to be closer to Kokh's soul. But this will not do. Everything must be honest, open and legal."[37]

No matter who was right, the scandals reflected one thing clearly. The tenuous coalition that had been formed in the spring of 1996, in order to secure a continuation of the Yeltsin regime, had finally broken down. Each of the clan leaders now used his own media empire to fight the others, and Anatolyi Chubais in particular, who had once been the favourite of the bankers, attracted much venom.

The main events in the subsequent battles have been outlined in Chapter 4 above, in our discussion of moral hazard. In early November, Chubais succeeded in convincing Boris Yeltsin that Boris Berezovskii must be fired from his post on the security council, and a week later Berezovskii retaliated by letting another book royalty scandal hit the media. This time, it was five prominent economists who had accepted an advance royalty of $90,000 each.

In addition to Chubais, who was the main target, the scandal also involved Alfred Kokh, who had already been forced to resign, and three other prominent participants in the privatization process. These were Maksim Boiko, who had replaced Kokh as head of the GKI, together with Pyotr Mostovoi, the head of the federal bankruptcy agency, and Aleksandr Kazakov, a previous privatization chief who had moved on to become Yeltsin's first deputy chief of staff.

It was in the midst of all this political infighting that Russia's financial markets were suddenly struck by fallout from the crisis in Southeast Asia.

The Asian crisis

When the financial crisis first began, it seemed as though Russia would be spared. There were quite a few confident statements made, from both political and financial circles, about the new stability that marked Russia's economic development. This, however, was a mood of optimism that would be brief indeed.

When the crisis finally did strike Russia, the impact was severe. The most visible results could be recorded in the stock market, where *The*

Moscow Times index dropped from a high point of well over 400 in October 1997 to just below 200 in early February 1998. But although investors were suffering heavy losses indeed, it was in another dimension that the real impact of the crisis would be felt.

Increasing capital outflows not only served to make a mockery of the anticipated Russian investment boom. Major outflows of capital from the market, for state securities in particular, added to the upward pressure on interest rates, which would seriously compound the already heavy burden of servicing the public debt. Thus, the complicated process of haggling between the government and the Duma over the budget for 1998 was set to worsen even further.

It would be some time, however, before the real gravity of the situation started to sink in. At a joint meeting with the World Bank in Hong Kong, in early September, the IMF characterized its lending to Russia as an act of "historical justice" and went on to talk about expected positive GDP growth of 1.5 per cent for 1997, and of 4.9 per cent for 1998.[38] In November, the Russian government was still optimistic, posting a 0.3 per cent growth in GDP for the first ten months of 1997,[39] and as late as December, the OECD was hoping for a 3 per cent positive growth in 1998.[40] Meanwhile, the financial situation was deteriorating at increasing speed.

In early November 1997, the IMF announced that it would withhold further disbursements of credits to Russia, pending an improvement in tax collection, and on 11 November, the Central Bank announced a hike in the re-finance rate, from 21 per cent to 28 per cent. The situation was worsening but it was still not critical. At the beginning of December, President Yeltsin made a personal appearance in the Duma, pleading – successfully – with the deputies to accept the budget for 1998 in a first reading. At about the same time, it was announced that arrears to the pension fund had risen to 82 trillion roubles.[41]

On 22 December 1997, Anatolyi Chubais admitted that federal budget revenue for the first ten months had stopped at 52.4 per cent of target, and that tax revenue was only 47.3 per cent of plan. Meanwhile, the sum total of tax arrears, including deferments, had risen from 70.5 to 102.9 trillion roubles. Servicing of the public debt had amounted to 39.2 per cent of government spending.[42] Three days later, the budget for 1998 was approved by the Duma in a second reading, but by now the financial crisis was beginning to have political implications.

In a classic move to shift the blame, the president issued a direct order, calling for all state sector wage arrears to be cleared before the end of the year. And on 30 December 1997, Prime Minister Viktor Chernomyrdin duly announced that the mission had been accomplished. A total of 14.5 trillion roubles had been transferred, including 3.2 trillion roubles in aid to regional authorities that accounted for about half of the arrears.[43]

What the actual truth of the matter was is a bit unclear. It is a fact that there were many places in the country where the promised money failed to show up, and on 19 January 1998, upon returning from a two-week holiday, Yeltsin blasted his government for having failed to comply with his order. Whether the money had in fact not been transferred, or if it had quietly disappeared *en route*, is beside the point here.

It is of far greater importance to note that the order to pay up had triggered a severe crackdown on some of the major tax dodgers. The Sidanko oil company, for example, claimed that by 31 December 1997, it had paid into the budget 5.6 trillion roubles in back taxes and Rosneft said it had contributed 0.37 trillion roubles.[44] The "temporary" Cheka had also added its share by threatening to seize the Omsk refinery and the Angarsk petrochemical facility, if the owners did not pay their tax arrears by 25 December 1997.[45] These *ad hoc* measures did have some impact, but it was chiefly of a political nature.

According to the Russian government, tax collection had improved dramatically during November–December 1997, and on 8 January 1998, the IMF announced that it was releasing a desperately needed tranche of $670 million. On 16 January, however, a government reshuffle indicated that scapegoats were being targeted. Prime Minister Viktor Chernomyrdin announced that the powers of Chubais and Nemtsov would be curtailed, as they were deprived of all control over finance and energy matters. Chubais, moreover, was placed alone in the hot seat, with full responsibility for future tax collection (only).

On 20 January 1998, the Russian economy was announced to have grown by 0.4 per cent in 1997, and a week later President Yeltsin announced a 12-point plan for economic recovery. While touching all the bases, from non-payments to trade policy and land reform, it was not so much the economic contents that attracted interest, as the fact that all ministers were clearly charged with well defined responsibilities, and warned that they would be "severely reprimanded" if they were to fail.[46]

The "tsar" had given yet another demonstration of his abilities in the old game of *divide et impera*, but it was hardly something that was designed to help the economy. On 29 January 1998, Illarionov warned that damage already done would lead to an increase in federal budget expenditure for 1998 by 3–5 per cent of GDP, mainly because of an increase in debt service by 10–15 per cent, but also owing to falling oil prices.[47] And it was set to get even worse.

On 2 February 1998, following a turbulent week on the financial markets, the Central Bank hiked the re-finance rate from 28 per cent to 42 per cent. In response, prices on the financial market fell sharply, driving up yields on one-year GKOS to 46–47 per cent and on OFZ bonds to 49 per cent.[48] (Inflation for 1997 had stopped at 11 per cent.)

Meanwhile, increasing pressure on the rouble had forced the Central Bank to reduce its currency reserves from $18 billion to $16 billion during January alone (there were also rumours of discreet "extra borrowing" in December, to the tune perhaps of $1 billion), and as investors were moving from shares to T-bills, the stock market was taking a heavy battering as well. On 2 February, *The Moscow Times* index dipped below 200.

On 5 February 1998, the budget for 1998 was approved in a third reading, and on that same day the president declared that he would stand behind his men: Anatolyi Chubais and Boris Nemtsov would be around until the year 2000!

On 17–19 February, Michel Camdessus visited Moscow to discuss the release of the next tranche of the IMF credit. The occasion prompted Yeltsin to deliver a speech were he said that "We need a growth that is supported by a massive inflow of investment". It was also announced that tax collection in January 1998 had been 40 per cent above January 1997, and on 20 February 1998 Central Bank chairman Sergei Dubinin said that there would be no further net borrowing in the first quarter: GKOs and OFZs would be issued only to re-finance maturing debt.

It now only remained to get the budget and the proposed new tax code passed by the Duma. The former problem was exacerbated as the president suddenly announced that the financial crisis had prompted a need for further cuts of 27.9 billion redenominated roubles, which were rejected by the Duma item by item. Despite heavy pressure from the Kremlin, on 28 February 1998 the budget was rejected as a whole.[49] Thus the problem of getting the tax code passed was also aggravated.

On 4 March 1998, however, the six-month budget battle was finally over, as the Duma gave its approval in a fourth reading. Some concessions were made, most notably in postponing debate on the tax code, but the president had refused to budge on the politically contentious issue of undertaking personnel changes in the government. The "young reform economists" remained in place.

Although Moody's announced a downgrade for Russia on 11 March, on 16 March the Central Bank announced a further reduction in the re-finance rate, from 36 per cent to 30 per cent. There was a growing sense that perhaps the worst was indeed over. The rouble had held steady and interest rates were beginning to come down.

The end of the dream team

In the midst of this growing optimism, Boris Yeltsin was suddenly taken ill. The illness as such was not so bad, but while the president was away old familiar rumours about his health started spreading, and there is probably nothing that irritates the "tsar" more than this. Upon returning to the Kremlin, he was thus bent on making a strong show of force. In the morning of 23 March 1998, it was announced that Prime Minister Viktor Chernomyrdin had been asked to step down. The formal reason given was dissatisfaction above all with the failure to comply with the order to pay back wages.

Irrespective of reason, this move not only marked the end of the "new regime" in Russia. By electing to dismiss the prime minister, and thus the government, as a whole, rather than merely some ministers, the president had triggered a constitutional process that would drag out for a full month to come. The economic price to be paid for the ensuing political gridlock would be of quite some magnitude.

According to the constitution, after dismissing the government the president had to submit a new prime minister for approval by the Duma. If his first choice were rejected, a new name would have to be submitted, and if that too were to be rejected, there would be a third round. Then it would be over. After having rejected the president's choice three times, the Duma would be dissolved and new elections called.

Entering into this process at a time when there were solid signs of at least the beginning of an economic recovery, when GDP might have started to grow, when the new tax code was on the table and when much of the groundwork had been laid for a sound fiscal policy, was foolhardy in the least. Getting the country out of the dark shades that had been cast by the financial crisis in Asia would have required political stability, not an absence of government.

Regrettably, however, Boris Yeltsin persisted in placing priority on his own personal power agenda. It was imperative that someone else should take the blame for the economic troubles. The subsequent political process would be a rather depressing show of the president's penchant for using confrontation to shift the blame.

Yeltsin could easily have struck a deal with the Duma, and composed a government that would have been agreeable to both sides. Thus it might also have been possible to move on with the economic recovery. But the president was bent instead on showing the Duma who was in charge. Thus yet another "chicken" game was triggered. By nominating the young Sergei Kiriyenko, he made sure that the first vote would be negative, by re-nominating the same Kiriyenko immediately upon conclusion of the first vote, he made sure that the second vote would also be negative, and by a snap third nomination of Kiriyenko, all options for negotiation were foreclosed.

It was now up to the Duma to decide if it wanted to go down with Kiriyenko, and thus risk losing cars, apartments, free travel and other privileges – such as immunity from prosecution – that are associated with being a member of the Duma. In consequence, the third vote was not about Kiriyenko at all, but about whether the Duma was ready to put itself out of business. And that it was not. The vote was secret, and overwhelmingly affirmative. On 24 April 1998, Sergei Kiriyenko was confirmed by the Duma as new prime minister of Russia. Yeltsin had triumphed again.

Via this performance, Russia's president had demonstrated not only his predilection for confrontation, but even more so his fears of having anyone close to power who might get ambitious. It does not take much imagination to realize that the real reason for the 23 March decision to dismiss the government as a whole was linked to the fact that Viktor Chernomyrdin had begun voicing interest in running for president.

It had all really been an elaborate trap, set by Yeltsin in order to see if there were any serious contenders for power. In the midst of speculation concerning possible constitutional tricks that might be deployed, in order to make an unconstitutional third presidential term look like a constitutional second term, the president suddenly announced that he had decided who would be his successor. This was an interesting manoeuvre, not only from a democratic point of view, but even more so for the simple reason that he refused to disclose the name of the anointed one.

Logically, there must have been several of the major players who felt that they were now being groomed for the very top. Among them – undoubtedly – was Viktor Chernomyrdin, who began speaking on radio in a manner that indicated obvious presidential ambitions. That proved to be his undoing. After having served Yeltsin loyally for several years, all while consistently denying any form of ambitions for higher office, his time in power had now come to an end.

This pattern of refusing to accept any heir apparent has a long tradition in Russian history. A couple of years before his death, for example, Peter the Great issued a decree saying that the tsar reserved the right to name his own successor, and then was silent on the matter until the very end. For good measure, he also followed the pattern of Ivan the Terrible in having his own son murdered. The tsar stood alone.

In 1934, Joseph Stalin effected a similar manoeuvre. At the famous seventeenth party congress, often known simply as the "Victors' Congress", some delegates were seeking to advance Sergei Kirov, the Leningrad party secretary, as an alternative to Stalin. Subsequently, Kirov was murdered. There is no doubt as to who committed the act – the assassin was apprehended and duly executed. Whether it actually took place on direct order from Stalin is a matter of some debate, which need not concern us here. The point lies in the pattern of autocracy. Once Kirov was gone, the dictator stood alone. And so it would remain until his death, with no heir apparent.

When Boris Yeltsin was first elected president of Russia, in 1991, he had a running mate – General Aleksandr Rutskoi – who became vice president. During the October 1993 revolt, Rutskoi was to be found among the insurgents, to the point even of swearing the oath as new president of Russia. Once the confrontation was over, and Yeltsin had won, a new

Russian constitution was adopted that made no provision for a vice president. The tsar again stood alone, with no heir apparent.

With the March 1998 events it was shown how shortsighted the new constitution really was. It does have a clause saying that in a case where the president is incapacitated, the prime minister will assume power, under an obligation to call new elections within three months. But at the end of March 1998 Russia had no prime minister, and what would have happened if the president had indeed been incapacitated at that time was – from a constitutional point of view – totally unclear.

To the country's president, however, that was not a problem. By ramming through the appointment of the Kiriyenko government, he had not only shown who was the real boss. With both Chernomyrdin and Chubais out of the way, the security of his autocracy had also been restored. Boris Yeltsin again stood alone, with no significant political figure in his vicinity who could get ambitious. It was, however, also guaranteed that if he were indeed to become incapacitated there would be a major crisis of succession.

Kiriyenko in power?

While the outcome of the struggle between the president and the Duma was a clear victory for the former, it was less obvious what the position would be for the nominal winner. Coming to power under conditions such as these, the 35 year old Kiriyenko would have to start out with a hostile Duma and with few friends of any political importance. John Helmer, writing for the *Moscow Tribune*, captured his predicament rather to the point:

> If Sergei Kiriyenko is an unelectable, stand-in prime minister, he's got either a very short, or a very long tenure. If Yeltsin decides he can survive and run again for re-election, Kiriyenko could be in office for almost six years. That's longer than any of Yeltsin's prime ministers to date. If Yeltsin doesn't run, and must choose someone he trusts to win the 2000 presidential election, Kiriyenko has got no more than 245 days. That's all the time left this year, including the Russian holidays.[50]

The reason for the deadline was that a new candidate would have to be groomed from the beginning of the New Year, in which the Duma election would offer an important test of strength for presidential candidates *in spe*.

Calculations of this sort were seriously complicated by the gubernatorial election in Krasnoyarsk, which took place right after the confirmation of Kiriyenko and was won by Aleksandr Lebed. Having secured, against all polls and odds, a solid 45 per cent of the votes in the 26 April 1998 first round, in the 17 May second round the general won comfortably, with close to 60 per cent of the votes.

There were several reasons for the Kremlin to be worried about this outcome. One was that Lebed had been fired from the security council without being offered something in compensation. The normal pattern of dismissals from Yeltsin's entourage had merely been to recycle – Anatolyi Chubais being a case in point: the general, therefore, could be expected to bear a real grudge, a grudge that was aggravated by his being an outsider, one who had not been allowed to take part in the plunder and looting of the economy.

A second reason for concern lay in the fact that economically the Krasnoyarsk region is one of the most powerful ones. One-fourth the size of the United States, it holds Russia's second-largest deposits of oil, gas, coal and metals, and it is home to several of the country's most profitable mining operations. Perhaps most importantly, it is home to Norilsk Nikel, one of the most controversial of all the privatized enterprises. As governor of this region, Lebed will have an important springboard – economically as well as politically – from which to launch a challenge against other contenders for power, or indeed against Yeltsin himself.

But perhaps the most important cause for Kremlin concern was linked to previous voting patterns, where Krasnoyarsk had been a mirror of the federation as a whole. In the 1995 Duma election, for example, communist and nationalist candidates scored 54 per cent in Krasnoyarsk, against 53 per cent overall, and in the first round of the 1996 presidential election Yeltsin scored 35 per cent both in Krasnoyarsk and overall. In a free and fair election, Lebed might thus be expected to repeat his high score nationwide, and therefore win the presidency.

Symptomatically, there had been a powerful process of political mobilization against his candidacy, including Moscow mayor Yurii Luzhkov and Oneksimbank tycoon Vladimir Potanin. But Lebed had shored up heavy support as well. Endorsement from former Soviet leader Mikhail Gorbachev perhaps did not count for much, but the fact that rival LogoVaz tycoon Boris Berezovskii weighed in on the general's side must have been bad news indeed to the Kremlin – and thus to Kiriyenko as well.

As if these political problems were not enough, the new government was immediately confronted with a number of pressing economic problems. Although some of the leading macroeconomic indicators – notably inflation, interest and exchange rates, and GDP – still gave some reason for cautious optimism, the financial sector was set in a process of accelerated deterioration.

According to Goskomstat, public sector wage arrears had grown by 17 per cent during March alone, to reach 8.9 billion re-denominated roubles, and according to the director of the Pension Fund, Vasilii Barchuk, pension arrears had also started growing again.[51] In May 1998, Goskomstat presented its revised first quarter data, showing that GDP growth had been zero and that wage and pension arrears had reached an all-time high of more than 60 billion roubles.[52]

On 21 April, only days before the third vote on Kiriyenko, the Duma began hearings on the government's (twice-revised) structural development programme for 1997–2000. In a comment, *Finansovye Izvestiya's* Yevgeniya Pismennaya offered a rather sombre portrayal of the achievements thus far:

> For example, already in the past year tax collection should have begun to improve visibly, the structural development budget should have begun implementation, the revenue base of the Pension Fund should have stabilized and the situation of public sector wage payments should have been improved. After having read through the Goskomstat materials, one may conclude that not one of these tasks has been achieved.[53]

In spite of the achievements of the Chubais administration that were outlined above, the revenue side of federal budget for 1997 had been fulfilled only to 77.2 per cent, and public debt had risen to 40 per cent of GDP. In an international comparison, the latter figure may not appear to be overly alarming, but it was set in a process of rapid increase and could be expected very soon to get seriously out of hand.

Appearing before the Duma, Kiriyenko was quite candid about the continued deterioration that had marked the first quarter of 1998. GDP growth had ceased, fixed capital investment in the first two months had been reduced by a further 7.5 per cent, and the balance of trade had fallen to a mere $150 million, compared to $1.5 billion in the same period in 1997. Most importantly, tax collection in money form stood at 18–19 billion roubles, rather than the budgeted 25 billion roubles. The latter was even worse than in 1997.[54]

The one real asset on which the new government could rely was the continued absence of major social unrest. The 9 April attempt to call into the streets a national protest movement was something of a non-event, and both 1 May and 9 May, traditional communist days of mass mobilization, served most of all to confirm the communist party's distinct lack of popular appeal.

Then followed the renewed crisis in Indonesia, which dealt a serious blow to Russia's financial markets. Over five days of trading, culminating with a 12 per cent drop on Monday, 18 May, the stock market lost about a quarter of its value. Seeing that the rouble again was coming under heavy pressure, on the following day the Central Bank hiked the re-finance rate from 30 to 50 per cent. In nominal terms, this was the highest rate since December 1996 but given the much lower inflation rate it was a punishing blow to all expectations for a halt to the investment decline.

In a parallel to the financial crisis, the Kiriyenko government was also forced to deal with the country's coal miners, who seemed finally to have had enough with not getting their wages on time – or at all. Entering into hunger strikes and blocking the Trans-Siberian railroad at several points, they presented a serious threat to the economy as a whole.

Recalling that the coal miners made a big contribution to the downfall of Mikhail Gorbachev, the government was understandably worried but the president remained aloof. In a characteristic move, he refused to accept any responsibility for the crisis, claiming on live television to have signed a decree that should have satisfied all parties. Young Kiriyenko was standing alone.

The first serious gusts of the approaching financial storm passed during the last week of May 1998.[55] It was felt in equities, in securities and in the exchange rate. On Tuesday, 26 May, GKO yields rose to 63 per cent, the highest level since January 1997. Investors began selling both stocks and securities and the rouble came under intense pressure. Panic was in the air.

The Kiriyenko government, having hardly had time to settle in its new offices, was slow in reacting and rebellious tycoons were adding fuel to the fire. One of the main Moscow papers, the *Nezavisimaya Gazeta*, which is controlled by Boris Berezovskii, was conducting a powerful campaign for a devaluation of the rouble. And the pyramid game that had been played in the market for state securities was beginning to wobble.

Wednesday proved to be the real crunch, when an attempt to auction off 8 billion roubles of GKOs failed miserably. After trying an extraordinary session, the government ended up having to contribute 2.4 billion roubles from the budget, in order to redeem 5.5 billion roubles in maturing debt. As a result, average yields were pushed up to a 22-month high, touching 90 per cent. In secondary trading, one GKO issue traded at an annualized yield of 231 per cent.

Equities were also being pummelled, with *The Moscow Times* index sliding to a low of 137, erasing all gains since December 1996. Some blue chips lost up to a quarter of their value in that one day. Moscow-based market analysts were excelling in doom and gloom: "We are seeing a meltdown. . . . Everything has been shot down." All was seen to hinge on a massive foreign bailout: "The writing is on the wall: only a big, fat foreign loan will save the rouble from a devastating collapse." Even World Bank president James Wolfensohn was talking of "a crisis".[56]

At the end of the day, the Central Bank announced that it was hiking the re-finance rate from 50 per cent to a forbidding 150 per cent, in order to cool off speculation against the rouble. Bank chairman Sergei Dubinin also announced that the bank had spent close to $1.5 billion on its rouble defence, bringing total reserves down to just above $14 billion, from a high of $24 billion in July 1997. Markets were hoping for a further loan package of no less than $10 billion.

On Thursday, the situation stabilized somewhat, with the stock market recovering more than 7 per cent and yields on securities dropping to 70 per cent. The Central Bank bought $500 million, thus shoring up its reserves somewhat. But with non-residents still holding about $20 billion in Russian treasury bills and Central Bank cash reserves (minus gold) standing at merely $10 billion, the situation was far from satisfactory. In addition, interbank lending rates around 400 per cent indicated a severe liquidity crisis.

On Friday, the IMF announced that it would release a previously frozen $670 million tranche of the $10.1 billion Extended Fund Facility that was agreed in March 1996. At the same time, however, Moody's announced a downgrade for Russia (from Ba3 to B1, or on a par with Lebanon but below Jamaica), and the markets obviously placed more trust in Moody's than in the IMF. According to the Central Bank, during the previous two weeks, $500 million to $700 million had been pulled out of the securities market by non-residents.

Friday also marked the political fallout from the crisis. The president had promised that "heads would roll", and so they did. The head of the government tax service, Aleksandr Pochinok, was fired, to be replaced by the former finance minister Boris Fyodorov. Seeking to restore some confidence in the country's rotten system of tax collection, the government was now huffing and puffing in all directions.

Major corporate tax dodgers were given until the end of June 1998 to come up with 5 billion roubles in back taxes, and about 1,000 Russian jet set celebrities were threatened with special tax revision.

The gist of the new campaign was clearly reflected in the media. While television showed Russian tax police, heavily armed and clad in black ski masks, making brutal raids all over Moscow, *The Moscow Times* published a cartoon of Boris Yeltsin wielding an executioner's axe and clad in a big apron, with the caption reading "Let's collect some taxes."

Speaking at a rally in Orenburg, moreover, former prime minister Viktor Chernomyrdin found it hard to conceal his glee at the predicament of his successor's government. Accusing Kiriyenko of acting too slowly, Chernomyrdin made it clear that the election race was now on, both for his own party in the 1999 Duma election and for himself in the 2000 presidential election. To the financial markets, these were hardly stability-enhancing prospects.

Then some good news finally arrived. At the beginning of June there were strong signals indicating that the G7 was pondering a package of relief measures, and the stock market rebounded. The government also succeeded in issuing a five-year, $1.2 billion Eurobond.

It was beginning to look as though the worst was over. GKO yields dropped to 45 per cent and equities continued to rise. On 4 June, the Central Bank announced that it was cutting the re-finance rate from 150 to

60 per cent. The market was clearly in a "show-me" mood, waiting for concrete news from the G7 finance ministers, due to meet in Paris on the following Monday.

When the third week of crisis opened, there was more bad news. The outcome of the Paris meeting was soothing noise about further help via the IMF – but no hard cash. On Tuesday, Standard & Poor's followed in the footsteps of Moody's by announcing a downgrade for Russia, and on Wednesday the Japanese Yen took a serious nosedive, spreading further shockwaves of "Asian flu".

In Moscow, the government tried to offer a total of 18 billion roubles in securities, of various durations, but succeeded in selling only 4.72 billion. Being forced yet again to use up its reserves (including much of the $1.2 billion Eurobond) in order to redeem maturing securities, it thus met to approve an increase of its foreign borrowing limit from $3.5 billion to $6 billion. A one-year GKO rose to 61 per cent and the stock market entered a new period of sharp falls, losing 14 per cent during the week.

Week four opened with another crash in the stock market, as *The Moscow Times* index slid to 124.5, down 60 per cent since the start of the year and touching a 20-month low. The one-year benchmark GKO rose to more than 70 per cent and there was renewed pressure on the rouble.

By now advocates for a massive international bailout were painting a series of grim scenarios about possible developments should the rouble be allowed to collapse. There were variations on the theme of a nationalist backlash, and upheavals in a nuclear superpower. US Deputy Treasury Secretary Lawrence Summers even threatened that "Russia's problem has the potential to become in turn Central Europe's and the World's." It was argued that the West simply could not allow the worst to happen.

The serious fears that were attached to a Russian devaluation mainly concerned Western exposure. Devaluation would not only damage foreign portfolios containing Russian securities. Even more importantly, it would compound the problems of servicing the foreign debt and thus enhance the risk of Russian defaults. And the latter would spell trouble. Big trouble. Contamination effects had already been noted in other emerging markets in the region, and even far-off Brazil had felt jitters of Russian origin.

And it was not only the sovereign debt that was in focus. Russian commercial banks had added their share by running up large debts to foreign banks, debts that would become more expensive after devaluation and might thus go into default. To make things even worse, they had also entered into forward rouble contracts with foreign hedge funds, implying that in the case of devaluation they would stand to make big losses.

In spite of the mounting pressure to undertake a bailout, both the IMF and the G7 seemed bent on holding out. They appear to have believed that for the first time in a long time they had the Russian government and the Russian Duma in a position where necessary and repeatedly promised reform measures would simply have to be enacted. Thus the stage was set for an international "chicken" game. And the markets were putting big money on Moscow to be the winner.

In order to improve relations with the Western creditors, on 17 June Yeltsin appointed Anatolyi Chubais to serve as international loan liaison officer. Although a serious provocation to the Duma, his personal contacts in Washington would be of great value. On the following day, Russia issued a 30-year $2.5 billion Eurobond, but according to Chubais a full $10–15 billion would be needed in order to avert financial collapse.

The IMF, however, was still holding back. On 18 June it delayed payment of a $670 million tranche of the previous $10.1 billion credit, citing problems with implementation of needed reforms.

On 23 June, the Russian government reacted by presenting an anti-crisis plan that was directed mainly at improving tax collection. Stating that the situation had now become "so acute that there are social and political dangers", President Yeltsin called on the Duma to take rapid action – or else! Two days later the IMF released the frozen tranche, but the situation was still deteriorating. On 29 June, the Central Bank raised its re-finance rate to 80 per cent.

At the beginning of July, Siberian miners resumed their pickets of the railroads and this time they were not only calling for wage arrears to be settled. Now they were also demanding Yeltsin's resignation. GKO yields were running between 130 and 140 per cent and *The Moscow Times* index was falling close to the 100 level where it had begun in September 1995, representing a drop of more than three-fourths from the high in October 1997.

On 13 July, the international lenders finally came through. Under heavy political pressure not to let Russia fail, the IMF had reluctantly taken the lead in organizing a joint $22.6 billion rescue package. Including previous commitments, the IMF would contribute $15.1 billion over 1998–99. The World Bank put up $6 billion and the Japanese government $1.5 billion.

On 20 July, the IMF approved its share and a first tranche of $4.8 billion was paid out. Markets seemed to have been right in gambling that Russia was simply too big, and too nuclear, to be allowed to fail. What they obviously had failed to reckon with, was that the "chicken" game would be continued. And in the second round both sides would lose. In a big way.

The reason was that the breathing spell that was intended to follow from the bailout was put to no good use whatsoever, at least not for Russia. On the one hand, the Duma continued to obstruct necessary legislation. Already in the days after the rescue had been announced, and *before* the IMF conformed its decision, it gutted the government's anti-crisis plan, defeating measures which according to Kiriyenko would have provided two-thirds of targeted revenues.

Although the president responded by vetoing the reductions in tax cuts and by decreeing new taxes, the market had been sent a strong signal. After a brief recovery the situation continued to deteriorate. On 12 August the Moscow interbank market was virtually paralyzed by liquidity shortages. The Central Bank imposed limits on the purchases of foreign exchange by banks.

On the following day *Financial Times* published a letter from financier George Soros, saying that Russia's financial crisis had reached a terminal stage and that the rouble must be devalued by 15–20 per cent.[57] At the same time, Moody's downgraded Russian sovereign foreign debt from B2 to CAA1, on par with many poor African countries.

Markets were now finally coming round to realizing the true nature of the pyramid games that had been played in the securities market. Expectations were that Russia would either devalue the rouble or default on its debt. What no one seems to have anticipated was that the Russian government would choose to do both.

In the night between 16 and 17 August 1998 the final round of the "chicken" game with the IMF was resolved, as the latter communicated its decision not to pour any more money down the Russian drain. The markets had thus been proven wrong. Despite all its nuclear weapons, Russia after all had not been too big to be allowed to fail! In the morning of 17 August markets were informed of the price of their failure.

At first sight the news was not all bad. The rouble corridor was widened, to allow fluctuations within a band of 6.3 to 9.5 roubles to the dollar, and much of the short-term foreign debt was frozen for 90 days. Technically, as Prime Minister Kiriyenko would insist, these moves were neither devaluation nor default. And with a more professional handling, the fallout could perhaps have been kept within reasonable limits.

As it was, however, the rouble entered a stage of free fall, where the Central Bank repeatedly had to invalidate trading on the currency exchange and go back to fixing yesterday's exchange rate. Even more important, the first signals of how the short-term debt would be restructured provided clear indications that the Russian government was bent on giving Russian banks preferential treatment *vis-à-vis* foreign investors.

An important reason behind the subsequently disastrous development was that in the midst of this latest round of crisis Boris Yeltsin chose to intervene in his own by now all too familiar way. On 21 August, the Duma called for the resignation of both Yeltsin and Kiriyenko. Two days later the president dismissed the government and launched yet another "chicken" game with the Duma.

The president's first choice for new prime minister was Viktor Chernomyrdin, who had been dismissed six months previously for mishandling the economy. Arguing that a re-appointment of Chernomyrdin would mean a return to the problems of crony capitalism that had caused the crisis, the Duma turned him down. Yeltsin immediately nominated him again, and the Duma again defeated him.

So far the stage appeared to be set for a repetition of the confrontation that had been played out in March, but in the third and final round the Duma members were in a different mood altogether. They were now bent on staying the course. By defeating Chernomyrdin they would force the president to dissolve parliament and call new elections. The communists in particular expected that their position would be greatly strengthened in a new Duma.

What went on in Yeltsin's mind is as usual subject to speculation. The fact that leave had been cancelled at several vital military units prompted rumours of an intended rerun of October 1993, i.e. a forcible dissolution of the Duma and presidential rule by decree. The latter, after all, had been a great success in the Russian president's relations with the West.

In the end, however, it was Yeltsin who flinched. By choosing in the third round to nominate Yevgenii Primakov, who had been one of several candidates proposed by the Duma, he avoided the showdown. The price, however, that had been paid for this latest round of playing "chicken" was nothing short of terrible.

The collapse of the rouble represented not only an immediate economic loss. There are even tougher long-term implications of thus destroying all confidence in the national currency that had been so painfully built up over the last couple of years. In equal measure, the collapse of the banking system represents a setback of perhaps decades before Russians will again trust banks to handle their money.

In relation to the international financial markets, the defaults on foreign debt means that Moscow can look forward to a protracted period of pariah status. Moody's downgraded Russia's sovereign debt to CCC-, which is below Congo and Nigeria. Exacerbating the problem, there are also suspicions of deliberate abuse.

There are rumours, for example, indicating that the fall of the Kiriyenko government was orchestrated by tycoon Boris Berezovskii, the reason being that he and the other top bankers feared that the government would strike a fair deal between domestic and foreign creditors.[58] According to then Deputy Prime Minister Boris Nemtsov, the Russian government had been preparing to bankrupt some of the politically powerful but economically weak banks and oil companies, allowing others, including Westerners, to take over: "They (the oligarchs) understood that the end was near, that there might be serious changes in ownership and that the current oligarchate might come to an end."[59] They thus pre-empted.

And there are suspicions being advanced both by the Federal Audit Chamber and by Prosecutor General Yurii Skuratov that parts of the $4.8 billion tranche paid out in July had quite simply been stolen.[60] All in all, it seems safe to conclude that the appointment of the Primakov government effectively marked the end of an era.

There was one vital feature of this last confrontation, which perhaps may help explain why Yeltsin was finally forced to climb down from

Olympus. On all previous occasions there had been substantial figures in his vicinity on whom he could dump the blame. There had been Yegor Gaidar; there had been Anatolyi Chubais and eventually even Viktor Chernomyrdin. But trying to blame the August *debacle* on Sergei Kiriyenko would have been a bit too much.

Young Kiriyenko had not been in power long enough to be a credible victim and he was, quite frankly, not a substantial enough figure to serve as a lightning rod for the president. As one Russian journalist framed it, one cannot make a scapegoat out of a bunny rabbit.[61]

Before turning to look at what lessons may be drawn from the close to seven years that passed between Yeltsin's speech in October 1991 and the appointment of the Primakov government in September 1998, we shall take a closer look at the mechanics of predation, i.e. at how the kleptocrats have gone about their business of plundering. And we shall have a few words to say about the frequently heard comparisons with previous American robber barons.

The mechanics of predation

Looking back at the accounts that have been presented above, about financial speculation and about variously rigged privatization deals, we may find an important common denominator in the blending of power and property. The outcome has been a peculiar hybrid system, which Yabloko party leader Grigorii Yavlinskii has called a "semi-criminal oligarchy",[62] and which has prompted Moscow mayor Yurii Luzhkov to say that Russia now faces "unlimited criminalization of the economy . . . and of the government itself".[63]

Noting that the difference – on a fundamental level – between this novel form of Russian "market" economy and the old Russian patrimonial society is not all that great, we have a powerful illustration of the often neglected fact that history matters. Much as the great tsars of the fourteenth and fifteenth centuries patronized their boyars with *pomestie* land in return for service, the present-day boyar capitalists have become dependent on straight links to the government for their own enrichment.

This is not intended to serve merely as an amusing historical parallel. Analytically, there lies a crucial point in the fact that in both cases, the boyars lack real security of tenure: both accumulating and holding on to wealth is conditional upon service and loyalty to the tsar. In the historical case, the point can hardly be disputed. In the current one, it hinges on our understanding of how Russia's economic system will continue to develop. Will it really be possible to achieve within the foreseeable future an effective separation of power and property, or indeed of power and money?

Whether the plight of the modern-day Russian service nobility represents a transitory problem or a powerful historical lock-in, i.e. a stable but inferior institutional equilibrium with deep historical roots, is a question that will have to await its answer for another few years. Indications from the first six-odd years of reforms, however, are that we may be faced with a powerful path dependence, expressed in an inability to develop the type of legitimate general enforcement mechanisms that are normally associated with the rule of law. We shall return to this at length in Chapters 8 and 9 below.

From an institutional perspective of rules, norms and enforcement mechanisms, the difference between the Russian past and the Russian present is of a primarily technical nature. Instead of land grants, the present-day boyars have been rewarded for their service and loyalty in monetary terms (cash or shares). The latter rewards have been offered in two different ways, one representing a siphoning off of money from the federal budget and the other a transfer of wealth out of government hands, in both cases over time to increasingly well defined recipients of government patronage.

Looking at these schemes from a perspective of the pure mechanics of predation, we may see clearly the pivotal role that has been played by the Russian federal budget. Or, more precisely, by the failure of the Russian government to cover its budget deficit in a sustainable and non-inflationary way.

In the first phase of high inflation, inflationary financing provided ample scope for speculation based on easy non-collateralized credit offered at negative real interest rates. In the second phase of low inflation, the government decided to raise revenue by selling state property, thus offering the power elites a new venue for enrichment, by controlling the conditions of the sales.

Feeding off the budget

Beginning with the flow dimension of this process, we may identify a number of ways in which favoured members of the neo-nomenklatura have been allowed to siphon off substantial shares of budget expenditure into their own coffers. As indicated above, there is an early stage of general handouts and a later one of more specifically targeted benefits.

In the early stage, high inflation provoked a rather peculiar tug-of-war where government fiscal austerity programmes were matched by lavish Central Bank lending. The main beneficiaries of the latter were to be found in the emerging Russian banking system. While state owned enterprises were abruptly cut off from the traditional form of direct finance via the state budget, commercial banks were allowed to borrow easy money from the Central Bank, money that could be put to highly profitable speculative use in the currency market.

The general bonanza peaked towards the end of 1995, when Russia had more than 2,500 banks, most of which were weak and seriously under-capitalized. Their life support system was high inflation, lax regulation and a friendly source of lavish credit. All that would end, but while the sun was still shining there was plenty of hay to be made.

As Illarionov underlines, there could be no *economic* rationale behind the massive credits that were granted during the summer and autumn of 1992:

> Their scale, as well as the total absence of any form of public control over their granting, objectively strengthens the point of view, according to which the reasons behind this lending were political and even criminal. It was during precisely this period of unlimited credit expansion that the financial foundations for many of the large Russian banks were laid.[64]

At first, this was a phase which benefited many actors but as the situation stabilized power and influence was concentrated in the hands of a smaller group of banks, which could then become more direct beneficiaries of government patronage. Putting it differently, they were in a better position to extort from the government, but that difference is academic. Unless we are interested in the legal aspects of the matter, demanding and supplying privilege really represents but two sides of the same transaction.

One specific mode of patronage took the form of a system of federally "authorized banks" (*upolnomochennye banki*), which was introduced in 1993 and allowed favoured commercial banks to handle the accounts of various government agencies, including the Ministry of Finance.[65]

The potential gains involved in this right were of many different kinds. One could be to simply delay a transfer for some time, parking the money for a couple of weeks in, say, the market for state securities and pocketing the gains. (This, incidentally, has also been a steady source of revenue for enterprises delaying wage payments.)

Another, and more serious abuse of the rights to handle budget transfers was by exploiting the fragmented nature of the Russian monetary system, where various money surrogates have become a prominent feature. To mention but one example of how this could be turned into a source of substantial profit, when asked to transfer a 100-billion rouble payment to the Tyumen region, the Oneksimbank issued a money surrogate for the amount, asking for a 25 per cent fee to turn it into cash.[66]

In order to complete the picture of unbridled rent seeking by the country's financial and political elites, we should note that their ambitions have not been limited to squeezing funds out of the budget. In addition, their subsequent use of these funds has been heavily geared into supporting other elite activities, which have little indeed to do with furthering the development of the Russian economy.

As Steven Rosefielde notes, the dominant Moscow banks "specialize in short term revolving commercial loans which finance lucrative domestic wholesale commodities trade, Mafiya business, exported resources, the importation of luxury goods for the new Russians and the asset seizing operations of deal-making tycoons".[67]

Noting that these very same banks have also been major beneficiaries of the government's deficit spending, the circle may be closed: "The state borrows funds to finance its deficit spending, but pays above-competitive rates for the loans as a device for concealing what Robert Reich would call corporate welfare. Instead of transparently gifting kleptocratic banks from the state treasury, government revenues are transferred under the guise of servicing its debt."[68]

It was in this latter dimension, i.e. in the market for state securities, that the elites found their real financial killing fields, and thus also where the consequences for the real sector of the economy would be the most detrimental. The effective crowding out of industrial investors from the financial markets will have long-term implications for the economy as a whole that are serious indeed.

The background to this development was linked to falling inflation rates, which meant falling seigniorage revenue and thus rising problems in financing the federal budget deficit. Seeking to solve the underlying problems by balancing revenues and expenditure would have meant a serious challenge to the predatory elites. Macroeconomic stability would have forced them to engage in constructive and competitive moneymaking, where the edge would have belonged to foreign operators.

Against this background it was logical that the government sought instead another easy way out, by borrowing money. It thus created a situation where the banks, being the only ones having sufficient loanable funds, could increasingly dictate their terms for buying state securities. (Needless to say, foreigners were effectively barred from taking part on equal terms.) The costs to Russian society would be quite substantial.

As we have noted above, in the spring of 1996 the situation went completely out of hand. Getting rich at the expense of the federal budget, the banks were now ready to deliver their end of the bargain. Faced with the real prospect of a communist presidential election victory, the "group of seven" leading bankers decided to throw their whole might – money as well as media – behind the incumbent. And they succeeded.

At a cursory glance, the 1996 Russian presidential race may be held up as something similar to a typical US presidential race. In both cases, "Big Money" played a big role in securing the political outcome. Yet there is also a profound difference. In the typical US case, candidates go to great lengths in order to secure contributions for their respective sides. In the Russian case, the financial elite as a whole decided that the sitting president must remain in power, at any cost.

Somewhat ironically, in this rather undemocratic endeavour they received massive support and praise from the democratic West. It is hard, for example, to see the $10.1 billion credit that was granted by the IMF in March 1996 as something entirely unconnected to the Russian presidential race. The morality, and perhaps even wisdom, of this approach may certainly be questioned.

The conclusion of what has been said above is that while in the US case money may be said to create power, in the Russian case the borderline has been erased. While moneymaking outside the central circles of power is not a promising venture, maintaining a central political position requires substantial financial backing. This blurring of the distinction between power and money has emerged as a defining characteristic of Russia's new economic system.

Turning now to look at the stock dimension of predation, we shall see a similar pattern of blurring the distinction between power and property, manifested in a process where favoured predators have been allowed – perhaps even encouraged – by the government to feed off the remains of the Soviet economy.

Handing out property rights

Keeping our focus directed at the pure mechanics of predation, the main vehicle throughout the process of redistributing wealth has been rigged privatization deals. This practice was already begun in the early stages of the grand privatization programme, when rules were twisted so that insiders were guaranteed *ex ante* that they would maintain control over "their" enterprises. The result was an unprecedented transfer of wealth, held up by some as a major success of the reform programme as such.

The following verdict by three prominent participants in the formation of the privatization programme – Maksim Boiko, Andrei Shleifer and Robert Vishny – is rather telling: "Workers in privatized enterprises received the most generous benefits ever, in any previous privatization. . . . The benefits of managers appear at first sight not to be particularly large, but were in practice enormous."[69]

While it was a substantial volume of property that was thus transferred into private hands, more or less for free, in the early stage it still represented a transfer of wealth to a rather large group of new "owners". It should be noted that this outcome was anticipated, as a necessary price to pay in order to overcome feasibility constraints. As two other prominent advisors – Richard Layard and Olivier Blanchard – put it, rather more bluntly, if insiders could not be offered sufficient bribes, privatization could not proceed.[70]

As the process proceeded, however, bribes to insiders were transformed from general handouts to specific privileges for specific actors; thus crystallizing the pattern of offering politically determined rewards to loyal boyars.

A glaring example of this type of patronage may be found in the notorious "loans-for-shares" programme that unfolded in late 1995.

The background to this development is linked to the rapidly deteriorating financial position of the Russian government. Faced with a projected budget deficit of about 73 trillion roubles, it was decided that privatization could no longer proceed as more or less free handouts to various insiders. It would have to contribute revenue to the budget. Thus began the second phase of privatization, which at once became known as "money privatization".

The outcome for 1995 as a whole may be divided into three different sources of revenue. In the budget it was expected that auctions and tenders for blocks of shares in 136 of the most attractive state enterprises would generate 4–5 trillion roubles – the actual outcome was only 1.5 trillion roubles. Offering blocks of shares in 29 enterprises as collateral for loans was expected to generate another 2–3 trillion roubles – in practice this brought in 5.1 trillion roubles. Finally, the sale of Lukoil convertible bonds did raise an expected 1.0 trillion roubles, while the planned sale of a 25 per cent stake in Svyazinvest, which was expected to generate 1.9 trillion roubles, never took place.[71]

All in all, money privatization succeeded in bringing in 7.6 trillion roubles, against an expected 8.7 trillion, which at first sight looks like something of a success. On closer inspection, however, this success was bought at a price that was paid in terms of a serious degradation of the economic relations between the country's political and financial elites.

At first, the political struggles focused on the process of pinpointing exactly which of the state owned enterprises should be sold. This triggered a harsh debate concerning "economic security" (*ekonomicheskaya bezopasnost*), the harshest part of which concerned the fate of the natural monopolies and the raw materials giants.

In March 1995, the GKI and the federal property fund presented a preliminary list of more than 7,000 "non-strategic" enterprises that could be put up for sale. In July, a second list of 3,054 "strategic" enterprises was presented, which would not be offered for sale on grounds that they were particularly important to the country's national security. During summer, a great number of those on the former list were also excluded, and by August, when the GKI presented its final list of enterprises that were to be auctioned off during September–December 1995, only 136 were left.[72]

The main point of interest here concerns not so much the straight sales, which were disappointing in the extreme,[73] as a result of the rather peculiar scheme of offering blocks of shares in state owned enterprises as collateral for loans to the Russian government. That project was taking shape already in April, at the suggestion of Vladimir Potanin, but it was only in September that a list of 29 key industries was presented, which would be auctioned off to a small group of very large banks.

The list contained the "commanding heights" of the Russian economy: all the oil giants, together with Gazprom – the world's largest gas company, Norilsk Nikel – the world's largest nickel smelter, Rostelekom – Russia's largest telecommunications company, UES – the electricity utility giant, etc.

Officially, the purpose of the programme was that the winner in each auction would grant credit to the government for a period of three years at LIBOR plus 0.5 per cent. In return they would gain control over management (and profits) in the various enterprises for a period of five years.[74] The purpose of the auctions was to determine which banks would be allowed to gain control over which enterprises. It was specifically stated that there was to be more than one bidder at each auction. Reality, however, would turn out somewhat different from plan.

The conditions for the auctions were spelled out in a presidential decree of 31 August 1995. There was to be broad-based competition from both domestic and foreign investors, and a minimum of one bid each from at least two investors was required for an auction to be valid. The state reserved the right to repay the credits, and thus to reclaim the collateral, but in case that was not done by a specified date (which was extended from 1 January to 1 September 1996) the winners would have the right to sell the shares and to keep one-third of the proceeds in excess of the credit granted. As the OECD points out, this "essentially included the right to keep the shares by arranging a sale to oneself at a price close to the value of the loan, an option that has been since chosen by several winners".[75]

In actual practice, only 12 auctions were held, almost all of which were surrounded by considerable controversy. (Pressure from ministries and from the enterprises themselves succeeded in removing the remainder from the GKI list.) In five of the 12, there was only one bidder, and in two foreigners were explicitly excluded. In some cases, enterprises organized their own auctions, in others major banks were responsible, and could then rig the procedures to suit their own bidders.[76]

The insider pattern was brought out clearly in the first of these auctions, held on 3 November 1995, when the highly profitable Surgutneftegaz oil company succeeded in having its own pension fund secure a 40 per cent stake. It did so after eliminating all competition on pure technicalities. A similar deal was concluded on 7 December 1995, when 5 per cent of Lukoil stock was offered for sale. The winning bid of $35.01 million came from the company itself, backed by Bank Imperial, defeating a competing bid of $35 million.

On 17 November, a majority 51 per cent of the votes (38 per cent of the shares) in Norilsk Nikel was secured by Oneksimbank, which was also the organizer of the auction. The starting bid was $170 million. After formally excluding foreign investors, and after disqualifying a competing domestic bid, Oneksimbank could accept its own offer of $170.1 million. On 7 December, it went on to organize and win another major auction, for 51 per cent of the Sidanko oil company, again after formally barring foreigners and disqualifying a domestic competitor.

On 8 December, Bank Menatep won 45 per cent of Yukos, Russia's second largest oil company. Already being in control of part of Yukos, Menatep secured the right to organize the auction and proceeded to disqualify several competitors on technicalities. The starting price was $150 million. Menatep put up $159 million.

The scandalous nature of these deals was disclosed when Russia's independent accounting office undertook an investigation, revealing massive fraud. Peter Reddaway summarizes its findings: "Not only were the assets undervalued and the winners predetermined, but the government actually deposited its own funds in the banks that won the auctions. So the banks made the loans using the government's own money, and the whole transaction was, for the Kremlin, not a major infusion of cash but a net loss."[77]

Since it was fairly obvious at the outset that the government would not be able or willing to pay back the loans, in practice the collateral was forfeit at the moment of the transaction.

Once it was made public that a small number of banks with close ties to the government – notably so Oneksimbank and Imperial – had made some real killings, there was an uproar. Moscow mayor Yurii Luzhkov stated that the activities of privatization chief Anatolyi Chubais were so dubious that they required criminal investigation.[78]

In January 1996, following an increasing torrent of criticism, Boris Yeltsin finally decided to fire Chubais. The official reason was that he had failed to deal with the growing problem of wage and pension arrears, but in unofficial Moscow it was generally thought that his real failure was that of having allowed the communists to score a victory in the December elections to the Duma. Be this as it may. As we know, the "radical reformer" would not stay out of favour for long. Nor would he keep his hands clean once returned to power.

Writing about the scandals that surrounded the loans-for-shares scheme, Illarionov points at the increasingly obvious pattern of dependence between the government and the country's financial elites:

> Having set a hardly realistic target for incomes from privatization at nine trillion rubles, the government became a prisoner of its own decisions. In order to fulfill the established plan, in the final analysis it was forced into radically reducing the price of government property offered for sale or as collateral, at the legally and morally not irreproachable auctions.[79]

Following these scandals, a special law was passed prohibiting further auctions of shares for loans, but that did not mean that the handouts of state property to favoured bankers were stopped. Far from it. The process would continue in 1996, when money privatization was expected to generate a further 12.4 trillion roubles,[80] and the beneficiaries would be picked from the very same circles as before.

In the first of these auctions, concerning a 34 per cent share in the Sidanko oil company, only one bidder appeared. The lucky winner was again Oneksimbank, whose former head, Vladimir Potanin, was now first deputy prime minister in charge of economics. In November 1996, Alfa Bank and Most Bank, both of which had also contributed heavily to Yeltsin's re-election campaign, pushed out a Western consortium that had been entrusted with privatizing the country's telecommunications sector, and in December, Bank Menatep organized an auction for a one-third stake in the Yukos oil company. The winner was a Menatep subsidiary, and the price about a quarter of what had been estimated by Salomon Brothers as a fair value.[81]

In 1997, however, as we may recall from above the games of power and property would undergo a radical transformation. The elite struggles that erupted in the late summer of 1997, concerning the latest round of privatization, provided public illustration of how important it is to maintain a good relation with the "tsar".

The analytical dimension of that process will be discussed further below. Here we shall merely note that if Russian history matters, it does so in the institutional sense of preserving a hierarchical and non-reciprocal relation of power, between the ruler and the ruled. If there is one thing that is sadly lacking for the Russian *noveau-riches*, it is security of tenure for their mostly ill-gotten gains. The reason has deep historical roots, defying comparisons with emerging capitalists in other countries at other times.

Russian Robber Barons?

One of the major differences between Russia and the West lies in the rapid accumulation of very great private wealth that has taken place among people who five or ten years ago may be realistically assumed to have had little idea of either business or finance. This is a phenomenon that really has no previous parallel, and which may be explained only within the context of the equally unparalleled Russian project of shock therapy.

As Rosefielde points out, the "entrepreneurs" of new Russia have not emerged from any form of capitalist class, nor are they primarily concerned with wealth creation:

> They are defrocked communists and their scions, who are trying to reconstitute and plutocratically expand the élite privileges and status they enjoyed as party members and state servants under Soviet socialism in conjunction with other aspirants, especially

the Mafia. They are a new breed of Czarist servitor in the sense that their power derives from state service, or state solicitude, but they lack the security that comes with hereditary wealth, titles and entitlements.[82]

The comparison that is frequently made between present-day Russian tycoons and the nineteenth century American Robber Barons should be seen against this background. It rests primarily on two fundamental misconceptions, both of which have far-reaching implications for the future of Russia.

First, it is an irrefutable fact that the Carnegies, Mellons, Rothschilds and Rockefellers were engaged in large-scale productive investment and technological advancement of the national economy. A generation later, the legacy of their activities was banks, railroads, steelmills and factories, together making up the basis of a modern industrialized society.

In sharp contrast, their modern Russian counterparts have been engaged in heavy predation and capital flight, of the kinds outlined above. What the next generation legacy of *their* activities will be remains to be seen, but judging from the record during the first six-odd years, an industrial waste-land specked with islands of speculative financial prosperity would seem to be the likeliest prospect.

Secondly, and even more importantly, it is an equally irrefutable fact that the American Robber Barons operated on the fringe of a society that was otherwise marked by the rule of law. They conducted a form of business that in some senses may perhaps have been immoral, but as a whole was not illegal, for the simple reason that legislation had not yet caught up with their operations.

In equally sharp contrast, the current Russian version of robber capitalism represents not something that is happening on the periphery, but activities that are anchored at the very heart of the system of power, within the "semi-criminal oligarchy". There can be little doubt that much of what is happening in present-day Russian wealth creation is both immoral and illegal. And it would be hard indeed to interpret the steady stream of legislation and presidential decrees as signs of laws being in the process of catching up with and overtaking crime.

The problem is not an absence of legislation, but an absence of enforcement and an associated absence of expectations for the rule of law to be established in the near future. To mention but one case in point, we may ask what type of business culture is engendered by a long string of unprosecuted contract killings. It is not simply a question of the loss of life, and the consequent suffering that is brought onto friends and relatives, but even more so a vital demonstration of what will happen to those who break the "criminal" code – in the true sense of the word.

At the heart of the problem lies the danger of a lock-in effect, of the emergence of a prisoners' dilemma situation where the use of violence becomes the dominant strategy. Why trust in the courts, when you must realistically assume that your business partners will place *their* trust in hit men? Why make long-term investments, when there is no long-term security of tenure?

The tragic fate of American businessman Paul Tatum, who was gunned down in early November 1995, in an underpass next to the Slavyanskaya Hotel in Moscow, provided one of many demonstrations for others to beware. Tatum went public with his problems and was going to take his partners to court. In return he was assassinated. Those responsible have not been brought to justice.

The criminal periods in American capitalism could be contained for the simple reason that the "Robbers" were never allowed to take over completely. Above all, they were not allowed to infiltrate and dominate the highest echelons of power, such as the Presidency, Congress or the Supreme Court. It may be argued that they never felt a need to do this, that lower level protection was sufficient, but that really amounts to the same thing, namely an effective separation of the country's leadership from its criminal structures.

Comparing the Robber Barons to the Wild West and the Gangland periods, we may find that throughout there were US legislators and marshals diligently at work, seeking to catch up. And finally they did catch up. This is certainly not to say that crime has been purged from American society, nor that there will be no more cases of high level corruption, merely that the rule of law has prevailed as the dominant system. (It is somehow symptomatic that in the end it was the IRS that succeeded in sending Al Capone to Alcatraz!)

It is this background that must be kept in mind when looking at the new society that is emerging in Russia. The highly distinctive blend of executive power, corrupt officials and criminal gangs that have become the true hallmark of Russian politics is definitely not a marginal phenomenon, happening on the fringe of a society that is otherwise built on the rule of law. Nor is it an arrangement that is conducive to investment and technological change.

Comparing the minute flows of foreign direct investment going into the Russian economy to the massive capital flight that takes place from Russia provides a clear indication of the market value of Russia's post-Soviet leadership.

The most distressing factor of all, in this rather grim scenario, is that there are strong negative and self-reinforcing spirals at work. If we accept, for example, that no real positive change in the economy will be possible until at least some rudimentary form of rule of law has been established to separate power, business and law enforcement, the problem may again be formulated in terms of a very simple prisoners' dilemma, where continued predation and "instant justice" is the dominant strategy.

Who wants to be the first to invest, when the others are engaged in plunder? Who wants to be the first to repatriate capital, when the others are putting their money in safe havens abroad? Who wants to be the first to trust in courts of law that are ignored by all the others?

One may certainly hope that the Russian clan leaders will some day get together with "their" politicians, lawmakers and judges, and agree that all will henceforth work together for the better of Russia, within the limits of the law, but it is hard indeed to make that happy vision of born again tax paying, church going and law abiding citizens seem credible.

The question that remains to be answered concerns *why* Russia's attempt at systemic change in the end produced such a deplorable outcome. Putting it more specifically, we may recall two questions asked by Mancur Olson in the introductory chapter to this book: a) why did the transition from state planning to market economy result in such a massive drop in output, and b) why did it come to be associated with such heavy criminality?

Seeking to answer these questions, in the final section of this book, we shall change tack somewhat, leaving the chronological perspective in order to adopt a more analytical stance. What are the lessons that may be drawn from the accounts that have been outlined above?

Notes

1. Bush, K. 1997. The Russian economy in October 1997, continually updated mimeo, p. 7.
2. ITAR–TASS, 8 October 1996.
3. Rutland, P. 1997a. Another year lost for the economy, *Transitions*, **3**(2), 79.
4. *Finansovye Izvestiya*, 6 February 1997.
5. *Finansovye Izvestiya*, 22 May 1997. On the realism of the 1997 budget, see e.g. Sokolov, V. 1997. Byudzhet na 1997 god stal zakonom, no realnost ego vypolneniya blizka k nulyu, *Ekonomika i Zhizn*, **11**, 8.
6. Quoted by Reddaway, P. 1997a. Beware the Russian reformer, *Washington Post*, 28 August.
7. OECD 1997. *Russian Federation 1997*. Paris: OECD, p. 71. On the Russian debt, see also Khakamada, I. 1997. Gosudarstvennyi dolg: struktura i upravlenie, *Voprosy Ekonomiki*, **4**.
8. The former was Ba2 and the latter BB-, which was better than Brazil and Argentina but below Poland and Hungary (OECD 1997, op. cit., p. 70).
9. Vavilov, A. and Trofimov, G. 1997. Stabilizatsiya i upravlenie gosudarst-vennym dolgom Rossii, *Voprosy Ekonomiki*, **12**, 76.
10. For technical details on the various Eurobond issues, see *Finansovye Izvestiya*, 31 July and 5 August 1997.
11. *Finansovye Izvestiya*, 11 February 1997.
12. Even normally optimistic market analysts in Moscow seem to have been a bit miffed by this relapse in bad old Soviet practice. See, e.g., interviews in *Moscow Tribune*, 2 April 1997, pp. 1–2.
13. *Ekonomicheskaya Gazeta*, **29**, 1997, p. 1.

14. In the words of analyst Florian Fenner, at Brunswick brokerage: "All the money they get now goes into paying pensions and wages – that is what happened with the Deutschmark issue. . . . They don't care how they do that, they just want to do it." (*New Europe*, 20–26 April 1997, p. 20.)
15. See further articles in *New Europe*, 20–26 April 1997, pp. 1, 3.
16. On 7 April, the exact figure was a total of 50.6 trillion roubles, of which 40.6 trillion was owed by industry (*Finansovye Izvestiya*, 17 April 1997).
17. The reason given for the massive monetary expansion was that the degree of monetization (M2 in relation to GDP) of the Russian economy had fallen sharply, to merely 12 per cent of GDP, compared to 68 per cent for the US, 90 per cent in France and 117 per cent in Japan (*New Europe*, 25–31 May 1997, p. 20). On this problem, see further Illarionov, A. 1996c. Teoriya "denezhnogo defitsita" kak otrazhenie platezhnogo krizisa v rossiiskoi ekonomike, *Voprosy Ekonomiki*, **12**.
18. *New Europe*, 22–28 June 1997, p. 16.
19. *Finansovye Izvestiya*, 9 September 1997.
20. *Finansovye Izvestiya*, 17 June 1997.
21. Gazprom paid a total of 14.7 trillion roubles in back taxes, of which 10 trillion was hard cash and the rest offsets against debts owed by military and other official organizations. In addition to this source of extra revenue, there was also the then newly issued $2 billion Eurobond (OECD 1997, op. cit., p. 74).
22. *New Europe*, 10–16 August 1997, p. 16.
23. *Finansovye Izvestiya*, 9 September 1997.
24. Illarionov, A. 1998. Effektivnost byudzhetnoi politiki v Rossii v 1994–1997 godakh, *Voprosy Ekonomiki*, **2**, 27.
25. Ibid., pp. 28–9.
26. Ibid., pp. 29–30.
27. Ibid., pp. 31–3.
28. Rutland, op. cit., p. 78. According to Boris Berezovskii, the business alliance on its own put up $3 million (*Financial Times*, 1 November 1996).
29. *The Economist*, Russia survey, 12 July 1997, p. 13.
30. OECD 1997, op. cit., p. 106.
31. *Finansovye Izvestiya*, 3 July 1997.
32. *Finansovye Izvestiya*, 10 July 1997.
33. *Finansovye Izvestiya*, 29 July 1997. In addition to Oneksimbank, the winning side also included a number of investment banks: Renaissance International, Deutsche Morgan Grenfell, Morgan Stanley and financier George Soros' Quantum Fund. Soros later told *Financial Times* that his share in the deal was $1 billion (*Finansovye Izvestiya*, 31 July 1997).
34. *Finansovye Izvestiya*, 5 August 1997.
35. *Finansovye Izvestiya*, 7 August 1997.
36. *Washington Post*, 2 October 1997. Adding to the trouble, Kokh would subsequently be charged also with illegally handing out Moscow apartments to government officials, including himself, while being deputy head of the GKI in 1993. The latter offence could render him up to 10 years in prison. (*Moscow Times*, 7 May 1998).
37. *New Europe*, 24–30 August 1997, p. 19.
38. *Finansovye Izvestiya*, 11 and 18 September 1997.

39. *Finansovye Izvestiya*, 25 November 1997.
40. *Finansovye Izvestiya*, 9 December 1997.
41. *Finansovye Izvestiya*, 4 December 1997.
42. *New Europe*, 11–17 January 1998, p. 17.
43. *New Europe*, 4–10 January 1998, p. 7.
44. *New Europe*, 25–31 January 1998, p. 18.
45. *Finansovye Izvestiya*, 4 December 1997, and *New Europe*, 4–10 January 1998, p. 18.
46. *New Europe*, 1–7 February 1998, p. 48.
47. *New Europe*, 8–14 February 1998, p. 17.
48. Ibid., p. 21.
49. Ibid., p. 7.
50. *The Moscow Tribune*, 30 April 1998.
51. *Finansovye Izvestiya*, 21 April 1998.
52. *Finansovye Izvestiya*, 14 May 1998.
53. *Finansovye Izvestiya*, 23 April 1998.
54. Ibid.
55. The financial data given below are taken from current issues of *The Moscow Times*.
56. Quotes from *The Moscow Times*, 28 May 1998.
57. *Financial Times*, 13 August 1998.
58. See, e.g., *The Moscow Times*, 25 and 27 August 1998.
59. *Financial Times*, 26 August 1998.
60. *The Moscow Times*, 22 September 1998.
61. I owe this quote to an anonymous referee.
62. Yavlinsky, G. 1998. Russia's phony capitalism, *Foreign Affairs*, **77**(3), 69.
63. Quoted in csis 1997. *Russian Organized Crime: Global Organized Crime Project.* Washington, DC: Centre for Strategic and International Studies, p. 2.
64. Illarionov, A. 1995. Popytki provedeniya politiki finansovoi stabilizatsii v SSSR i v Rossii, *Voprosy Ekonomiki*, **7**, 10.
65. Tompson, W. 1997. Old habits die hard: fiscal imperatives, state regulation and the role of Russia's banks, *Europe-Asia Studies*, **49**(7), 1172.
66. Quoted by Reddaway, P. 1997b. Possible scenarios for Russia's future, *Problems of Post-Communism*, September/October, p. 43.
67. Rosefielde, S. 1998b. Klepto-banking: systematic sources of Russia's failed industrial recovery, in Stern, H. (ed.), *The Nigerian Banking Crisis in Comparative Perspective*. New York: Macmillan.
68. Ibid.
69. Boyko, M., Shleifer, A. and Vishny, R.W. 1993. *Privatizing Russia*, Brookings Papers on Economic Activity, No. 2, p. 152.
70. Layard, R. and Blanchard, O. 1993. Overview, in Blanchard, O. (ed.), *Post-Communist Reform*. Cambridge, Mass.: MIT Press, p. 5.
71. Radygin, A. 1996. Privatizatsionnyi protsess v Rossii v 1995 g., *Voprosy Ekonomiki*, **4**, 5.
72. Ibid., pp. 7–8.
73. Three-quarters of all revenue from this source was derived from 30 "special auctions", indicating that in the end there was little left of the initial ambitions of selling blocks of shares in thousands of enterprises. The reasons for this outcome are discussed by ibid., pp. 8–9.

74. *Nezavisimaya Gazeta*, 16 November 1995.
75. OECD 1997, op. cit., p. 139.
76. See further ibid., pp. 140–41.
77. Reddaway 1997a, op. cit., p. C4.
78. Ibid.
79. Illarionov, A. 1996a. Upushchennyi shans, *Voprosy Ekonomiki*, **3**, 88.
80. Radygin, op. cit., p. 5.
81. Bush, op. cit., p. 11.
82. Rosefielde, S. 1997. Russian market kleptocracy, unpublished.

IV

Lessons to be learned

CHAPTER EIGHT

A Russian path dependence

In the introductory chapter of this book, it was argued that Russia's process of post-Soviet reforms presents something of a laboratory for studying institutional change, and we made a point of how Russian scholars have begun discovering the tools of institutional theory. Returning now to that approach, we shall widen the perspective somewhat, in order to look at the Russian experience as a whole, i.e. to incorporate the main features of what was said in Chapter 2 about the burden of history.

Perhaps the most important reason for attempting this comprehensive view is linked to the analytical importance of making a distinction between the respective causes that lie behind successes and failures. Looking back at economic scholarship during the past decades, it is rather striking that – in growth theory in particular – success has been more attractive than failure. In a 1995 article on the experience of the Asian "miracle" economies, for example, William Easterly notes that

> Economists find it much more appealing to study what the successes did right than what the failures did wrong: from 1969 to the present there have been 717 articles on Singapore in economic journals. On the Central African Republic, a country of similar population size but opposite performance, the number of articles over this period was: 1. It is not really clear why large positive outliers should contain more information than large negative outliers.[1]

With the Asian crises that began in the summer and autumn of 1997, this may be set to change. Previous beliefs in a variety of "miracles" may give way to reflection on what causes economies to fail. From a scholarly point of view, this is all for the better. To begin with, such a shift of emphasis may have a salutary effect on our understanding of the world around us, and thus on how future policies of international co-operation should be devised.

Here the focal point must be aimed at the need to explain *persistent* failure. One has only to think of all the proud pronouncements that were made in the late 1960s and early 1970s, about how the Third World would catch up with the industrialized world, in order to see that something went wrong. Exactly what went wrong with Third World development policies is an intriguing topic, which so far has failed to receive adequate answers.

Commenting on this latter failure, Douglass North offers an explanation which at the same time is a plea for institutional theory: "The disparity in the performance of economies and the persistence of disparate economies through time have not been satisfactorily explained by development economists, despite forty years of immense effort. The simple fact is that the theory employed is not up to the task."[2]

Leaving the question of definitions of "failure" aside for the moment, there are good reasons why a study of cases where institutional conflicts cause failure would be more revealing of the underlying dynamics of institutional change than a study of cases where institutions are supportive of a positive development.

Most importantly, looking at cases of failure may help us understand the way in which norms are created – and preserved – which stand in the way of successful changes in the formal rules, i.e. "reforms". Since it is only the formal rules that may be directly influenced by policy, situations of this kind, which result in lock-in effects, offer a real litmus test for the validity of generally held assumptions about the universal applicability of economic policy.

Are the laws of economics really like the laws of engineering, such that one set of policies has equal applicability in all social settings, and in all cultural contexts? Or is it perhaps rather the case that the real challenge to reformers, who are bent on social engineering, lies in the informal dimension, in norm systems that may be at the very limits of, or perhaps even beyond the scope of economic policy?

Given what has been said in previous chapters, this question may emerge as largely rhetorical. Yet, there is much left to be said about the *way* in which such blocking norms may be formed and about how they influence attempts to change the formal rules of the game.

In the present chapter we shall therefore return to take a second and closer look at Russia's historical experience, this time with the help of some tools out of the institutional toolbox. Thus prepared we shall be ready, in the following chapter, to approach the main theme of the book as a whole, namely to investigate the institutional dimension of the economic reforms that have been undertaken under the leadership of Boris Yeltsin.

Before proceeding to the theoretical toolbox we shall, however, take a brief look at some of the main features of the Russian case, features which may be of particular relevance to our search for the driving forces behind a deeply rooted Russian path dependence.

The Russian case

The most immediate relevance of the Russian case lies in the repeated failures, of at times well intended reformers, that were mapped out in Chapter 2 above. In general, one might say that the reading of Russian history, while fascinating in its own right, can also be a rather dismal experience. Having finished a chapter on terror under the Mongols, one is led via the madness of Ivan the Terrible into the Time of Troubles and the near collapse of Muscovy. And having built expectations for success in a chapter on Peter the Great and Catherine the Great, one is plunged into stories of peasant rebellions, of terror and assassination, of revolution and renewed terror.

This is certainly not to say that the historical development of other European countries is marked by continuous peace, harmony and progress, merely that there are in the Russian case patterns of repetition that we do not encounter elsewhere. We may, for example, recall from above the repeated pattern of tsars beginning their rule as liberal reformers only to end up in isolation and orthodox conservatism – in the case of Alexander II, symptomatically the greatest of the reformers, even in assassination.

From an institutional perspective, this legacy offers excellent opportunities to look for what may be called "revealed institutional preference". We have a number of attempts made in the same direction of introducing formal rules that are modelled on a Western pattern, all of which ended in reversal.

An intuitive hypothesis seeking to explain these reversals would be that serious conflicts resulted between newly introduced formal rules and existing informal norms, which were marked by a remarkable resilience. An optimistic interpretation of such conflicts would be that there were systematic faults in policy design, such that reforms were introduced without due consideration of possible responses from relevant actors.

On a superficial level, this would imply that incentives were created for actors to engage in, say, rent seeking, but on a deeper level we would look for a failure by the reformers to undertake a transformation of the informal norm systems, in such a direction that norms could fill their fundamental function of supporting and providing legitimacy for the new rules.

A stronger and more pessimistic version of the same hypothesis might be that there were features in the norm systems which were so deeply rooted and stood in such firm opposition to the attempted changes in the formal rules, that reversal was all but predictable. The latter would represent what some writers have referred to as "pathological institutions" or "pathological path dependence". The latter are problems that will be referred to repeatedly below.

There is a fine dividing line here, setting these analytical categories aside from simple determinism. The distinction may be brought out by moving from "Russia cannot change" to "Russia cannot change, unless . . ." By seeking to uncover what may lurk behind this "unless" we may learn something important not only about Russia's ability to undertake fundamental institutional change, but also about the interplay between rules, norms and enforcement mechanisms from a more general perspective.

In order to illustrate, we may recall the previously mentioned case of the Russian nineteenth century philosopher Pyotr Chaadaev who caused "great alarm in the salons" when he wrote that Russia's history was sterile and her contribution to European culture of no value.

His clarion call was that Russia could not change *unless* she embraced the rationality, the values and the liberties of Western Europe – heretically summarized in a need for *rapprochement* with Catholicism. In the late 1990s, economists argue that Russia cannot change *unless* she introduces a functioning tax system, based on stable rules and legitimate enforcement mechanisms. In neither case is there a deterministic statement of *inability* to change. But in both cases the "unless" goes to the very roots of the informal norm systems, namely those of rules, rights and legitimacy.

In the following we shall use the term "revealed institutional preference" to capture situations where the informal norm system, following an external shock of radical changes from above in the formal rules, responds either by not moving or by gravitating back to previously well known patterns.

This formulation is not only less provocative than that of "pathological institutions". It also allows for some dynamics, in the sense that we do not need to assume a total rejection of the reform out of hand. By assuming that some parts (only) of society may follow the lead of the reformers, by reorienting their mental models and thus also their expectations, we will have an outcome that is marked by increasing polarization, which in the end leads to reversal. If this process is repeated several times, with similar outcomes, we may talk of a revealed systemic preference for a certain type of institutional arrangement.

Anticipating our discussion in the following chapter, Russia's twentieth century history has particular relevance to this argument, in the sense that this troubled century has witnessed two grandiose attempts at "systemic change". The first case was associated with the Bolshevik attempt to create a new social order, the second with the neo-liberal dream of pulling out from under the rubble of the collapsed Soviet order a system of modern democracy, resting on market economy and the rule of law.

Both ambitions were fundamental in the true sense of the word, seeking to rewrite the most basic rules of the game. At the same time, however, they also stood in stark contradiction to each other, representing extreme swings of the pendulum and thus offering truly laboratory-like conditions for studying the introduction – in turn – of both market-suppressing and market-conforming formal rules.

Although the Bolshevik "revolution" had little to do with the alleged storming of the Winter Palace in October 1917, from an institutional perspective it did represent a true revolution, setting out to erase all those steps towards democracy, market economy and the rule of law that had been taken since the reforms of Alexander II, to the point even of trying to create a new "Soviet man".

And the programme of sweeping reforms that was announced by President Boris Yeltsin in October 1991 was no less revolutionary, seeking – in turn – to erase all traces of the *communist* order, by re-introducing money and property, by dismantling much of the controlling and redistributive functions of the state, and – most importantly – by unleashing a brutal form of individualism that is totally alien to Russian tradition.

It is hardly surprising that many writers have found good cause to draw parallels between these two "reform" programmes. Commenting on the haste that was implied by shock therapy, for example, the Hungarian economist László Szamuely asks a rather pertinent question: "Does it not resemble Stalin's famous slogan: Let's fulfill the five year plan in four years?"[3] And others have been even harsher.

In an article about the institutional responses of the Russian banking system, Juliet Johnson juxtaposes a statement by Lenin from *State and Revolution* with a quote from one of the leading foreign advisors to the Gaidar government. While to Lenin the task was "to smash the old bureaucratic machine at once and to begin immediately to construct a new one . . . this is not utopia", in 1992 "it must be remembered that there is an abyss between a command economy and a market economy . . . first the old system must be destroyed . . . then the foundations of the new market economic house must be built on the other side of the abyss."[4]

And in the opening lines to their previously quoted reckoning with the shock therapists, Lynn Nelson and Irina Kuzes strike the tune by placing 1917 and 1992 in the very same category of ill-prepared forcible changes from above:

> In January 1992, for the second time this century, a new Russian government that was determined to radically restructure the economy launched a program of reforms based on economic vision imported from the West. In both cases, Russia hoped to establish a robust economic system through plans developed and administered by an élite cadre of planners who worked to insulate themselves from close public scrutiny. In the 1990s, as well as after the October revolution, hasty improvisations were required to implement directives whose theoretical assumptions did not mesh well with prevailing social and economic conditions in Russia.[5]

Several comments are due in this context. First of all, while the parallels between the two cases are compelling in an overall perspective of how the respective leaderships decided that Russian society must be *forced* to accept reform, there are also important distinctions with regard to the *way* in which they went about implementing their respective programmes, distinctions which are of a fundamental importance.

Secondly, the violent swings that occurred in 1917 and 1991 represent one of those patterns of repetition that go far back in Russian history. Much as Yeltsin's reforms were driven by a perceived need to uproot all remnants of the failed Soviet order, Lenin's "revolution" was based on a perceived need to uproot all traces of the tsarist order, and Peter the Great set out to cleanse Russia of all traces of its Byzantine past. Symptomatically, all three have been branded as both heroes and traitors, or even as the Antichrist.

While both of these observations are sufficiently important to merit further discussion below, it is in a third dimension that the comparison between 1917 and 1991 becomes particularly relevant to the argument pursued here, namely with respect to how we understand and define failure.

While the communist system was long held up – admired even by some – as an alternative to capitalism, today it is generally condemned as a total failure. Applying that label to Russia's latest attempt at systemic change is perhaps – still – a bit more controversial, but if we recall all the proud pronouncements of rapid successes that were made in 1992, it is hard indeed to avoid concluding that something has gone seriously wrong.

The details of that "something" will be the focus of our discussion in the following chapter. For the moment we shall pursue the question of failure, by making a distinction between collective and individual outcomes. Once we recognize that response to a reform initiative will take the form of strategies that are pursued by individual actors, we must also ask under which conditions their individually rational choices will lead to a collectively rational outcome.

That question proceeds in two steps: a) are actors faced with opportunities to engage in predatory behaviour, and b) if so, to what extent are they ready to exploit such possibilities?

In retrospect, the Bolshevik experiment may be seen as a failure because it thwarted the prospects for constructive economic effort and thus in the end brought about the system's collapse from within. This understanding, however, presupposes a certain ranking of priorities on behalf of the Soviet leadership. If we assume, for example, that Stalin unleashed the horror of forcible collectivization in order to improve production, then it must surely be seen as a massive failure. But if we assume instead that he did so in order to break peasant resistance to Soviet power, then it was quite successful.

What this example illustrates is that when looking at the questions of success and failure from the perspective of those designing the reform policies, it is important to make clear whether we assume a democratic or a dictatorial leadership. In the latter case, the failure of Bolshevism is no longer as apparent. Though Lenin might have died embittered and disillusioned, he did get quite far in the direction he had originally envisioned. And when Comrade Stalin was finally called before his Creator, he had plenty of reasons to feel – for himself – that his rule had been one of great successes.

Looking back at Russia's history of autocracy, we may thus suspect that what an outside observer might at first sight condemn as a series of failures, from the point of view of successive autocrats might well have been perceived as successes – and rationalized as such in their own private mental models. Needless to say, their respective ways of understanding the needs for change would be influenced accordingly.

Leaving the question of leadership aside, it is by placing the yardstick for measuring success and failure in focus that our attention will be directed at the above-mentioned distinction between individual and collective rationality that is at the core of the prisoners' dilemma, and which has been repeatedly referred to in previous chapters. A definition of "reform failure" that agrees with this perspective would be a design of formal rules which create incentives for actors to move against the common good, without promoting such informal norms that might block this type of collectively destructive behaviour.

In order to set the stage for our following discussion, we shall take a brief look at two themes that are not only highly characteristic of the Russian case in general but also have a great deal of relevance to the specific argument that is pursued here. First, we have the violent swings between reform and reversal, and the general apathy that tends to follow in the wake of failed reform attempts, and then the isolation that has marked rulers implementing reforms from above, on the assumption that society must be *forced* to accept change.

On the former count we may turn to a study by Tim McDaniel, which charts a history of "cyclical breakdowns", of attempted reforms that harbour within themselves the seeds of their own failure: "Reform in Russia: over the centuries it has always failed, sometimes to be replaced by a reactionary regime (Alexander III's reversal of Alexander II's 'great reforms' of the 1860s and 1870s), and sometimes culminating in the collapse of the system (1917 and 1991)."[6]

What McDaniel shows, without making specific reference to this area of research, is a powerful Russian path dependence, entrenched in a Russian ideology, as represented in a set of private mental models of the surrounding world. His work has been strongly influenced by the Russian semioticist Yurii Lotman's writings about the Russian binary logic of oppositions. Where Western tradition has given rise to pluralism, power sharing and argumentation, Russia's Orthodox tradition has rested on posing absolute alternatives, with no room for compromise.

Where there is no neutral zone, man has to take sides, and the winning side must be the absolute victor. After having fully crushed his opponent, the victor also seeks to radically annihilate the past. Lotman's own conclusion goes to the very heart of the problem: "True forward movement requires coming to terms with, and not simply rejecting, the past, for absolute rejection leads only to fruitless cycles of negation."[7]

In his historical account, McDaniel shows how repeated Russian attempts to break out of the bad equilibrium consistently led the system to revert to its original institutional position. This is well in line with our assumption of revealed institutional preference. Each such failed undertaking, moreover, was accompanied by high social costs and a protracted period of disorder, known in Russian as *smuta*.

Returning to present-day Russia, it is easy enough to find support for the thesis that a failed reform is followed by a moral crisis and widespread social apathy. To name but one example, we may recall from previous chapters the steadily worsening problems of wage and pension arrears. While there can be little doubt that these problems have been both real and serious, to date it has been difficult to organize open protests of any substantial order.

A case in point arose in the spring of 1997, when the Russian labour unions attempted – on 27 March – to call a massive national protest. While the communists had hoped to see 20 million angry workers taking to the streets, the actual turnout was maybe a tenth of that. This level of resignation is all the more remarkable in light of the preceding campaign, where the chauvinist parts of the press had excelled in slogans against the "genocidal" Yeltsin regime, against Anatolyi Chubais who was compared to Adolf Hitler, and against the West in general, where the IMF in particular was held up to be aiming for the final extermination of the Russian people.[8] Even sober *Izvestiya* expressed worry about a pending "Albanian" scenario.[9]

The poor turnout provided confirmation for those in power that Chubais had indeed been correct when he "proudly compared the government's policy with the actions of a surgeon who operates on a patient without anesthesia".[10] For reasons that are very specifically Russian, it turned out that the patient did take the pain without protesting.

Writing about the remarkable ability of the Russians for adaptive preference formation, for passively accepting almost everything as "normal", Vladimir Shlapentokh emphasizes the real importance of the 1996 re-election of Boris Yeltsin:

> By re-electing Yeltsin, Russians in effect endorsed various pathological developments in Russian society and invited the Kremlin to continue the policies which were significantly responsible for them. The results of the election sent a signal to the political and economic élite that corruption and crime, the colonial character of the Russian economy, the technological decline in the country and many other negative developments were accepted.[11]

What lies at the heart of this matter is the firewall that has been erected between the rulers and the ruled, or between the few rich and the very many poor. As Stephen Holmes puts it, "the pathological disconnection of the Russian government from the Russian people is simultaneously a disturbing insulation of the rich from the poor".[12] Recalling our previous historical perspective, this is a distressingly familiar phenomenon.

Yeltsin is certainly not the first tsar to reside in splendid isolation in the Kremlin, while the people are suffering hardship and members of the intelligentsia – who might have provided valuable support for successful reforms – are becoming increasingly frustrated, and thus also increasingly alienated. We have here the contours of an important component in a Russian path dependence, the nature of which will be discussed further below.

One might certainly ask how it was possible for Yeltsin to be re-elected in the first place, given his track record. Shlapentokh blames the communists for not presenting a realistic alternative programme: "Yeltsin would have been easily defeated by almost any decent candidate not connected to the communists, or even to the former communists, if they had followed the examples of their East European comrades in arms."[13]

But there is also a deeper moral to the story, which says that with strongly adaptive preferences among the electorate, the incumbents need not fear being held accountable.

Russian post-Soviet politics may thus be reduced to elite infighting, again in splendid isolation from the electorate. Holmes captures the essence of the problem: "Elections in Russia, in fact, do not create power. For the most part, they mirror the power that already exists. . . . What Russia's electoral charades bring home is something we already knew: democratic procedures are of value only if they establish some sort of dependency of public officials on ordinary citizens."[14]

We have here the contours of another important component in a Russian path dependence, one which will also be pursued at length below. Before proceeding to the theoretical dimension we shall, however, have another few words to say about the question of determinism. Although the famed Russian patience has served so far to protect the regime from violent protests, it should also be noted that following Yeltsin's re-election this patience has become stretched, and may well be approaching a point where it finally breaks.

In the spring and summer of 1998, as the economic crisis was deepening, the escalating non-payments of wages provoked open protests from the country's traditionally radical coal miners. As was mentioned above, on 12 May massive strikes began which a few days later escalated to blockades on several points of the vitally important Trans-Siberian Railroad. The strikes spread rapidly across the country and began causing great losses to industry. One of the big Siberian aluminium smelters, for example, was losing $5 million a day.[15]

The government's readiness to take remedial action was nevertheless limited to words only. The first round of the conflict could be resolved by promises that back wages would be paid out, but once it transpired that those promises had been hollow new pickets went up. Beginning on 1 July, daily newscasts could show angry miners banging their hard-hats against the pavement both at the Kremlin and at the Moscow White House. And this time their anger was firmly directed against Yeltsin himself.

Thus, recognizing that patience may not last forever, the danger of a social explosion may not be entirely discounted. So, where does that leave us with respect to Russia's ability to change? Will widespread and violent protests be conducive to constructive institutional change, or would a massive outbreak of violence be merely repetition of an old pattern of the *russkii bunt*, i.e. senseless violence with no political objective?

The answer to this question has considerable bearing on the issues that will be discussed at length below, namely to what extent communication between the rulers and the ruled may influence public policy. At first sight, the answer might seem to be the discouraging one that things simply *will* not change, but that is a conclusion of which we must be wary.

From a scholarly point of view it is agreeable indeed to refute determinism, and to argue that no matter how powerful specific lock-in effects may be there is always a solution. This line of argument, however, also logically implies that poor outcomes are the result of poor policy choices.[16]

Looking back at the evolution of Russia's economic policies from 1992 up until the financial meltdown that took place in the early autumn of 1998, it follows that heavy responsibility must be placed on the shoulders of Boris Yeltsin and the men around him, who were in charge of shaping the reform programme: if 1991 was indeed a crucial fork in the road of Russia's long-term historical progression, the reformers certainly failed to choose the right path.

Much of the anger that has been directed at the Russian reformers, and at their foreign advisors, has its roots in this observation. No matter how much credence you are willing to give to the generally presented argument, that late in 1991 shock therapy was the *only* road ahead, it would seem difficult indeed to argue that all that has happened since has been nothing but further steps on that same solitary and predetermined road.

Given what has been said in previous chapters, about the logic of haste which prompted the implementation of shock therapy, there might seem to be a contradiction here; one cannot at the same time condemn a policy and abstain from presenting an alternative. That argument, however, is valid only if we look at some of the immediate decisions, such as price liberalization. As will be argued in the following chapter, it has no bearing whatsoever on subsequent events.

Let us assume for the moment that it *could* have been done differently, and join with Richard Pipes in hoping that one day it *will* be done differently:

"Sooner or later – I fear that it will be later rather than sooner – Russians will come to realize that there are no rapid fixes to their difficulties, and that ahead of them lies the arduous task of building a modern state and a modern economy from the bottom up."[17]

His formulation of an "arduous task of building" indicates in which direction we must be looking: no quick fixes, no prescription of universal economic cures, and no rapid transitions, but instead a fundamental societal reconstruction, entailing a transformation of social norm systems and the promotion of trust in legitimate rules of the game, upheld by a legitimate government.

All of this in turn implies that we must return to the dimension of history, in order to ask – more specifically – *how* history matters. Having arrived thus far, we are ready to venture into the realm of "path dependence", of a theory that seeks to explain how decisions taken in the past may influence decisions that are taken in the present.

The theory of path dependence

In his original article on the subject, Paul David uses the example of typewriter keyboard design as an illustration of how economic development may be locked into technologically inferior alternatives.[18] Why do all desktop computers still come with a top row of letters that reads QWERTYUIOP, despite the fact that superior designs have been suggested? The answer shows how path dependence may arise.

The QWERTY keyboard was associated with a machine that was constructed by Christopher Sholes of Milwaukee in 1867 (year of patent application) and went into production with the Remington arms maker in 1873. One of the advantages of that specific keyboard design was that it allowed a salesman to quickly type out the brand name of the new machine: TYPE WRITER.

In 1932, however, a rival design, the "Dvorak Simplified Keyboard", was introduced which allowed a number of world records for speed typing to be set. In the 1940s, the US Navy undertook tests showing that higher typing speed would allow the cost of retraining typists to use the DSK keyboard to be amortized within ten days of full-time work. Nevertheless, it is still QWERTY that is the standard. David offers three explanations to this puzzle, all of which are fairly straightforward.

The first concerns technical *interrelatedness* between the hardware and the "software" that resides in the typist's memory, and the second the fact that there were *system scale economies*. The logic is simple. Given that employers would have no incentive to train their own typists – the human capital is too mobile – they would prefer to purchase hardware for which there was a ready supply of software. And given that typists would seek to acquire the skill that was in highest demand, the market would converge on one standard.

By historical chance this standard happened to be QWERTY, which initially had only a slender lead over competing designs. This "lock-in" was further entrenched by a third feature, namely the fact that while hardware conversion costs fell rapidly, the software came to be marked by a *quasi-irreversibility of investments*, as the costs of retraining typists did not come down. Thus machines had to be adapted to humans, who were locked in by their investments in learning.

The compelling message of this illustration is threefold. First, historical accidents play a greater role in determining the growth paths and the technological development of various economies than is generally thought. Secondly, despite freedom of competition and free access to information, such growth paths may remain locked into inferior choices over an extended period of time, and, thirdly, "irreversibilities due to learning and habituation" play an important role in the creation of such lock-in effects.

In a later contribution, David elaborates on the theme of "history matters" by issuing a challenge to the economics profession. Departing from the general belief in strict "laws of nature" that marked the eighteenth century, he shows how not only the natural but also the social sciences – notably so economics – came to be profoundly influenced in the direction of indifference to the role of history.

From Adam Smith onwards economists have been drawn further and further into modelling, where the influence of initial conditions is reduced to the point of insignificance. And by assuming that social change, like that of nature in the world of Darwin, always is "slow, gradual and continuous", economics could be made amenable to analysis by mathematical techniques of infinitesimal calculus. In the end we are left with a situation where "much of modern economics remains essentially *ahistorical*".

By referring to the growing interest that physicists and philosophers of physics have begun, in the past couple of decades, to show for matters of causation, i.e. to ask not only *how* but also *why* things happen, David argues that the inattention by economists to matters of causal explanation "has impoverished modern economic theory" and goes on to make a plea for "historical economics", which would be aimed at "understanding the reasons why particular sequences of events in the past are capable of exerting persisting effects upon current conditions".[19]

Two remarks of great relevance for our subsequent argument are due here, namely: a) that "historical economics" thus defined is essentially different from modern economics taking an interest in history, the difference resting in the recognition of path dependence, and b) that the belief in "the laws of economics" has been one of the most salient features of Western economic advice to the various Russian governments that have served under Boris Yeltsin.

Returning to the theory of path dependence, an early follower of David's, Brian Arthur, set out to explain how "small historical events can lead one technology to win out over another".[20] In a 1988 article he identified four self-reinforcing mechanisms which may combine to produce an outcome where it is the inferior technology that wins.

The first is large set-up or fixed costs, implying that unit costs will decrease as production expands. The second is learning effects, meaning that an increased prevalence of the product will lead to improved quality or lower cost. Thirdly, co-ordination effects will arise from co-operation with economic agents who are involved in similar ventures, and fourthly, adaptive expectations will secure that increased prevalence on the market enhances consumer beliefs in further prevalence.

The final outcome will be marked by the following four properties: a) there will be multiple equilibria, so that the outcome of the process is indeterminate, b) inefficient solutions are possible, so that an inferior technology may win out, c) a lock-in can occur, which may prove difficult to break out of, and d) there is path dependence, so that small and/or chance historical events may determine the chosen path.

In a later contribution, Arthur emphasizes that the notion of multiple equilibria lies at the very core of what path dependence is about: "I became convinced that the key obstacle for economics in dealing with increasing returns was the indeterminacy introduced by the possibility of multiple equilibria." And the possibility of different equilibria in turn follows from the presence of increasing returns. What remains is to ask how to analyze the path that leads the system towards one or the other of these equilibria: "What was needed therefore was a method to handle the question of how one equilibrium, one solution, one structure, of the several possible came to be 'selected' in an increasing returns problem."[21]

In a foreword to Arthur's book, Kenneth Arrow outlines the troubles generations of economists have had in coming to terms with the presence of increasing returns, which create trouble for elegant theories that are based on assumptions of constant returns, and he compliments Arthur for contributing a solution: "It is in this context that Brian Arthur's precise and fully modelled papers caused us all to understand clearly and specifically what kinds of models have what kinds of implications."

And by pointing at the role of learning processes, he also emphasizes that both formal rules and informal norms are at play:

> Increasing returns have more than one source. Arthur . . . shows how the transmission of information based on experience may serve also as a reinforcement for early leading positions and so act in a manner parallel to more standard forms of increasing returns. A similar phenomenon occurs even in individual learning, where again successes reinforce some courses of action and inhibit others . . .

> There are in all of these models opposing tendencies, some toward
> achieving an optimum, some toward locking in on inefficient forms
> of behavior.[22]

The bulk of work that has followed in these footsteps has been devoted to
problems of technological change,[23] which is of marginal importance to
the argument pursued here. Given that our focus is aimed primarily at the
relevant norm systems, we must move into less well charted territory,
namely to look at how actors deal with decision making under uncertainty
by constructing their own "cognitive models" of the surrounding world,
models which may become firmly entrenched and resistant to change.

The importance of the latter is clearly recognized by David: "If we
would understand the behavior of historical actors who were obliged to
make choices in conditions of Knightian uncertainty, more attention will
have to be devoted to learning about the cognitive models they call upon
when interpreting their society's visions of its past and forming expectations
about its future. Even for economists, then, '*mentalité* matters'."[24]

Commenting on the shift of focus from technological to institutional
change, North points out that in the latter case two forces combine to form
the path of change, namely increasing returns and imperfect markets with
significant transactions costs. With competitive markets and no increasing returns to institutions, institutions would not matter. As competition
eliminates inefficient solutions, actors would be forced to continually and
correctly update their mental models, or face the consequences.

With increasing returns, however, all of the four self-reinforcing mechanisms that were outlined by Arthur apply and they do so in equal measure
(almost) to institutional development; North illustrates by using the example
of the large set-up costs of the US Constitution, and the ensuing effects of
learning, co-ordination and adaptive expectations that have marked the
development of the US political system.

The reasonable success and efficiency of this path hinges, however,
on the presence of competitive markets and conditions which "roughly
approximate the zero-transactions-cost model". This is where we are
approaching factors that have a great deal of relevance to the Russian case:

> But if the markets are incomplete, the information feedback is
> fragmentary at best, and transaction costs are significant, then the
> subjective models of actors modified both by very imperfect feed-
> back and by ideology will shape the path. Then, not only can both
> divergent paths and persistently poor performance prevail, the his-
> torically derived perceptions of the actors shape the choices that
> they make.[25]

So, then, history matters not only because increasing returns may influence
the creation and preservation of specific institutional arrangements. Under

conditions of imperfect competition, imperfect information and high costs of transacting, actors may also be locked into mental models of the world around them that profoundly influence future decision making.

Before turning to look in greater detail at the role of the institutional matrix that captures all of these features, we shall round off the discussion of path dependence with some rather provocative thoughts.

Although writing about problems that are located in an entirely different context, Vincent Ostrom makes a point that is of great relevance to our argument as well:

> From a long-run perspective, economic stagnation has political and social roots and reveals failures of co-operation, co-ordination and organization. Pathological institutions often are the result of a human propensity to make great experiments which generate monumental failures because of the perpetrator's unrealistic assumptions concerning knowledge, information and incentives.[26]

In a comment to Ostrom's portrayal of "pathological institutions", Thráinn Eggertsson points out that the roots of the problem may lie at a considerably deeper level: "However, long-run economic failures also may reflect an inability to experiment at all – a social paralysis where institutions thwart economic progress and trap communities at levels of low income."[27]

Is it perhaps the case, as Eggertsson hints, that there may be instances of "pathological path dependence", where public policy is powerless: "The strong version of path dependence can be compared to the discovery of debilitating genes in specific human groups, and the implications for structural policy are devastating. . . . If one were to select the single most important policy implication of the new institutionalism, it is the notion of reform-resistant path dependence that endures for centuries."[28]

With this we conclude our look at the theory of path dependence and the possibilities of historical lock-in. Given the frequent reference that has been made above to the role of institutions, the time has now come to look in somewhat greater detail at what institutions are really about, and at the specific role they have played in shaping a Russian path dependence.

Back to institutions

The basic role of institutions is given as follows by North, in the opening lines to his presentation of the theory of institutional change:

> Institutions are the rules of the game in a society or, more formally, are the humanly devised constraints that shape human interaction. In consequence they structure incentives in human exchange,

whether political, social or economic. Institutional change shapes the way societies evolve through time and thus is the key to understanding historical change.[29]

Briefly put, it is people who make the rules that govern their interaction with other people, and it is people who respond to an introduction of new rules by, for example, forming organizations that may serve to exploit opportunities for gain – productive or redistributive – that are embedded in the new rules.

As we have outlined above, if a reform fails it is thus either the result of a failure in the design of the new rules, such that actors may develop efficient ways to engage in, say, rent seeking, or to the fact that informal norms fail to respond in a supportive mode, the extreme of the latter being where a gulf is opened up between the rulers and the ruled, such that we are faced with a "pathology" of the Ostrom–Eggertsson kind, namely an inability to experiment at all.

Thus placing the emphasis on human choice and human response implies a need to think of the role of expectations, of learning and of previous experiences on both sides of the fence: on one side those who devise the new rules and on the other those who respond to them. In a democratic setting this relationship is supposedly marked by a high degree of trust, which is derived from accountability and positive experience. But in a setting which is marked by negative experience and a lack of accountability, learning of a different kind will result.

A Russian case in point may be taken from the time of Peter the Great, when a sudden wholesale introduction of a system of formal rules that were copied from the West – in administration it was a virtual blueprint of the Swedish "college" system[30] – created a gulf in Russian society that would persist up until the Bolshevik "revolution".

On one side of the fence was the autocracy and the Westernized parts of the bureaucracy in Petersburg, that understood – at least vaguely – what the reforms were really about, and on the other were the bulk of the people, notably so the peasants but also the provincial bureaucracy that felt at a loss when faced with all the novelties.

Peter's battle against the Church certainly added to the problem, but the real dilemma lay in the combination of strong central power and weak regional administration. Marc Raeff captures the essence of Peter's failure to achieve a sustained transformation as follows: "Throughout his regime these [government agencies], created supposedly for the sake of greater efficiency, acted as a barrier between the ruler and the ruled. Communication and the passage of information between them were nearly impossible, and this led to mutual ignorance, suspicion, and eventually to a dramatic break."[31]

The agent of subsequent violent reaction was an initially small group of enlightened members of the upper classes, which in the nineteenth century would swell and come to constitute the celebrated Russian intelligentsia.

Perched on the fence between the autocracy and the provincial masses, they were angry young men seeking a mission for themselves but not being allowed to find one in the service of the state: "Unable to find a meaningful active role in Russian society, persecuted by the government and constricted by censorship, the members of the intelligentsia were finally driven into revolutionary action."[32]

The strongly path dependent reason for the exclusion from the sphere of public policy of these potentially supportive and progressive intellects was rooted in the historical role and self-image of the autocracy: "In the final analysis, the source of all authority and of all favours remained the arbitrary and unchallengeable personal power of the autocrat. Such a situation served to undermine the very *raison d'être* of legal and bureaucratic order. It also was the root of the failures of many attempts at fundamental political reform and of the search for a *Rechtsstaat*."[33]

The simple fact that a mere five years after Peter's death most of his reforms had been restored to the *status quo ante* illustrates not only what was said above about reversals; given that his reforms were essentially market-conforming, aimed at promoting greater rationality and efficiency, it also illustrates our previous point about the assumed general validity of the "laws" of economics. Seeking to explain Peter's failures, it would seem more rational to heed Paul David's plea for "historical economics", with particular emphasis on learning and the formation of expectations.

Before proceeding to a more detailed look at the implications of this example, we shall have a few words to say about the problem of persistent failure, which is inherent in the formation of a negative path dependence.

The puzzle of underperformance

North was quoted above saying that for decades economic theory had not been up to the task of explaining development failures in the Third World. Pursuing this argument he formulates the analytical challenge that is involved here: "The central puzzle of human history is to account for the widely divergent paths of historical change," and then goes on to wonder why there is so little convergence: "Wouldn't the political entrepreneurs in stagnant economies quickly emulate the policies of more successful ones? How can we explain the radically different performance of economies over long periods of time?"[34]

He also makes reference to his own intellectual development in approaching this problem. While *The Rise of the Western World*,[35] which was co-authored with Robert Thomas in 1973, uses an institutional approach to tell what is essentially a success story, with *Structure and Change in Economic History*,[36] published in 1981, he abandons the efficiency view and allows for institutions to be devised by rulers in their own interests, thus allowing for the existence of inefficient institutions.

North's key question, about the failure of some societies to copy the successes of others, is also formulated by Avner Greif, writing about the economic differentials between North and South in Italy that emerged in the thirteenth century and which have proven to be remarkably resilient over the centuries: "Why do societies fail to adopt the organization of economically more successful ones?"[37] Why indeed?

The fact that we do encounter cases of sustained economic differentials between countries or between regions has been given a great deal of attention in recent years. A prominent example is Robert Putnam's study of how different levels of "civicness" led to the economic divide in Italy.[38]

In the South, or the "Mezzogiorno", we have a strongly hierarchical society based on dependency, personalized trust and mafia control, all of which produces a specific form of "criminal capitalism".[39] In sharp contrast, society in the North is marked by horizontal relations, by trust in general rules and by a "social capitalism" that has produced not only some of the highest per capita incomes within the European Union, but also strong political movements, such as the Lega Nord, which advocate a secession by the North from the rest of Italy, to form a sovereign "Padania".

The Italian problems that are discussed by Putnam and others provide an eminent illustration of what has been said above about multiple equilibria and the danger that a specific society may be locked into a bad equilibrium out of which it proves hard to break. Putnam explicitly recognizes the parallel between his work and North's previous study of differences between the post-colonial development paths in North and South of America, but his reference to the works of David and Arthur is only a passing one.[40]

Before proceeding, two observations are due. On the one hand we have the – perhaps predictable – fact that Putnam's presentation of low degrees of "civicness" in the Mezzogiorno has been met by accusations of determinism, of "condemning" the Italian South to lasting underdevelopment. On the other is his tentative prediction that "Palermo may represent the future for Moscow".[41] Both of these have a great deal of relevance to our discussion in the following chapter, where we turn to look at Yeltsin's policies.

But what, then, is it that creates and sustains a path dependence which is based on inefficient institutions?

In North's formulation, there are two driving forces behind such a process. One relates to the formal rules in the pay off matrix: "The increasing returns characteristic of an initial set of institutions that provide disincentives to productive activity will create organizations and interest groups with a stake in the existing constraints."

The other emphasizes the emergence of informal norm systems: "The subjective mental constructs of the participants will evolve an ideology that not only rationalizes the society's structure but accounts for its poor performance. As a result the economy will evolve policies that reinforce the existing incentives and organizations."[42]

These observations highlight the need to focus on the interplay between formal rules and informal norms, and at the enforcement mechanisms that are to provide legitimacy for the former. Let us look at these in turn, and see how they may help us structure what has been said above about Russian history.

Formal rules

Looking simply at the formal rules that govern human interaction, there are good reasons to take a pessimistic view of the future of civilization. From the classic prisoners' dilemma, via Olson's free rider problem, to North's institutional matrix which rewards piracy, we have many reasons to predict that society would break down. In the end there would be a Hobbesian war of all against all, where economic actors behave according to the principle of *homo, homini lupus*, and where life becomes "short, nasty and brutish".

Nevertheless, back in 1776 Adam Smith could tell us that "It is not from the benevolence of the butcher, the brewer, or the baker that we expect our dinner, but from their regard to their own interest". If all producers strive to maximize their own gain, says Smith, they will be led, as if by an "invisible hand", to promote the interests of society.

Ever since, the logical conclusion that private markets should be liberated and interference by government limited has been the creed of liberal economics and a standard component in undergraduate economics teaching.

So, how may we explain the seeming paradox that is embodied here? The simple solution is that strong social norms prevent the extremes of defection from occurring. Even if the institutional matrix is such that piracy *does* carry high rewards, in a "civilized" society few people would actually be ready and willing to engage in that kind of activity.

In a less extreme illustration, there are many cases where actors will refrain from pursuing short-term individual gain simply because past learning has taught them that in repeated transactions, with a limited number of participants and perfect information about the past performance of other actors, co-operation is in their own best interest. Experiments in game theory have shown that with repeated games, defection ceases to be a dominant strategy. Actors resort instead to "tit-for-tat", i.e. to responding in kind.

Two important questions arise here. First, we must ask under which conditions these assumptions are valid, i.e. what does it take for defection to become – or remain – a dominant strategy? This again highlights the vital role of learning, of the availability of information and of the role of trust in other players. Secondly, from a policy point of view it is perhaps even more important to ask under what conditions – if at all – it is possible to devise policy measures that serve to promote such norms, which may block defection. This, as we shall see below, is where the question of "pathological institutions" may enter the picture.

Returning to the Russian case, we are faced with a cultural context that throughout the centuries has been very different from that of the Western world, and which to this day remains a world apart in Russian self-images: "The sense of isolation and uniqueness bequeathed by Orthodox Christianity unfortunately survives. Present-day Russians still feel themselves to be outsiders, a nation *sui generis*, belonging neither to Europe nor Asia," writes Richard Pipes in 1996.[43]

To begin with, the main feature of old Muscovy, as we may recall from Chapter 2 above, was the very absence of formal rules, notably so with respect to private property and individual rights. As always, the mirror of language provides an excellent reflection. The Russian word for the old nobility – *dvoryanie* – is derived from the word for "household" (*dvor*), implying that even the nobility were considered part of the family of the prince and thus subject to his "fatherly" discipline.

The Russian story of rule aversion, as told by Edward Keenan, has important roots in the old village community, the *mir*. In a brief portrayal, this was an institutional arrangement that was marked by highly conservative features, exhibiting strong norms against individual initiative, which in turn served to block many options for progress. Many of Russia's subsequent troubles may be traced back to these roots.[44]

Leaving the question of norms aside for the moment, the main reason behind the emergence of this very special arrangement was linked to the harshness of nature. Living constantly on the brink of disaster, the early Russians simply had to develop a set of practices which were up to the task of securing survival.

In the *economic* dimension, the survival strategy of the *mir* was marked by a need to employ all available resources – land, man and beast – to the fullest extent possible. Since the economic potential of the individual households varied over time, depending on natural variations in size as well as in the distribution of age and sex, frequent redistributions of land were found to be necessary. Households with an increasing number of strong young males were allocated more land, at the expense of widows, the elderly and households with many females. In return, the strong households were forced to shoulder a larger share of the common burden, e.g., by taking in widows or cripples.

From an analytic perspective, this was a highly peculiar economic system, marked by narrow boundaries beyond which the individual household was unable to influence its own welfare: while those who worked hard to improve their own lot were burdened by increasing communal obligations, the unfortunate knew that they would never be allowed to fall below a certain minimum level. It is hardly surprising that this institutional arrangement gave rise to a rather special understanding of a range of basic economic concepts, chiefly with regard to private property but also in questions relating to income differentials and individual responsibility.

In the *political* dimension, the *mir* developed such institutional arrangements necessary to handle these economic tasks. Forcing a young man to marry an old widow, or depriving a hard working family of a good part of its surplus, required a harsh authoritarian structure. The *mir* was consequently governed by the elders, whose decisions could not be questioned. Neither opposition nor appeals for help from the outside were tolerated. The need for unity (*sobornost*) was strongly felt and the dangers of internal divisions (*raskol*) always seen as highly threatening.

The institutions that developed on such premisses were, by necessity, informal. Since rules and enforcement mechanisms were formed in order to guarantee survival of the collective, the individuals could not be granted any formal rights. Thus the exercise of power assumed an arbitrary nature.

In discussing the autocracy's obsession with secrecy, Keenan points at the scholar's problem in approaching old Russian political culture: ". . . the abiding deep structures of that culture have not found systematic expressions either in legislative or in descriptive codifications: as a result they must be extracted from the historical record by unconventional means."[45]

Here we are approaching the very core of the Russian dilemma. From Peter the Great onwards, the aim of Russian reformers would be firmly pointed in the direction of seeking to establish formal rules of the game. In Peter's own case the ambition, as Raeff put it in Chapter 2 above, was to introduce "the concept of the active, creative, goal-directed state."

The ultimate purpose of this ambition was to enhance Russia's military power, by harnessing the full potential of the country's resources behind the tsar, but in so doing Peter could not help but taking some steps towards what is nowadays known as the "civil society".

Rules and regulations were laid down that sought to imbue the system with a greater sense of purpose and rationality. There was the Entail Law of 1714 and the introduction of wages to replace the old practice of *kormleniya*, which had allowed officials to live off the land (i.e. off the backs of the peasants), but the most important step on that road was the introduction, via the Table of Ranks in 1722, of regulated promotion – an act which Pipes has called "one of the most important pieces of legislation in imperial Russia".[46]

Compared to the old Muscovite practice of *mestnichestvo*, a ranking system of "extreme complexity and refinement" which had been administered by the nobility itself and served as a source of constant feuding,[47] this was a big step ahead. There would still be room for a great deal of corruption and nepotism in dealing with the "Herald Master", who was in charge of promotions to higher rank, but at least now there were rules laid down by the state and thus less room for discretion.

From a perspective of learning and the formation of "cognitive models", two other steps are important to note. One was the introduction, in 1703, of Russia's first newspaper, the *Vedomosti*, which broke with the old tradition of making state secrets out of all news, foreign as well as domestic; the other was the introduction of mandatory education for young nobles. While the first served to make information available, the latter was designed to enhance their ability to process that information.

All of this served not only to promote a greater degree of predictability, but also to create demands and expectations from below for a continued erosion of the autocracy's grip over society.

Under Peter III and Catherine II further important steps were taken in the direction of introducing rights for the nobility, notably so with the abolition of mandatory service in 1762 and the granting of the Charter of the Nobility in 1785. And the process of fundamental legislation was proceeding apace, if yet only on the drawing board.

In the great nineteenth century debate between the slavophiles and the *zapadniki*, the main demand from the latter was not Westernization *per se*, but again the introduction of rights. The fact that constitutions were allowed in two newly incorporated Russian provinces – Poland (until 1830) and Finland – but not in Russia proper, added fuel to the fire.

With the great reforms under Alexander II, this process culminated in a legal reform that, as we may recall from above, went some way towards introducing due process. The new court system was public, adversarial and open to all. There was trial by jury, which could include newly freed peasants, and there were judges with security of tenure and rights of discretion. From a formal perspective, these were truly important steps, aimed at providing a basic autonomy for the legal system.

An important illustration of the fact that the autocracy was at least partly ready to heed its own new rules may also be found in the fact, mentioned above, that although the growing wave of terrorism that marked the latter part of the nineteenth century was dealt with severely, executions of terrorists and revolutionaries were not accompanied by confiscation of property. The sanctity of private property had finally sprouted some roots, if ever so slender.

By the early twentieth century, most of the formal building blocks needed for democracy, market economy and the rule of law were in place.

With the "October Manifesto" of 1905, Tsar Nicholas II allowed the first steps to be taken on the road towards representative democracy, based on free and universal elections to a new State Duma. Although the rights thus granted were seriously circumscribed, the occasion represented the first time since the rise of Muscovy that the people would have at least some say in the running of their country. Perhaps this could have evolved into true popular representation.

In the economic sphere, both money and property had been introduced and rapid industrialization was proceeding apace. Following the disasters of War Communism, the mid-1920s proved that even the Bolsheviks were able to pursue successful economic stabilization, to balance the budget and to create a strong rouble. Had this been allowed to continue, a mixed economy of sorts might have been the result.

Finally, in the legal sphere, progress towards the rule of law was crowned by the power sharing agreement that was laid out in the October Manifesto. If the tsar had been more receptive to demands from liberal *zemstvo* politicians to introduce some kind of constitutional order, Russia might perhaps have evolved into a constitutional monarchy.

The simple fact that none of this was to be is hardly explicable by Lenin alone, nor even by Stalin. As will be argued in more detail below, putting the formal building blocks in place was a necessary but far from sufficient condition for a successful "Westernization". There remained substantial problems in the norm systems, which made the road ahead slow and susceptible to reversals. We are reminded here of Oliver Williamson's previously quoted distinction between "getting the property rights right", and "getting the institutions right".

The distinction between the latter cases may be reflected in the difference between rewriting laws and transforming the legal culture that supports specific legislation, say, the principle of *pacta sunt servanda*. Without success on the latter count, the former will be reduced to a rather futile academic exercise. This observation brings us to the role of informal norms in the institutional matrix.

Informal norms

The role of social norms in a democratic, market-oriented setting is a topic that has attracted a considerable amount of scholarship. One of many applications has been to show how the introduction of norms against some forms of individually rational behaviour may be a cost-effective way of escaping the collectively irrational outcome of the prisoners' dilemma. A trivial but illuminating case is that of littering, where campaigns such as "Keep America Clean" will yield better results than relying exclusively on the imposition of stiff fines for defection.

We shall not pursue this track further, for the simple reason that it deals chiefly with cases where social norms fill an important supportive function (cf. Jon Elster's "Cement of society"[48]). In the Russian case, we are interested in looking for cases where norms have evolved that stand firmly in the way of introducing such formal rules that are prevalent in the Western-type societies.

Analytically, this is considerably more complicated than comparing different systems of formal rules – the crux of the matter being that we are forced to enter the realm of psychology where neat mathematical modelling is of limited use.

A serious attempt to analyze how individuals deal with decision making under uncertainty by forming mental models has been made by North and

Arthur Denzau. Using tools from cognitive psychology, they argue that "the diverse performance of economies and polities both historically and contemporaneously argues against individuals really knowing their self interest and acting accordingly. Instead people act in part upon the basis of myths, dogmas, ideologies and 'half-baked' theories."[49]

In this interpretation, "institutions" remain the formal and informal rules of the game, while "mental models" are "the internal representations that individual cognitive systems create to interpret the environment," and ideologies become "the shared framework of mental models that groups of individuals possess".[50] Here the crucial dimensions of analysis concern the processes of "internal representation" and of interpersonal co-ordination of the mental models.

The scope of this discussion may be extended to include neurobiological research, where David Ingvar has shown that in order to deal with the daily barrage of information that we are all subjected to, the human brain has developed a "memory of the future", a form of screening mechanism which filters out information that is not consistent with the individual's perception of what the future will look like.[51] With this filter, the task of "interpreting the environment" will be greatly facilitated, but also the more difficult to influence. The risk of entrenchment is obvious.

Denzau and North also address the issue of multiple equilibria, by bringing into the picture North's previous analysis of institutions: "Individuals with common cultural backgrounds and experiences will share reasonably convergent mental models, ideologies, and institutions; and individuals with different learning experiences (both cultural and environmental) will have different theories (models, ideologies) to interpret their environment."[52]

As the prospects for multiple equilibria to arise are linked to the process of convergence among the different mental models, we are pointed not only in the direction of cognitive psychology – "The process of representational redescription would require an understanding of exactly how the progression in human cognition occurs"[53] – but perhaps even more so towards learning and informational processes:

> Mental models are shared by communication, and communication allows the creation of ideologies and institutions in a co-evolutionary process . . . The path-dependence of the institutional development process can be derived from the way cognition and institutions in societies evolve. Both usually evolve incrementally but the latter, institutions, clearly are a reflection of the evolving mental models. Therefore, the form of learning that takes place is crucial.[54]

Returning again to the Russian case, we may note that Keenan indirectly recognizes a lock-in effect, phrased as "distinctive and interconnected patterns of behavior". Noting that this social system was preserved over centuries, and may help explain many aspects of later reform failures, we must nevertheless be wary of condemning it as a failure.

Placed within the context outlined by David, the fateful decision made by early Muscovy, to go into farming in a region that was ill suited for such endeavours, may be seen as the "accident" that set off a self-reinforcing process marked by increasing returns and path dependence.

Though it rested on an economically inferior equilibrium, this solution proved to be remarkably resistant to change. And in the mental models of the participants it was undoubtedly rationalized as a great success. Keenan even argues that it actually *was* an achievement: "Indeed, I would argue that, in historical perspective, the creation of a distinctive and strikingly effective political culture in the hostile and threatening environment that was the womb of Russian political culture was that nation's most extraordinary achievement."[55]

The main point in this argument lies in the implications it has concerning the influence of the harsh environment on the formation of communal norm systems, or "shared mental models", where the key features were the need to keep the collective welded together, to endure hardship (*terpenie*), to avoid risk and to strive for stability.

In the mirror of language, we may note that the Russian word "*mir*", while denoting the village community also may be translated as "peace" and "world". The implicit logic is simple: the village *is* the world and there peace must reign.

In this context, it is understandable that the self-image of the individuals – their mental models – came to be dominated by an experience of weakness and vulnerability in the face of nature, combined with a feeling of security in the collective. As a result, individual patterns of behaviour became highly unpredictable. After times of severe hardship follow various kinds of lascivious behaviour: unbridled drinking and eating coupled with sleeping on the warm stove. This unreliability in its turn gave rise to danger: hardship and authoritarian discipline breed resentment, at times resulting in explosions of violence which threaten the very survival of the collective.

What we have here is an asymmetric social relationship, where the individual draws security from the collective but returns distrust and suspicion. If we recognize that the collective is no actor in itself, it follows that the real objects of distrust and suspicion will be neighbouring households. Assuming further that this basic asymmetry is translated into social values, we may see the contours of a game where the individual may derive positive utility not only from his own success but perhaps even more so from his neighbour's failure. (There are plenty of Russian anecdotes illustrating such attitudes.) The fact that he depends for his survival on those very neighbours serves to further augment his feeling of resentment.

This kind of *mentalité* has also been portrayed by the great Russian writers, most notably so in the works of Dostoyevsky. In his "Notes from Underground", for example, we have a vivid account of suspicion, aggressiveness and vengeance, coupled with self-pity and self-despiction.

Writing on this topic in a more scholarly fashion, the Russian historian Boris Mironov implicitly follows North in pointing at the interaction between the formal and informal rules of the institutional matrix and the associated ideology or value system: "The regulating principles of familial and communal life were institutionalized not only in the peasants' social, economic, and familial relations within the commune, but also in their ideals, ethical outlooks, and value systems."[56]

The authoritarian type of mentality that developed within this social context is described in the following way:

> The traits most characteristic of the authoritarian personality are emotionality, irrationality of behavior, and, closely tied to these, a readiness to rely on any kind of superior force (which might appear in the form of a god, fate, or a leader) on the one hand and, on the other, constant revolt in relation to weak authority. Other traits of the authoritarian personality include an inability to cooperate; an inclination towards anarchy, destructiveness, cynicism, and hostility and enmity towards people; painstaking observance of accepted norms of behavior; aggression against those who violate these norms; faith in superstitions and in mythical predestination of the material world; and a preconceived notion that the outside world is filled with terrible things.[57]

Mironov argues that this Russian *mentalité* is distinguished by "conservatism, aggression, contempt both for the intelligentsia and for different ethnic groups, and conformity and stereotypy of thought or dogmatism". He supplements that portrayal by showing how the individual households were run – by the *bolshak* – in much the same way as the *mir* itself: "The patriarchal peasant family was akin to an absolute government, only with a smaller constituency."[58]

The hierarchy within the household was passed on to future generations through a special form of relationship between children and parents: "In the peasant's view, parental responsibility before their children is lacking. However, the children's responsibility before their parents exists in an exaggerated manner . . . Violence was recognized as a completely normal and important form of interaction."[59]

The strongly authoritarian control that is exercised by the rulers of the *mir* over its members is also underlined by Mironov: "It regulated the behaviour of its members primarily through absorption of the peasant's personality – enslavement or domination, one might say – and through control of the member's economic and other activities."[60]

293

Without phrasing it in economic terms, he also emphasizes that demand from below plays a crucial role: "The drawbacks of the commune as a social organization – its repression of initiative, absorption of the individual personality, traditionalism, collective responsibility, and so on – were, from the peasants' point of view, its benefits."[61]

The latter is a fundamental point, implying that throughout much of its early history the Russian social order – the patrimonial state – was reproduced on demand from below, within a set of mental models that were shared by the vast majority of the peasant population. Mironov is very clear in this respect: "The authoritarianism of the family and commune found external support in Orthodoxy and autocracy, while internally it rested on the ignorance and, most important, the ethical outlook of the peasantry."[62]

The implications for reforms from above are quite clear: "Indeed, one important reason the Russian state enjoyed only limited success with its reforms since the eighteenth century was the durability of the peasant family and commune. These reforms were not initiated from below, within the primary social groups – the family and the commune – and they contradicted the traditional mode of the peasants' lives."[63]

Maintaining our ambition to avoid determinism, we must underline that there was nothing to say that this institutional arrangement was the *only* way available to solve the problems originally imposed by a harsh nature. There are other societies which have faced at least as harsh natural conditions (albeit of different sorts), but have chosen different solutions. Keenan clearly recognizes this simple fact:

> Cultures that, under conditions similar to those that influenced Russian culture, develop a similarly pessimistic view of man may devise various general patterns of control designed to save the community – and the individual – from man's allegedly dangerous innate proclivities. It can, as was the case in much of Northern – later Protestant – Europe, develop controls that through socialization and cultural "transcription" are internalized . . . the necessary social control is achieved through internalization in the individual and reinforced by non-violent psychological means.[64]

So, the path that was chosen by the early Muscovites was not the only one available. The decision to go into farming was not a given one, nor was the chosen mode of controlling the members of the community. But once these decisions had been made, they became path dependent.

The opting for a solution that was clearly sub-optimal set off a self-reinforcing process where increasing returns reproduced the practice of redistribution and where the associated feelings of resentment from below and of distrust from above gained firm representation in mental models on all sides. The resultant "Muscovite view of man"[65] would have a lasting influence on Russia's path dependence, standing firmly in the way of such norms that enable legitimate government and enforcement.

Moving from the world of Muscovy into the Russian imperial period, we must ask how the mental models of the Russians responded to the new rules that were suddenly imposed from above (and from without). Raeff emphasizes the monolithic nature of the drive for modernity: "The central [agencies] of the state were assigned positive tasks and given the monopoly of authority in practically all areas of Russian life. Little was left to the autonomous initiative and action of the individuals and of constituted groups."[66]

The ability of actors to respond by forming new organizations that might serve to exploit benefits from the new rules was thus seriously circumscribed. With service to the tsar still being both mandatory and life-long, we must look instead at the informal dimension, where vital transformations would have to take place.

The challenge was substantial. It was under Peter that the notion of separating the state from the Crown began to take root. The tsar spoke of "the common good" and "the benefit of the whole nation" and he actively sought to promote a sense of connection between private and public good. The increased freedom of information was part of this, as was the new practice of attaching explanations to imperial decrees. In short, one might say that the tsar sought to make citizens out of his subjects.

The outcome, which Pipes calls "the central tragedy of modern Russian politics", was determined by an autocracy that failed to understand the implications of its own new venture:

> It was clearly contradictory to appeal to the public sentiments of the Russian people and at the same time deny them any legal and political safeguards against the omnipotence of the state. A partnership in which one party held all the power and played by its own rules was obviously unworkable. And yet this is exactly how Russia has been governed from Peter the Great to this day.[67]

Returning to the framework of path dependence, there was nothing that forced Peter to invite a discussion of the *bien public*, but once it had been done a self-reinforcing process was started where demands for rights grew ever louder, never to be heeded by the tsar. With each round of this game, learning took place that reinforced distrust as a fundamental feature of mental models on both sides of the fence.

Under Catherine the Great the nobility was finally free to adapt to the new visions that were held up under the aegis of her "small enlightenment", at least technically so. They could leave state service and form their own ventures, but the first to do so would be very much alone on "the market". Thus, we are still faced with a situation where response will take place mainly in the form of adapting expectations rather than in forming organizations.

And this would persist for some time yet to come. As we may recall, Catherine did toy with the idea of abolishing serfdom, which she found repulsive, but then there was the Pugachev rebellion and the French revolution both of which had the effect of reinforcing deep-seated fears of the popular masses. Thus the gap between the autocracy and the nobility, not to mention the intelligentsia, continued to widen.

Throughout the nineteenth century, as we have seen above, the name of the game was increasing polarization. The autocracy repeatedly attempted reform, only to reverse itself. The intelligentsia was shut out, and the peasantry was tied to the land. New classes that emerged, such as industrialists or merchants, could find no place. With learning thus producing divergent mental models, the course towards violent upheavals was fixed.

Enforcement mechanisms

Looking at the rapid erosion of the Russian legal system that has accompanied the reforms of the 1990s, one is tempted to speculate that in the institutional triad it really is the third leg, that of legitimate enforcement mechanisms, which plays the main part. Recalling our example of campaigns against littering, for example, it is rather obvious that in the absence of effective sanctions against those who do defect, no attempt at introducing norms against such behaviour will stand much chance of success.

In a more relevant parallel, we may ask when it is rational to pay your taxes. The simple answer is that with an increasing number of people who do pay their taxes, there will be two mechanisms supporting the rationality of making tax payments: a) the expected return – in terms of public goods – will grow, and b) the risk of getting caught – in the case of evasion – will also increase. But the process obviously works in the other direction as well, and perhaps it is even more powerful in the negative case of approaching general defection.

An important factor determining in which direction the system will evolve may again be found in the norm systems. If citizens experience that the tax system is fair and efficient they will have no problems making a contribution, but if they were to find out that crooks are successful in evading their share of the burden the supportive norms will erode and universal defection becomes a serious threat.

The main function of enforcement may therefore be taken to be the creation of legitimacy for the formal rules by promoting trust. In a situation where there are few actors, focus will be on learning about the past behaviour of the others and on credible group pressure on potential defectors. This is fairly straightforward, but when there is a large number of players we have a problem even theoretically: "Third party enforcement means the development of the state as a coercive force able to monitor property rights and enforce contracts effectively, but no one at this stage in our knowledge knows how to create such an entity."[68] This is a crucial point, which will be discussed at length below.

What is at stake in the economic dimension is the ability of actors to capture the gains from trade that are inherent in specialization and large scale. Effective institutions will serve to reduce the costs of transacting and producing, by raising the benefits of co-operation and the costs of defection. Thus the potential gains may be realized. The story of the rise of the Western world is essentially one about how this was successfully achieved.[69]

In the first stage economies were small, involving local exchange within the village and thus small-scale production (or hunting–gathering). Transactions by implication were personalized and repeated. All the relevant actors were known to each other, possessed a reasonably shared set of mental models and knew how to deal with defectors. Thus there was no need for third party enforcement. Transaction costs were low, but in return the low degree of specialization made transformation costs high.

The second stage was marked by an expansion of the market, to include actors at growing distances from the village, perhaps even involving caravans or overseas travel by ship. This expansion of the choice set implied a dramatic growth of the potential gains from specialization, but it also led to an increase in the costs of transacting. Entering into trade with unknown parties meant that actors would have to invest more resources in measurement and enforcement, problems that were often met – with varying degrees of success – by the imposition of religious norms.

Long distance trade, in particular, placed these problems in focus. While the potential gains from geographic specialization were substantial indeed – namely, plantation agriculture – there arose a serious agency problem, in terms of needing a trusted person to take charge of arriving cargo, and an equally serious enforcement problem, in making sure that agreements were honoured and that goods were not stolen *en route*.

In order to solve these problems, where the potential gains from defection were very large, traders resorted to the use of kinship ties, bonding, exchange of hostages or merchant codes of conduct.[70] The costs and restrictions associated with the latter weighed heavily.

It was only in the third stage, that of impersonal exchange with third party enforcement, that economic development really took off. An excellent example is the above mentioned thirteenth century commercial revolution in the city states of Venice, Florence and Genoa, which laid the foundations for the lasting economic differentials between North and South of Italy, analyzed by Putnam.

The trigger for the subsequent trajectory of rapid economic growth was provided by the state, which stepped in as a guarantor of contracts and property rights. Thus all the instruments of modern market economy that rest on trust and credibility, such as money, banking and credit, could be deployed. The consequent reduction in transaction costs made it possible for merchants to enter into ventures that were marked by increasing returns, and with repeated transactions learning took place which told traders that it was indeed rational to trust in the rules of the game. The rest is a success story.

The failure of the Italian South to follow the example of the North, by emulating this successful example of institutional change, illustrates the complexity of the problem of imitation. Despite massive efforts by Rome to turn things around, to this day "criminal capitalism" has remained a defining characteristic for the economy of the Mezzogiorno.

One is reminded here of what Robert Lucas once wrote about imitation in the case of the Asian "miracle" economies: "But simply advising a society to 'follow the Korean model' is a little like advising an aspiring basketball player to 'follow the Michael Jordan model'."[71] If it were that easy, Jordan would be no star, indeed there would be no stars anywhere below the heavens.

Turning back to the Russian case, an important reason behind the failure to develop competitive markets and a democratic order rests in the fact that enforcement has traditionally been geared to the purely punitive dimension, designed to support unaccountable power rather than legitimate rules. The classic statement by Grand Prince Vasilii III, that "All are Slaves", reflected the total lack of rights that marked all levels of Muscovite society, as well as the associated arbitrary administration of punishments. This was a pattern that would be preserved well into the imperial age.

Under Peter the Great the drive for greater rationality, for communication and for stable rules, was associated with the introduction of the world's first organized secret police, which based much of its work on denunciations, and with the tsar's strong preference for personally beating his nobles. Peter being a strong man, such beatings could at times result in serious injuries.

It would not be until with the 1785 Charter that the nobility was exempt from corporal punishment and it would be almost another century, until 1861, before the peasantry was freed from serfdom.

Against this background it is hardly surprising that the Russian language exhibits the previously quoted double translation of the English word for "justice": *yustitsiya* for that which is administered from above, and *spravedlivost* for that which should prevail among equals. This is not a suitable mental environment for the promotion of legitimate legislation, no matter how well intended the legislators.

As a case in point we may recall the trial against Vera Zasulich, the young terrorist who had taken a shot at the governor of St Petersburg. Although the trial took place under conditions laid out in the legal reform of 1864, the verdict was rendered not on the basis of the law but on the consciences of the jurors who felt that the terrorist had been morally right in her action.

Thus placing morality before the law not only frustrated the legislators, it also confirmed any suspicions the autocracy might have had that granting rights for the people was the wrong way to go.

As we may recall from above, the last words that Alexander II had received from his dying father, Nicholas I, had been to "Hold on to everything!", and after his own assassination in 1881, many of his reforms, now branded as "criminal errors", would be reversed. And when Nicholas II was petitioned by liberal *zemstvo* politicians, he waved off their demands for a constitution as "senseless dreams".

Before proceeding to look at Russia's twentieth century, which will be the topic for discussion in the following chapter, it may be of some use to sum up here the experiences that have been collected thus far, in the hope that taken together they perhaps form at least the outline for a theory of revealed institutional preference.

Outline of a theory

In a 1994 article about the role of institutions in Russia's economic reform process, Michael Intriligator finds it "necessary to establish the relevant economic, legal, political and social institutions so as to prevent the further collapse of the Russian economy," and then goes on to argue that "privatization, price liberalization, and other aspects of the current economic reform program will not create these institutions".[72]

The main thrust of his argument is that despite surviving negative attitudes to a major role for government, the new Russian government must assume a more active role in creating, with external assistance, the institutions in question. This is a crucial dimension of the problem, which illustrates the limits to widely held beliefs in *laissez-faire*.

In his previously quoted 1995 article, Mancur Olson notes that "Some enthusiasts for markets suppose that the only problem is that governments get in the way of the market and that private property is a natural and spontaneous creation". This view, however, is branded as "unquestionably and drastically wrong". The reason given goes to the heart of the matter:

> Though individuals may have possessions without government, the way a dog possesses a bone, there is no private property without government. Property is a socially protected claim on an asset – a bundle of rights enforceable in courts backed by the coercive power of government.[73]

These statements indicate where the roots of the Russian predicament lie, namely in the path dependent absence in Russian tradition of a state which is ready, willing and able to shoulder a role as legitimate guarantor of the rules of the game. Intriligator notes that in order to solve this problem "it will be necessary to resolve the conflict between the Yeltsin government and the parliament".[74] Yes, but how?

In Western tradition, the universal embrace of Roman law, blended with common law, provides a basis for contracts and constitutionalism. In the market economies, repeated games have taught actors that defection is not a rational strategy, and with learning taking place there has been a convergence of mental models such that norms like *pacta sunt servanda* have become internalized both in the political culture and in a code of business ethics. And the legal system has been up to the task of coping sufficiently well with defectors for basic norms to be preserved.

The Russian case, as it has been presented above, represents a diametric opposite. Pipes emphasizes how the suppression of private property, which was the true hallmark of the patrimonial society, had devastating consequences for the emergence of laws:

> In the words of C. B. Macpherson, "What distinguishes property from mere momentary possession is that property is a claim that will be enforced by society or the state, by customs or convention or law." Thus property posits common or statutory law and all that goes with them. "Property and law are born together and must die together," wrote Jeremy Bentham nearly two centuries ago. "Before the laws there was no property; take away the laws, all property ceases."[75]

An immediate consequence of this absence of both state, property and legitimate laws was that the notion of "rights" also disappeared, and with it the need for any formal rules of the game. Such laws that were made had their point firmly aimed at suppressing the subjects, and thus were deprived from the outset of any chance of winning legitimacy.

The theoretical problems that arise in seeking to construct a state that is able to function as a legitimate third party enforcer go back to Hobbes and Locke and have been underlined not only by North, as quoted above, but by many others as well, notably so by those interested in the role of constitutions.

Referring to the advice frequently given to the post-socialist economies, that they must "get prices right", Barry Weingast, for example, notes that "something is missing", and argues that that "something" is lodged firmly in the political dimension:

> Juxtaposed to the problem of "getting prices right" is what I call the *fundamental political dilemma of an economic system*: a government

strong enough to protect property rights is also strong enough to confiscate the wealth of its citizens. Thriving markets require not only the appropriate property rights system, an unfettered price mechanism, and a law of contracts, but a secure political foundation that limits the ability of the state to confiscate wealth by altering those rights and systems.[76]

Weingast's solution being that of "market-preserving federalism", he goes on to look at experiences from England and the United States, which again is the success story. Given what was said in our previous chapter, however, about the problems of fiscal federalism under Yeltsin, the Russian case clearly does not belong in that category.

Assuming that the reason for this is lodged in the "political foundation", we are pointed in the direction of credible commitment, the pre-conditions for which are given as follows by North: "Establishing a credible commitment to secure property rights over time requires either a ruler who exercises forbearance and restraint in using coercive force, or the shackling of the ruler's power to prevent arbitrary seizure of assets."[77]

Discussing the same problem in another context, he distinguishes between "motivational credibility", where the ruler succeeds in structuring the game so that it is in everybody's interest – including his own – to follow the rules, and "imperative credibility", whereby he decides to bind himself irreversibly by handing over powers to his subjects.[78]

Again, the former would represent the direction of a success story, and it is not surprising to note how Greif describes the start of the Italian success: "The political institutions of Genoa and Venice that crystallized during the twelfth century . . . were endogenous, self-enforcing organizations. They were self-enforcing in the sense that in the short run inter-clan co-operation was fostered and no clan was induced to challenge the system."[79]

In the Russian case, repeated games have taught actors on both sides of the fence what value may be realistically ascribed to contracts that might become self-enforcing, and the very notion of "imperative credibility" has foundered on the inability of the autocracy to realize that communication with the citizenry requires the granting of basic rights.

Rounding off the argument we may return to Weingast, when he turns to argue that as rules may be "disobeyed or ignored", a constitutional arrangement is needed which may help in policing the sovereign. Two interrelated characteristics are posited, which must be achieved by a society that is seeking to establish the rule of law: on the one hand "institutions that limit and define the legitimate boundaries of state action", and on the other a "set of shared beliefs among citizens who react against the state when the latter attempts to transgress the boundaries defined by those institutions".[80]

This takes us close to the completion of our story in the present chapter. Why has it not been possible for Russia's rulers to promote a set of such "shared beliefs", or "shared mental models", among their subjects? Pipes points at the profound influence of serfdom, which, although not analogous to slavery, did serve to deprive the peasants of all legal rights, including rights to the land they tilled. Like slavery, it had the effects of instilling in the peasant an instinctive contempt for law and property, coupled with resistance to authority and an absence of any sense of patriotism:

> The most harmful legacy of Russia's past may well lie here. Its people were given no opportunity to develop either respect for property and law, or a sense of belonging to a national community. They were taught to obey when there was no choice and to rebel when there was: the one thing they were not taught was the responsibilities and the benefits of citizenship.[81]

Looking at this historical legacy from the perspective of "shared mental models", we may recall from above two assumptions of crucial importance to the theory of institutional change: a) that both cognition and institutions evolve incrementally, and b) that institutions develop as a reflection of the evolving mental models.

Against this background it follows that Russia's successive attempts at modernization, from Peter the Great onwards, have foundered on the absence of a common ideology out of which a set of norms could have emerged to support market-oriented change. Periodic attempts by the autocracy to achieve a co-ordination of the mental models of different groups in society, by inviting change and by making information available, failed to produce learning of the kind that might have led to internal redescription.

The "revealed institutional preference" rests in the dimension of distrust. The consistent refusal to grant rights reflects a failure to achieve credible commitment, which in turn led to a preservation of the path dependence in the mental models. The production of ideology from above is a crucial dimension of this process, which has been referred to only *en passant* in this chapter.

In the following chapter, however, we shall have much more to say about the role of Orthodoxy in old Russia and about the role of marxism–leninism in the Soviet Union. There are important parallels here, which may be usefully interpreted within the path dependent framework that has been outlined above.

Notes

1. Easterly, W. 1995. Explaining miracles: growth regressions meet the gang of four, in Ito, T. and Krueger, A. O. (eds), *Growth Theories in the Light of the Asian Experience*. Chicago: University of Chicago Press, p. 268.

2. North, D.C. 1990. *Institutions, Institutional Change and Economic Performance.* Cambridge: Cambridge University Press, p. 11.
3. Szamuely, L. 1993. Transition from state socialism: whereto and how?, *Acta Oeconomica*, **45**(1–2), 8.
4. Johnson, J.E. 1994. The Russian banking system: institutional responses to the market transition, *Europe-Asia Studies*, **46**(6), 973, n. 11.
5. Nelson, L.D. and Kuzes, I.Y. 1995b. *Radical Reform in Yeltsin's Russia: Political, Economic and Social Dimensions.* Armonk, NY: M.E. Sharpe, p. 3.
6. McDaniel, T. 1996. *The Agony of the Russian Idea.* Princeton, NJ: Princeton University Press, p. 147.
7. Ibid., p. 17.
8. See, e.g., various issues of *Sovetskaya Rossiya*.
9. *Izvestiya*, 4 March 1997.
10. McDaniel, op. cit., p. 179.
11. Shlapentokh, V. 1997. *Bonjour*, stagnation: Russia's next years, *Europe-Asia Studies*, **49**(5), 877.
12. Holmes, S. 1997. When less state means less freedom, *Transitions*, September, pp. 74–5.
13. Shlapentokh, op. cit., p. 870.
14. Holmes, op. cit., p. 73.
15. Reuters, 22 May 1998.
16. The role of good versus bad policies as a determinant of sustained economic differentials between countries is discussed at length in Olson, M. 1996. Big bills left on the sidewalk: why some nations are rich and others poor, *Journal of Economic Perspectives*, **10**(2).
17. Pipes, R. 1996. Russia's past, Russia's future, *Commentary*, June, p. 37.
18. David, P.A. 1985. Clio and the economics of QWERTY, *The American Economic Review*, **75**(2).
19. David, P. 1993. Historical economics in the long run: some implications of path dependence, in Snooks, G.D. (ed.), *Historical Analysis in Economics.* London: Routledge, p. 29 and *passim*.
20. The following summary is from North 1990, op. cit., pp. 93–4, citing Arthur, W.B. 1988. Self-reinforcing mechanisms in economics, in Anderson, P.W., Arrow, K.J. and Pines, D. (eds), *The Economy as an Evolving Complex System.* Reading, Mass.: Addison-Wesley.
21. Arthur, W.B. 1994. *Increasing Returns and Path Dependence in the Economy.* Ann Arbor: University of Michigan Press, p. xv.
22. Ibid., pp. ix–x.
23. See, e.g., Arthur, W.B. 1989. Competing technologies, increasing returns, and lock-in by historical events, *Economic Journal*, **99**.
24. David 1993, op. cit., p. 39.
25. North 1990, op. cit., pp. 95–6.
26. Cited by Eggertsson, T. 1996a. No experiments, monumental disasters: why it took a thousand years to develop a specialized fishing industry in Iceland, *Journal of Economic Behaviour and Organization*, **30**(1), 2.
27. Ibid.
28. Eggertsson, T. 1996b. Rethinking the theory of economic policy: some implications of the new institutionalism, paper prepared for a workshop on "Economic

Transformation, Institutional Change, Property Rights, and Corruption", arranged by the NAS/NRC "Task Force on Economies in Transition", Washington, DC, 7–8 March 1996, pp. 22–3.

29. North 1990, op. cit., p. 3.
30. Peterson, C. 1979. *Peter the Great's Administrative and Judicial Reforms: Swedish Antecedents and the Process of Reception*. Lund: Bloms boktryckeri.
31. Raeff, M. 1976. Imperial Russia: Peter I to Nicholas I, in Auty, R. and Obolensky, D. (eds), *An Introduction to Russian History*. Cambridge: Cambridge University Press, pp. 129–30.
32. Ibid., p. 129.
33. Ibid., p. 130.
34. North 1990, op. cit., pp. 6–7.
35. North, D.C. and Thomas, R.P. 1973. *The Rise of the Western World: A New Economic History*. Cambridge: Cambridge University Press.
36. North, D.C. 1981. *Structure and Change in Economic History*. New York: Norton.
37. Greif, A. 1994. Cultural beliefs and the organization of society: a historical and theoretical reflection on collectivist and individual societies, *Journal of Political Economy*, **102**(5), 914.
38. Putnam, R.D. 1993. *Making Democracy Work: Civic Traditions in Modern Italy*. Princeton, NJ: Princeton University Press. A similar approach is used by Francis Fukuyama, pointing at the important role that is played by the level of trust in a society (Fukuyama, F. 1995. *Trust: The Social Virtues and the Creation of Prosperity*. New York: The Free Press).
39. See further Leonardi, R. 1995. Regional development in Italy: social capital and the Mezzogiorno, *Oxford Review of Economic Policy*, **11**(2).
40. Putnam, op. cit., pp. 179–81.
41. Ibid., p. 183.
42. North 1990, op. cit., p. 99.
43. Pipes, op. cit., p. 35.
44. Keenan, E. 1986. Muscovite political folkways, *The Russian Review*, **45**, 123–8. For the sake of completeness, it should be noted that in addition to the *mir*, Keenan also discusses the political culture of the court and the bureaucracy of Muscovy. We shall return to the latter below. See also Hedlund, S. and Sundström, N. 1996a. Does Palermo represent the future for Moscow?, *Journal of Public Policy*, **16**(2), 134–9.
45. Keenan, op. cit., p. 116.
46. Pipes, R. 1974. *Russia under the Old Regime*. New York: Scribner, p. 124.
47. See further ibid., pp. 90–95.
48. Elster, J. 1989. *The Cement of Society: A Study of Social Order*. Cambridge: Cambridge University Press.
49. Denzau, A.T. and North, D.C. 1994. Shared mental models: ideologies and institutions, *Kyklos*, **47**, 3.
50. Ibid., p. 4.
51. Ingvar, D. 1995. "Memory of the future": an essay on the temporal organization of conscious awareness, *Human Neurobiology*, **4**.
52. Denzau and North, op. cit., pp. 3–4.
53. Ibid., p. 21.
54. Ibid., pp. 20, 22.

55. Ibid.
56. Mironov, B.N. 1994. Peasant popular culture and the origins of Soviet authoritarianism, in Frank, S.P. and Steinberg, M.D. (eds), *Cultures in Flux: Lower Class Values, Practices, and Resistance in Late Imperial Russia*. Princeton, NJ: Princeton University Press, p. 63.
57. Ibid., pp. 54–5.
58. Ibid., pp. 55–6.
59. Ibid., p. 57.
60. Ibid., p. 60.
61. Ibid., pp. 61, 63.
62. Ibid., p. 62.
63. Ibid., p. 70.
64. Keenan, op. cit., pp. 126–7.
65. Ibid., p. 125.
66. Raeff, op. cit., p. 123.
67. Pipes 1974, op. cit., pp. 128–9.
68. North 1990, op. cit., p. 59.
69. For a brief account, see North, D.C. 1991. Institutions, *Journal of Economic Perspectives*, **5**(1), 98–102 and *passim*.
70. Important contributions to this area of research have been made by Avner Greif, in several papers about the Mahgribi traders. See, e.g., Greif, A. 1993. Contract enforceability and economic institutions in early trade: the Maghribi traders' coalition, *The American Economic Review*, **83**(3), and Greif 1994, op. cit. The role of merchant guilds has been analyzed in Greif, A., Milgrom, P. and Weingast, B.R. 1994. Coordination, commitment, and enforcement: the case of the Merchant Guild, *Journal of Political Economy*, **102**(4), and the role of the Champagne Fairs in Milgrom, P.R., North, D.C. and Weingast, B.R. 1990. The role of institutions in the revival of trade: the medieval Law Merchant, private Judges and Champagne Fairs, *Economics and Politics*, March.
71. Lucas, R.E. 1993. Making a miracle, *Econometrica*, **61**(2), 252.
72. Intriligator, M.D. 1994. Reform of the Russian economy: the role of institutions, *Contention*, **3**(2), 153.
73. Olson, M. 1995. Why the transition from communism is so difficult, *Eastern Economic Journal*, **21**(4), 458.
74. Intriligator, op. cit., p. 155.
75. Pipes 1996, op. cit., p. 33.
76. Weingast, B.R. 1993. Constitutions as governance structures: the political foundations of secure markets, *Journal of Institutional and Theoretical Economics*, **149**(1), 287. (Emphasis in the original.) See also Greif, Milgrom and Weingast, op. cit.
77. North 1991, op. cit., p. 101.
78. North, D.C. 1993a. Institutions and credible commitment, *Journal of Institutional and Theoretical Economics*, **149**(1), 14.
79. Greif, A. 1995. Political organizations, social structure, and institutional success: reflections from Genoa and Venice during the commercial revolution, *Journal of Institutional and Theoretical Economics*, **151**(4).
80. Weingast, op. cit., p. 305.
81. Pipes 1996, op. cit., p. 34.

CHAPTER NINE

Victory for the kleptocrats?

One of the main questions that will be addressed in this chapter is that of rent-seeking, or redistributive activities, or plain thieving. While in a superficial sense these are activities that may be found in all societies and at all times, there may also be systemic causes which explain the great variations that may be observed in the *extent* of such negative behaviour across times and across societies.

On the one hand we have differences in formal rules, such as high marginal tax rates, market-suppressing regulations or plain legal loopholes, which create temptations for actors to steal. On the other is the dimension of readiness to resist such temptations, which may be conditioned by cultural norms, social cohesion or the legitimacy of government.

An ideal society, where all actors engage in productive activities only and where stealing is unthinkable, will certainly never exist, at least not in any significant size. Yet, there is a large interval where public policy may influence whether society will gravitate towards the crime-free or the totally anarchic extremes of the spectrum. This is where the Russian story again assumes great relevance.

In Russia under the old regime there were plenty of options for actors to help themselves to the property of others, and few if any norms condemning such behaviour. When asked, for example, to answer in the shortest possible way the question "What goes on in Russia?" the conservative Russian historian and courtier to Alexander I, Nikolai Karamzin used to answer in one word: "thieving" (*voruyut*).[1]

The reason behind this sorry state of affairs was a combination of available opportunities and a lack of blocking norms, which – taken together – made thieving an individually rational strategy. This, moreover, was something that held not only for predatory elites in Moscow or St Petersburg.

To the provincial bureaucracy, which was effectively cut off from the closed world of lucrative elite positions in the capital, there was little alternative but to engage in bribery and self-seeking on their own. Thus the vast majority of Russian officialdom sank deep into corruption. The great Russian novelists provide plenty of insights into this world, and it is logical that no social norms emerged to effectively condemn and preclude such behaviour.

To the peasantry, stealing lay even closer at hand. As we have noticed above, their sense of property was weak if at all existent and their readiness to revolt against authority always simmering just below the surface. Landlords were regarded as an alien element in what was taken to be *their* countryside, and the notion of a state, or of public property, made little if any sense at all. Here the norm systems were even less geared into preventing theft.

Chekhov has written a beautiful short story, *Zloumyshchlennik*, about a peasant who is brought before the magistrate for having removed a nut from a nearby railroad. He had needed the nut for a sinker when fishing and refused to comprehend what the magistrate had to say about the risks of a train being derailed and of people being killed if nuts and bolts were removed from the rails. When he is led out of court, after being sentenced to jail, the peasant mutters to himself that there is nothing to be said even about being hanged, if only it is for something one has done, for something that is on one's conscience.

The moral of both these cases is that of drawing a line between stealing from public and from private pockets, a distinction which in turn reflects the weak development in Russia of a sense of society or of citizenship. As we have noted above, without a state that is legitimate in the eyes of its citizenry, there can be no laws, and without laws there can be no property. Thus Mancur Olson's previously quoted statement, that without government there can be no private property.

When we turn now to look in greater detail at Russia's twentieth century, these latter observations will be the focus of our analysis. Russia's Soviet period has been described above as a kleptocracy and the prevalence of plunder under the Yeltsin regime by now ought to be part of common knowledge.

Our task then becomes to investigate if these latter patterns are path dependent phenomena, having their roots in old Muscovy and/or imperial Russia, or if they may be explained by more specific causes. This obviously entails a need for a broader investigation than simply looking at options for and a readiness to engage in plunder. As we shall see below, however, when looking at the pre-conditions for fundamental institutional change to be successfully implemented, the issues of enforcement and norms take on a pivotal importance.

In the previous chapter it was argued that Russia's twentieth century forms an ideal laboratory for a study of the pre-conditions for successful institutional change. The main argument was that we have two major attempts at "systemic change" – undertaken by Lenin and by Yeltsin – which are fundamental in the true sense of the word. Here we may add two further reasons, which support that argument.

The first is that in stark contrast to reforms undertaken in the previous two centuries, neither of the latter represented reforms that were initiated within the existing order. On the contrary, in both cases the old order had collapsed – prodded by the incoming leaders – and in both cases the new leadership set out to create from scratch, thus revealing basic preferences about institutional arrangements.

Secondly, the formal directions of the respective reform programmes were diametrically opposed to each other. While the nature of the Bolshevik programme was essentially market-suppressing, that of Yeltsin's neo-liberals was market-conforming. We have an ideal situation, therefore, where a similar set of questions may be posed against a background of radically different formal parameters.

In the following we shall begin by looking at the Bolshevik experiment, searching for patterns of revealed institutional preference that may provide further support for our previous outline of a theory of Russian path dependence.

With the link between Imperial and Soviet Russia having been thus investigated, we shall turn to Boris Yeltsin's programme, again with the ambition of looking for path dependent choices, but also to look for points where at least some parts of the path dependence might perhaps have been broken. Bearing this latter possibility in mind, we shall also maintain our previous ambition of cautioning against determinism.

Systemic change I: Lenin and the Bolsheviks

In the night of 24–25 October 1917, Bolshevik Red Guards and Red Sailors occupied strategic positions in Petrograd. Although subsequent myths – brilliantly filmed by Eisenstein – about the heroic storming of the Winter Palace have little foundation in fact, these were decisive hours indeed, heralding the end of Russia's "democratic parenthesis" and the advent of a new social order.

In our initial brief account of the Soviet kleptocracy, the essence of the communist transformation of Russian society was pictured with the help of János Kornai's "genetic program". We saw how the monopoly on power together with the official ideology form the "body and soul" of the system, which then produce a need to suppress private property. (The following building blocks in his chain are bargaining, soft budget constraints and the distinctive "quantity drive".)

Bearing that portrayal in mind, we shall proceed here to look at the Bolshevik programme from a more detailed institutional perspective of rules, norms and enforcement mechanisms. And we shall structure the discussion according to our previous schema of "zones of confrontation", i.e. to see how the newly installed executive power would go about arranging its relations to the legislature, to the judiciary, to the financial system and to the entrepreneurial sector.

All power to the Soviets?

Although subsequent Soviet ideology would make much of "Great October", we may recall from above that the real watershed came not in October 1917 but in January 1918, at the first session of the newly elected Constituent Assembly. Having won only 175 seats, against the 350 won by the rival Socialist Revolutionaries (the SRS), the Bolsheviks found themselves in a minority, and when the first vote went against them the assembly was dispersed by Red Guards, never to meet again.

This was the first step on the road towards establishing a power monopoly. Although no decree was ever issued to formally prohibit the other two socialist parties, there is a striking continuity in both words and deeds pointing in the direction of the Bolsheviks claiming all power not for the "workers" but for the party and its hard-line leadership.

In his "April Theses" of 1917, Lenin had argued that the aim was "not the 'introduction' of socialism as an *immediate* task, but immediate transition merely to *control* by the Soviet of Workers' Deputies".[2] And it would not be long before the true ambitions behind that statement were revealed.

Although both Mensheviks and SRS were included when the second "All-Russian Congress of Soviets" proceeded, in October 1917, to elect a new "Executive Committee", the Bolsheviks reserved a majority of seats for themselves. And when the all-powerful "Council of People's Commissars" was formed, it consisted of Bolsheviks only (the SRS held three temporary seats, until March 1918).

In May 1921, Lenin could finally discard all pretence: "We shall keep the Mensheviks and the SRS, whether open or disguised as 'non-party', in prison."[3] Thus the stubborn refusal to engage in any form of power sharing, which had been so characteristic of the old autocracy, was continued, albeit in a new garb.

At first, however, the Bolshevik hold on power was tenuous indeed. In April 1918 the brutal peace with Germany was concluded at Brest-Litovsk, which provoked open rebellion from the SR left wing. Terror and counter-terror followed, which escalated into a civil war between "red" and "white" armies that well nigh brought about a total collapse of Russian society. By August 1918 there were some 30 different governments seeking to rule the remaining Russian territories.[4]

Nevertheless, while the civil war was still raging the Bolshevik leadership proceeded to take its second step on the road to monopoly power, namely to secure control over society and to streamline the internal working of the party. In the former case, the initial slogans of worker control, and of all power to the Soviets, were soon shown to have been mere tactical ruses.

All aspects of Soviet society were to be placed under "one-man management", known as *edinonachalie*, and that one person was to be accountable upwards only. Lenin argued already in 1918 that neither "railways nor transport, nor large-scale machinery and enterprises in general can function correctly without a single will linking the entire working personnel into an economic organ operating with the precision of clockwork," and in 1929 *edinonachalie* was established by the party central committee as a vital principle of organization.[5]

The process of internal party streamlining culminated in the spring of 1921, with the prohibition against factions within the party. The leadership of the single remaining party had thus succeeded not only in securing for itself a monopoly on political power, but also in reserving for itself the *formal* right to speak with a single voice. Remaining dissent within the party leadership would delay the actual completion of this streamlining, but not for long.

The third step on the road to what Lenin would call "democratic centralism" was to bring the judiciary under control, and here the Bolsheviks wasted no time declaring their true intentions. Already on 7 December 1917, the new government issued Decree No. 1, which said that old laws would be observed "only insofar as they had not been repealed by the Revolution and did not contradict revolutionary conscience and the revolutionary concept of justice". Thus, says the Russian jurist Aleksandr Yakovlev, "the theoretical grounds and the political and moral justifications for the Great Terror . . . were laid down".[6]

Although the Soviet state would differ from the Russian empire in the formal sense of adopting constitutions – in 1924, 1936 and 1977 – these were something essentially different from what is normally implied by a constitution in a society that rests on the rule of law. The Bolsheviks were certainly not going to accept any independent judicial controls over their exercise of power, and even the more routine-oriented aspects of the actual administration of justice would be marked by what has been referred to above as "telephone justice", i.e. discretion.

The final touch in the ambition to secure a monopoly on political power was to block all production of uncensored information. This again was a bit longer in the making. The Bolsheviks had already secured total control over the press by August 1918, which precluded all outside challenges to the party, but since the 1920s was also a time of debate within the party, it was not possible to achieve an immediate and total uniformity in the output of information.

It was only once Stalin had gained the upper hand in his struggles against opposition within the leadership that the curtain could be conclusively pulled down. In 1930, many of the scholarly journals in the social sciences were closed and the production of meaningful statistics ceased. The information blackout would last until 1956, when the production of a statistical yearbook was resumed.

Viewed from our institutional perspective, the aim of these changes in the rules of the game was pointed firmly in the path dependent direction of depriving the formal rules of any meaningful content, or of suppressing rules altogether. Behind the Soviet façade of constitutions, elections, trade unions and a variety of outwardly democratic government bodies, true power was lodged at the top of the party hierarchy (the new autocracy). And the exact relation between party and state organs was never codified, nor were the provisions for co-optation to the supreme organ of power, the politburo.

Soviet law, as adopted by the communist party, was purposely designed to function as an instrument in the hands of the executive power, ever so flexible in supporting what for the moment was held to be in the interests of "building socialism". The consequences bear a great deal of similarity to what has been said above about the old regime. Most importantly, as the Russian jurist Vadim Granin points out, "Part of this legal ideology was a rejection of the notion that man is endowed with inalienable rights."[7]

Symptomatically, Granin also underlines the instrumental and discretionary nature of Soviet legislation: "Couching its statutes in general abstract terms and regularly enforcing unpublished regulations, secret ministerial instructions and administrative orders undisclosed to the general public, the political élite could invoke the judicial system whenever their interests were involved."[8]

The practical outcome of these ambitions to suppress both the legislature and the judiciary was a hybrid form of rule: on one side a state apparatus which was run according to rules that in any serious case were of little consequence, and on the other a party apparatus which recognized no externally enforceable rules, but relied instead on its own internal and often clandestine informal rules.

This effective placing of the executive power above the law recalls not only Count Benckendorff's previously quoted statement about laws being made for the subjects only. Even more so, it recalls the secrecy and conspiratorial politics of old Muscovy, which later become known as *neglasnost*. The essence of the latter game, as Edward Keenan puts it, was that "those who needed to know [the] rules knew them, and those who had no need to know were kept in ignorance".[9]

As we have noted above, official secrecy would last until Peter the Great embarked on his skewed project of communicating with his subjects, and long after Peter's time provincial judges would still have to write to St Petersburg in order to learn about applicable laws. Against this background, the Soviet practice of ruling by decrees and by the issuing of semi-secret instructions represents continued path dependence in the exercise of power. Actors were led to invest in skills that would help them play this game, and mental models would be adjusted to rationalize that behaviour.

Summing up our argument so far, the establishment of Bolshevik rule represented a *de facto* restoration of the old autocracy, albeit dressed up as rule by the people, combined with a retrogression to a world without open rules and with no legitimate enforcement mechanisms.

It is important to note that the path dependence that is manifested here does not represent a straight and simple continuity. By the time the Great War broke out, developments in several respects already appeared to be deviating from the path.

This was so even in the judicial sphere, where, as Peter Solomon notes, over the 50 years that had passed since the legal reforms of Alexander II, Russian courts of law had remained strong and independent. This at least was the case in the higher courts in the civil realm. Criminal courts were a different story, as was the continued ability of the regime to find ways of resolving problems in reliable forums. Thus, "In short, fifty years of reform brought into focus the limits of change possible under an authoritarian government."[10]

We are thus again faced with a conflict between the path dependent desire for unaccountable power and the "reformist" ambition of introducing autonomy for the judiciary. And in this conflict the Bolshevik leadership would reveal the very same institutional preference that had marked the old autocracy. And given their set example, other political actors would not be slow in realizing that continued investment in skills that would make them better "pirates" was the rational way to go. And it should be rather obvious what this in turn meant for the formation of norms and mental models among the population.

Turning now to look at the economic sphere, we shall see how a parallel suppression of money and property served to restore the essence of the old patrimonial system as a whole.

Control is better than trust

The sudden success in gaining power, the subsequent civil war and red terror, and the obsession with holding on to power, even at the price exacted by the Germans at Brest-Litovsk, certainly had a formative influence on Bolshevik economic policy. Yet, as in the case of power, there are some patterns of decisions that did serve, in the midst of pressing needs, to reveal basic institutional preferences. The most important of these lies in the order of battle, where the assault on the financial system went before that of nationalizing enterprises.

Being convinced that money circulation within the big banks constituted the lifeblood of the economy, manifested in his previously quoted statement that socialism would be unrealizable without the big banks, Lenin's first priority was to strike at the financial sector. And the ambition was not to destroy, but to capture and use the financial system for his own purposes. The latter, however, would turn out in a shape and form that was rather special.

Action was swift and immediate. On 20 November 1917 armed bands seized the State Bank. On 27 December 1917 all commercial banks were nationalized and merged – together with the State Bank – into the People's Bank of the Russian Republic, and in February 1918 the process was completed with a repudiation of all foreign debt.

These moves not only secured that the Bolshevik regime would be regarded as a pariah on the international financial markets, thus necessitating internal capital accumulation, which in turn would place relations to the peasantry in – deeply tragic – focus. It also marked the origin of the monobank system and of the pseudo nature of the Soviet currency, both of which have been described at length above.

The desire expressed by Lenin to take over the financial system was coupled with early ambitions of doing away with money altogether. According to a resolution adopted at the second "All-Russian Congress of Soviets", for example, transactions between state enterprises should be undertaken on command, without payments being made. Alec Nove points at the implications of this decision: "In making this proposal, the congress expressed the desire to see the final elimination of any influence of money upon the relations of economic units."[11]

The subsequent hyperinflation was certainly not intentionally unleashed, but it was received in ever larger party circles as an efficient tool with which to crush the money economy, and the collapse of the currency that took place in 1920 was not seen by all as a disaster. As we know, monetary relations would return under NEP, and the currency would be stabilized, but the freedom of choice that follows with the use of money would also provoke serious discontent and discord within the Bolshevik leadership.

The choice that was facing the party may be formulated as money versus control. By allowing trade (i.e. money) the food crisis could be greatly alleviated, which was imperative, but Lenin also pointed at the inherent danger: "Freedom of trade . . . inevitably leads to white-guardism, to the victory of capital, to its full restoration."[12] At first, there seems to have been expectations for a limited retreat to suffice, for forcible requisitions to be replaced by an ordered "commodity exchange" (*produktoobmen*), but as 1921 rolled on trade and money relations gained an unstoppable momentum. And in October Lenin changed tack, urging the party to "learn to trade" (*Uchites torgovat!*).

That retreat, however, was to be a temporary one. By the end of the 1920s, vacillation on the monetary front was over and the basic roles of money as a means of exchange and a measure of value were suppressed (with the previously mentioned exceptions). For decades to come, the Soviet state would run budgets that were formulated in roubles but which in essence rested on direct administrative commands, dressed up *ex post* in money transfers in and out of state coffers. To those who were charged with supervising this system it implied a generation of unlearning by not doing.

A somewhat less obvious component in the Bolsheviks' economic strategy concerned the ownership of the means of production. The first steps towards suppressing private property were taken quickly, but nevertheless rather hesitantly. The new organ that was created by the Bolsheviks to run the economy, the VSNKh, was given rights of confiscation, requisition, sequestration and syndication, but its directives of implementation were pretty vague.

With the exception of the railroads and the merchant navy, which had been nationalized already by January 1918, the process of expropriation proceeded mainly on the local level and on local initiative. More than two-thirds of all nationalizations that had taken place by June 1918 had been local, directed at single plants rather than at entire industries. It is interesting to note that the central authorities tried in vain to gain control over this process, and there are sources indicating that the wholesale expropriation of private capital that took place in June was due to "external forces", i.e. to prevent further spontaneous actions.[13]

Given these ambivalent developments in the spheres of both money and property, it might seem that the Bolsheviks at first were content with retaining control over the "commanding heights" of banking, big industry and foreign trade. Plenty of conflicting statements from Lenin may also be advanced to support interpretations of the NEP both as a retreat and as an advance. Against this background, Nove concludes that "the evidence, though mixed, is still consistent with the intention to maintain a mixed economy for a considerable period".[14]

Again recalling the "genetic" logic of Kornai's programme, there would seem to be a problem here. Having established a monopoly on power, the suppression of property would have to follow logically. That problem, however, may be resolved by defining the second step in the chain as one of gaining *control* over the factors of production, and here the Bolsheviks appeared to believe that the "commanding heights" would suffice. Once this was shown to have been a false belief, Kornai's logic would be allowed to run its full course, irrespective of human or other costs.

From a perspective of revealed institutional preference, it is not money and property *per se* that are placed in focus, but the underlying desire for control. As Lenin is reputed once to have said, "trust is fine, but control is better". War Communism had provided an illustration of what could be achieved in this sense. As László Szamuely concludes, in a pioneering study, "Its main features outline a model of the centralized directive system of planned economy in its purest historical form ever implemented."[15] And it was something very close to that same model which was soon to re-emerge.

The decisive breaks with any potential ambitions of allowing a mixed economy arrived towards the end of the 1920s, with the introduction of mandatory central planning in the autumn of 1928, and the launching of forced collectivization in the winter of 1929–30. The combined effect of these two moves was to remove all scope for legitimate private enterprise and thus to reintroduce a total dependence by the subjects on the state, both as an employer and as a provider. Thus the "Soviet Model" was completed, and the essence of the patrimonial state restored.

Rounding off this discussion, we may return to our introductory presentation of Mancur Olson's suggested "theory of power". The essence of his approach was to combine a removal of both money and property with the introduction of market-contrary policies and an army of watchers, who were charged with controlling the property of the autocracy (or the politburo). Since the latter was the only bearer of property rights, it was also the only actor having an encompassing interest in optimizing the use over time of the country's productive resources.

With the bureaucrats having narrow interests in helping themselves to the property of the autocracy, and being faced with a collective action problem in seeking to overthrow the autocrat, collusion among the guards was destined to lead not only to endemic corruption. It would also serve to produce norms rationalizing and supporting such behaviour. The latter, as we shall see below, was the really crucial dimension of the Bolshevik system.

Rephrasing the same in more directly institutional terms, the formal rules that were established (or suppressed) by the Bolsheviks prompted actors to develop skills that related to manipulating power relations and engaging in redistributive activities. Being effectively locked into the party-controlled monolith, the only constructive activities that remained within the private sphere were the "soft" versions of exit and voice that were described in Chapter 1 above.

Given this re-creation of dependence on a central power which recognized no judicial limitations on itself and which dispensed its own justice on a discretionary basis, it follows that actors wanting to make a career, or at least secure a decent living, would have to deal with the high set-up costs and the cognitive dissonance that was bound to follow from the mandatory public pledge of allegiance to marxism–leninism.

While the suppression of both politics and economics that was entailed by the two series of moves that have been described above was important enough in its own right, it was therefore not in the formal but in the informal dimension of the institutional matrix that the real consolidation of Soviet power, that of blending the "body and soul" of the system, would take place. And here the path dependence that resided in the mental models of the population would prove to be strong indeed.

Creating Soviet man

As we may recall from above, Russian tsars and grand princes had invested heavily in promoting Orthodoxy as the moral basis of society. Beginning in 1326, when the Metropolitan of the Russian Orthodox Church decided to move his see from Vladimir to Moscow, the Church and the state entered into a mutually beneficial relation where the Church agreed to provide ideology in return for tax exemptions and generous donations.

To the Church, the benefits at first were massive indeed. Being exempt from paying tribute to the Mongols, and being patronized in the wills of Russian princes, abbeys and monasteries became major landowners, which in turn implied a steady growth in the needs for serf labour. At one point, the St Sergius Monastery of the Trinity had 100,000 "souls" cultivating lands that were scattered over 15 provinces, and there are foreign travel accounts from the sixteenth century which indicate that clergy owned one-third of all land. It was therefore not surprising that monasteries were among the first to demand charters that would fix the peasants to the land.[16]

In the early phase, when the Muscovite state was still weak and the Mongols were strong, the Church managed to enjoy both wealth and independence. It stood in well with the khan at Sarai and could often serve as an effective mediator between conflicting interests. With the gradual strengthening of the state, however, resentment of Church privileges was growing. The clergy were making use of a substantial part of the labour force and they were not paying taxes. As the tsar began making overtures towards confiscating its riches, the Church agreed to merge its interests with those of the state. Richard Pipes captures the essence of the contract that was implicit here:

> Traditionally partial to strong imperial authority, in the first half of the sixteenth century, under threat of expropriation, the Russian Orthodox Church placed its entire authority behind the Muscovite monarchy, filling its mind with ambitions which on its own it was incapable of conceiving. The entire ideology of royal absolutism in Russia was worked out by clergymen who felt that the interests of religion and church were best served by a monarchy with no limits to its power.[17]

Following the religious schism of the 1660s,[18] the power of the Church to resist was broken and under Peter the Great it went into quiet submission. In retrospect, the pact it had entered into with the state had proven to be a disaster. Having first sacrificed its independence in order to retain its wealth, in the end it found itself being deprived of its riches as well.

To the Muscovite state, however, and to the subsequent Russian Empire, the services that were rendered by the Church were both lasting and invaluable.

The main outcome of its ideological groundwork was that of bestowing the Moscow tsar with the combined honour of being both a worldly and a spiritual supreme. In the former case, substantial efforts were made to prove that the genealogy of the tsars was unbroken all the way back to Roman Emperor Augustus, thus claiming for Moscow the imperial legacy of Rome; and in the latter, the tsars were held up to have divine authority, to be not only the rulers of the purest and the most pious kingdom on earth but also the sovereigns over all Orthodox Christians, at times even over all of Christianity.

The effects, however, of these labours were not limited to enhancing the legitimacy and self-esteem of the autocracy. The withdrawal of the Church from all matters of current worldly existence, and its distinct lack of interest in everyday ethics, would also have a profound effect on the formation of mental models among the peasants, who after all made up the vast majority of the population.

There were several themes being played out. One was the search for an Inner Light, for an inner rather than an outer freedom, which is captured in the idea of the Hesychasm.[19] Another was the dilemma that lies in loathing violence while being unable to stand up to it, which is contained in the legend of the martyr-saints Boris and Gleb. The combined impact of these themes was to teach the people submission and to refrain from resistance in the face of violence.

Adding the traditional insistence on all available truth being contained in the Bible, which obviated any further search for knowledge, the Church also stood in the way of providing education to the people. This in turn served for centuries to block the emergence of communication and the sense of rationality, which might have created a demand for basic rights rather than myths and otherworldly rewards.

But perhaps most importantly, the increasing isolation of the Orthodox Church brought in its wake intolerance, and a perceived need to guard against all forms of heresy, against both inner and outer enemies. The feelings of suspicion that were thus aroused are captured, *inter alia*, in Mironov's previously quoted portrayal of the authoritarian personality that was developed within the *mir*. Recalling what has been said above, about the role of learning and the internal redescription of mental models, we may begin to appreciate the path dependence that was thus created.

Completing the picture, we may note that until the early twentieth century it was impossible for a Russian to leave the Orthodox Church. Given that being Russian was thus essentially the same as being Orthodox, it follows that the ideological influence of the Church was not to be easily avoided.

When the Bolsheviks in their turn set out to legitimate their rule, this Orthodox heritage would come to play an important role indeed. Looking merely at the outer forms of the new ideology, we find striking reminiscences of the old. Above all we have the same fascination with rituals. The icon procession in the Orthodox mass was replicated in Red Square processions, where the Lenin mausoleum served as a new form of iconostasis, where pictures of politburo members served as a new set of icons, and where the 1 May and 7 November line-ups on the roof of the mausoleum bore an eerie resemblance to the last supper of Christ.

And it was certainly no coincidence that the suffering and martyrdom of Christ would come to serve as a mainstay of the Bolshevik ambitions towards legitimization. It was begun in August 1918, when a young girl by the name of Fanny Kaplan took a shot at Lenin. A mere week after the incident, Zinoviev depicted Lenin as "a saint, an apostle and a prophet". Thus the professional revolutionary leader was inscribed in the tradition of Boris and Gleb, of Russian princes who were canonized because of their suffering and martyrdom.[20]

The simple fact that Lenin survived the shot made no difference. The myth caught on and much effort went into elaboration, into consciously inscribing Lenin in Russian history. The icon corner, the *krasnyi ugolok*, that was to be found in every Russian hut was replicated in "Lenin corners", where pictures of Lenin served as new icons and new objects of veneration. And the subsequent lying in state of the deceased leader replicated a tradition that had begun with Peter the Great (barring enbalmment and eternal life).

Perhaps most importantly, however, when the party's department for agitation and propaganda went about their task of actively creating a supportive norm system, they showed great dexterity in targeting different social groups with different versions of the message of marxism–leninism.[21]

To the *peasants*, the message was that nothing much had really changed. There was a new icon, in the figure of Lenin, but otherwise all would remain the same. The subjects were expected to show the same deference to and the same beliefs in the divine authority of the "eternally living" (*vechno zhivoi*) leader. Under Stalin, this was complemented with an appeal to the old image of the just tsar, the *batyushka*. The active ingredients in this message were the myths of Holy Russia.

To the *workers*, or the urban population, the message was radically different. Their task would be that of modernity, of being the builders of socialism and thus of the future. And for some time at least this messianic challenge was potent indeed. Stakhanovite worker heroes were held up as futuristic icons, and Lenin was cast in the role of master architect.

Perhaps the best illustration of the ideological distinction between peasants and workers may be found in Mukhina's classic 1937 statue "Worker and Kolkhoz Woman" (*Rabochii i kolkhoznitsa*), which was erected at the permanent VDNKh exhibition in Moscow and which also served as the official logo of Mosfilm. While the male worker exudes power and a promise of a bright future, the peasant woman – following a half step behind – has connotations of Mother Russia being passively led into this future by the vanguard of the proletariat.

The symbolic exclusion of the peasantry from the active building of socialism had obvious foundations in fact. When the Bolsheviks issued their decree on land, which was made into law at the beginning of 1918, events in the countryside were firmly in the hands of the peasants themselves. With the redistribution of land being supervised by the old *mir*, the outcome, as Nove points out, was paradoxically reactionary.

Whatever modernization had taken place with the Stolypin reforms in 1906–11 was now to be effectively undone. Those families that had opted to set themselves up as independent farmers, and had gotten their share of communal land, were returned to the communal fold, and thus to the traditional techniques of cultivation: redistribution of scattered strips of land and three-field cultivation with wooden plows. By 1925, more than 90 per cent of the Soviet peasantry belonged to some 350,000 village communities.[22] Their eventual incorporation into the Soviet "model" would be bloody indeed.

Moving to the other end of the ideological spectrum, we find the *party cadres*, whose implied mission was to serve as a new clergy, professing a new ideology that was cast in strangely familiar old forms. Although appeals were made to a new set of fathers of learning, the old insistence on all truth being contained in the Bible was replicated in the new claims of "scientific socialism". And the rigidity of the new faith would be every bit as powerful as the old. Perhaps even more so.

Having been elaborated over a very short time span, and largely by one man, marxism–leninism was suddenly elevated to the status of true faith. And the guardians of that new faith were constantly exhorted to be on their guard against potential heretics, exhortations that in the 1930s in particular would have deeply tragic consequences.

Even the Communist International may be held up as a striking replication of vital mental structures of Muscovy under Orthodoxy. Again Moscow was consciously presented as the last remaining bastion of purity, with an implied responsibility for the faithful (i.e. the toiling masses) in the world as a whole. Stretching the analogy, the breaking of relations with first Yugoslavia and then Albania may be seen as a parallel to the heresy of the Orthodox churches that fell from grace at Florence in 1439.

Thus far we have dealt chiefly with the output side of the new ideology. In order to complete the picture, a few words must now also be said about the demand side, i.e. about the impact at the receiving end. While recognizing that this is a topic for a serious investigation in its own right, which goes way beyond the scope of our present study, a few general comments can be made, which have a great deal of relevance to the arguments that are pursued here.

Understanding the Bolshevik programme as an extreme case of social engineering, the ultimate goal of the new faith, which was implied in the creation of a new socialist man, may in a sense be understood as an attempt to create a Marxian version of the "invisible hand". Nove's pointed characteristic is rather illustrative:

> If one assumes that the "new man", unacquisitive, "brilliant, highly rational, socialized, humane", will require no incentives, problems of discipline and motivation will vanish. If it is assumed that all will identify with the clearly visible general good, then the conflict between general and partial interest, and the complex issues of centralization/decentralization, can be assumed out of existence.[23]

There are a couple of important points contained in this portrayal. On the one hand we have the issue of creating norm systems that render formal enforcement mechanisms superfluous. One case where this has been achieved, to some considerable degree, is the Israeli kibbutz. Symptomatically, however, kibbutzim are very stringent in screening potential new members for deviating norms, thus illustrating the importance of ideology and "shared mental models". Early attempts by the Bolsheviks to introduce agricultural communes of a similar kind were a disappointment and would soon be dropped altogether.

The other point concerns the appeal to the "general good". As we may recall from above, ever since the times of Peter the Great there have been many attempts made along these lines but given the refusal of the autocracy to grant rights to the subjects, the notion as such has failed to take roots in Russian soil. And Soviet appeals to the common task of "building socialism" would not be much different.

Whether the Bolsheviks actually did believe that their massive investment in agitation and propaganda would have the officially desired effects is beside the point here. Knowing that reality turned out quite differently we are left asking what effects agitprop *did* have, and here we may usefully recall what Jon Elster has written about "states that are essentially by-products".[24]

The logic is that states of mind like trust, love and altruism can come about only as by-products of other actions. Ordering a person to laugh might, for example, indeed produce laughter, but if so only because the command itself is seen to be laughable. And while it may be argued that the US practice of expecting citizens to serve as jurors will have the beneficial by-product of promoting loyalty to the legal system, if jurors were told that this was the real aim, they would not take their tasks seriously and thus the purpose would be defeated.

Recalling our introductory discussion of the Soviet kleptocracy, we may see more clearly the relevance of these observations to the Soviet case. The rigidity and the totalitarian nature of marxism–leninism implied that the subjects were indeed ordered to exhibit certain states of mind that were associated with being a "Soviet man", a *sovetskii chelovek*. Since failure to comply would result in negative consequences, subjects were forced into public faking of the desired states, which in turn could not help but produce a psychologically stressful cognitive dissonance.

In order to deal with the latter, people would not only draw a line between their private and public spheres, they would also resort to various dissonance-reducing strategies, which served to rationalize at least part of their public behaviour. Thus we are back to the internal redescription of mental models, and to the "memory of the future".

Many writers, notably so Aleksandr Zinoviev, have pointed at the complexities of the dual mental universe that resulted. Vadim Granin, who was cited above, emphasizes the difficulties that lie in seeking to discover what might have been the "true" ideology of the Soviet citizenry: ". . . people have for their entire lives held two sets of beliefs, one to be espoused fervently in public, the other to be shared solely with family and close friends".[25]

It is against this background that we must see the main role of enforcement under the Soviet system. If we recall what was said in the previous chapter about the role of communication and learning in the shaping of informal norms, and in the internal redescription of mental models, it is obvious that this dimension harboured a major threat to uncontested party rule. If people had been allowed to communicate, they would have achieved a co-ordination of their mental models and all hopes for legitimization of the Soviet government would have dissipated into thin air.

The relative success that lies in maintaining the system for so long may be explained mainly by the efforts of the KGB to prevent horizontal communication between disgruntled citizens. Lodging complaints in the vertical direction, to newspapers or party committees, was always encouraged, much as the private soldier will always be allowed to complain to the general. But allowing a group of workers to discuss party policy – freely and critically – at their workplaces would have been the same as allowing groups of privates to openly question army policy. The latter case is normally referred to as mutiny, and it is frowned upon.

By clamping down hard on any sign of unauthorized horizontal communication, the KGB succeeded, on the one hand, in producing a sense of "pluralist ignorance". As an individual, I might experience a disturbing discrepancy between what I do see and what I am told to see, but it will not be possible to compare notes with others. And since I can never be sure about the extent of such discrepancies, there will always be a lingering doubt. Maybe it is only in my village, or at my workplace that things are not going so well?

On the other hand, by allowing people to say and do pretty much what they wanted as long as they were in private, the KGB secured the additional benefit of promoting the dual value system that was so characteristic of the Soviet system. The active encouragement of "soft voice" in public and the tacit permission of open voice in private served to defuse some of the discontent that was bound to follow from repression and thus to help prolong the life-span of the system.

In a 1998 interview, the Russian sociologist Leonid Kesselman explained the Soviet legacy in terms that closely resemble the arguments that have been pursued above. On the one hand, the formal rules were such that stealing was an open option: "Everybody was stealing, and everybody was paying somebody off. It was the only way to survive given the peculiarities of Soviet economics." On the other, the legitimacy of the government was so weak that stealing from the public purse would not be censored by other subjects: "People know that stealing from the state and taking bribes is illegal, but they don't see it as corruption; they see it as a social norm."

And in this view of the state as an essentially alien factor the subjects were destined to develop, or preserve, their highly characteristic dual vision of reality: "Russians have always lived with two sets of rules: formal ones that were largely ignored, and informal ones that were obeyed. Pilfering from the workplace was allowed if you paid tribute to your superior, who in turn was allowed to accept bribes if he in turn paid off a communist party official."[26]

In conclusion, the path dependence that links old Russia with the Soviet system may be seen to rest, above all, in the continued failure of the state to serve as a guarantor of the rule of law. Though there were differences in the respective modes of repression and censorship, the continued absence of rights, reciprocity and participation looms large. And actors under both regimes logically would invest in skills that improved their performance under such rules. And the associated processes of learning would serve, on both sides of the fence, to rationalize these collectively irrational types of behaviour.

Was it a success? To those who succeeded in climbing within the party hierarchy there undoubtedly must have been strong feelings of achievement involved. Assuming that some of the kleptocrats would have stood little chance of success under an open regime, they were truly successful (provided they escaped being purged). But for the remainder of those who were forced to adapt their skills and expectations, success was that of the winning prisoner in the classic dilemma. Early gains made at the expense of others were soon enough to be outweighed by the deteriorating performance of the system as a whole.

Let us turn now to look at the drastic change in course that followed in the wake of the failed August 1991 *coup*. Will we see the same path dependence being preserved, into the new system of democracy, market economy and the rule of law? And, perhaps even more importantly, will we see the same old kleptocrats emerge in a similar role of predatory winners?

322

Systemic change II: Yeltsin and the neo-liberals

When Boris Yeltsin completed his crushing of the Soviet system, great expectations were generated both within the country and in the West. The main catchword in his October 1991 speech was that of turning Russia into a "normal" society, thus implying that behind the Soviet façade Russian society was in no fundamental way different from Western societies. And the main theme of the "Washington consensus", which would drive the efforts of the IMF and the World Bank, was very much the same, namely that Russia in itself was no different from other countries that had been "cured" by the Washington Twins.

In the following pages we shall seek to address this crucial issue of "normality". We shall question if the Russian reformers who gathered around Boris Yeltsin were correct in assuming that democracy, market economy and the rule of law – all representing the wished-for "normal" society – were indeed to be found under the Soviet rubble. And we shall ask if there might have been some more fundamental obstacles at hand, which would have required measures of a somewhat greater sophistication than simply destroying the old system and trusting in *laissez-faire* to do the rest.

Provocatively put, the question concerns whether Russia in 1992 was indeed fundamentally different from those societies of Western Europe and North America that would serve as role models for the "transition". Given that the Russian reformers and their foreign supporters would proceed on the assumption that this was *not* the case, the question assumes some considerable importance. From our institutional perspective, three observations are due.

First of all, the formal rules of the new game were rewritten in a *laissez-faire* direction, i.e. to be market-conforming. Essentially, however, this implied much more of a dismantling of the old control systems than the creation of a set of new rules that might support market transactions. The continued absence of relevant legislation would soon enough become a serious impediment above all to investment and thus to economic growth.

Secondly, where the Bolsheviks had invested massively in reshaping the country's norm systems, Yeltsin's reformers would largely ignore this aspect, assuming that the Russian people did have the same values as the peoples of Western Europe and North America and would thus automatically support the reforms. We shall not burden the reader with further catalogues of metaphorical statements from the Russian reformers, and from their foreign advisors, to this effect. They are readily available.[27]

Thirdly, and perhaps most importantly, where the Bolsheviks had established a dictatorial enforcement system, based on discretion, denunciation and detailed control, the reformers of the 1990s assumed that *laissez-faire* would somehow spontaneously produce institutional arrangements that draw the line between the jungle and an ordered society. If you need a constitution, just take one from abroad and have it translated!

In the following we shall return to the same perspective of "zones of confrontation" that has been put to repeated use above. We shall investigate how the new executive power – Boris Yeltsin – went about arranging his relations to the legislature, the judiciary, the financial markets and the enterprise sector. And again we shall begin by looking at the dimension of power.

Unaccountable power

During the Soviet era, Western scholars engaged in a series of at times harsh debates concerning whether or not it was warranted to label the system as "totalitarian". Without going into the details of the various arguments, we may note that the main issue concerned what degree of serious content there was in the variety of formally democratic institutions that adorned the system: general elections, parliament, government, labour unions, courts of law, etc.

When we turn now to contemplate Boris Yeltsin's years as president in "the new Russia" it is striking how relevant that question remains. The variety of labels that have been suggested to describe Russia's new political system is indicative of the confusion that reigns in this respect. Is it "democracy", "Yeltsinocracy", "kleptocracy", "oligarchy", "clan rule", a "mafiya state", or indeed a "pedocracy", as it has been branded by communist party leader Gennadii Zyuganov – with reference to the "young reform economists"?

While recognizing that the choice of labels to some extent reflects political preferences and attitudes on the observer's side, on a deeper level we still have the question of what actual content may be found within the democratic institutions of "new Russia".

An illuminating parallel may be drawn here to the period leading from 1905 to 1917, when Russia had succeeded in introducing most of the institutions that are *formally* necessary for democracy, market economy and the rule of law. Although that process was put to an effective end by the Great War and the Bolshevik *coup*, as we may recall from above there were numerous inherent problems which made it far from certain that a lasting deviation from the path dependence was imminent.

The conclusion is well in line with the main thrust of institutional theory. While certainly necessary, changes in the formal rules are far from sufficient in order to guarantee a sustainable change of path, or a shift to a superior equilibrium.

By the time Boris Yeltsin went into his second term in office, Russia had developed most if not all of the formal institutions that are normally associated with democracy. Free and fair elections had been held twice for the post of president and twice for a popular assembly, the bicameral Federal Assembly. A constitution had been adopted by referendum, guaranteeing freedom of speech and organization, etc. There was no more censorship, no more political prisoners and no fears of being wantonly apprehended by the internal security service.

It is also symptomatic that the struggles between Yeltsin and the Duma increasingly were fought with weapons out of the democratic arsenal; threats by the Duma to impeach the president were answered by counter-threats of dissolution and new elections.

Moving behind the façade, however, there is one key question that needs to be asked. Did Boris Yeltsin ever even *intend* to promote a development towards real power sharing? Was he aiming to promote a political culture where problems are solved via negotiations and compromises, which are respected by all parties and may thus form a solid basis for both democracy and market economy?

Leaving the question of intentions aside for the moment, there is an obvious test of actual success. Have we been witnessing the emergence of stable and transparent rules of the game, and of well functioning enforcement mechanisms that enjoy a high degree of legitimacy with actors in all spheres of society, in politics as well as in the economy? This would have marked a true departure from the path dependent preferences for rule in isolation, for the subordination of justice and for the refusal to grant rights to the subjects.

When Russia embarked on its path of post-Soviet reconstruction, the officially declared ambitions were consonant with making this departure, and that was also the condition upon which support from the West was forthcoming. Five years later, however, Yeltsin's re-election marked a path dependent triumph of the traditional Russian patterns of autocracy, where might is right, where power is unaccountable and where agreements are made under duress, to be honoured only up to the point where one side gets the upper hand. More specifically, Yeltsin's victory meant that discretion once again had been placed before rules, and that power had degenerated into a tradable commodity.

In the following we shall argue that this deplorable outcome far from being pre-determined was the result of a series of decisions taken by the president, in situations that were marked not by pressing needs but by considerable latitude. (We reach determinism only via the additional and rather far-fetched assumption that Boris Yeltsin was the only possible leader, and that his actions were beyond control or influence.) We shall thus follow a track of revealed institutional preference, and guard against the common practice by so many commentators – both Russian and Western – of blaming everything on the "evil" opposition.

In order to support this argument, we shall look at two interacting themes in the Russian president's exercise of power. One lies in the "chicken" games that were played out between the executive and the legislature, and the other in the effective farming out of the economy that was to provide a real bonanza for the country's financial elites.

Beginning with the long series of confrontations between president and parliament – first the Supreme Soviet and then the Duma – we have ample illustrations of how easily political confrontation in an environment of low trust may degenerate into "chicken" games. The case of October 1993 is certainly not the only illustration of this point, but given the bloody outcome we may usefully recall all the attempts that were made by various actors – albeit to no avail – in order to bring about a compromise.

The outcome of the October events around the White House was also in tune with Lotman's understanding of the total victory. The opposition leaders were thrown in jail, the Supreme Soviet was replaced by the new Duma, and Yeltsin's team immediately went to work rewriting the draft of the proposed constitution, in order to eliminate a number of concessions that had been made under duress over the preceding months.

As the past was thus again to be eradicated, the president again had sufficient leeway to act according to preference, and this is where intentions enter the picture. As we may recall from above, Yeltsin would make no efforts to support the reforms he liked to profess being committed to. He would watch jealously over his own new constitution, but in all other areas the reformers were left to fight their own – losing – battles.

If viewed against the visions of democracy that had been held up in the autumn of 1991, the Duma elections of 1993 and 1995 were certainly major disappointments. But viewed from the president's personal point of view, that conclusion is far from obvious. On the contrary, by maintaining an atmosphere of confrontation he could maximize the returns to his unquestioned skills in playing that game. And a similar logic may be applied to many of the parliamentarians, whose skills were of a similar nature.

The one really obvious loser from these games was Russia, but as we have shown repeatedly above the *bien public* has never had much of a constituency in that country's path dependence. The 1996 presidential election provided ample illustration of the extent of the havoc that the games of power have been allowed – by all sides – to wreak on the economy. And the spring of 1997 is no less illustrative in this respect.

Not only was Yeltsin's decision to re-appoint Anatolyi Chubais the greatest provocation imaginable to the – democratically elected – opposition in the Duma. It was equally striking that the new reform team under Chubais–Nemtsov started out following the unhappy example of the previous Gaidar team in portraying itself as a "kamikaze government". It would seem hard indeed to dispute the path dependent nature of these events.

Again the president and his men had revealed a total disregard for matters of trust and credibility; at least if the country's own legislature and its own citizenry are to be included in the picture. As Peter Rutland puts it,

"Yeltsin does not seek a dialogue with society: he seeks to browbeat it into compliance with his populist rhetoric."[28] And the West not only applauded his actions. It even began pouring massive amounts of Western tax dollars into the pockets of the Russian kleptocracy.

The sudden and wholesale dismissal of the Chernomyrdin government in March 1998 threw the country into even deeper chaos and pushed the confrontation between the president and the Duma to the brink. Although the latter did flinch in the end, the economy meanwhile had paid a terrible price. And five months later, when the Kiriyenko government in its turn was thrown out, the president predictably was bent on running yet another "chicken" game.

This time, however, it was Yeltsin who ended up as "chicken". Whether this was owing to the gravity of the economic situation, or simply to the increasing weakness of the "tsar" is beside the point here. Similarly, we shall leave for our concluding chapter all speculation concerning the future course, into a world beyond Yeltsin.

Let us recall instead what was said in Chapter 4 above, about the involvement of the West in Russia's reform programme. Four main points are relevant.

To begin with, irrespective of the nature of his actions, Western governments persisted in providing unqualified political support for Boris Yeltsin. Following the collapse of the Kiriyenko government that policy was finally subjected to harsh criticism, but by then it was late in the day, with much damage already done to the project of establishing democracy in Russia.

Assume, if you will, that Western governments had insisted instead on constituency building and on democratic anchoring of the reform policies. Might not the Russian legislature then have developed along a path of increasing responsibility? Refusing to accept this possibility is tantamount to saying that from the very outset of Yeltsin's reforms Russia was doomed to embark on its course of self-destruction.

Secondly, irrespective of economic policies and actual achievements, Western financial institutions persisted in providing *de facto* untied credits to Yeltsin's governments. Following the August 1998 collapse of the rouble and the freezing of parts of the foreign debt, that policy was also subjected to harsh criticism, but again it was late in the day and much damage already done to the project of establishing market economy in Russia.

Assume, if you will, that the IMF had upheld its traditionally stringent rules and had thus prevented Russia from sliding deep into uncontrollable debt, foreign as well as domestic. Might not Russia's nascent financial markets then have been forced to engage in sound financial operations, with the associated learning of constructive skills? Refusing to accept this possibility in equal measure implies that Russia was doomed from the outset to be plundered.

Thirdly, irrespective of the rapidly mounting problems of non-payments of wages and pensions, it is hard to recall either the IMF or any other Western "partner" pointing out to the Russian government the moral hazard that lies in thus grossly undermining whatever legitimacy that government might have been able to win in the eyes of its population.

Assume that the Western partners had chosen to complement their consistent harping about financial austerity with some equally stern words about *pacta sunt servanda* and about the basic responsibilities of the state *vis-à-vis* its citizenry, might this not have prevented the strategy of systematic non-payments from becoming *the* main vehicle of inflation-fighting?

Fourthly, irrespective of revelations about personal corruption and scandalous links between business and politics, Western donors persisted in targeting a select group of individuals, leading to the unhealthy formation of what Janine Wedel calls "cliques and clans" on both sides of the fence. Yet again, that policy would eventually be subjected to severe criticism, but that too would be late in the day with much damage already done.

Assume that aid had been made available on a competitive basis only, with outside evaluation, might not the extent of high level corruption then have been curtailed? (At the very least, there would have been fewer tax dollars to play around with!)

The latter observations bring us over to the second of the two themes indicated above, namely that of the role of Russia's "tycoons" or "oligarchs", a topic which has become a real favourite in both Russian and foreign publications. An important trend-setter in the genre was a 1996 interview in *Financial Times*, where Boris Berezovskii, one of the leading tycoons, boasted that he and six others together controlled more than 50 per cent of Russia's GDP.[29]

The factual truth of that statement is beside the point here. Our focus must instead be directed at the undisputed influence that these magnificent seven have had over the formation of Russia's economic policy. In particular, this pertains to the main vehicles that have been used for predation: privatization, borrowing and payments out of the federal budget.

One of the first to approach Russia's new political system from the angle of oligarchy was Thomas Graham, at the time a high-ranking diplomat at the American embassy in Moscow, who created quite a stir when he turned, shortly before the important December 1995 election, to one of the major Moscow newspapers with an article about Russia's new political landscape.[30]

The essence of Graham's "clan theory" was to argue against the use of traditional terms like "democracy", "dictator" and even "political parties". According to him, the power struggle in Moscow could be understood only if seen as a struggle between different "clans", over which the real "tsar", Boris Yeltsin, presided in splendid isolation.

His portrayal was of different interest groups, all of which were centred on single political figures that were struggling for power. Each of these "clans" was linked to financial, trade and industrial structures, had guaranteed access to the media, control over armed formations, state or private, and links to similar regional groups.

One of the clans in question was headed by Prime Minister Viktor Chernomyrdin, drawing support from the Russian gas giant Gazprom, whose former head he had been. Another belonged to the mayor of Moscow, Yurii Luzhkov, mainly supported by the capital's powerful financial interests. A third was the clan of the hard-line generals, led by Yeltsin's personal bodyguard Aleksandr Korzhakov. On its way out there was a fourth "reform clan", composed of various former spokesmen for reform but lacking powerful leadership, and on its way up was a fifth oppositional military clan under General Aleksandr Lebed.

If we compare Graham's clan theory to the Soviet political system, which in turn was often compared to a "mafiya" or a "kleptocracy", we may find important common ground that relates to the role of enforcement. While there is important similarity in the fact that neither of the two is marked by the rule of law, there is also an important difference. The Russian kleptocracy is operating without the supreme arbiter that was the politburo of the communist party. The latter in particular would have considerable implications.

Instead of one single kleptocracy, or one homogenous predatory state, we now have a number of competing kleptocracies, or predatory elites. Returning to Mancur Olson's perspective, this implies that the transfer from Gorbachev to Yeltsin implied one really fundamental change. As the old system collapsed, the single centre of power, which had possessed an encompassing interest in securing the long-run viability of the system, was replaced by a number of actors with narrow interests only.

We are therefore back to a situation which is marked by roving bandits, with short time horizons and little security of tenure. We may thus also see where one of the main failures of the Yeltsin regime would be recorded. Having successfully destroyed the party/KGB enforcement mechanism, the leadership of "the new Russia" failed to make a credible commitment to the rule of law. Thus the country could be farmed out to the oligarchs, the outcome of which has been described at length above.

The path dependent failure of the new Russian state to develop credible and legitimate enforcement mechanisms is reflected in the seemingly ambivalent relations that emerged between the executive and the judiciary.

In the formal sense, there are good grounds on which to claim that Russia started out in the right direction, on the road towards a system of justice that rests on the rule of law. A constitution was adopted; a constitutional court was created and courts of law were delivered from party tutelage. There was also substantial work, and much foreign advice, vested in the production of new law codes, which agree better with the needs of the market economy.

Nevertheless, Russian reality a few years later tells us that critical items are still missing. When the Primakov government was installed, the number of contract killings in Moscow alone was running at the rate of about 300 per year.[31] Private enterprise was forced to rely on tens of thousands of private security firms, employing hundreds of thousands of security people who were charged with guarding against each other, and prisons were filled to the brim because the state had no money to pay for the holding of trials. Against this background, it is hard to talk of anything but a near-total privatization of justice.

And it is equally hard not to see the link back to the way in which President Yeltsin decided to run the country. As Rutland puts it, implementation of the reforms has faltered not because of strong social opposition, but because of a failure of political leadership, and that failure is encapsulated in the person of Yeltsin: "Yeltsin is not the solution, he is the problem. And he is the problem because he is the state."[32]

Far from promoting the stability and transparency that is consonant with the rule of law, the outcome of Yeltsin's leadership was fluidity and massive discretion. As it had been under the old regime and under Soviet rule, Russia again was to be ruled by decree, of which the current president signs about 1,500 a year.[33] Economic policy in particular came to rest almost exclusively on this fragile basis and to investors the lack of enforceable rights was to be a constant topic for complaints.

Given what has been said above about the role of enforcement in promoting and sustaining norms that may provide legitimacy for the formal rules, which in turn provide confirmation for actors that trusting in the rules is indeed rational, this outcome was deplorable indeed. Turning now to look at the financial sphere, we shall find important reasons that may help explain how and why this came about.

To tax and spend

Moving into the third of our four "zones of confrontation", systemic change under Yeltsin implied that the previous essentially de-monetized command system was to be replaced by monetized market co-ordination. This in turn implied a need to introduce a stable national currency, to promote the emergence of financial institutions that would make it possible to govern via economic policy, and to create a basis for running a federal budget that is in reasonable balance.

In all three of these dimensions the needs for trust and credibility loom large. In the absence of such supportive mental models we are back to barter and primitive enforcement.

The purely technical aspects of the problem of creating – or resurrecting – a financial sphere in the Russian economy have been dealt with above. We have pointed at the need to compensate for the loss of revenue from privatized, formerly state owned enterprises by creating a functioning tax system, and at the associated need to work out the problems of fiscal federalism.

Here we shall focus on the question of rationality that has been repeatedly referred to above, namely to ask in general terms to what extent and under which conditions individual actors will find it meaningful to make a contribution out of their own pockets towards the common good.

In a perceptive paper presented in 1994, Jeffrey Sachs pointed at the dangers that were inherent in the Russian transition: "Several simple examples of immediate relevance to Russia illustrate the risks of state collapse. The Russian state is threatened by at least six types of contagious antisocial behavior: a flight from the ruble, tax evasion, criminality, regional separatism, foreign debt overhang, and panic by government creditors."[34]

Each of these six types of behaviour has the characteristics of a prisoner's dilemma. When nobody else pays taxes, it is not rational to do so. When nobody else trusts in the law, it is not rational to do so, etc. By identifying a number of such dilemmas, Sachs showed that the Russian economy had been locked into a bad equilibrium, from which there was no easy escape.

His own conclusion was that "Russia is in a state of deep crisis that could send the country into a spiral of self-reinforcing destructive behaviours: criminality, regional separatism, tax evasion and flight from the currency".[35] By the end of summer 1998, Russian reality had caught up with this prediction. Crime was rampant, the regions were increasingly ignoring the federal centre and the financial markets had suffered a major meltdown.

The key to understanding this outcome lies in the financial sector, where the exercise of power was blended with the growing influence of money. Which would be the rational strategy to pursue for actors who were suddenly presented with this radically new set of opportunities?

In a 1997 article about the failure of financial stabilization in Russia, Barry Ickes, Peter Murrell and Randi Ryterman introduce the notion of "informal profit seeking", to describe practices aimed at "the production of wealth that can be hidden from official view". Their point, appropriately made, is that the high incidence of barter and quasi money reflects a rational strategy designed by enterprises primarily to avoid paying taxes. The relevance to our perspective lies in the fact that informal profit seeking is seen to "work best when the stock of social capital in a country is characterized by a low level of rule obedience and a high level of trust in personal relations".[36]

Given the illegal nature of the actions in question, actors must be able to trust *both* that their partners will not experience a suggested rule breaking deal as unethical, *and* that they will not at some later stage defect by calling it to the attention of the authorities. This not only presents a textbook example of how repeated games of the prisoners' dilemma may result in learning what promotes trust in the partners with whom you engage. It also illustrates how path dependence may be started.

If we return to the criteria that were listed by Brian Arthur in the previous chapter, we have high set-up costs in terms of crossing the line into crime. We have investments in skills of evasion that exhibit increasing returns, we have co-ordination and learning as the practice spreads, and we have adaptive expectations that it will persist. The outcome is that the economy is locked into an inferior equilibrium, where the path dependence is strong above all in the mental models of the participating actors.

Referring to the World Value Survey, Ickes, Murrell and Ryterman find that Russian social capital is indeed highly compatible with this form of behaviour. It is shown that the level of interpersonal trust is moderately high (on a par with Germany) and that civic behaviour is very low (Russia ranks 31 out of 33 countries surveyed).

If we make an additional distinction between interpersonal and impersonal trust, these findings may be usefully compared with one of the conclusions reached by Robert Putnam from his Italian investigations: "The absence of civic virtue is exemplified in the 'amoral familism' that Edward Banfield reported as the dominant ethos in Montegrano, a small town not far from Pietrapertosa: 'Maximize the material, short-run advantage of the nuclear family; assume that all others will do likewise.' "[37]

The essence of this "amoral familism" was seen to lie in "the striking lack of 'deliberate concerted action' to improve community conditions,"[38] which in turn lies at the heart of Robert Leonardi's previously cited presentation of the "criminal capitalism" of the Italian South.[39] The preservation over centuries of this path dependence again illustrates the importance of the informal dimension of the institutional matrix.

While the Russian and Sicilian cases are marked by a low degree of rule obedience and a high degree of interpersonal trust, the Italian North features high degrees of both rule obedience and impersonal trust, i.e. trust in the authorities that uphold the rules you obey. Phrased in this way, the interaction between trust and rule obedience becomes obvious, and then we are back again to North's basic point about institutions, namely that it is the norms in a society that provide legitimacy for the rules.

Trust not only is very much a question of a state of mind. It also falls into the category of what Elster refers to as states that cannot be willed.[40] Trust may emerge as a by-product of positive experience, but it cannot be willed, or developed by command. Recognizing this in turn brings us back to the question of learning, which is of crucial importance in the preservation of path dependence.

North points at the dynamic interaction between learning and incentives in a process of *successful* institutional change: "The incentives embedded in the institutional framework direct the process of learning by doing and the development of tacit knowledge that will lead individuals in decision-making processes to evolve systems gradually that are different from the ones that they had to begin with."[41]

But he also emphasizes the obstacles that may *preclude* successful change: "We must also learn from failures, so that change will consist of the generation of organizational trials and the elimination of organizational errors. There is nothing simple about this process, because organizational errors may be not only probabilistic, but also systematic, due to ideologies that may give people preferences for the kinds of solutions that are not oriented to adaptive efficiency."[42]

Looking more closely at the role of communication in Russia's path dependence, we may find a superficial pattern of pendulum movement. Increasing openness from Peter the Great onwards followed in the steps of secrecy under the old regime, and the renewed openness under Yeltsin followed upon a period of renewed secrecy under Soviet rule. On closer inspection, however, we may find that under both periods of increasing openness, the regime largely ignored the calls for participation that were issued from below.

Openness, or *glasnost*, is thus not to be equated with communication. The path dependence lies not in the formal rules of censorship as such, but in the consistent refusal of the autocracy to communicate with its subjects. And without rights of participation, subjects can never become citizens. Thus the country's social capital will remain frozen at a low level of "amoral familism".

At this point it may be worth recalling Lotman's previously quoted conclusion that true forward movement requires coming to terms with, and not simply rejecting, the past. Placing this into McDaniel's perspective of cyclical breakdowns, Russia's path dependence has been one of consistent absolute rejection, leading to Lotman's fruitless cycles of negation.

Viewed against this background, a successful transition to a post-Soviet order of democracy, market economy and the rule of law implied a dual and interconnected challenge of transforming both the informal norms and the enforcement mechanisms that had been associated with Soviet rule.

In the former case, the new regime would have to achieve an "internal redescription" of the mental models of the actors at large, which, *inter alia*, would have required making a clean break with all that Lotman has presented as defining characteristics of the binary oppositions. Putting it simply, it implied replacing the traditional Russian notion of *kto kogo* (who beats whom?) by the classic legal principle of *pacta sunt servanda*.

Given that this transformation would have to take place in domains that cannot be willed, the second part of the challenge, that of creating a state which was both able and willing to function as a third party enforcer – *within* the limits of the rule of law – assumed pivotal importance. And it was here that the main failure of the project of systemic change as a whole would be recorded. Let us look at just one more illustration.

Following a particularly violent outburst in *Nezavisimaya Gazeta*, where Anatolyi Chubais was openly accused of aiming to take full control over Russia as a whole,[43] the president called the country's six leading bankers to a special disciplinary meeting in the Kremlin. This type of *ad hoc* intervention by the autocracy represents something vastly different from what is normally understood as legitimate enforcement mechanisms. And it says something important about the path dependent mode of autocratic rule.

Rounding off this discussion, we shall return to the economic dimension. Creating a government that is able to uphold the rule of law is not merely a question of forming a legitimate constitutional contract, something that would be a tall order in its own right in a country that is marked by a low degree of rule obedience.

Compounding this difficulty we must also take into account the fiscal crisis that has been described at length in previous chapters. Handing the economy over to a host of competing predatory clans not only caused inequity and destitution, which is clearly detrimental to growth. Even more importantly, it eroded the state's ability to provide such public goods that make democracy and market economy possible. Well-funded and reasonably honest legal institutions would rank high on this list. Stephen Holmes points at the crucial link between money and liberalism:

> An insolvent state, in the pertinent sense, is one that cannot extract, in a way that is widely deemed to be fair, a modest share of social wealth and then channel the resources extracted into the creation and delivery of public services, rather than into the pockets of incumbents and their cronies. The Russian state is an illiberal state partly because it is insolvent. And it is insolvent because it is corrupt – because norms of public service are weak, and potential taxpayers do not trust the government. Thus, one of the principal lessons of the new Russian illiberalism is that individual rights are unprotectable without the power to tax and spend.[44]

As we have noted above, holding elections in no way changes the outcome of the game. The simple reason is that so few care enough for democratic politics to make a difference. As Vladimir Shlapentokh notes, "Indeed, most Russians now accept many aspects of their life which would have seemed to them almost horrible 10 years ago as completely 'normal'."[45]

When plunder is rational

In order to sort out how and why Russia finally *did* end up in the predicament that had been held up by Sachs as a danger, we shall return again to our previous discussion of the role of the state as a third party enforcer. When the Russian reforms were launched, the general consensus was that once all remnants of the communist order had been crushed, the "invisible hand" would guide Adam Smith's "butcher, baker and brewer" to work for the common good.

What really did come about has been succinctly summarized by George Soros, stating at a 1998 conference that first "the assets of the state were stolen, and then when the state itself became valuable as a source of legitimacy, it too was stolen".[46] There is an important distinction here between common theft, or even stealing from the state, and *using* the machinery of the state for private rent seeking or otherwise predatory purposes.

There is also, in this respect, important path dependence in the transition process. Following North's previous institutional analogy, those who had invested in becoming skilled pirates under the Soviet system – by exploiting the state machinery – were poised to continue their predation under the new rules. Especially after the appointment of the Primakov government in September 1998, it was striking how many of the very same old hands were still in positions of power. *Plus ça change, plus ça reste le meme!*

Writing in the spring of 1998, shortly before the financial meltdown which put an end to the liberal dream of a "new Russia", Grigorii Yavlinskii underlined precisely this continuity: "Far from creating an open market, Russia has consolidated a semi-criminal oligarchy that was already largely in place under the old Soviet system. After communism's collapse, it merely changed its appearance, just as a snake sheds its skin."[47] And he went on to explicitly refute the frequently heard comparison with the American robber barons:

> Unfortunately, those who believe that the capitalism of the robber barons will eventually give way to a market economy that benefits all in society, as occurred in the United States at the turn of the century, are mistaken. America had an established middle class with a work ethic and a government that remained largely free from robber-baron infiltration. The American tycoons were still investing in their own country. Russia's robber barons are stifling their homeland's economic growth by stealing from Russia and investing abroad. In the late 1990s, Russia has no emerging middle class, and the oligarchy, which is deeply involved in the government, can alter policy for its private benefit.[48]

There are two important observations contained in this portrayal. First, we may recall from above Barry Weingast's call for "a set of shared beliefs among citizens" who react against the state when the latter attempts to transgress boundaries that are designed to limit and define the legitimate scope for state action. Against this background, the observation of the missing middle class is relevant indeed. And we should be careful here to distinguish between a group of people enjoying middle incomes, and a distinct social class exhibiting the values and habits normally associated with being "middle class".

It is the latter that has been distinctly missing throughout Russian history, and it was its continued absence that made it possible for the state to be "stolen". There was, quite simply, an insufficient constituency with encompassing interests in preventing this from happening.

Secondly, looking at the behaviour of the Russian oligarchs it is important to note that from their individual points of view, their behaviour has been quite rational. They were faced with a state that not only refused to accept responsibility for enforcing the rule of law, but also encouraged rent seeking in exchange for political support. Thus, following the logic of Olson's narrow interests, it would have been irrational indeed for them to pass up the opportunity to steal, above all so if the machinery of the state was available to help out with the thieving.

The question for the future then becomes if and when they will become legitimate. This yet again brings us back to the problem of credible commitment, to the old familiar discussions of Hobbes on the Leviathan and of Montesquieu on a social contract, and to the equally well known problem of collective action.

Within small groups voluntary agreements will be sufficient to achieve order, but as the group grows larger the incentive to defect increases while the power of social sanctions is diluted. This is the essence of the collective action problem as it has been described to us by Mancur Olson. The prevalent interpretation in a Western context has been that small groups will be successful in lobbying for special interests, at the expense of a more diffuse "general public".

But it has a great deal of relevance to the problems we are dealing with here as well, namely to the prospects for the rule of law to emerge as a result of *laissez-faire*: "So logic tells us that the collective good of law and order, like other collective goods, can never be obtained through voluntary collective action in really large groups."[49]

Again the problem is that of credible commitment, in an environment where there is no independent judiciary and no other effective means of credibly "shackling" the political leadership: "The autocrat can promise that he will not impose any future taxes or confiscations that would make current investments unprofitable, but given his incentive to make that promise even if he intends to break it, the promise may not be credible."[50]

History provides plenty of illustration to the problems that are brought out here. In a study of Western European development in the period from 1050 until 1800, for example, J. Bradford De Long and Andrei Shleifer contrast the performance of city-states that have experienced merchant-friendly rule with those that have been marked by "strong princely rule". Their conclusions come close to what has been said above about Muscovy.

Ruling princes "saw the legal order as an instrument of control rather than as a constraint on their actions". They lived in "parasite cities", which were "centers of neither trade nor urban industry but instead the homes of bureaucrats and the favored dwelling places of landlords". And under their rule, property was always potentially insecure: "Subjects do not have rights; they have privileges, which endure only as long as the prince wishes."[51]

Seeing that in all of the latter cases, change for the better was indeed possible, we must conclude that the same should apply to Russia. The question is what it takes.

Assuming that credible commitment and constituency building together composed *the* crucial challenge to the Yeltsin government, the choice of shock therapy becomes even more astounding. Adding just one more illustration to what has been said above, we may recall a comment made by then acting Prime Minister Yegor Gaidar in late 1992, in response to a presentation of the dire predicament of the small business sector: "So what? One who is dying deserves to die."[52]

It is hard to find a better reflection of the posture of the Russian government, and it is easy to understand how the political process was destined to degenerate into the repeated rounds of "chicken" games that have been described in previous chapters. When the game of "chicken" is the only game in town, there will be little room for compromise, trust and consensus to emerge. Let us round off this discussion by recalling briefly the main patterns of economic policy that were outlined in Section III above.

In the *first* phase, the reformers set out to annihilate both the command economy and the communist party that had acted as its enforcement mechanism. Their total disregard for dialogue, credibility and trust served to trigger the destructive games that were played by the government against other actors in the economy. The collapse of both GDP and investment illustrates how productive activities were crowded out by redistributive actions. (Some relevant figures will be presented in our concluding chapter.)

As had been the case under Soviet rule, there were many short-term winners. Politics and financial operations, in particular, provided fertile grounds on which to claim achievement. But this was not Schumepeterian creative destruction; it was a case of simple predatory wealth redistribution. The subsequent collapse of the Moscow bubble economy brought home that the seeming success had really been a question of roving banditry, of rent seeking and conspicuous consumption.

In the *second* phase, continued emphasis on predation and redistribution led to the policy of unrestrained borrowing. While the short-term costs of high inflation had been borne primarily by savers and wage earners, the real costs of the games that were now being played in the securities market were manifested primarily in a crowding out of productive industrial investment. Adding to the damage, we may also recall how the Central Bank ran its own destructive games, against both the government and the commercial banks.

The predatory nature of the new elites that were formed within the alliance between the government and the big banks has been illustrated in a number of ways: in the vast array of give-away privatization deals, in the continued squeeze on the real economy, in the largely illegal capital flight, and in the effective ransoming of the future that is implied by massive borrowing for current needs.

In the *third* phase, however, as the options for easy gains were exhausted, the predators were increasingly forced to turn on each other. Prodded by the IMF to improve tax collection, the government reversed its previous policy of exchanging economic favours for political support.

It could have sought consensus on a new tax system, but resorted instead to punitive measures leading, *inter alia*, to responses from below in the form of the killing of a number of tax inspectors.[53] Similarly, it could have sought consensus on a working budget, but decided instead to continue the policy of aggressive sequestration and to submit proposed budget cuts under a thin veil of threats and intimidation.

While these moves provided ample illustration of preserved path dependence in confrontation and rule evasion, they also had a rather discouraging effect on the crucially important processes of learning and internal redescription of mental models.

Here we may return to our previously cited passage from Plautus, about men being to other men as wolves: "*Lupus est homo homini, non homo, quom qualis sit non novit.*" The point concerns the qualification that is inserted in the second part, namely that "Men are like wolves to each other, not men, *as long as they do not know each other.*" This is the same message that is contained in the repeated game solution to the prisoner's dilemma, but it may also be turned in the other direction.

If in repeated games people learn that others are indeed *not* to be trusted, then the resulting frustration may be expected to reinforce mental models of distrust. The "memory of the future" will hold images of continued confrontations that may be rationally approached only by distrust and defection.

Thus yet another "window of opportunity" in Russia's long history seems to have finished in one of Lotman's binary oppositions. In a situation where the old system had collapsed, the new regime set out not to create but to destroy, to eradicate all remnants of the past. As a result, the state abdicated from its responsibility to act as a third party enforcer.

And the real tragedy of it all is that given this abdication, the kleptocrats who went about plundering the remnants of the Soviet economy acted rationally. Some certainly have succeeded in accumulating and exporting enough wealth to remain as winners even after the collapse of August 1998, but again the majority were winners only in the sense of the prisoner's dilemma. The most immediate loser in the crash was the nascent middle class, the members of which had been led to believe that they had secure jobs and that Russian roubles were real money. Restoring that confidence will be a task of Herculean proportions.

Perhaps the greatest paradox of all, however, is that by embarking on shock therapy the Russian reformers showed that they themselves were as much part of the Russian path dependence as the system that they so wanted to change. They did not trust others enough to engage in serious dialogue, in Polish-style round table negotiations on the political transformation, or for that matter in calling the constituent assembly that had been at the top of the agenda during the previous "systemic change" of 1917–18. By choosing instead the path dependent strategy of *"kto kogo"*, they ensured that they themselves in return would not be trusted.

With this we have concluded the bulk of our presentation. It only remains, in the final chapter, to say a few words about the damage that has been done and about the likely prospects for the future.

Notes

1. Pipes, R. 1974. *Russia under the Old Regime*. New York: Charles Scribner, p. 287.
2. Carr, E.H. 1952. *The Bolshevik Revolution* (Vol. II). London: Macmillan, p. 270. (Emphasis in the original.)
3. Hough, J. and Fainsod, M. 1979. *How the Soviet Union is Governed*. Cambridge, Mass.: Harvard University Press, p. 87.
4. Kochan, L. and Abraham, R. 1990. *The Making of Modern Russia*. Harmondsworth: Penguin, p. 316.
5. Nove, A. 1982. *An Economic History of the USSR*. Harmondsworth: Pelican, pp. 57, 213.
6. Yakovlev, A.M. 1995. The rule-of-law ideal and Russian reality, in Frankowski, S. and Stephan, P.B. III (eds), *Legal Reform in Post-Communist Europe: The View from Within*. Dordrecht: Martinus Nijhoff, p. 10.
7. Granin, V. 1998. Soviet legacy of Russian legal reform, *Parker School Journal of East European Law*, 4(2), 187.
8. Ibid., p. 189.
9. Keenan, E. 1986. Muscovite political folkways, *The Russian Review*, **45**, 145.
10. Solomon, Jr, P.H. 1997. Courts and their reform in Russian history, in Solomon, Jr, P.H. (ed.), *Reforming Justice in Russia, 1864–1996: Power, Culture and the Limits of Legal Order*. Armonk, NY: M.E. Sharpe, p. 17.
11. Nove 1982, op. cit., p. 64.
12. Ibid., p. 84.
13. Ibid., p. 53, quoting a report by Kritsman who had hoped that "capital (i.e. the capitalists) would be in some sense in the service of the proletarian state".
14. Ibid., p. 54.
15. Szamuely, L. 1974. *First Models of the Socialist Economic System*. Budapest: Akademiai Kiado, p. 22. It should be noted that this was written before the Khmer Rouge experience in Cambodia.
16. Pipes 1974, op. cit., pp. 226–7.
17. Ibid., p. 232.

18. See further Billington, J.H. 1970. *The Icon and the Axe: An Interpretive History of Russian Culture.* New York: Vintage Books, Section III.
19. Ibid., p. 51.
20. On the emergence of the Lenin cult, see further Tumarkin, N. 1983. *Lenin Lives! The Lenin Cult in Soviet Russia.* Cambridge, Mass.: Harvard University Press.
21. See further Gerner, K. and Hedlund, S. 1989. *Ideology and Rationality in the Soviet Model: A Legacy for Gorbachev.* London: Routledge, chs. 4–5.
22. Nove 1982, op. cit., p. 106.
23. Nove, A. 1983. *The Economics of Feasible Socialism.* London: Allen & Unwin, p. 10.
24. Elster, J. 1983. *Sour Grapes: Studies in the Subversion of Rationality.* Cambridge: Cambridge University Press, Section II.
25. Granin, op. cit., p. 184.
26. Quoted by Whitmore, B. 1998. Russia's top crime fighter, *Transitions*, **5**(3).
27. See, for example, Nelson, L.D. and Kuzes, I.Y. 1995b. *Radical Reform in Yeltsin's Russia: Political, Economic and Social Dimensions.* London: M.E. Sharpe, *passim.*
28. Rutland, P. 1997b. Yeltsin: the problem, not the solution, *The National Interest*, Autumn, p. 34.
29. *Financial Times*, 1 November 1996.
30. *Nezavisimaya Gazeta*, 23 November 1995.
31. Rutland, op. cit., p. 30.
32. Ibid., p. 32.
33. Ibid., p. 35.
34. Sachs, J. 1995. Russia's struggle with stabilization: conceptual issues and evidence, in *Proceedings of the World Bank Annual Conference on Development Economics 1994.* Washington, DC: The World Bank, p. 59.
35. Ibid., p. 63.
36. Ickes, B.W., Murrell, P. and Ryterman, R. 1997. End of the tunnel? The effects of financial stabilization in Russia, *Post-Soviet Affairs*, **13**(2), 119.
37. Putnam, R.D. 1993. *Making Democracy Work: Civic Traditions in Modern Italy.* Princeton, NJ: Princeton University Press, p. 88, quoting Banfield, E.C. 1958. *The Moral Basis of a Backward Society.* Chicago: The Free Press, p. 85.
38. Putnam, op. cit., p. 91.
39. Leonardi, R. 1995. Regional development in Italy: social capital and the Mezzogiorno, *Oxford Review of Economic Policy*, **11**(2).
40. Elster, op. cit., pp. 44–52.
41. North, D.C. 1990. *Institutions, Institutional Change and Economic Performance.* Cambridge, Mass.: Cambridge University Press, p. 81.
42. Ibid.
43. *Nezavisimaya Gazeta*, 13 September 1997.
44. Holmes, S. 1997. When less state means less freedom, *Transitions*, **4**(4), 70.
45. Shlapentokh, V. 1997. Bonjour, stagnation: Russia's next years, *Europe-Asia Studies*, **49**(5), 871.
46. Quoted by Yavlinsky, G. 1998. Russia's phony capitalism, *Foreign Affairs*, **77**(3), 69.
47. Ibid.

48. Ibid., pp. 69–70.

49. Olson, M. 1991. Autocracy, democracy, and prosperity, in Zeckhauser, R.J. (ed.), *Strategy and Choice*. Cambridge, Mass.: MIT Press, p. 135.

50. Ibid., p. 153.

51. Bradford De Long, J. and Shleifer, A. 1993. Princes and merchants: European city growth before the Industrial Revolution, *Journal of Law and Economics*, **36**, October, 673, 675, 679.

52. Quoted by Nelson, L.D. and Kuzes, I.Y. 1995a. Privatization and the new business class, in Lane, D. (ed.), *Russia in Transition: Politics, Privatization and Inequality*. London: Longman, p. 129.

53. According to the Russian tax authority Gosnalogsluzhba, in 1996 26 of its inspectors were killed, 74 injured, 6 kidnapped and 164 threatened with physical violence. Eighteen of its offices suffered bomb blasts or shooting incidents (Ickes, Murrell and Ryterman, op. cit., p. 113).

CHAPTER TEN

Whither Russia?

At the time of writing this concluding chapter, Boris Yeltsin is still president of Russia and the Russian government is led by Yevgenii Primakov. Exactly what this means is difficult to say. At the time of Yeltsin's most recent "chicken" game with the Duma, which he actually ended up losing, there were rumours abounding that he was about to resign. Again, however, like so many previous rumours about his weak health leading to a transition of power, they were proven wrong. Russia's president seems to be stubbornly bent on serving out his term. Whether he will actually succeed in that ambition is beside the point here.

It is only by looking beyond Yeltsin that we can break free from the current uncertainties and thus, perhaps, also be able to say something meaningful about the future course of Russia. Irrespective of who will be the next man in the Kremlin, there are a few basic realities of life that will somehow have to be addressed. The most important of these concerns the country's financial elites.

In previous chapters we have seen the tycoons engage in games of plunder and rent seeking that brought them tremendous short-term benefits, but also had two rather serious by-products. One was the collectively irrational outcomes that were manifested above all in the real sector of the economy. We shall return to these in a moment. The other concerns the security of their ill-gotten gains, and really goes to the very heart of the matter at hand.

Any attempt to construct a positive scenario for a future Russian economic recovery must address the question of credible commitment, which has been the focus of our discussion in previous chapters. Putting it simply, how may those who presently control the country's main economic assets be persuaded that capital repatriation and productive investment in the Russian economy really is in their own best interests?

Two possible approaches might generate a solution that is positive for Russia. One is the "strong man" scenario, whereby a new leadership accepts the responsibility of acting as a third party enforcer. It would not have to rest on the rule of law, indeed that would be most unlikely, but it needs to be credible in the eyes of those who play the big money games. The other is the "market" solution, implying that with repeated rounds of the game the players by themselves come to the realization that a joint agreement on a positive-sum game is the rational way to go.

In the former case we are dealing with a more general problem in the exercise of power, which is common to all the "transition economies". In a recent book about institutional design in post-communist countries, Jon Elster, Claus Offe and Ulrich Preuss emphasize the tendency for transition governments to focus on maximizing control rather than investing scarce power resources in devolution, institution building and power sharing.

The driving force behind this tendency is related to the "conditions of breakdown and transformation", not the least of which is a massive time pressure. It is argued that the obsession with discretionary power spending "appears to be as rational in its motivation as it is tragic in its consequences". The rationality lies in government perceptions. Investing in rule making will not only appear less rewarding, in terms of tangible benefits, than ruling by decree. It will also bring "self-binding" of the rule maker, together with the "empowering" of others that lies in power sharing.

Given that the government will perceive its environment as both hostile and uncertain, any ambition of sharing power will harbour a risk of losing power, and is thus to be avoided. The outcome is not encouraging:

> As a consequence, establishing binding rules and entering into lasting arrangements must appear virtually suicidal to any holder of economic or political resources in an institutionally insecure and low trust environment. What results is the pathology of permanent *ad-hoc* tinkering through an often hyper-centralized practice of ruling by unilateral decrees, rather than authority building through self-binding and other-empowering rules that demarcate spaces for autonomous action.[1]

In the general case, a vicious circle is suggested where governments seek to compensate for limited governing power by relying on decrees rather than on institution building, which in turn makes power all the more contested and precarious. In the specifically Russian case, these arguments must be placed within the framework of path dependent patterns of rule aversion and preference for autocratic rule in isolation. The implication is that what in many other post-socialist states has been a transitory problem of power, in Russia represents just one more instance of revealed institutional preference.

The "strong man" scenario is critically dependent on this observation. In order to have a successful outcome, we must rule out the more spectacular intuitive aspects of this scenario, such as renationalization or punitive crusades against the tycoons. Such possibilities are certainly in the cards, and they would agree with path dependent preferences for confrontation and the suppression of property rights. But they would not lead to any improvement in economic performance.

For the latter to happen, the "strong man" will have to credibly commit himself to impartially upholding the rules of the game and to sharing at least some of his power. The latter is important for the simple reason that without some form of credible "shackling" we are back to the classic danger of an autocrat turning into a wilful usurper of property rights. The prospects for this to come about must be viewed against the background of the long series of such temptations that Boris Yeltsin has shown himself incapable of resisting.

The alternative solution, that of the "market" sorting things out by itself, comes in two versions. One would be to simply institutionalize oligarchy as the overriding rule of the game. If credibly arranged, this would have the benefit of making sure that the oligarchs as a group are vested with an encompassing interest in the long-term development of the economy. Thus the presently roving bandits could be turned into a collective stationary bandit.

The other would be to achieve a separation of power from money, without a strong man to dictate the rules. This borders on the happy solution of introducing democratic government, but is not quite the same. It would have to include the Duma as a formal rule maker but in the end it hinges on the tycoons being ready and willing to accept and rely on outside enforcement.

In both of the latter cases the temptation to defect would be tremendous, and the experiences of violence among the various elites hardly forms a fertile ground for inspiring trust. Nevertheless, we must also be aware that the only remaining alternative to these scenarios is that of going back to Hobbes and the war of all against all. The traditional option of "muddling through" is no longer feasible, for the simple reason that under such a regime the Russian economy will eventually self-destruct.

In the remainder of this concluding chapter we shall address the classic question of "Whither Russia?" from these perspectives, and we shall do so within the framework of Russian path dependence that has been outlined above. Where may we expect to find suboptimal solutions that are marked by increasing returns? And where do we have mental models that are incompatible with the requirements for progress?

Before delving deeper into these various options, there is, however, one dimension of the Yeltsin years that has been referred to repeatedly above but remains to be more properly addressed, namely the damage that has already been done to the stock of both physical and human capital. If we are to hope for yet another "new regime" in Russia, which is capable of addressing the issue of credible commitment and economic recovery, what are the initial conditions from which it will have to depart?

Damage already done[2]

The moral and social costs that have been inflicted on Russian society by what Tim McDaniel has called Yeltsin's "surgical dictatorship"[3] represent a whole complex of detrimental factors. Writing towards the end of 1996, when President Yeltsin had been successfully (?) re-elected, *Finansovye Izvestiya's* economic commentator, Yevgenii Vasilchuk, provided a rather disturbing picture of a country that was "moving rapidly towards complete intellectual and industrial degradation, financial disorder, the formation of a criminal élite, and regional disintegration from the federal center".[4]

In this rather sombre kaleidoscope, it may be of some use to make a distinction between the hardware and the software of the system. On both counts there are grounds for serious worry. In the former dimension we have seen the combination of plunder via privatization and the collapse of productive investment leading to unprecedented industrial degradation. In the latter, the human capital in a broader sense has also taken a serious beating, as the abdication of the state from its role of providing basic public goods has led to a degradation of health, skills and perhaps even moral fibre.

The hardware

Beginning with the hardware, Table 10.1 provides a summary overview of the performance of the real sector of the Russian economy during the first six years of reforms. (The turbulence that broke out following the August events makes it rather pointless, at the time of writing, to enter an estimate for 1998.)

The first impression is rather stunning. By the end of 1996, Russia's GDP had declined by close to 40 per cent and industrial production by slightly

Table 10.1 Performance of the real sector, 1992–7 (%)

	1992	1993	1994	1995	1996	1997
GDP	−14.5	−8.7	−12.6	−4.0	−4.9	0.4
Industry	−18.1	−14.1	−20.9	−3.3	−4.0	1.9
Investment	−37.1	−21.1	−29.3	−6.0	−15.0	−5.0

Source: EBRD 1998. *Transition Report Update.* London: EBRD, p. 63.

more than 50 per cent.[5] In comparison, we may note that during the Great Depression of 1929–33 the US economy lost 30.5 per cent of GDP.[6] And that depression, as we have noted above, has been known ever since as a great disaster.[7] In 1997 there were some signs indicating that the Russian decline might be bottoming out, but following the August 1998 crash, a renewed downward spiral was set in motion.

It may be useful here to recall all the negative things that had been – rightly – said about the Soviet command economy. Against this background it was logical indeed to expect that scrapping the old command structures and paving the way for markets *should* have led to substantial improvements. Instead, however, we have been witnessing a protracted period of unprecedented hyperdepression, the end of which, moreover, is still not in sight.

This observation becomes all the more intriguing if we place the Russian economy in a wider context, noting that there have been many voices arguing that Russia really *ought* to have performed better than a number of its previously socialist neighbours, both within and outside the former Soviet Union.

In a 1995 study of the Russian economic transformation, IMF economists Vincent Koen and Michael Marrese pointed at all the advantages Russia had over other transition economies: vast deposits of natural resources, a huge domestic market, a potential for substantial gains in terms of trade, lagging sectors with a great potential for efficiency improvement, a total absence of restitution problems and – perhaps most important of all – overwhelming interest and support from the West.[8]

Today we may conclude that while many countries in Central Europe have managed their respective transitions relatively well, with only brief dips in output, Russia's project of "systemic change" ended in abysmal failure and its future course looks bleak indeed. While the arguments that have been presented in previous chapters explain *why* the advantages held up by Koen and Marrese were not sufficient, it is still interesting to note how the widespread belief in Russia's capabilities caused many other observers to raise some fairly serious questions.

To name but one example, in its 1995 *Economic Survey of Europe* the UN Economic Commission for Europe found that the unexpected depth and persistence of the Russian recession was a puzzle still to be explained:

> However, the deep fall in output is still intriguing because the very collapse of communist regimes was supposed to bring about a substantial and rapid improvement in economic performance and standards of living, precisely because the traditional communist system was commonly regarded as so wasteful and inefficient. Removal of the command system and transition to a market economy was thus seen as an efficiency- and welfare-improving socio-economic

innovation. It is therefore somewhat surprising that most experts now tend to regard the registered fall of output in the transition economies as something quite natural and largely inevitable.[9]

In addition to the sheer magnitude of the decline, there are three particular dimensions of the Russian case, which combine to make it even more striking. One is the political process of seeking in various ways to deny or rationalize the decline in output, which is referred to by the ECE above. A second is the potential for exceedingly serious long-term consequences of what has already come to pass, and the third is the impact of massive capital flight.

Beginning with the attempts to deny and rationalize, there was a first line of defence drawn, which simply held that it was all an illusion, a statistical artifact of no real consequence. This argument was supported above all by the fact that casual visitors to Russia thought they could see for themselves that things simply had to be going in the right direction.

Moscow (which is very different from Russia) was simmering with life. Widespread construction and reconstruction provided a boomtown image. The streets were being filled by luxury Western cars, and the number of trendy nightclubs, posh restaurants and luxury hotels was growing in leaps and bounds. The old Soviet capital, once so gray and drab, was being transformed into a showcase of luxury and progress. Behind the façade one could envision the growth of a Russian middle class, which in turn would come to provide stability for the new Russian democracy.

These impressions of progress were to have a regrettable influence over both the mass media and the political establishment in the West, and thus also over Western policy making on Russia. Decisions on further credits, say, would be conditioned by a belief that positive economic developments were actually taking place, and that a Russian middle class was in the process of developing, which would have a strong vested interest in preventing a return to the old system.

Following the August 1998 collapse of the Moscow bubble economy there is precious little left of all these happy visions. The nascent middle class has been dealt a savage blow and all the newly constructed shopping malls and banking palaces are left as monuments of sorts over the broken dreams of a coming Russian boom.

Still, it must be recognized that the ambitions of presenting a Russian success story also had a more scholarly methodological dimension, which might deserve at least brief mention.

In one approach it was claimed that official Russian output statistics reflected neither the service sector nor the rapidly growing private sector. Thus the fall in output was overstated. In principle this is correct, but only in principle. The fact that much economic activity falls outside recorded GDP figures is not an exclusively Russian phenomenon. The Western market economies also have their shares of "black" or underground activities (as did the old Soviet economy) that are neither taxed nor recorded and the extent of which may thus be determined only indirectly. If Russia is different, it is thus a quantitative rather than a qualitative difference.[10]

A more specific argument, which gained some considerable popularity, was to say that the fall in GDP must be exaggerated because no corresponding fall could be seen in electrical power generation. The problem with this approach was that one cannot assume all sectors of the economy to have the same power requirements. An aluminium smelter, for example, will have far greater power consumption than a textile factory. And, as we shall see in a moment, the fall in output has been proportionately lower in the power-intensive sectors. Thus data on power consumption will understate the total drop in output.

Once it was no longer tenable to deny that output was indeed falling sharply, a second line of defence was drawn, arguing that the decline really was for the better. Above all, it was held that much of the previous output had been of so little use that losing it really was no loss at all. The Soviet economy had, for example, churned out massive amounts of tanks and other military hardware, which had added nothing to the welfare of the population.

While there was a bit more substance to this approach, it still failed to consider the welfare implications of shutting down military production only to have it replaced by – nothing much. Is it really an improvement, for example, to convert high-tech factories that had produced SS-20 missiles into producers of mechanical waffle irons?

There is certainly merit in discussing the welfare aspects of transforming the structure of Russian industrial output, and there are dimensions where, even granted the massive drop in output, consumers today are unquestionably better off. That discussion, however, calls for a more serious approach than simple proclamations of what is in some sense good or bad. We shall not pursue it further here.

Let us return instead to the official figures and to the second of the three dimensions mentioned above, that of potentially serious long-term consequences.

Recalling Table 10.1 above, it is not so much the figures on decline in GDP and industrial production that give rise to concern. The real trouble for the long term lies in the veritable collapse of investment. Over the first six years of reforms, the volume of investment in the Russian economy fell by more than 70 per cent! In contrast to GDP and industrial production, moreover, the decline continued unabated throughout 1997, bringing the fall close to three-fourths. (Foreign direct investment, as we may recall from above, has also been pitifully small.)

There are obvious conclusions to be drawn from these figures. When the Soviet economy was subjected to shock therapy, much of the infrastructure

Table 10.2 Annual change in Russian industrial production, 1992–7 (%)

	1992	1993	1994	1995	1996	1997★
Natural gas	−3	−5	−6	−0.4	−1	−
Electricity	−5	−5	−9	−3	−2	−1
Coal	6	−8	−12	−1	−2	−
Oil extraction	−6	−9	−7	−4	−2	−
Oil refining	−10	−13	−14	1	1	−
Ferrous metallurgy	−16	−17	−17	10	−2	4
Non-ferrous metallurgy	−25	−14	−9	3	−4	17
Chemicals and petrochemicals	−22	−21	−24	8	−7	−1
Wood and paper	−15	−19	−30	−0.7	−17	−4
Construction materials	−20	−16	−27	−8	−17	−12
Machine building	−15	−16	−31	−9	−5	4
Food industry	−16	−9	−17	−8	−4	−7
Light industry	−30	−23	−46	−30	−22	10

★ 1997 is January 1997–January 1998 (fuels lumped together are reported at
−0.5 per cent)
Sources: Goskomstat 1998. *Rossiiskii statisticheskii ezhegodnik: ofitsialnoe izdanie
1997.* Moscow: Goskomstat Rossii, p. 330; *Sotsialno-ekonomicheskoe polozhenie
Rossii,* Yanvar 1998 goda. Moscow: Goskomstat Rossii, p. 11.

and much of the physical capital stock was both worn down and technologically obsolete. And much also was infungible. Thus there were massive
needs for investment and for technological change.

Against this background it is striking to note what little interest the
various Russian governments that have served under Boris Yeltsin were to
show for such needs. The games that were played in the securities market
served to crowd out productive investment in industry and the way in
which mass privatization was designed served to block all prospects for
outside strategic investors taking over. Throughout, Yeltsin's governments
persisted in arguing that *laissez-faire* would force industrial managers to
adjust and improve.

Looking back at this track record, there are two aspects that make the
potential long-term consequences perhaps even more serious than figures
at first hand would indicate. One of these concerns what has come to be
known in the Russian debate as the "primitivization" (*primitivizirovanie*) of
the Russian economy.[11] After several years of attempted restructuring, we
may clearly identify a distressing trend which shows that the higher the
degree of processing within a specific industry, the greater has been the fall
in production.

From Table 10.2 we can see how the extractive branches have increased
in relative importance. Natural gas, electricity, coal and oil extraction have

all shown a modest rate of decline. In contrast, the accumulated fall in output for ferrous and non-ferrous metallurgy is around 40 per cent. Chemicals, wood and paper, construction materials and machine building have declined by between 56 per cent and 63 per cent. The food industry has declined by 44 per cent and light industry is on the way to being completely wiped out, following a decline of close to 84 per cent. And these figures still fail to take into account the renewed decline that followed after the events of August 1998.

The figures given in Table 10.2 exhibit a clear pattern where the primary sector of the economy (the extractive branches), despite a steady decline, is increasing its share of total output at the expense of the secondary sector (manufacturing). The increasing divergence between these two sectors recalls a phenomenon that is known as the "Dutch disease".

The concept as such was introduced to describe what followed in the wake of the discovery and exploitation of the Dutch Groeningen gas field. At first sight, one might wonder why this should have been a problem. It did, after all, mean substantial extra export earnings for the Dutch economy.

The "disease" relates to the impact on the other sectors of the economy. With increasing exports of natural gas the real exchange rate appreciated, which in turn led to increasing difficulties for domestic industries facing import competition. As long as the export boom is in progress this might not be an obvious problem, but once it subsides there is a distinct risk that the manufacturing industries that failed to cope with the adverse development in their terms of trade will not return. The increasing dependence of the Russian economy on oil and gas conjures up precisely this danger.

The third of the three particular dimensions of the Russian depression that were mentioned above concerns capital flight, perhaps the most contentious issue of all that has beset the Russian reform debate. In a survey of what has happened in this field, Vladimir Tikhomirov points at two interesting patterns.[12] The first concerns the actors that have been responsible and the ways in which capital has been taken out of the country, and the second the wide range of estimates that have sought to quantify the magnitude of the problem.

The first official Russian recognition of capital flight as a problem came in the aftermath of the collapse of the Soviet Union, when the focus of discussion was aimed at how the communist party had succeeded in transferring large sums of money into secret accounts in foreign banks. In March 1992, the Russian government hired a private US corporate investigations firm, Kroll Associates, in order to track down and repatriate money that was illegally held abroad. A year later, however, the Russian parliament ordered the investigation to be shelved. It had become far too sensitive.

While the Kroll investigation was still in progress, the Russian debate came round to realizing that many circles other than the old party network were undertaking illegal money transfers. This realization also meant that the role of the new political elite was placed in focus. Since it is not possible for Russian citizens or businesses to open accounts in foreign banks without special permission, and since Russian commercial banks are not permitted to transfer large amounts of money abroad without proper authorization, the question of how it was actually done was bound to arise.

Tikhomirov identifies foreign trade as the "major gateway" for capital flight from post-Soviet Russia. With rapid privatization of the previously state controlled foreign economic relations, the Russian state not only lost an important source of hard currency revenue, it also gave up its means of control over foreign capital flows. The various ways in which private actors sought to exploit the new opportunities were intimately linked to the development of the domestic economy.

In the first phase, when the country's financial and banking system was still underdeveloped, barter trade was the order of the day. Imperfect adjustment to world market price levels implied that goods thus exported from Russia could often be sold at higher prices than those imported to Russia. The Russian exporter would therefore receive extra payments from the foreign partner, payments that were credited to private accounts abroad.

As Russia's financial markets developed, the use of barter trade became obsolete and actors began operating a variety of illicit financial operations, such as "sham credits", where Russian companies would either fail to receive payments for exported goods, or fail to receive imports after making all the required payments. The foreign partner, often set up by Russians, would then simply disappear, leaving the Russian company with "losses".

As the Russian government began tightening its controls, actors also moved up the ladder of sophistication, increasingly relying on double invoicing. With Russian exporters selling at a discount and Russian importers paying a premium, substantial excess profits were generated for foreign partners, who kept part for themselves and deposited the remainder in various private Russian accounts abroad.

The negative impact on the Russian economy of such undertakings will not have to be spelled out in any greater detail. We have the obvious ones of siphoning off funds from the treasury and of slowing down needed restructuring of industry, but also a more subtle effect of blocking the ambition to establish enforceable rules of the game. Since capital flight involves illegal transactions, it will reinforce old patterns of personalized relations, based on trust that neither party will turn to the authorities. And it will feed traditional patterns of high-level corruption. In the longer run, the latter two effects are probably more detrimental than the diversion of funds.

Turning to the *volumes* of capital flight, Tikhomirov presents a series of estimates from various sources where over time there has emerged a clear pattern of systematic differences. At the lower end of the scale we will find Russian government sources. At the upper end we have spokesmen for the Russian security establishment, and somewhere in the middle various foreign sources are to be found.

The span between the extremes has at times been tenfold or more. In 1996, for example, First Deputy Prime Minister Oleg Lobov put the figure for 1990–95 at more than \$35 billion, while Aleksandr Lebed, then newly appointed secretary of Yeltsin's security council, claimed it to be as high as \$400 billion.[13] Going further into the numbers would require a substantial discussion of methodology, which would take us far astray. We will thus leave this for others.

Suffice it to say that no matter which set of figures we choose to accept, capital flight has far exceeded foreign direct investment in the Russian economy. By thus voting with their feet, Russian actors have actively contributed to what some observers have called the "de-industrialization" of the Russian economy.[14] And, as Tikhomirov points out, their actions have been conditioned by the design of the reforms:

> In this regard it is necessary to stress that to a large extent all of the negative factors that currently deter both local and foreign investors from investing in the Russian economy were themselves a consequence of the way post-Soviet reforms in Russia were conducted. The philosophy of post-communist Russian reformers based on the idealization of a "pure market" that was seen as a remedy for most of Russia's ills made them almost totally deaf to the social needs of the population. Even the notion of "economic crime" was considered by many decision-making Russian economists to have become irrelevant with the development of a "pure market".[15]

Summing up our discussion of the "hardware", we may note that in the economic growth literature successful economies are often portrayed as being in a process of climbing a "quality ladder". As the economy develops, the technology content in the production of goods and services becomes ever more sophisticated as does the human capital component.

In the Russian case, we have a deplorable process of climbing back down this quality ladder. The primary sector of the economy is expanding relative to the secondary sector and the virtual collapse of the financial sector that followed in the wake of the August devaluation of the rouble in one fell swoop wiped out much of the market for high-tech employment of young urban professionals.

Given that Russia is unlikely to attract substantial foreign direct investment in the foreseeable future, and that a series of defaults on foreign debt will preclude further borrowing abroad, there seems to be little hope for any substantial restructuring and upgrading of the physical capital stock to take place. For the young generation that is about to enter the labour market this presents a rather gloomy picture of future prospects.

An economy that is based on exporting oil, gas and scrap metals will not have any great demand for a workforce with higher education and specialized skills. Taking trips to Turkey or Dubai in order to bring home consumer goods for resale in street markets may be lucrative indeed to the individuals concerned, but it adds little to the development of the economy at large. And while growing your own food in dacha plots – as around 100 million Russians currently do – may help the household survive the winter, it is not really something that one normally associates with modern agricultural undertakings.

For ambitious young people emigration is therefore set to become an increasingly attractive option, thus posing a serious long-term threat of brain drain.

The software

Turning now to the "software" side of the reform process, we may find several factors that feed into this rather gloomy outlook for Russian human capital. When the reform programme was launched, there was an outspoken realization of pending hardship. The "kamikaze" attitude of the Gaidar government reflected a belief that unless tangible improvements could be shown within a few months, a wave of social unrest would sweep the reformers out of office.

Although the social situation a few years later would turn out to be far worse than anyone could have imagined, the feared backlash has failed – so far – to materialize. Despite all the negative developments that have been described above, notably so the chronic problem of non-payment of wages and pensions, the level of open social discontent, in the form of strikes, mass demonstrations or even riots, has been remarkably low.

From a scholarly perspective, it must be stressed that the relationship between poverty and revolt is far from clear-cut, but to the layman the absence of massive social protests nevertheless remains remarkable. While it may be interpreted as a manifestation of the legendary Russian ability to endure, *terpenie*, it also puts to serious test how far that endurance may be stretched before it snaps.

In the following we shall look at two separate dimensions of hardship. One is the poverty that has followed from a reduced ability on the part of the population to support itself via gainful employment, and the other deprivation that has resulted from a reduced ability of the state to maintain social safety nets. Let us begin with the former.

Post-Soviet poverty

As we may recall from our previous discussion, the Russian reformers had seriously underestimated the force of one-shot inflation that would follow upon price liberalization. And they were certainly not ready to face the protracted period of high and variable inflation that has been described

Table 10.3 Annual change in real wages, real incomes and real pensions, 1992–7 (%)

	1992	1993	1994	1995	1996	1997★
Real wages	−33	0.4	−8	−28	6	4
Real incomes	−47	16	12	−16	0	0
Real pensions	−48	31	−3	−19	9	4

★ 1997 is January 1997–January 1998.
Sources: Goskomstat 1998. *Rossiiskii statisticheskii ezhegodnik: ofitsialnoe izdanie 1997.* Moscow: Goskomstat Rossii, p. 139; *Sotsialno-ekonomicheskoe polozhenie Rossii,* Yanvar 1998 goda. Moscow: Goskomstat Rossii, p. 200.

above. They had thus also underestimated the impact of rising prices on the incomes and savings of the population.

What actually came to pass was a redistribution of both income and wealth that has indeed been significant and the future implications of which, both for the country's economic performance and for the living conditions of the population, give rise to serious concern. Table 10.3 provides a summary overview of the development of real wages, incomes and pensions. Recognizing that this is an area of great complexity, we shall not aim here for any greater degree of sophistication, merely to provide an impression.

There are several aspects to Table 10.3 which merit comment. The first concerns the distinction between real wages and real incomes, which is of some methodological importance.

Figures in the row for real wages reflect what enterprises have reported, and are therefore subject to a number of problems. On the one hand, we may suspect that there is under-reporting for the simple reason of personal tax evasion income (though wages also are costs offsetting revenues and thus reducing taxable profits). Thus we might be led to believe that reality is a bit better than what is reflected in the data. On the other hand, however, under conditions of high inflation and frequent delays in making wage payments, we have a serious problem in measuring the real value of what the household actually gets. Reality, therefore, may actually be worse than shown by the figures above.

Turning to figures given in the row for real incomes we have information provided by the households themselves, in Family Budget Surveys, which should be more reliable. The FBS have been conducted regularly since 1922, based on a very large sample of the population. In 1970–85, about 60,000 Soviet households were in the pool, increasing to about 90,000 in 1988–90. The Russian sample in 1995 was about 50,000 families.

Although the size and regularity of these surveys provide us with an extremely rich potential source of data, here as well there are numerous methodological problems. The main line of criticism concerns the sampling frame, which was developed according to Soviet needs. On the one hand, urban areas and workers in large enterprises were over-represented, thus providing an upward bias. On the other, certain sensitive social groups, such as the KGB, senior party officials and bureaucrats, as well as military officers, were excluded, which would provide a downward bias. We shall not go further into any of these methodological issues.[16]

Let us return instead to the drastic fall in the real incomes of households that was reported for 1992. This fall reflects not only the influence of inflation on wages, pensions and other benefits, but also significant cut-backs in different benefit systems, as well as periodic withholding of state budget expenditure. While the combined impact of these various effects should certainly not be trivialized, it must be pointed out that the statistics do overstate the immediate impact on the population's purchasing power.

To name but one reason, in 1990 and 1991 wages had gone up consider-ably, without any corresponding increase in the output of consumer goods. Thus a part of the massive drop in real incomes that was recorded in 1992 reflected a deflation of fictitious purchasing power. The disappearing lines in front of shops that were suddenly filled with consumer goods provide an obvious indication of such adjustment.

This said, it should also be pointed out that aggregate figures fail to reflect the substantial redistribution of both wealth and incomes that resulted from high inflation. At a casual glance, the Russian population might be divided into two disproportionate groups. On the one hand we have a rather small group of winners, often known as the "new Russians", who were mainly young urban professionals well placed to exploit the unpre-cedented possibilities for private wealth creation that were opened up with liberalization. For a few years they were making good money indeed. They had secure jobs, new cars and refurbished apartments. They believed in both the rouble and in the Russian banking system. They looked at the future with confidence. And they were dead wrong.

On the other hand we have a much larger group of losers, in the form of those who are often referred to as "ordinary people". All those who lived on fixed incomes – state wages, pensions or other benefits – were forced to see their real incomes fall rapidly, and all those who had a modest amount saved in the bank saw their savings wiped out. The result was considerable poverty, for a people that over the decades had become used to the state guaranteeing a certain minimum existence level.

As was the case with reported data on wages, incomes and pensions, it is difficult to arrive at a precise and reliable image of the extent of redistri-bution. Using data from the FBS sample to compute Gini-coefficients we should recall that important upper-income groups are excluded and that lower-income groups are under-represented, thus providing a bias towards understating inequality. This notwithstanding, there is still clear evidence of a drastic redistribution, one, moreover, that would not be of a passing nature.

The Gini-coefficient based on official statistics rose from 0.251 in 1986 to 0.409 in 1994, after which it fell back somewhat to 0.381 in 1995 and 0.373 in 1997. Looking at the decile ratio that is measured between the highest and the lowest income deciles, as reported by Goskomstat, we may also find a dramatic widening, from 4.5 times in 1991 to 15.1 times in 1994, after which it again narrowed somewhat, to 13.5 in 1995 and 13.0 in 1997.[17]

In a more detailed analysis, Jeanine Braithwaite has studied differences between the "old" and the "new" poor in Russia, showing that while poverty certainly existed in the Soviet Union as well it got significantly worse during the first years of post-Soviet reforms. She also shows that the recovery in both wages and incomes that is reported for 1993 was due to distributional shifts, as represented in a sharply deteriorating Gini-coefficient.[18]

There are several ways of providing a more detailed image of poverty. One is the "headcount index", which measures the percentage of the population with incomes below the poverty line. Data from the FBS show this index declining from 1950 until 1980, and then remaining fairly stable throughout the 1980s; thereafter a steep increase set in. The figures for 1980 and 1991 were 11.25 and 11.40. In January 1992 it rose to 30.18, reflecting the initial shock of price liberalization. Throughout 1992 it fell back, to stop at 15.69 in December, but for most of 1993 and 1994 it would remain between 20 and 35, indicating that the initial shock was not a passing one.[19]

Another way of looking at poverty is to measure the "poverty gap", which is defined as the cost of bringing the incomes of all the poor (provided they could be identified) up to the poverty line. While the headcount index only measures how *many* fall below the poverty line, the poverty gap measures how *deep* they fall, and from this perspective Russian poverty assumes an even starker image. Measured in relation to GDP, the poverty gap in 1989–91 was between 0.53 per cent and 0.60 per cent. In January 1992 it rose to 1.20 per cent and then it continued to rise, reaching 1.74 per cent in December 1992 and peaking at 4.1 per cent in October 1993.[20]

Following the initial shock of high inflation, the Russian general public also fell prey to assorted swindlers. During 1993 a number of investment funds started to appear, promising wonders to gullible savers. In principle, they worked like Ponzi games. The money that was raised from sales of shares was not invested. Part of it was simply pilfered, and the remainder used to pay dividends on old shares. It lies in the nature of such games that while the initial gains may be rapid indeed, sooner or later a collapse must follow.

The outstanding example in this genre was the MMM investment fund, which managed, via highly professional television advertisements, to attract 10 million small savers. Those who were involved from the start saw the value of their shares climbing exponentially, but few managed to get out in time. When the inevitable crash arrived, on 29 July 1994, MMM shares fell from a high of 115,000 roubles to merely 950 roubles. Desperate people gathered under riotous conditions outside the closed fund offices.

The combination of high inflation and deceits of this kind soon enough led a large number of Russians to turn against the very idea of market economy. For the majority of the Russian people, their own poverty began to stand out in ever greater contrast not only to the openly demonstrated wealth of the newly rich *bisniz*-men, but also to the equally openly demonstrated desire of corrupt politicians and officials to line their own pockets.

There are two potentially harmful long-term consequences that may follow from what has been detailed above. One concerns squandered political capital. Following the crash in August 1998, the group of winners from Russia's economic reforms has been narrowed down even further. With the bulk of the nascent middle class also being suddenly thrown out into the streets, to join those already dissatisfied, there is precious little left in terms of a potential constituency to support further reform activity. It will be hard indeed for a new Russian regime to sell "market economy" as a programme for future prosperity.

The other consequence is more theoretical, and concerns the link between distribution and growth. New approaches in growth theory have shown a negative correlation, i.e. that inequality may be harmful to growth.[21] Seen from this perspective, Russia's economic recovery potential must be adjusted even further downwards.

Social safety nets

Perhaps the most striking feature of all in what has been said above about the decline in output is the fact that unemployment has remained very low. To some extent this reflects differences between Russian and Western methodology. According to the official Russian standard (job-seekers who are registered at employment bureaux), the number of unemployed is around two million. According to the broader ILO standards the figure rises to around seven million, but that is still below 10 per cent.[22] Compared to the figure on output decline it is remarkably low. Why?

The fact that people continue to go to work though they are no longer receiving wages, and though they might not even have meaningful things to do, at first sight is a remarkable phenomenon, not to be expected in any Western country. It does, however, have a number of serious explanations that relate to the way in which the old Soviet society functioned.

It has often been claimed that while the introduction of market economy did bring higher prices, at the same time the population was freed from the eternal standing in line, which would be a compensatory welfare factor. While there is some obvious truth in this statement, it cannot be taken at face value. One objection is that to poor people the opportunity cost of standing in line is not very high. Thus it may be rational for them to prefer some such rationing of goods that are made available at low prices.

Even more importantly, however, the image of Soviet society as one where people are forced to stand in endless lines for just about everything is a serious misrepresentation of reality. To foreign journalists wanting to provide an account of the daily life of a Soviet consumer there were certainly plenty of stores with empty shelves that could be used to illustrate this, but in reality much of the distribution of consumer goods found other ways, most notably through the workplace.

In their company canteens employees received a cooked meal for lunch and often a food packet to take home. Large industries frequently had their own agricultural undertakings, which provided their employees with basic necessities. Even the military devoted part of its time to the production of foodstuffs for its own units.[23]

Moreover, this type of striving for self-sufficiency concerned not only foodstuffs. Enterprises often bartered with each other, thus making it possible to run special stores where employees could be offered scarce consumer goods. The communist party even made use of special sales of desirable consumer goods, as a way of attracting people to party meetings or propaganda lectures.

This function of the Soviet workplace as a channel for the distribution of consumer goods formed part of a bigger pattern, where it was the enterprise rather than the state that answered for much of the provision of public goods. As a result, the workplace effectively constituted a socio-economic system of its own, to which employees went for a host of reasons over and above that of simply working.

Via their employers, Soviet citizens were provided with healthcare, childcare and pensions. Employees often lived in company apartments. They visited movie theatres run by their enterprise and took their holidays in its resorts. It was common that pensioners continued to show up at their old place of work, to be provided with meals and perhaps even parcels to take home. The smaller the town, the more important these functions became. In many places, particularly in Siberia, where whole towns were built around a single enterprise, the dependence increased even further.

As long as industry was state owned, it did not matter much whether it was the enterprise or the state that had the technical obligation to pay, but with privatization the situation underwent drastic change. Since it is in no way possible to run a private enterprise with social obligations of the kinds mentioned above, privatization would have to be accompanied by programmes designed to shift such expenditures onto public sector budgets. But despite much talk and much support from abroad, little has come of this.

Russia's low unemployment rate should thus be seen as the result not of successful restructuring but of a fairly general failure to restructure the responsibilities for public sector activities. The outcome has been one where the Russian workforce continues to be dependent on a broad range of social services from enterprises that find themselves increasingly incapable of providing sufficient finance for such services.

This brings us to the central question of how the Russian population manages to cope. In a Western market economic context, where money is the conventional measure of the welfare of households and individuals, the figures that have been presented above on the development of wages and incomes would have represented true disaster. But in Russia there have been mitigating factors. Most Russian households somehow do manage to get by.

The simplest answer to the question of *how* they manage to do so is that the service life of nondurables is being extended. Clothing is being patched and repatched. Utensils receive makeshift repairs. Old bottles are being reused, etc. In a more sophisticated approach, however, Richard Rose and Ian McAllister have addressed the same question, using data from Russian nationwide household surveys – the "New Russia Barometer" – that were conducted in January 1992 and in April 1994.[24] Their ambition is twofold. On the one hand, they set out to investigate if the economic transformation has caused a rapid fall in the significance of non-market as against modern market determinants of money income. On the other they look at the importance of money in sustaining welfare.

On the former count, the picture that transpires is well in line with expectations. Regression analysis on data from the 1992 survey showed that of the 35 per cent of variations in income that could be explained, non-market influences accounted for one-fourth and modern influences for three-fourths. In 1994, 24 per cent of income variations could be explained by the latter, while the former accounted for less than four per cent. It was thus clear that in determining money incomes, non-market influences had been squeezed out.[25]

On the second count, however, the results are not what might have been expected. Seeking to identify household survival strategies that are based on both monetized and non-monetized activities, Rose and McAllister begin by recognizing the highly peculiar nature of life under the old Soviet system. They present a picture of households that are moving between nine different "economies", divided into three different categories.

To begin with, there are two *official economies*, which are both legal and monetized. This is official employment or pensions. Secondly, there is a group of four *social economies*, being illegal and non-monetized. These include growing your own food and making your own repairs, providing help among friends and relatives, exchanging free favours, and standing in line for more than half a day per week. Thirdly, there are three *uncivil economies*, which are illegal and monetized, representing work in the second economy, receiving tips and bribes, or using hard currency.

In the 1992 survey it was found that 94 per cent of all households derived income from the "official" economies, that 96 per cent were active in one or more of the "social" economies, and that 48 per cent were also involved in one or more of the "uncivil" economies. The average household was active in 3.7 out of the 9 economies listed above.[26]

The reasons that lie behind this image were linked to the incomplete monetization of the economy under the Soviet system. Households were simply forced to enter into a broad spectrum of unofficial activities.[27] This applied even to those who might derive a relatively high wage from their official employment. As Rose and McAllister put it, "Socialization into a non-market economy taught Russians survival skills rarely required in a modern market economy."[28]

With the transition to market economy, one would have expected these practices to be rendered obsolete, and that money should now be an adequate measure of welfare. As a first test of this hypothesis, Russian households in employment were asked if they were making enough money to meet their basic needs. In 1992, less than a third answered in the affirmative. In 1996, that figure had fallen to less than one-sixth, indicating that the link between money and welfare is weak.[29]

This interpretation is strengthened by a further question, asking households if they are able to get by without drawing on savings or getting into debt. In 1992, 63 per cent of all households questioned answered in the affirmative. In 1994 that figure had actually increased, to reach 77 per cent.[30]

In sharp contrast to various claims that following Boris Yeltsin's reforms Russia has now become "a market economy", Rose and McAllister show that old patterns of daily survival have undergone remarkably little change. Given that measured money income is derived from both official and unofficial sources, the impact of the economic transformation has been remarkably weak.

Having lived in a society where the state was distrusted and seen as both intrusive and oppressive, Russian households had developed considerable skills in looking after themselves. Rose and McAllister refer to this survival strategy as "household privatization", since it is outside official national accounts, and they find it strikingly persistent:

> The absence of any influence by income or other variables on sustaining welfare suggests that the capacity of Russian households to get by depends on idiosyncratic characteristics of families best identified by anthropological studies rather than categoric attributes relied upon by bureaucratic officials and social scientists.[31]

Noting that shocks have been felt across all income levels, and may not be related to "unalterable characteristics" such as old age, they also find reason

to expect that the problems are likely to be short-term rather than permanent: "Short-term problems are real problems, but they are also problems
that can be coped with by many strategies that Russians learned in a non-
market economy."[32]

Some years later, the continued decline of the Russian economy has led
to the emergence of a host of new problems that are clearly beyond the old
coping strategies, such as the provision of food, energy and medicines for
the country's remote northern areas, or the rising incidence of poverty-
related disease such as tuberculosis. Though there are very real grounds for
worry here, detailing such new forms of hardship will have to be the topic
for another study.

What next?

Turning now to look at possible future developments, we shall again resist
the obvious temptation to enter into Kremlinological speculations about
who will be the winners in the 1999 Duma election or the 2000 presidential
election. Let us return instead to our previous comparison with the Great
Depression in the United States. Will Russia be able to imitate the American
recovery? Economic as well as political arguments speak against such hopes.

From the *economic* perspective, it is important to note that while the
American depression followed as a reaction to the boom of "the roaring
twenties", the current Russian hyperdepression followed upon a prolonged
period of steadily falling growth rates and a steadily increasing technology
gap.[33] The implication is that where recovery in the American case could be
driven by increasing demand, the Russian problem is of a long-term structural nature.

From the *political* perspective, we may add that the American depression
could be broken with the help of a strong programme for economic recovery, namely Franklin D. Roosevelt's famous "New Deal". Roosevelt's programme rested on credibility and succeeded by securing widespread popular
and political support creating self-fulfilling expectations about progress.

The significance of the latter psychological dimension is also brought home
by Jeffrey Sachs, who refers to Roosevelt's classic statement that "the only
thing we have to fear is fear itself," and goes on to point at the crucial role
of leadership in forming expectations: "[Roosevelt] understood the importance of psychology – that people have to have the courage to keep seeking
a cure, no matter what the cure is. America had lost its will to recover, and
Roosevelt was certain that regaining it was the first order of business."[34]

Sachs sees it as "no accident" that historically almost all major programmes of economic stabilization have been identified with particular
leaders, from Hamilton in the United States (1790), to Schacht in Germany
(1923), Erhard in Germany (1948) and Balcerowicz in Poland (1990). The

implication is that the technical dimension of devising a reform programme cannot be seen in isolation from the political dimension of ensuring popular support and expectations for success.

In the Russian case we have seen how Boris Yeltsin initially was placed in the rare position of almost unquestioned political and moral authority, and we have seen how he squandered that capital by lapsing into old autocratic ways of rule. Thus, great expectations were rewarded by massive failure. For the future we must question whether it is realistic to assume that a new leader in the Kremlin will be able to provide the vision and leadership that is needed in order to mend what has now been broken.

There are purely technical problems involved here, which are of some considerable magnitude. The country's financial system needs to be rebuilt; the tax system needs to be reformed, etc. Yet, it really is not in the technical dimension that we must look for possible ways out of the crisis. Recognizing that it was bad politics that drove the Russian economy into a brick wall, our focus must remain directed at the role of the executive power.

In the autumn of 1991, deliverance from communism and Soviet power provided a powerful rallying point for the country's democratic forces. Seven years later it is difficult to see what might constitute a new point of departure. The challenge to a new leadership again lies in the dimension of credible commitment. It will have to convince the Russian population that it must break out of its current state of gross disillusionment, and it must convince the financial elites that co-operation and constructive effort is in their own best interest. Neither of these tasks will be easy to achieve.

The problems of corruption and rent seeking that have been described at length above are serious not only in the sense that they consume real resources. Given that actors may be expected to adjust to the rules of the game, by investing in skills that make them better rent seekers and by evolving norms that rationalize such behaviour, there is a distinct risk of the economy being locked into a bad equilibrium, which in turn will have a negative influence on long-term performance.

Writing about how past allocations of talent may influence future reward structures Daron Acemoglu captures the essence of this danger in a general case:

> However we have also obtained the additional result that if an economy starts with too much rent seeking at a point in time, it may be condemned to the steady state equilibrium with high rent seeking unless shocked by an exogenous event. Initial differences can thus have important long run effects. Moreover reversing the adverse effects of a misallocation is difficult because such a misallocation also leads to an unfavorable future reward structure.[35]

Recognizing that the Russian case is one where corruption and rent seeking are strongly path dependent phenomena, the risk of a lock-in becomes even greater. The collapse of the Soviet Union and the ascension to power of Boris Yeltsin quite clearly provided an exogenous event that *might* have shocked the system into a superior equilibrium. The question now is whether this can be repeated in some other form? Putting it more specifically, by what means can a new leadership achieve credible commitment?

In the ideal case, this is where we would look to the legal dimension for constitutional arrangements, but in the Russian case that is not a promising venue.

Of all the problems that have been detailed above it is likely to be the degradation of the legal system which in the long run will turn out to be the most devastating. The near-total privatization of the state's previous monopoly on the use of force has brought Russia from dictatorship to statelessness, and it is far from clear that this really represents an improvement. As Stephen Holmes underlines, "Today's Russia makes it excruciatingly plain that liberal values are threatened just as thoroughly by state incapacity as by despotic power. 'Destatization' is not the solution: it is the problem."[36]

When Russia embarked on its programme of becoming a "normal society", the establishment of the rule of law was an important component and much Western effort has gone into supporting that ambition. Regrettably, as Kathryn Hendley has shown, much of this effort was misdirected. In a distinct parallel to the equally misdirected "Washington Consensus" on how the economic reforms should be implemented, the ambitions to reform Russia's legal system rested on a "Development Argument", saying that law and legal institutions must be reshaped in a rapid and top-down fashion.

There are three important assumptions or expectations embedded in this argument. One is the existence or emergence of a market, and of a state that is capable of enforcing the law. Another is the readiness of Russian actors to rely on a newly introduced legal system, and a third that the new legal system should be essentially Western, resting on rules applied across the board by politically neutral agencies. In contrast to such expectations, Hendley argues that "institutional changes have not prompted Russian economic actors to shift from a reliance on networks of personal relationships to a reliance on law."[37]

The simplest of all reasons that may help explain why Russian enterprises have failed to rely on law is that Russian managers have failed to be convinced of the usefulness of law. This in some part is a result of their past experiences: "Russian enterprise managers have had a different experience of law, which taught them that their personal connections (political and otherwise) could trump any apparent legal obligation."[38]

But the format of Western assistance has also been misguided. There have been cases of elegant legislation, which may live up to the highest standards of Western law schools but nevertheless come across to Russian "consumers" as incomprehensible and therefore useless. Above all, Western legal assistance has blended into the Russian path dependence of top-down legislation. Thus Russian actors have perceived it, logically, as more of the same. Despite the fundamental changes that have been introduced, many Russians still "perceive the role of law as unchanged, as a sword still brandished by the state, rather than as a shield protecting society".[39]

There have been many studies undertaken in recent years, reflecting a general failure of the reformers' ambitions to introduce such generally accepted rules and enforcement mechanisms that make impersonal relations between economic actors possible and fruitful. It has been shown that managers persist in relying on a variety of traditional means, such as connections that may help in applying pressure. Or they turn to extra-legal assistance, in the form of what has become known in Russian as a "roof", a *krysha*. Vertical integration has also been developed as a way of internalizing potential problems.

In one study, Hendley, together with Barry Ickes, Peter Murrell and Randi Ryterman, conducted detailed structured interviews with four respondents in each of fifteen manufacturing enterprises based in Moscow and Yekaterinburg. Their conclusions were that Russian enterprises make little use of law and legal institutions in their relations with other actors. Though formal contracts were used, this was more a matter of routine than one of substance. Lawyers were employed but played a peripheral role. Arbitration (*arbitrazh*) courts were held to be poor on enforcement.[40]

In a comparative study of Hungarian and Russian experiences, Hendley and Cheryl Gray posit three conditions for a successful transition to the rule of law. These are good laws, sound supportive institutions, and market-based incentives that create a demand for law and legal institutions. While each of the three is necessary, they are sufficient only if achieved in combination. Using this yardstick, Hungary is found at least to be moving in the right direction, while Russia has failed to achieve even the first condition of good laws: "It is hard to imagine a legal system that would have made changes in the ownership structure and management of companies more difficult than the Russian corporate laws that governed the privatization and immediate post-privatization process."[41]

Problems relating to the quality of Russian corporate law are placed in focus also in a study by Katharina Pistor. She traces the nature and quality of legal rules issued in the post-socialist Russia not only to Russia's legal tradition but also to policy choices made by the Russian reformers. She argues that comprehensive legal reform was delayed in favour of speedy economic reforms based on *ad hoc* decisions and decrees with detrimental consequences for the development of property rights and governance structures.[42]

One of the conclusions reached by Hendley is strikingly similar to the arguments that have been pursued above about the difference between formal and informal rules of the game:

Rewriting the rules of the game is necessary but not sufficient. Rhetoric about the importance of law currently falls on deaf ears. Russians have not been persuaded of the usefulness of law. Without greater attention to state-building and the development of legal culture, Russia stands in grave danger of becoming a country with an excellent legal system on paper, but one that remains largely irrelevant to business.[43]

With this we are getting ready to conclude the argument and to rest our case. In previous chapters we have seen how Russian enterprises failed to adjust in the way that had been expected by the reformers. We have seen a retrogression by the executive power to old autocratic ways, and we have seen a disillusioned population resort to familiar old survival strategies.

In all of these respects we have seen path dependent choices being made. From a Western perspective it may be difficult to understand, for example, why Russian managers fail to rely on the fine new legislation that has been made available. Why do they go through all the tremendous trouble of seeking to apply personal pressure rather than relying on the law, and how can they be willing in the process also to forego the expansion of the choice set that lies in doing business on an impersonal basis?

The simple answer is that they have invested in skills that exhibit increasing returns, and they have evolved mental models that are marked by a deep distrust of rules and of third party enforcement. Briefly put, they are behaving in a rational path dependent manner. And the path dependence goes way back. As Michael Newcity rightly emphasizes, one must be wary of linking the pervasive lawlessness that characterizes current Russian society merely with 75 years of communism:

> There is in fact a continuity in the Russian legal tradition. Many of the current characteristics of the Russian legal system – overlapping, contradictory, and ambiguous statutes, decrees, and orders; bureaucratic arbitrariness; courts that are often incompetent or corrupt; and a popular disrespect for the law – characterized pre-revolutionary Russia as well. Popular attitudes towards the law and legal institutions were distrustful and cynical then, just as they are today.[44]

The ambition to introduce a system of Western rule of law simply by changing the system disk was flawed, for the same reason that the parallel ambition of introducing market economy simply by undertaking sweeping liberalization was flawed. The fault lies with the reformers – and their advisors – who never even *attempted* to provide legitimacy for their new formal rules. Thus they also forfeited any prospects of achieving an internal redescription of the mental models of the population, which in turn might have produced a new set of supporting informal norms.

It now only remains to conclude by returning to the two future scenarios that were presented very briefly at the outset of this chapter, namely the "strong man" and the "market" solution. Does either of these present a likely future development? Or should we prepare instead for some rather negative scenario, of which there are quite a few around?

In previous chapters we have referred repeatedly to the role of credible commitment, arguing that this really is the crucial dimension in which Russia's long-term troubles have been lodged. A typically Western remedy would lie in the adoption of a constitution, which after all is the primary vehicle of commitment, defining and constraining the actions of the state. It is logical, therefore, that the role of constitutions has played a prominent part in the debates on economic transformation.

Writing on this subject, Joel Hellman points at problems of "time-inconsistency" in policy making. Time-inconsistent policies arise when actors recognize that policy-makers have incentives to deviate from their declared policies, and to do so at a point where actors have already borne the costs of adjusting to that policy. Expecting that such deviations will indeed occur, actors will adjust their decision making accordingly, thus leading to a suboptimal outcome. This may be avoided only if the policy-makers can find a way of credibly binding themselves, by way of a set of rules that limit their discretionary power.

Applied to economic policy, the problem lies in convincing actors of the rationality in making short-term sacrifices in order to secure long-term gains. How can they be sure that the expected gains will not be confiscated *en route*, say, by a government that finds itself under severe fiscal pressure? As Hellman notes, the answer again is that of credible commitment:

> In the absence of such a commitment, individuals will discount the potential gains from reform by the political risk that current policies will be reversed in the future, thus weakening the initial gains for reform and reducing the willingness to invest in the reforming economy. To be successful, economic reform requires more than a well-designed plan, but a state that has the capacity to make a credible commitment to that plan.[45]

At this point we are about to close the circle. From above we may recall all that was said by North and Weingast about the problems that lie in finding a solution to the practical problem of *how* to achieve credible commitment, and especially the comments that were made about the need for shared mental models that support constitutionalism.

While it is rather obvious that these problems will take on extra difficulty in a country in transition, the Russian case is complicated even further by path dependent obstacles that stand in the way of both the formal and the informal components that must form part of a solution.

Against this background it might be useful also to say something about the frame of reference that has been used in the transition debate as a whole, and which has also been implicit in much of what has been said above.

The ideal Western model, and thus the standard of success for countries in transition, has its roots in Adam Smith's consumer sovereign invisible hand and John Locke's social contract. We have economic efficiency in combination with a form of social justice that requires individuals to honour the rights of others and to avoid coercion, and governments to administer only to the extent approved by an informed democratic citizenry.

Knowing that none of the successful great Western powers, or indeed Japan, have lived up to the full standards of this ideal, holding it up as a role model for ambitious reformers of states in transition may actually cause more harm than good. Has it, for example, been a wise move by Western advisors and political leaders to support the Russian reformers in their beliefs in a "pure market", and in the resultant ambitions of scaling back the state, to the point of near collapse?

Stephen Holmes follows this line of thought in arguing that Western advice on constitutional matters has been more of an obstacle than a help. His point is similar to that of Elster, Offe and Preuss, namely that the ship must be rebuilt at sea. Under conditions of simultaneous political and economic reform, combined with unprecedented social change, special provisions must be made. In the ideal case, legislators should not negotiate the rules while the game is in progress, and the constitution in particular must always be treated as a strategic rather than a tactical weapon. But what if the case is not ideal?

Holmes argues that it is "a great mistake to cry out against the politicization of constitution-making", and also calls it "a mistake to import German perspectives on constitutional law, particularly a fondness for unamendable provisions and an overly prestigious Constitutional Court, empowered, for example, to overturn procedurally correct constitutional amendments passed by the political branches on the ground of incompatibility with the constitution".[46]

His advice is that politicians must indeed be able to renegotiate the rules while the game is in progress. Any attempt to prevent such readjustments in the name of constitutionalism is tantamount to courting political disaster. The logic of the argument departs from the assumption that the main challenge facing a transition government is to pursue effective reforms while maintaining public confidence and remaining democratically accountable. Thus, the "core institution of the fledgling democracies" will be the parliament, and it will need to be supported rather than undermined.

For a host of reasons, not the least of which is a lack of experience in democratic politics, deputies will be at a disadvantage in relations with the general public. Strong governments will find it easy to shift blame for various shortcomings onto parliament. By overlegitimating the unelected justices of a constitutional court, or by frequently referring complicated issues to resolution by popular referendum, reformers may further erode what little legitimacy that body might possess. In Holmes' mind, feeding the "spirit of anti-parliamentarism" represents an "immensely dangerous development".

His main line of criticism concerns the difference between negative and positive constitutionalism:

> Negative constitutionalism is the political equivalent of libertarianism in economics. Libertarians believe that freedom will come when the state is prevented from interfering in civil society, when government simply leaves people alone. Negative constitutionalists believe that freedom will be secured when the constitution erects safeguards against abuses of power. These attitudes are well meaning but ultimately simplistic.[47]

The solution to the problem lies in interim arrangements, in stopgap constitutionalism. In the same vein as Michael Intriligator above, Holmes sees the need for a strong government that is able to promote the necessary institutional change and to enforce individual rights. Somalia is held up as a useful warning of what happens when the state is no longer able to "intervene", and the total absence of rights for stateless peoples (such as migrating Kurds or Vietnamese boatpeople) illustrates that "it is absurd to associate the establishment of rights with the radical weakening of the state."[48]

Sensible as all this may sound, we are still left wondering what the implications are in the concrete Russian case. Looking back at what has been said above about the Russian reform process, we may see that the Russian reformers have committed pretty much all of the mistakes that Holmes warns about. They have fostered an atmosphere of extreme anti-parliamentarism and they have created a constitution that is all but impossible to amend. And the behaviour of President Boris Yeltsin has been a perfect illustration of what Elster, Offe and Preuss had to say above, about "the pathology of permanent *ad-hoc* tinkering through an often hyper-centralized practice of ruling by unilateral decrees".

While it is quite likely that Western advice and Western pressures have served to reinforce these patterns of behaviour, in the economic as well as the legal dimensions, it remains a fact that the Russians were in no way forced to listen to the advice, and they were only in a very minimal way dependent on the financial aid. The only reasonable explanation, therefore, is that there was a perfect match between supply and demand. Thus the main cause behind the failure of the reforms must be sought on the Russian side, in path dependent modes of behaviour.

With the Primakov government, the Russian readiness to listen to advice from the West is set to change. It was interesting, for example, at the beginning of November 1998 to hear Yurii Maslyukov, the old Gosplan chairman and new deputy prime minister with responsibility for the economy, state that he did not need the advice of the IMF on how to wash his hands. "I am perfectly capable of handling that myself!" The remaining question is if he is equally capable of handling the economic crisis.

Again projecting the perspective beyond Yeltsin, what may we realistically expect? If a "strong man" is to prevail, he will somehow need to make a credible commitment to a programme that is designed to run not only downtown Moscow but the Russian Federation as a whole, with all the associated difficulties of fiscal federalism. With a deteriorating socio-economic situation, the temptation to meet pressing needs by resorting to rule by decree will be even greater than it was during the Yeltsin years, and thus the path dependence will be preserved. Whether there will also be components of violence, of open rebellion or forceful repression, is an open matter. Suffice it to say that such options would in no way improve the performance of the economy.

If, on the other hand, a "market" solution of sorts is to be reached, all that was said above by Holmes, concerning relations to the democratically elected Duma, will need to be taken into consideration. If the Russian oligarchs, and foreign investors, are to be convinced of the wisdom of investing in Russia, they must be offered some tangible evidence that some Russian institution is credibly charged with acting as a third party enforcer.

It is quite possible to envisage some form of stopgap measures being implemented that would slowly bring the ship around. It would have to entail adjusting the rules as the game is being played, but it would also have to rest on greater legitimacy than the backroom dealing that has marked the breakdown of fiscal federalism. In short, it would need to involve increasingly responsible elected parliamentarians.

While success along this route is not impossible, it will have to be what Pipes referred to, in Chapter 8 above, as an "arduous task of building a modern state and a modern economy from the bottom up."

Again, the problem is not mainly of a technical but of a political nature. And here there are many question marks. Will the Russian population prove capable of enduring long enough for positive change to set in? Will Russia's financial elites prove capable of resisting temptations to defect from the collectively rational path? And will all those republics and regions that in the past were able to survive mainly owing to help from the federal budget prove capable of quietly waiting for the federal budget to be resurrected?

Let the sole remaining question be asked by McDaniel: "The great question now is whether, after the terrible mistakes of Yeltsin's regime, there can still emerge a new form of order, one that will be a pragmatic vision in accord with Russian culture and institutions. Or will order once again take the form of a model imposed from above in the name of historical inevitability. Only the former choice . . . will save Russia from yet another tragic repetition of the logic of explosion."[49]

It is very far from clear whether there actually is an answer to any of these crucial questions.

Notes

1. Elster, J., Offe, C. and Preuss, U.K. 1998. *Institutional Design in Post-communist Societies: Rebuilding the Ship at Sea.* Cambridge: Cambridge University Press, pp. 33–4.
2. The following draws on Hedlund, S. and Sundström, N. 1996b. The Russian economy after systemic change, *Europe-Asia Studies,* **48**(6).
3. McDaniel, T. 1996. *The Agony of the Russian Idea.* Princeton, NJ: Princeton University Press, p. 171.
4. Quoted by Rutland, P. 1997a. Another year lost for the economy, **3**(2), 81.
5. Comparing present Russian measures of GDP with earlier Soviet measures presents a particular problem, which will not be addressed here. (See, for example, Kudrov, V. 1995. National accounts and international comparisons for the former Soviet Union, *Scandinavian Economic History Review & Economy and History,* **43**(1).)
6. The exact figures show a fall (measured in 1958 prices) from $203.6 billion in 1929 to $141.5 billion in 1933 (US Department of Commerce 1975. *Historical Statistics of the United States: Colonial Times to 1970.* Washington, DC: Bureau of the Census, pp. 224–5).
7. Steven Rosefielde makes the following striking comparison: "A rising chorus of voices contend, evidence to the contrary notwithstanding, that the standard of living in Eastern European countries is higher now than it was under communism and that this accomplishment is attributable to the liberalization achieved under the G-7's guidance. Although one can easily anticipate the guffaws provoked by claims that the Great Depression of 1929 raised living standards and was a macroeconomic triumph, the same kinds of preposterous assertions regarding the former communist states are being credulously accepted by statesmen and academics alike." (Rosefielde, S. 1995. Eastern European economic reform: transition or mutation?, *Atlantic Economic Journal,* **23**(4), 327.)
8. Koen, V. and Marrese, M. 1995. *Stabilization and structural change in Russia, 1992–4,* IMF Occasional Paper, No. 127, p. 54.
9. ECE 1995. *Economic Survey of Europe in 1994–95.* New York and Geneva: Economic Commission for Europe, pp. 10–11.
10. Note also that there are established ways of checking for systematic errors. One may, for example, compare figures for GDP that are computed on the supply side (total output) to figures computed on the demand side (consumption and investment). This has been done both for Russia and for other transition economies, without any systematic faults being discovered. (See, for example, Bartholdy, K. 1995. Are growth estimates for Eastern Europe too pessimistic?, in *The Transition Report.* London: EBRD; Gavrilenkov, Y. and Koen, V. 1994. *How large was the output collapse in Russia?,* IMF Working

Paper, No. 94/154; and Troschke, M. and Vincentz, V. 1995. *Zuverlässigkeit und problematik der statistischen Berichterstattung in Russland, Weissrussland und der Ukraine*, Osteuropa-Institut München Working Papers, No. 176.)

11. It should be noted that "primitivization" refers mainly to the massive degradation of the military-industrial complex. As anyone who ever visited the Soviet Union may easily recall, the civilian sector never did progress much beyond the "primitive". Nevertheless, it is far from clear that the ongoing destruction of the technological and human capital that was embodied in military production represents a step forward for the Russian economy as a whole.

12. Tikhomirov, V. 1997. Capital flight from post-Soviet Russia, *Europe-Asia Studies*, **49**(4).

13. Ibid., p. 602.

14. Götz, R. 1994. Deindustrialisierung Russlands: unabwendbares Schicksal oder Problem der Struktur- und Währungspolitik?, *Aktuelle Analysen des Bundesinstituts fur ostwissenscahftliche und internationale Studien*, No. 50.

15. Tikhomirov, op. cit., p. 609.

16. For details, see Klugman, J. and Braithwaite, J.D. 1997. Introduction and overview, in Klugman, J. (ed.), *Poverty in Russia: Public Policy and Private Responses*. Washington, DC: The World Bank, pp. 14–19.

17. Ibid., p. 9. *Sotsialno-ekonomicheskoe polozhenie Rossii 1995*, No. 12, p. 260. *Sotsialno-ekonomicheskoe polozhenie Rossii*, Yanvar 1998 goda, p. 203.

18. Braithwaite, J.D. 1997. The old and new poor in Russia, in Klugman, J. (ed.), *Poverty in Russia: Public Policy and Private Responses*. Washington, DC: The World Bank, p. 63.

19. Ibid., pp. 33–6.

20. Ibid., pp. 34–5, 50. On methodology and definitions of the poverty line, see also Foley, M.C. 1997. Static and dynamic analyses of poverty in Russia, in Klugman, J. (ed.), *Poverty in Russia: Public Policy and Private Responses*. Washington, DC: The World Bank.

21. See, e.g., Persson, T. and Tabellini, G. 1994. Is inequality harmful for growth?, *The American Economic Review*, **84**(3).

22. See further Commander, S. and Yemtsov, R. 1997. Russian unemployment: its magnitude, characteristics, and regional dimensions, in Klugman, J. (ed.), *Poverty in Russia: Public Policy and Private Responses*. Washington, DC: The World Bank.

23. Hedlund, S. 1989b. *Private Agriculture in the Soviet Union*. London: Routledge, ch. 3.

24. Rose, R. and McAllister, I. 1996. Is money the measure of welfare in Russia?, *Review of Income and Wealth*, **42**(1). In the former case, interviews began a mere three weeks after the introduction of reforms. In the latter, there had been ample time for the consequences of the macro reforms to impact on household micro behaviour, thus making comparisons fruitful. In both cases it is households rather than individuals that stand in focus, the rationale being that Russian households traditionally tend to pool all incomes.

25. Ibid., p. 83.

26. Ibid., pp. 83–4.

27. See also Katsenellenboigen, A. 1977. Coloured markets in the Soviet Union, *Soviet Studies*, **29**(1).

28. Rose and McAllister, op. cit., p. 85.
29. Ibid.
30. Ibid., p. 86.
31. Ibid., p. 88.
32. Ibid., p. 89.
33. After the massive industrialization efforts of the 1930s, when double-digit growth rates were recorded, there was a protracted period of steady decline. Towards the end of the 1970s, per capita growth in Soviet GDP was approaching zero.
34. Sachs, J. 1995. Russia's struggle with stabilization: conceptual issues and evidence, in *Proceedings of the World Bank Annual Conference on Development Economics 1994*. Washington, DC: The World Bank, p. 63, quoting Wills, G. 1994. What makes a good leader?, *The Atlantic Monthly*, April, p. 76.
35. Acemoglu, D. 1995. Reward structure and the allocation of talent, *European Economic Review*, **39**, 27.
36. Holmes, S. 1997. When less state means less freedom, *Transitions*, **4**(4), 67.
37. Hendley, K. 1997. Legal development in post-Soviet Russia, *Post-Soviet Affairs*, **13**(3), 228–9.
38. Ibid., p. 230.
39. Ibid., p. 237.
40. Hendley, K., Ickes, B.W., Murrell, P. and Ryterman, R. 1997. Observations on the use of law by Russian enterprises, *Post-Soviet Affairs*, **13**(1).
41. Gray, C.W. and Hendley, K. 1998. Developing commercial law in transition economies: examples from Hungary and Russia, in Sachs, J.D. and Pistor, K. (eds), *The Rule of Law and Economic Reform in Russia*. Boulder, Col.: Westview Press, pp. 181–2.
42. Pistor, K. 1998. Company law and corporate governance in Russia, in Sachs, J.D. and Pistor, K. (eds), *The Rule of Law and Economic Reform in Russia*. Boulder, Col.: Westview Press.
43. Hendley, op. cit., p. 246.
44. Newcity, M. 1998. Russian legal tradition and the rule of law, in Sachs, J.D. and Pistor, K. (eds), *The Rule of Law and Economic Reform in Russia*. Boulder, Col.: Westview Press, p. 45.
45. Hellman, J.S. 1998. Constitutions and economic reform in the post-Communist transitions, in Sachs, J.D. and Pistor, K. (eds), *The Rule of Law and Economic Reform in Russia*. Boulder, Col.: Westview Press, p. 57.
46. Holmes, S. 1995. Conceptions of democracy in the draft constitutions of post-Communist countries, in Crawford, B. (ed.), *Markets, States, and Democracy: The Political Economy of Post-Communist Transformation*. Boulder, Col.: Westview Press, p. 74.
47. Ibid., pp. 77–8.
48. Ibid., p. 79.
49. McDaniel, T. 1996. *The Agony of the Russian Idea*, Princeton, NJ: Princeton University Press, p. 21.

References

Abalkin, L. 1997. Insitutionalno-evolyutsionnaya teoriya i ee prikladnye aspekty, *Voprosy Ekonomiki*, **3**.

Acemoglu, D. 1995. Reward Structure and the Allocation of Talent, *European Economic Review*, **39**(1).

Allison, G. and Yavlinsky, G. 1991. *Window of Opportunity: The Grand Bargain for Democracy in the Soviet Union*. New York: Pantheon Books.

Arthur, W.B. 1988. Self-reinforcing mechanisms in economics, in Anderson, P.W., Arrow, K.J. and Pines, D. (eds), *The Economy as an Evolving Complex System*. Reading, Mass.: Addison-Wesley.

Arthur, W.B. 1989. Competing technologies, increasing returns, and lock-in by historical events, *Economic Journal*, **99**.

Arthur, W.B. 1994. *Increasing Returns and Path Dependence in the Economy*. Ann Arbor: University of Michigan Press.

Banfield, E.C. 1958. *The Moral Basis of a Backward Society*. Chicago: The Free Press.

Bartholdy, K. 1995. Are growth estimates for Eastern Europe too pessimistic?, in *The Transition Report*. London: EBRD.

Belyakov, G. *et al.* 1995. Poterya tempa pri potere kachestva, *Kommersant*, 23 May.

Berliner, J.C. 1957. *Factory and Manager in the USSR*. Cambridge, Mass.: Harvard University Press.

Bhat, G.N. 1997. The consensual dimension of late Imperial Russian criminal procedure: the example of trial by jury, in Solomon, Jr, P.H. (ed.), *Reforming Justice in Russia, 1864–1996: Power, Culture and the Limits of Legal Order*. Armonk, NY: M.E. Sharpe.

Billington, J.H. 1970. *The Icon and the Axe: An Interpretive History of Russian Culture*. New York: Vintage Books.

Birman, I. 1980. The financial crisis in the USSR, *Soviet Studies*, **22**(1).

Bogachov, V. 1989. Eshche ne pozdno, *Kommunist*, **3**.

Boycko, M., Shleifer, A. and Vishny, R.W. 1993. *Privatizing Russia*, Brookings Papers on Economic Activity, No. 2.

Bradford De Long, J. and Shleifer, A. 1993. Princes and merchants: European city growth before the Industrial Revolution, *Journal of Law and Economics*, **36**.

Braithwaite, J.D. 1997. The old and new poor in Russia, in Klugman, J. (ed.), *Poverty in Russia: Public Policy and Private Responses*. Washington, DC: The World Bank.

Brown, A. 1993. The October crisis of 1993: context and implications, *Post-Soviet Affairs*, **9**(3).

Bush, K. 1997. The Russian economy in October 1997, continually updated mimeo.

Carr, E.H. 1952. *The Bolshevik Revolution* (Vol. II). London: Macmillan.

Clark, B. 1995. *An Empire's New Clothes: The End of Russia's Liberal Dream*. London: Vintage.

Coase, R.H. 1992. The institutional structure of production, *The American Economic Review*, **82**(4).

Commander, S. and Yemtsov, R. 1997. Russian unemployment: its magnitude, characteristics, and regional dimensions, in Klugman, J. (ed.), *Poverty in Russia: Public Policy and Private Responses*. Washington, DC: The World Bank.

CSIS 1997. *Russian Organized Crime: Global Organized Crime Project*. Washington, DC: Centre for Strategic and International Studies.

David, P.A. 1985. Clio and the economics of QWERTY, *The American Economic Review*, **75**(2).

David, P. 1993. Historical economics in the long run: some implications of path dependence, in Snooks, G.D. (ed.), *Historical Analysis in Economics*. London: Routledge.

Denzau, A.T. and North, D.C. 1994. Shared mental models: ideologies and institutions, *Kyklos*, **47**.

Easterly, W. 1995. Explaining miracles: growth regressions meet the Gang of Four, in Ito, T. and Krueger, A.O. (eds), *Growth Theories in the Light of the Asian Experience*. Chicago: University of Chicago Press.

EBRD 1997. *Transition Report Update*. London: EBRD.

ECE 1995. *Economic Survey of Europe in 1994–95*. Geneva: Economic Commission for Europe.

Eggertsson, T. 1996a. No experiments, monumental disasters: why it took a thousand years to develop a specialized fishing industry in Iceland, *Journal of Economic Behaviour and Organization*, **30**(1).

Eggertsson, T. 1996b. "Rethinking the Theory of Economic Policy: Some Implications of the New Institutionalism". Paper prepared for a workshop on "Economic Transformation, Institutional Change, Property Rights, and Corruption", arranged by the NAS/NRC "Task Force on Economies in Transition", Washington, DC, 7–8 March, 1996.

Elster, J. 1985. *Sour Grapes: Studies in the Subversion of Rationality*. Cambridge: Cambridge University Press.

Elster, J. 1989. *The Cement of Society: A Study of Social Order*. Cambridge: Cambridge University Press.

Elster, J., Offe, C. and Preuss, U.K. 1998. *Institutional Design in Post-communist Societies: Rebuilding the Ship at Sea*. Cambridge: Cambridge University Press.

Fairlamb, D. 1996. When love's too blind, *Institutional Investor*, September.

Filippov, M. and Ordeshook, P.C. 1997. Who stole what in Russia's December 1993 elections?, *Demokratizatsiya*, **5**(1).

Fischer, S. 1982. Seigniorage and the case for national money, *Journal of Political Economy*, **90**(2).

Foley, M.C. 1997. Static and dynamic analyses of poverty in Russia, in Klugman, J. (ed.), *Poverty in Russia: Public Policy and Private Responses*. Washington, DC: The World Bank.

Fukuyama, F. 1995. *Trust: The Social Virtues and the Creation of Prosperity*. New York: The Free Press.

Gaidar, Y. 1995. Russian reform, in Gaidar, Y. and Pöhl, K.O. (eds), *Russian Reform/International Money*. Cambridge, Mass.: MIT Press.

Gavrilenkov, Y. and Koen, V. 1994. *How large was the output collapse in Russia?*, IMF Working Paper, No. 94/154.

Gerner, K. and Hedlund, S. 1989. *Ideology and Rationality in the Soviet Model: A Legacy for Gorbachev*. London: Routledge.

Gerner, K. and Hedlund, S. 1993. *The Baltic States and the End of the Soviet Empire*. London: Routledge.

Gerschenkron, A. 1962. *Economic Backwardness in Historical Perspective*. Cambridge: Harvard University Press.

Giersch, H., Paqué, K.-H. and Schmieding, H. 1992. *The Fading Miracle: Four Decades of Market Economy in Germany*. Cambridge: Cambridge University Press.

Gligorov, V. 1995. Gradual shock therapy, *East European Politics and Societies*, **9**(1).

Goldman, M. 1996. *Lost Opportunity: What has Made Economic Reform in Russia so Difficult?*. New York: Norton.

Goldman, M. 1999. Can you get there from here: what must Russia do to become a normal market economy?, unpublished.

Gorbachev, M.S. 1987. *Perestroika i novoe myshlenie dlya nashei strany i dlya vsego mira*, Moscow.

Goskomstat 1998. *Rossiiskii statisticheskii ezhegodnik: ofitsialnoe izdanie 1997*. Moscow: Goskomstat Rossii.

Götz, R. 1994. Deindustrialisierung Russlands: unabwendbares Schicksal oder Problem der Struktur- und Währungspolitik?, *Aktuelle Analysen des Bundesinstituts fur ostwissenschaftlische und internationale Studien*, No. 50.

Granin, V. 1998. Soviet legacy of Russian legal reform, *Parker School Journal of East European Law*, **4**(2).

Gray, C.W. and Hendley, K. 1998. Developing Commercial Law in transition economies: examples from Hungary and Russia, in Sachs, J.D. and Pistor, K. (eds), *The Rule of Law and Economic Reform in Russia*. Boulder, Col.: Westview Press.

Greif, A. 1993. Contract enforceability and economic institutions in early trade: the Maghribi Traders' Coalition, *The American Economic Review*, **83**(3).

Greif, A. 1994. Cultural beliefs and the organization of society: a historical and theoretical reflection on collectivist and individual societies, *Journal of Political Economy*, **102**(5).

Greif, A. 1995. Political organizations, social structure, and institutional success: reflections from Genoa and Venice during the Commercial Revolution, *Journal of Institutional and Theoretical Economics*, **151**(4).

Greif, A., Milgrom, P. and Weingast, B.R. 1994. Coordination, commitment, and enforcement: the case of the Merchant Guild", *Journal of Political Economy*, **102**(4).

Gros, D. and Steinherr, A. 1995. *Winds of Change: Economic Transition in Central and Eastern Europe*. London: Longman.

Grossman, G. 1963. Notes for a theory of the command economy, *Soviet Studies*, **15**(2).

Grossman, G. 1977. "The Second Economy" of the USSR, *Problems of Communism*, **26**(5).

Hedlund, S. 1987. Soft options in central control, in Hedlund, S. (ed.), *Incentives and Economic Systems: Proceedings of the Eighth Arne Ryde Symposium*. London: Croom Helm.

Hedlund, S. 1989a. Exit, voice and loyalty – Soviet style, *Coexistence*, **26**(2).

Hedlund, S. 1989b. *Private Agriculture in the Soviet Union*. London: Routledge.

Hedlund, S. and Sundström, N. 1996a. Does Palermo represent the future for Moscow?, *Journal of Public Policy*, **16**(2).

Hedlund, S. and Sundström, N. 1996b. The Russian economy after systemic change, *Europe-Asia Studies*, **48**(6).

Hellman, J.S. 1998. Constitutions and economic reform in the post-communist transitions, in Sachs, J.D. and Pistor, K. (eds), *The Rule of Law and Economic Reform in Russia*. Boulder, Col.: Westview Press.

Helmer, J. 1997. Russia: Regions Pressure Kremlin into Policy Shift – An Analysis. *Johnson's Russia List*, 4 November.

Hendley, K. 1997. Legal development in post-Soviet Russia, *Post-Soviet Affairs*, **13**(3).

Hendley, K., Ickes, B.W., Murrell, P. and Ryterman, R. 1997. Observations on the use of law by Russian enterprises, *Post-Soviet Affairs*, **13**(1).

Hernández-Catá, E. 1995. Russia and the IMF: the political economy of macro-stabilization, *Problems of Post-Communism*, **42**(3).

Hewett, E.A. 1990. The new Soviet plan, *Foreign Affairs*, **69**(5).

Hirschman, A. 1970. *Exit, Voice and Loyalty: Responses to Decline in Firms, Organizations and States*. Cambridge, Mass.: Harvard University Press.

Hollander, P. 1981. *Political Pilgrims – Travels of Western Intellectuals to the Soviet Union, China and Cuba 1928–78*. Oxford: Oxford University Press.

Holmes, S. 1995. Conceptions of democracy in the Draft Constitutions of post-communist countries, in Crawford, B. (ed.), *Markets, States, and Democracy: The Political Economy of Post-Communist Transformation*. Boulder, Col.: Westview Press.

Holmes, S. 1997. When less State means less freedom, *Transitions*, **4**(4).

Hough, J. and Fainsod, M. 1979. *How the Soviet Union is Governed*. Cambridge, Mass.: Harvard University Press.

Ickes, B.W., Murrell, P. and Ryterman, R. 1997. End of the tunnel? The effects of financial stabilization in Russia, *Post-Soviet Affairs*, **13**(2).

Ickes, B.W. and Ryterman, R. 1992. The interenterprise arrears crisis in Russia, *Post-Soviet Affairs*, **8**(4).

IEA 1995. Tendentsii ekonomicheskogo ravzvitiya Rossii, *Voprosy Ekonomiki*, **6**.

Illarionov, A. 1995. Popytki provedeniya politiki finansovoi stabilizatsii v SSSR i v Rossii, *Voprosy Ekonomiki*, **7**.

Illarionov, A. 1996a. Upushchennyi shans, *Voprosy Ekonomiki*, **3**.

Illarionov, A. 1996b. Bremya gosudarstva, *Voprosy Ekonomiki*, **9**.

Illarionov, A. 1996c. Teoriya "denezhnogo defitsita" kak otrazhenie platezhnogo krizisa v rossiiskoi ekonomike, *Voprosy Ekonomiki*, **12**.

Illarionov, A. 1998. Effektivnost byudzhetnoi politiki v Rossii v 1994–1997 godakh, *Voprosy Ekonomiki*, **2**.

IMF World Bank, OECD and EBRD 1990. *The Economy of the USSR*. Washington, DC: The World Bank.

IMF World Bank, OECD and EBRD 1991. *A Study of the Soviet Economy*, vols. 1–3. Paris: OECD.

Ingvar, D. 1995. "Memory of the future": an essay on the temporal organization of conscious awareness, *Human Neurobiology*, **4**.

Intriligator, M.D. 1994. Reform of the Russian economy: the role of institutions, *Contention*, **3**(2).

Johnson, J.E. 1994. The Russian banking system: institutional responses to the market transition, *Europe-Asia Studies*, **46**(6).

Katsenellenboigen, A. 1977. Coloured markets in the Soviet Union, *Soviet Studies*, **29**(1).

Kazantsev, S.M. 1997. The judicial reform of 1864 and the procuracy in Russia, in Solomon, Jr, P.H. (ed.), *Reforming Justice in Russia, 1864–1996: Power, Culture and the Limits of Legal Order*. Armonk, NY: M. E. Sharpe.

Keegan, W. 1993. *The Specter of Capitalism: The Future of the World Economy after the Fall of Communism*. London: Vintage.

Keenan, E. 1986. Muscovite political folkways, *The Russian Review*, **45**.

Khakamada, I. 1997. Gosudarstvennyi dolg: struktura i upravlenie, *Voprosy Ekonomiki*, **4**.

Klugman, J. 1997. *Poverty in Russia: Public Policy and Private Responses*. Washington, DC: The World Bank.

Klugman, J. and Braithwaite, J.D. 1997. Introduction and overview, see Klugman, J. (1997).

Kochan, L. and Abraham, R. 1990. *The Making of Modern Russia*. Harmondsworth: Penguin.

Koen, V. and Marrese, M. 1995. *Stabilization and structural change in Russia, 1992–94*, IMF Occasional Paper, No. 127.

Kornai, J. 1992. *The Socialist System: The Political Economy of Communism*. Oxford: Clarendon Press.

Kudrov, V. 1995. National accounts and international comparisons for the former Soviet Union, *Scandinavian Economic History Review & Economy and History*, **43**(1).

Lainela, S. and Sutela, P. 1994. *The Baltic Economies in Transition*. Helsinki: The Bank of Finland.

Lavigne, M. 1995. *The Economics of Transition: From Socialist Economy to Market Economy*. London: Macmillan.

Layard, R. and Blanchard, O. 1993. Overview, in Blanchard, O. (ed.), *Post-Communist Reform*. Cambridge, Mass.: MIT Press.

Layard, R. and Parker, J. 1996. *The Coming Russian Boom: A Guide to New Markets and Politics*. New York: The Free Press.

Leonardi, R. 1995. Regional development in Italy: social capital and the Mezzogiorno, *Oxford Review of Economic Policy*, **11**(2).

Lipton, D. and Sachs, J. 1992. *Prospects for Russia's economic reforms*, Brookings Papers on Economic Activity, No. 2.

Lucas, R.E. 1993. Making a miracle, *Econometrica*, **61**(2).

Matlock, J.F. 1995. *Autopsy on an Empire*. New York: Random House.

McDaniel, T. 1996. *The Agony of the Russian Idea*. Princeton, NJ: Princeton University Press.

Milgrom, P.R., North, D.C. and Weingast, B.R. 1990. The role of institutions in the revival of trade: the medieval Law Merchant, private judges and Champagne Fairs, *Economics and Politics*, March.

Millar, J. (ed.) 1987. *Politics, Work, and Daily Life in the USSR*. Cambridge: Cambridge University Press.

Mironov, B.N. 1994. Peasant popular culture and the origins of Soviet authoritarianism, in Frank, S.P. and Steinberg, M.D. (eds), *Cultures in Flux: Lower Class Values, Practices, and Resistance in Late Imperial Russia*. Princeton, NJ: Princeton University Press.

Nelson, L.D. and Kuzes, I.Y. 1995a. Privatization and the new business class, in Lane, D. (ed.), *Russia in Transition: Politics, Privatization and Inequality*. London: Longman.

Nelson, L.D. and Kuzes, I.Y. 1995b. *Radical Reform in Yeltsin's Russia: Political, Economic and Social Dimensions*. Armonk, NY: M. E. Sharpe.

Newcity, M. 1998. Russian legal tradition and the rule of law, in Sachs, J.D. and Pistor, K. (eds), *The Rule of Law and Economic Reform in Russia*. Boulder, Col.: Westview Press.

North, D.C. 1981. *Structure and Change in Economic History*. New York: Norton.

North, D.C. 1990. *Institutions, Institutional Change and Economic Performance*. Cambridge, Mass.: Cambridge University Press.

North, D.C. 1991. Institutions, *Journal of Economic Perspectives*, **5**(1).

North, D.C. 1993a. Institutions and credible commitment, *Journal of Institutional and Theoretical Economics*, **149**(1).

North, D. 1993b. Towards a theory of institutional change, in Barnett, W.A., Hinich, M.J. and Scofield, N.J. (eds), *Political Economy*. Cambridge, Mass.: Cambridge University Press.

North, D. 1995. Economic performance through time, *The American Economic Review*, **84**(3).

North, D.C. and Thomas, R.P. 1973. *The Rise of the Western World: A New Economic History*. Cambridge: Cambridge University Press.

Nove, A. 1974. Some observations on Bukharin and his ideas, in Abramsky, C. and Williams, B.J. (eds), *Essays in Honour of E.H. Carr*. London: Macmillan.

Nove, A. 1982. *An Economic History of the USSR*. Harmondsworth: Pelican.

Nove, A. 1983. *The Economics of Feasible Socialism*. London: Allen & Unwin.

OECD 1995. *The Russian Federation*. Paris: OECD.

OECD 1997. *Russian Federation 1997*. Paris: OECD.

Offe, C. 1996. *Varieties of Transition: The East European and East German Experience*. Cambridge: Polity Press.

Olson, M. 1982. *The Rise and Decline of Nations*, New Haven: Yale University Press.

Olson, M. 1991. Autocracy, democracy, and prosperity, in Zeckhauser, R.J. (ed.), *Strategy and Choice*. Cambridge, Mass.: MIT Press.

Olson, M. 1995. Why the transition from communism is so difficult, *Eastern Economic Journal*, **21**(4).

Olson, M. 1996. Big bills left on the sidewalk: why some nations are rich and others poor, *Journal of Economic Perspectives*, **10**(2).

Owen, T.C. 1998. Autocracy and the rule of law, in Sachs, J.D. and Pistor, K. (eds), *The Rule of Law and Economic Reform in Russia*. Boulder, Col.: Westview Press.

Peck, M. and Richardson, T.J. (eds) 1991. *What is to be Done? Proposals for the Soviet Transition to the Market*. New Haven: Yale University Press.

Persson, T. and Tabellini, G. 1994. Is inequality harmful for growth?, *The American Economic Review*, **84**(3).

Peterson, C. 1979. *Peter the Great's Administrative and Judicial Reforms: Swedish Antecedents and the Process of Reception*. Lund: Bloms boktryckeri.

Pipes, R. 1974. *Russia under the Old Regime*. New York: Charles Scribner.

Pipes, R. 1994a. *Communism: The Vanished Specter*. Oslo: Universitetsforlaget.

Pipes, R. 1994b. Was there private property in Muscovite Russia?, *Slavic Review*, **53**(2).

Pipes, R. 1995. *Three "Whys" of the Russian Revolution*. New York: Vintage Books.

Pipes, R. 1996. Russia's past, Russia's future, *Commentary*, June.

Pistor, K. 1998. Company law and corporate governance in Russia, in Sachs, J.D. and Pistor, K. (eds), *The Rule of Law and Economic Reform in Russia*. Boulder, Col.: Westview Press.

Popov, G. 1987. S totchki; zreniya ekonomista, *Nauka izhizn*, **4**.

Portes, R. 1994. Transformation traps, *Economic Journal*, **104**.

Putnam, R.D. 1993. *Making Democracy Work: Civic Traditions in Modern Italy*. Princeton, NJ: Princeton University Press.

Radygin, A. 1996. Privatizatsionnyi protsess v Rossii v 1995 g., *Voprosy Ekonomiki*, **4**.

Raeff, M. 1976. Imperial Russia: Peter I to Nicholas I, in Auty, R. and Obolensky, D. (eds), *An Introduction to Russian History*. Cambridge: Cambridge University Press.

Reddaway, P. 1995. Is Chernomyrdin a crook?, *Post-Soviet Prospects*, **3**(8).

Reddaway, P. 1997a. Beware the Russian reformer, *Washington Post*, 28 August.

Reddaway, P. 1997b. Possible scenarios for Russia's future, *Problems of Post-Communism*, September/October.

Reddaway, P. 1997c. Questions about Russia's "dream team", *Post-Soviet Prospects*, **5**(5).

Robinson, G.T. 1932. *Rural Russia under the old régime*. New York: Longmans, Green.

Roland, G. 1994. On the speed and sequencing of privatization and restructuring, *Economic Journal*, **104**.

Rose, R. and McAllister, I. 1996. Is money the measure of welfare in Russia?, *Review of Income and Wealth*, **42**(1).

Rosefielde, S. 1995. Eastern European economic reform: transition or mutation?, *Atlantic Economic Journal*, **23**(4).

Rosefielde, S. 1997. Russian market kleptocracy, unpublished.

Rosefielde, S. 1998a. *Efficiency and Russia's Economic Recovery Potential to the Year 2000 and Beyond*. Aldershot: Ashgate.

Rosefielde, S. 1998b. epto-banking: systematic sources of Russia's failed industrial recovery, in Stern, H. (ed.), *The Nigerian Banking Crisis in Comparative Perspective*. New York: Macmillan.

Rostowski, J. 1993. The inter-enterprise debt explosion in the former Soviet Union: causes, consequences, cures, *Communist Economies & Economic Transformation*, **5**(2).

Rutland, P. 1996. A fragile peace, *Transitions*, **2**(23).

Rutland, P. 1997a. Another year lost for the economy, *Transitions*, **3**(2).

Rutland, P. 1997b. Yeltsin: the problem, not the solution, *The National Interest*, Autumn.

Rutland, P. 1998. A flawed democracy, *Current History*, **97**, October.

Sachs, J. 1994a. Betrayal, *The New Republic*, 31 January.

Sachs, J. 1994b. Life in the economic emergency room, in Williamson, J. (ed.), *The Political Economy of Policy Reform*. Washington, DC: Institute for International Economics.

Sachs, J. 1995. Russia's struggle with stabilization: conceptual issues and evidence, in *Proceedings of the World Bank Annual Conference on Development Economics 1994*. Washington, DC: The World Bank.

Schelling, T. 1980. *The Strategy of Conflict*. Cambridge, Mass.: Harvard University Press.

Schroeder, G. 1979. The Soviet economy on a treadmill of "Reforms", in US Congress, Joint Economic Committee, *Soviet Economy in a Time of Change* (Vol. I). Washington, DC: US Government Printing Office.

Schroeder, G. 1987. Anatamy of Gorbachev's economic reform, *Soviet Economy*, **3**(3).

Selyunin, V. 1988. Istoki, *Novyi Mir*, **5**.

Selyunin, V. and Khanin, G. 1987. Lukavaya tsifra, *Novyi Mir*, **2**.

Senik-Leygonie, C. 1992. The breakup of the Soviet Union, *Economic Policy*, October.

Shevardnadze, E. 1991. *The Future Belongs to Freedom*. London: Sinclaire-Stevenson.

Shlapentokh, V. 1997. *Bonjour*, stagnation: Russia's next years, *Europe-Asia Studies*, **49**(5).

Shleifer, A. and Boycko, M. 1993. The politics of Russian privatization, in Blanchard, O. *et al.* (eds), *Post-Communist Reform*. Cambridge, Mass.: MIT Press.

Shmelyov, N. 1987. Avansy i dolgi, *Novyi Mir*, **6**.

Shmelyov, N. 1988. Novye trevogi, *Novyi Mir*, **4**.

Shmelyov, N. 1997. Neplachezhy – problema nomer odin rossiiskoi ekonomiki, *Voprosy Ekonomiki*, **4**.

Simis, K. 1982. *USSR: The Corrupt Society. The Secret World of Soviet Capitalism*. New York: Simon & Schuster.

Sokolov, V. 1997. Byudzhet na 1997 god stal zakonom, no realnost ego vypolneniya blizka k nulyu, *Ekonomika i Zhizn*, **11**.

Solomon, Jr, P.H. 1997. Courts and their reform in Russian history, in Solomon, Jr, P.H. (ed.), *Reforming Justice in Russia, 1864–1996: Power, Culture and the Limits of Legal Order*. Armonk, NY: M. E. Sharpe.

Sutela, P. 1996. Fiscal federation in Russia, in Dallago, B. and Mittone, L. (eds), *Economic Institutions, Market and Competition: Centralization and Decentralization in the Transformation of Economic Systems*. Cheltenham: Edward Elgar.

Szamuely, L. 1974. *First Models of the Socialist Economic System*. Budapest: Akademiai Kiado.

Szamuely, L. 1993. Transition from state socialism: whereto and how?, *Acta Oeconomica*, **45**(1–2).

Tikhomirov, V. 1997. Capital flight from post-Soviet Russia, *Europe-Asia Studies*, **49**(4).

Tompson, W. 1997. Old habits die hard: fiscal imperatives, state regulation and the role of Russia's banks, *Europe-Asia Studies*, **49**(7).

Troschke, M. and Vincentz, V. 1995. *Zuverlässigkeit und problematik der statistischen berichterstattung in Russland, Weissrussland und der Ukraine*, Osteuropa-Institut München Working Papers, No. 176.

Tulin, D. 1995. The IMF and the World Bank prevents what?, *Transition*, **6**(9–10).

Tumarkin, N. 1983. *Lenin Lives! The Lenin Cult in Soviet Russia*. Cambridge, Mass.: Harvard University Press.

US Department of Commerce 1975. *Historical Statistics of the United States: Colonial Times to 1970*. Washington, DC: Bureau of the Census.

Vaksberg, A. 1991. *The Soviet Mafia*. New York: St Martin's Press.

van Brabant, J.M. 1998. *The Political Economy of Transition: Coming to Grips with History and Methodology*. London: Routledge.

Vasilchuk, Y. 1995. Razogrev ekonomiki stavit krest na popytke finansovoi stabilizatsii, *Finansovye Izvestiya*, 20 June.

Vavilov, A. and Trofimov, G. 1997. Stabilizatsiya i upravlenie gosudarstvennym dolgom Rossii, *Voprosy Ekonomiki*, **12**.

Voslensky, M. 1984. *Nomenklatura: Anatomy of the Soviet Ruling Class*. London: Bodley Head.

Waller, J.M. 1997. Author's rebuttal to the Department of State, *Demokratizatsiya*, **5**(1).

Wedel, J.R. 1997. Cliques, clans and aid to Russia, *Transitions*, **4**(2).

Wedel, J.R. 1998. *Collision and Collusion: The Strange Case of Western Aid to Eastern Europe 1989–98*. New York: St Martin's.

Weingast, B.R. 1993. Constitutions as governance structures: the political foundations of secure markets, *Journal of Institutional and Theoretical Economics*, **149**(1).

White, S. 1996. *Russia Goes Dry: Alcohol, State and Society*. Cambridge: Cambridge University Press.

Whitmore, B. 1998. Russia's top crime fighter, *Transitions*, **5**(3).

Williamson, O.E. 1995. The institutions and governance of economic development. *Proceedings of the World Bank Annual Conference on Development Economics 1994*. Washington, DC: The World Bank.

Wills, G. 1994. What makes a good leader?, *The Atlantic Monthly*, April.

Yakovlev, A.M. 1995. The rule-of-law ideal and Russian reality, in Frankowski, S. and Stephan, P.B. III (eds), *Legal Reform in Post-Communist Europe: The View from Within*. Dordrecht: Martinus Nijhoff.

Yavlinsky, G. 1998. Russia's phony capitalism, *Foreign Affairs*, **77**(3).

Index